Winner of the 1991 Los Angeles Times Book Award for History

Winner of the First Annual Southern Book Critics Circle Award, 1991

Winner of the 1991 Helen B. Bernstein Award for Excellence in Journalism

"An absorbing chronicle of the past that shaped the present, *The Promised Land* is both gracefully written and heartfelt. Lemann's work has helped frame the national debate on some of the most vexing issues of the day."
—Henry Louis Gates, Jr.

"Brilliant . . . if we would understand the problem—which is the first step toward fully wanting any programs to succeed—*The Promised Land* is, along with Taylor Branch's *Parting the Waters*, one of the two indispensable books."
—Garry Wills, *New York Review of Books*

"Nicholas Lemann's well-written, thoughtful, and controversial account of race, poverty and public policy in America will continue to provoke discussion. *The Promised Land* is must reading for anyone interested in the problems of urban migration and the way policy makers addressed them."
—William Julius Wilson, University of Chicago

"Indispensable . . . *The Promised Land* is an important cornerstone in the effort to understand why so many travelers never reached the land of milk and honey."
—*Time*

"*The Promised Land* is a compelling and powerful book that should be read by anyone interested in the continuing history of racial oppression and conflict in the United States. Lemann successfully interweaves personal narratives of African-American migrants and their families with the discouraging story of politics and public policy in Chicago and Washington."
—David Brion Davis, Yale University

Nicholas Lemann
THE PROMISED LAND

Nicholas Lemann was born and raised in New Orleans and has been a magazine writer since he was a teenager. He has worked at *The Washington Monthly*, *Texas Monthly*, and the Washington *Post*, and since 1983 has been a national correspondent for *The Atlantic*. In addition, he writes regularly for *The New York Review of Books*, *The New Republic*, and other publications. He lives near New York City with his wife, Dominique Browning, and their two sons.

THE PROMISED LAND

The Great Black Migration and How It Changed America

Nicholas Lemann

Vintage Books
A Division of Random House, Inc.
New York

To my mother and father

VINTAGE BOOKS EDITION, MARCH 1992

Copyright © 1991 by Nicholas Lemann

All rights reserved under International and
Pan-American Copyright Conventions. Published in
the United States by Vintage Books, a division of
Random House, Inc., New York, and simultaneously in
Canada by Random House of Canada Limited, Toronto.
Originally published in hardcover by
Alfred A. Knopf, Inc., New York, in 1991.

Library of Congress Cataloging-in-Publication Data
Lemann, Nicholas.
The promised land: the great Black migration
and how it changed America
Nicholas Lemann.—1st Vintage Books ed.
p. cm.
Includes index.
ISBN 0-679-73347-7 (pbk.)
1. Afro-Americans—Migrations—History—
20th century. 2. Rural-urban
migration—United States—History—
20th century. I. Title.
E185.6.L36 1992
973—dc20 91-50493
CIP

Author photograph © 1992 by Rex Miller

Manufactured in the United States of America
10 9 8 7

Contents

CLARKSDALE

THREE OR four miles south of the town of Clarksdale, Mississippi, there is a shambling little hog farm on the side of the highway. It sits right up next to the road, on cheap land, unkempt. A rutted dirt path leads back to a shack made of unpainted wood; over to the side is a makeshift wire fence enclosing the pen where the hogs live. Behind the fence, by the bank of a creek, under a droopy cottonwood tree, is an old rusted-out machine that appears to have found its final resting place. The vines have taken most of it over. It looks like a tractor from the 1930s with a very large metal basket mounted on top. Abandoned machinery is so common a sight in front of poor folks' houses in the South that it is completely inconspicuous.

The old machine, now part of a hoary Southern set-piece, is actually important. It is the last tangible remnant of a great event in Clarksdale: the day of the first public demonstration of a working, production-ready model of the mechanical cotton picker, October 2, 1944. A crowd of people came out on that day to the Hopson plantation, just outside of town on Highway 49, to see eight machines pick a field of cotton.

Like the automobile, the cotton picker was not invented by one person in a blinding flash of inspiration. The real breakthrough in its development was building a machine that could be reliably mass-produced, not merely one that could pick cotton. For years, since 1927, International Harvester had been field-testing cotton-picking equipment at the Hopson place; the Hopsons were an old and prosperous planter family in Clarksdale, with a lot of acreage and a special interest in the technical side of farming. There were other experiments with mechanical cotton pickers going on all over the South. The best-known of the experimenters were two brothers named John and Mack Rust, who grew up poor and populist in Texas and spent the better part of four decades trying to develop a picker that they dreamed would be used to bring decent pay and working conditions to the cotton fields. The Rusts demonstrated one picker in 1931 and another, at an agricultural experiment station in Mississippi, in 1933; during the late 1930s and early 1940s they were field-testing their picker at a plantation outside Clarksdale, not far from the Hopson place. Their machines could pick cotton, but they couldn't be built on a factory assembly line. In 1942 the charter of the Rust Cotton Picker Company was revoked for nonpayment of taxes, and Mack Rust decamped for Arizona; the leadership in the development of the picker inexorably passed from a pair of idealistic self-employed tinkerers to a partnership between a big Northern corporation and a big Southern plantation, as the International Harvester team kept working on a machine that would be more sturdy and reliable than the Rusts'. With the advent of World War II, the experiments at the Hopson plantation began to attract the intense interest of people in the cotton business. There were rumors that the machine was close to being perfected, finally. The price of cotton was high, because of the war, but hands to harvest it were short, also because of the war. Some planters had to leave their cotton to rot in the fields because there was nobody to pick it.

Howell Hopson, the head of the plantation, noted somewhat testily in a memorandum he wrote years later, "Over a period of many months on end it was a rare day that visitors did not present themselves, more often than otherwise without prior announcement and unprepared for. They came individually, in small groups, in large groups, sometimes as organized delegations. Frequently they were found wandering around in the fields, on more than one occasion completely lost in outlying wooded areas." The county agricultural agent suggested to Hopson that he satisfy everyone's curiosity in an orderly way by field-testing the picker before an audience. Hopson agreed, although, as his description of the event makes clear, not with enthusiasm: "An estimated 2,500 to 3,000 people swarmed over the plantation on that one day. 800 to 1,000 automobiles leaving their tracks and scars throughout the property. It was always a matter of conjecture as to how the plantation managed to survive the onslaught. It is needless to say this was the last such 'voluntary' occasion."

In group photographs of the men developing the cotton picker, Howell Hopson resembles Walt Whitman's self-portrait in the frontispiece of *Leaves of Grass*: a casually dressed man in a floppy hat, standing jauntily with a hip cocked and a twig in his hand. In truth he was more interested in rationalizing nature than in celebrating it. Perhaps as a result of an injury in early childhood that kept his physical activity limited, Hopson became a devoted agricultural tinkerer. His entrancement with efficiency was such that after he took over the family plantation, he numbered the fields so that he could keep track of them better. The demonstration was held in c-3, a field of forty-two acres.

The pickers, painted bright red, drove down the white rows of cotton. Each one had mounted in front a row of spindles, looking like a wide mouth, full of metal teeth, that had been turned vertically. The spindles, about the size of human fingers, rotated in a way that stripped the cotton from the plants; then a vacuum pulled it up a tube and into the big wire basket that was mounted on top of the picker. In an hour, a good field hand could pick twenty pounds of cotton; each mechanical picker, in an hour, picked as much as a thousand pounds—two bales. In one day, Hopson's eight machines could pick all the cotton in c-3, which on October 2, 1944, was sixty-two bales. The unusually precise cost-accounting system that Hopson had developed showed that picking a bale of cotton by machine cost him $5.26, and picking it by hand cost him $39.41. Each machine did the work of fifty people.

Nobody bothers to save old farm equipment. Over the years the Hopsons' original cotton pickers disappeared from the place. Nearly forty years later, a family son-in-law discovered the one rusty old picker that sits in the pigpen south of town; where the other ones are today, nobody knows. Howell Hopson had some idea of the importance of his demonstration in c-3, though. In his memorandum, he wrote that "the introduction of the cotton harvester may have been comparable to the unveiling of Eli Whitney's first hand operated cotton gin. . . ." He was thinking mostly of the effect on cotton farming, but of course the cotton gin's impact on American society was much broader than that. It set off some of the essential convulsions of the nineteenth century in this country. The cotton gin made it possible to grow medium- and short-staple cotton commercially, which led to the spread of the cotton plantation from a small coastal area to most of the South. As cotton planting expanded, so did slavery, and slavery's becoming the central institution of the Southern economy was the central precondition of the Civil War.

What the mechanical cotton picker did was make obsolete the share-cropper system, which arose in the years after the Civil War as the means by which cotton planters' need for a great deal of cheap labor was satisfied. The issue of the labor supply in cotton planting may not sound like one of the grand themes in American history, but it is, because it is really the issue of race. African slaves were brought to this country mainly to pick cotton. For hundreds of years, the plurality of African-Americans were connected directly or indirectly to the agriculture of cotton; at the time of the demonstration on the Hopson plantation, this was still true. Now, suddenly, cotton planters no longer needed large numbers of black people to pick their cotton, and inevitably the nature of black society and of race relations was going to have to change.

Slavery was a political institution that enabled an economic system, the antebellum cotton kingdom. Sharecropping began in the immediate aftermath of the end of slavery, and was the dominant economic institution of the agrarian South for eighty years. The political institution that paralleled sharecropping was segregation; blacks in the South were denied social equality from Emancipation onward, and, beginning in the 1890s, they were denied the ordinary legal rights of American citizens as well. Segregation strengthened the grip of the sharecropper system by ensuring that most blacks would have no arena of opportunity in life except for the cotton fields. The advent of the cotton picker made the maintenance of segregation no longer a matter of necessity for the economic establishment of the South, and thus it helped set the stage for the great drama of segregation's end.

In 1940, 77 per cent of black Americans still lived in the South — 49 per cent in the rural South. The invention of the cotton picker was crucial to the great migration by blacks from the Southern countryside to the cities of the South, the West, and the North. Between 1910 and 1970, six and a half million black Americans moved from the South to the North; five million of them moved after 1940, during the time of the mechanization of cotton farming. In 1970, when the migration ended, black America was only half Southern, and less than a quarter rural; "urban" had become a euphemism for "black." The black migration was one of the largest and most rapid mass internal movements of people in history — perhaps *the* greatest not caused by the immediate threat of execution or starvation. In sheer numbers it outranks the migration of any other ethnic group — Italians or Irish or Jews or Poles — to this country. For blacks, the migration meant leaving what had always been their economic and social base in America and finding a new one.

During the first half of the twentieth century, it was at least possible to think of race as a Southern issue. The South, and only the South, had to contend with the contradiction between the national creed of democracy and the local reality of a caste system; consequently the South lacked the optimism and confidence that characterized the country as a whole. The great black migration made race a national issue in the second half of the century—an integral part of the politics, the social thought, and the organization of ordinary life in the United States. Not coincidentally, by the time the migration was over, the country had acquired a good measure of the tragic sense that had previously been confined to the South. Race relations stood out nearly everywhere as the one thing most plainly wrong in America, the flawed portion of the great tableau, the chief generator of doubt about how essentially noble the whole national enterprise really was.

The story of American race relations after the mechanical cotton picker is much shorter than the story of American race relations during the period when it revolved around the cultivation and harvesting of cotton by hand: less than half a century, versus three centuries. It is still unfolding. Already several areas of the national life have changed completely because of the decoupling of race from cotton: popular culture, presidential politics, urban geography, education, justice, social welfare. To recount what has happened so far is by no means to imply that the story has ended. In a way it has just begun, and the racial situation as it stands today is not permanent—is not, should not be, will not be.

O NE OF the field hands who used to pick cotton on the Hopson place sometimes in the early 1940s was a woman in her late twenties named Ruby Lee Daniels. She was tall and slender, with prominent cheekbones and wispy hair—there was supposed to be Indian blood in her mother's family. Ruby had spent most of her life on cotton plantations as a sharecropper, but now she was living in Clarksdale and working, occasionally, as a day laborer on the plantations. The planters often needed extra hands at picking time. Anyone who wanted to work would go at six in the morning to the corner of Fourth and Issaqueena streets, the main commercial crossroads of the black section of Clarksdale. Trucks from the plantations would appear at the corner. The drivers would get out and announce their pay scales. The Hopson place always paid at the high end of the going rate—at the time, two dollars for a hundred pounds of cotton.

Picking was hard work. The cotton bolls were at waist height, so you had to work either stooped over or crawling on your knees. Every soft puff of cotton was attached to a thorny stem, and the thorns pierced your hands as you picked—unless your entire hand was calloused, as most full-time pickers' were. You put the cotton you picked into a long sack that was on a strap around your shoulder; the sack could hold seventy-five pounds, so for much of the day you were dragging a considerable weight as you moved down the rows. The picking day was long, sunup to sundown with a half hour off for lunch. There were no bathrooms.

On the other hand, compared to the other kinds of work available to a poor black person, picking paid well. A good picker like Ruby could pick two hundred pounds of cotton a day. Before the war, when the rates were more like seventy-five cents or a dollar a hundred, she would have made two dollars or less for a day of picking. Now that Hopson had gone up to two dollars a hundred, she could make four dollars a day. Most of the jobs she had held outside the cotton fields were in "public work" (that is, being a maid in white people's houses), and that paid only $2.50 a week.

Even four dollars a day for picking cotton was nothing, though, compared to what you could make in Chicago, where many people Ruby knew, including one of her aunts, had moved since the war started. In Chicago you could make as much as seventy-five cents an hour working in a laundry, or a factory, or a restaurant or a hotel, or one of the big mail-order houses like Spiegel and Montgomery Ward, or, if you were a man, in the stockyards. You could get overtime. Some of these jobs were supposed to be as hard as picking cotton, but people were making sums unheard of among black unskilled workers in Mississippi. Anybody in Ruby's situation in Clarksdale at the time couldn't avoid at least toying with the idea of a move to the North. Ruby was thinking about it herself.

The ostensible reason she hadn't moved was that she was married and her husband was away fighting, so she had to wait for him to come home. Ruby was not exactly an adoring, patient war bride, though. She had never been very much in love with her husband, and by disposition she was not the passive type; she had a tough edge. Quite often in those days, black people would do things that white people considered irrational, or, at best, impulsive. Ruby would do many such things herself, in the course of her long life. But in her case, and perhaps many others, the real motivation was a desire to live with a basic human complement of love and respect. When she had this, she was kind and sweet, though she had too good a sense of humor ever to ascend to full church-lady saccharinity; when she didn't, which was most of the time, she could be angry and sarcastic and even mean, and could make what looked in hindsight like big, obvious mistakes.

The real reason Ruby hadn't moved to Chicago was that in her husband's absence, she had fallen in love with another man, a married man who was unwilling to abandon his wife and children in Clarksdale. Certainly the idea of moving was not itself in any way a deterrent to Ruby. She had been moving for all of her life already.

Ruby was born Ruby Lee Hopkins, on November 23, 1916, in Kemper County, Mississippi, near the Alabama border. She was one of a set of identical twins born out of wedlock to a fifteen-year-old girl named Ardell Hopkins. When Ruby's grandfather, George Hopkins, found out that his daughter was pregnant, he picked up his shotgun and went out looking for the young man who had gotten her in that condition, intending to kill him. When the young man, whose name was Sam Campbell, heard about this, he joined the Army and went off to fight in World War I. Ruby and her twin sister Ruth didn't meet their father until twenty years later.

The family history, as Ruby heard it, was sketchy. Her grandfather's grandmother had been a slave whose last name was Chambers, but she was sold to a white family named Hopkins who changed her name to match theirs; shortly afterward, according to family legend, she had given birth to a white-looking child whose father was the master. This child was Ruby's great-grandfather. Quite often in those days, poor black families in the South didn't pass on to their children too much information about slavery, because they considered it an unpleasant memory and one that might induce a lack of self-esteem if dwelt upon at length. Many people of Ruby's generation were left with a vague picture of horrors — whippings, sales that broke up families, sexual oppression, material privation — and a feeling that you were better off not knowing the details, so long as you were aware that things were better now.

Ruby's grandfather was a small farmer in Kemper County, barely getting by. Shortly after Ruby was born, a white man named Charlie Gaines appeared in the county. He was a manager on a big cotton plantation outside the town of Hill House, a few miles outside of Clarksdale; he had come all the way across Mississippi to recruit black people to come to Hill House as sharecroppers. His sales pitch was simple: a promise of prosperity. It convinced George Hopkins. In January 1917, when Ruby was six weeks old, George moved the family to Hill House to start over.

Hill House, and Clarksdale, are in a part of Mississippi called the Delta — a flat alluvial plain two hundred miles long and fifty miles wide that runs between the Yazoo and Mississippi rivers from Memphis down to Vicksburg. The Delta is the richest natural cotton-farming land in the United States. Its dark black-brown topsoil, deposited over eons of springtime floods, is more than fifty feet deep. Like an oil field or a silver mine, the soil of the Delta is the kind of fabulous natural resource that holds the promise of big, big money, and so the agricultural society that grew up on top of it was dominated by farming tycoons, not yeomen.

The Delta is remote, even now, and in its state of nature it was wild — swampy in some places and densely forested in most others, and populated by Choctaws and panthers and bears. It was the last area of the South to be settled; the mythic grand antebellum cotton plantation did not exist there. The leading planter families of the Delta consider themselves to be members of the Southern upper class — which is to say that they are Episcopalian, of British or Scotch-Irish extraction, and had ancestors living in the upper South before 1800 — but they were never so well established somewhere else as to have precluded a move to the Delta when it was frontier. The patriarch of the Hopson family, Joseph J. Hopson, came to the Delta from Tennessee in 1832, and he was one of the first white settlers. The Hopson plantation didn't begin its operations until 1852. Most of the other big plantations in the Delta were founded after the Civil War. John Clark, for whom the town of Clarksdale is named, arrived in 1839, and laid out the town's streets in 1868. Clarksdale had no rail line until 1879, wasn't incorporated until 1882, and had no paved streets until 1913.

The reason the Delta was quiescent before the Civil War wasn't just that the land was substantially uncleared and undrained, though clearing and draining it was a tremendous undertaking; it was that the Mississippi River flooded so often. Floods ruin crops. The river had made the land rich, but for the land to make men rich, its link to the river had to be severed. It was two decades after the end of the war before a marginally reliable system of levees was in place. Even then the Delta never became grand. It is a purposive country, the purpose being to grow cotton. The landscape is long and wide. Trees appear in lines, to demarcate the fields. The turn rows undulate only when they have to make their way around creeks. The planters' houses, most of them, are quite modest, with small lawns and a few shade trees, evidence of a desire not to divert too much arable land to other uses. The big money made in the Delta is usually spent outside the Delta, on parties in Memphis and tours of Europe and Eastern prep schools.

Before the Depression, cotton was the least mechanized type of American agriculture, and extremely labor-intensive. During the decades following the end of the Civil War, the acreage planted to cotton steadily increased, in the Delta and all through the Southern cotton belt, peaking in 1929. This created an enormous demand for field hands, which was met mainly through the expansion of the tenant-farming system whose most common form was sharecropping. The number of tenant farmers in the South grew in lockstep with the number of acres of cotton fields. In 1930, by the estimate of a commission investigating the sharecropper system, eight and a half million people in the ten chief cotton-producing states were living in tenant-farming families. The Delta, as home to the biggest and richest plantations in the cotton belt, was the capital of the sharecropper system — at least in its most extreme form, in which all the sharecroppers were black and lived in self-contained plantation communities that were home, in many cases, to hundreds of people, and where the conditions were much closer to slavery than to normal employment.

There used to be a misty, romantic tone to Southern whites' descriptions of how sharecropping got started. After the Civil War, the story went, the planters, weary and penniless, returned to the smoldering ruins of their plantations, determined to make a cotton crop. But there was no one to pick the cotton — the slaves, after freedom, had taken an extended vacation. They spent their days roaming aimlessly through the countryside or lolling about in the town squares, egged on by carpetbaggers, scalawags, and the occupying troops. The novels of Thomas Dixon, on which the film *Birth of a Nation* is based, are the mother lode of such lore.

Finally, the story continues, the former slaves ran out of food, and they began to drift back to their former owners and beg for a chance to cultivate the land again. The owner would explain that he had land but no money to pay out in wages, so he offered a deal, which the former slaves eagerly accepted: I'll provide you with land, housing, seed, and provisions, you make a cotton crop, and when we sell it we'll split the proceeds. Everyone put shoulder to the wheel, and social and economic order was restored.

The story has the overspecificity of a myth. Both of the Delta's best-known writers of the sharecropper period, David Cohn, a literary lawyer-businessman, and William Alexander Percy, a cotton planter and poet, claim that sharecropping was invented on a particular plantation: Cohn says the inventor was a General Hargreaves and the location "his plantation home in the Mississippi Delta"; Percy, with typical grandeur, says it was his own grandfather, on Trail Lake, the family plantation outside of Greenville. In both cases there is a worked-up social vision underlying the story that today seems obviously self-justifying and self-deluding. The planters are always kind, responsible, and disinterested; Percy, who had a more elaborately patrician self-concept than Cohn, makes it sound as if his family's entire purpose on earth was to help black people. The story cannot make sense, either, unless black people are congenitally incapable of an independent existence. Whites' accounts of the origins of share-cropping never mention the never-realized idea of giving the ex-slaves forty acres and a mule for each family. The reason blacks accepted the bargain of the sharecropper system, as white people tell it, was not that they could get no decent land to farm, but that they, practically alone among all the peoples in the world, lacked the basic ability to manage a simple agrarian way of life on their own.

The most obvious flaw in the idea of sharecropping as a benevolent, voluntary system is that for most of its reign, black sharecroppers were not citizens. When the sharecropper system began, just after the war, Mississippi was under military occupation; when it was readmitted to the Union, in 1870, blacks could, and did, vote and hold political office, and the Republican Party ran the state. Even then, in accordance with long-standing custom, black people living on plantations inhabited a world entirely apart from white society. Some different form of race relations might have evolved under Reconstruction — but Republican rule in Mississippi lasted only five years. Like the establishment of sharecropping, the restoration to power of the all-white Democratic Party in the South was a development of such magnitude to whites that it became encrusted in legend; many towns have their own specific, mythic stories of the redemption of the white South. In Clarksdale it is the story of the "race riot" of October 9, 1875.

Even then Clarksdale was dominated by relatively well-off, educated whites rather than rednecks. The Ku Klux Klan, in its several incarnations over the years, has never been an officially sanctioned presence there. During Reconstruction, Clarksdale's most prominent white citizen, James Lusk Alcorn, the "sage of Coahoma County," a former Confederate general, United States senator, and governor of Mississippi, was a Republican, though not a radical Republican like Adelbert Ames, the young man from Maine who was governor of Mississippi during the final phase of Reconstruction. Alcorn had rented land on his plantation to freed slaves, and the Klan rewarded him for this gesture by burning the plantation down.

The prelude to the race riot was a Republican county convention held at the courthouse in Clarksdale. After the Civil War, the Reconstruction government of Mississippi had first enfranchised blacks and then written a new state constitution that created a lot of new government jobs that went to blacks — all events that recurred in Mississippi, courtesy of the forces of Northern liberalism, a hundred years later. Alcorn and a few other practical-minded, economically ambitious ex-Confederates became Republicans "with the hope that the tide of ignorance might be controlled from within," as a segregation-era history of Mississippi put it. But by 1875 they had become disillusioned, believing (as, again, most of their counterparts in the white Clarksdale planter-businessman class of the late twentieth century would believe) that the true mission of the government's new agencies was to swell the voter rolls in service of liberal political interests in Washington, and that many of the new black officials were unqualified and incompetent.

Alcorn and his white Republican allies appeared at the county convention of 1875 bearing arms, and Alcorn delivered a fierce denunciation of the blacks who held most of the political offices in the county. In particular he accused the black county sheriff, John Brown, a recent arrival in the Delta from the abolitionist hotbed of Oberlin, Ohio, of stealing $60,000 in county funds. The convention broke up in confusion without the issue's being resolved.

In the meantime, a black man named Bill Peace, a former slave who had served in the Union Army during the war and then returned to his old plantation, had persuaded his former owner to let him start a security force in order to prevent blacks from stealing hogs and cattle from the place. As a white old-timer remembered it years later, "This turned out like things generally do when a negro is placed in power; he soon had a regiment of five thousand negroes." In the wake of the brouhaha at the Republican county convention, the whites in Clarksdale began to hear rumors that Bill Peace, now calling himself General Peace, was readying his troops to sack, plunder, and burn the county, and murder all the white people.

A former Confederate general named James R. Chalmers arrived on the scene and organized a white militia. An engagement occurred at a bridge on the Sunflower River, which meanders through the center of Clarksdale. All the surviving accounts of the battle come from the reminiscences of whites taken down many years later, and they share a basic implausibility: they all say that a small band of whites numbering in the dozens drew itself into a line and, by this act alone, engendered complete panic among five thousand heavily armed blacks. The blacks ran; the whites aimed their rifles, but General Chalmers commanded them not to fire, saying, "Do not shoot these negroes, boys, we need cotton pickers."

The whites marched into Clarksdale, which then consisted solely of John Clark's country store, and camped for the night. At dawn a messenger appeared and announced that two blacks had shot and killed a white plantation manager. General Chalmers took his men to the plantation and caught two suspects. He ordered them taken to the county jail, but they never arrived there—the rumor was that they were killed by their guards en route and their bodies thrown in a lake. Chalmers's militia spent the next couple of days marching to various settlements in the county where General Peace's army had supposedly been sighted, but the army was nowhere to be found. John Brown, the black sheriff, escaped across the Mississippi River. He eventually settled in Kansas, never to be heard from in Clarksdale again. All in all there were six black casualties over the several days.

So ended the race riot, if it was a race riot. A month earlier there was another riot, also involving a rumored armed black uprising that never materialized, in the Delta town of Yazoo City. Exactly the same script was played out in a third Delta town, Rolling Fork, at the same time. All over Mississippi white militias began, in response to similar shadowy incidents, to take the law into their own hands. Governor Ames, sensing his authority crumbling, asked Washington to send federal troops to Mississippi to restore order, and was refused. It was in this atmosphere that the election of November 3, 1875, took place, in which many blacks were prevented from voting by force or by threats, in which violence broke out at several county seats, and in which the Democrats swept the Republicans out of office forever. Governor Ames was impeached and the positions in state government held by black officials were abolished. In the late 1880s Mississippi and the other Southern states, emboldened by Washington's post-Reconstruction hands-off attitude toward the South, began to pass the "Jim Crow" laws that officially made blacks second-class citizens. The Mississippi constitution of 1890, which effectively made it impossible for blacks to vote, was a model for the rest of the South. After its passage, the new political order of legal segregation was fully in place.

Segregation's heyday and sharecropping's heyday substantially coincided. Together the two institutions comprised a system of race relations that was, in its way, just as much a thing apart from the mainstream of American life as slavery had been, and that lasted just about as long as slavery did under the auspices of the government of the United States. The Mississippi Delta, which was only a footnote in the history of slavery because it was settled so late, was central to the history of the share-cropper system, especially the part of the system that involved blacks working on large plantations. The Delta had the largest-scale farming of the quintessential sharecropping crop, cotton. It was in the state that had the quintessential version of Jim Crow. The intellectual defense of share-cropping emerged from the Delta more than from any other place. The study of sharecropping by outsiders took place more in the Delta than in any other place. The black culture associated with sharecropping — including that culture's great art form, the blues — found its purest expression in the Delta. The Delta was the locus of our own century's peculiar institution.

The greatest days of the Delta were during World War I. The veneer of civilization had by then been pretty well laid down. There were clubs, schools, libraries, businesses, and solid homes in the towns. Agricultural prices were high nationally all through the 'teens, and World War I created an especially great demand for cotton. In 1919 the price of Delta cotton went to a dollar a pound, its all-time high relative to inflation. Land prices were as high as a thousand dollars an acre, which meant that all the big plantations were worth millions. In 1920 disaster struck: the price of cotton fell to ten cents a pound. The Delta began struggling on and off with economic depression a decade earlier than the rest of the country.

Before the cotton crash, though, the Delta's main problem was that black people had begun to migrate to the North to work in factories. The main transportation routes out of the Delta led straight north. The Illinois Central Railroad, which was by far the most powerful economic actor in Mississippi, had bought the Delta's main rail system in 1892; its passengers and freight hooked up in Memphis with the main Illinois Central line, which ran from New Orleans to Chicago, paralleling the route of U.S. Highway 51. U.S. Highway 61, paralleling the Mississippi River, passed through Clarksdale; U.S. 49, running diagonally northwest through the Delta from Jackson, Mississippi, met 61 on the outskirts of Clarksdale. These were famous routes. The Illinois Central trains were household names: the Panama Limited, the City of New Orleans, the Louisiane. One of the canonical blues songs is called "Highway Forty-

Nine." The closest cities to Clarksdale were Jackson, Memphis, New Orleans, and St. Louis, but none of them was fully removed from the social orbit of Southern segregation, or in a state of flat-out industrial expansion. The main place where all the routes out of Clarksdale really led was Chicago—job-rich Chicago.

Chicago was home to the *Chicago Defender*, the country's leading black newspaper, with a wide readership in the rural South. Robert S. Abbott, the *Defender*'s publisher, a small, round, well-dressed man who artfully combined the roles of race crusader and businessman, launched what he called "The Great Northern Drive" on May 15, 1917. The object of the drive was to exhort Southern blacks to come to Chicago, in order to make money and live under the legal benefits of citizenship. Abbott invented slogans ("The Flight Out of Egypt") and promoted songs ("Bound for the Promised Land," "Going Into Canaan") that pounded home a comparison to the events described in the Book of Exodus for his audience of extremely religious children of slaves. He persuaded the railroads to offer "club rates" to groups of blacks migrating to Chicago. At the same time strong-back businesses like the stockyards and packing houses, desperately short of labor because of the war, hired white labor agents and black preachers to tour the South recruiting. Black porters on the Illinois Central, who at the time were a prosperous, respected elite in black America, spread the word (and passed out the *Defender*) on their stops in Mississippi towns. E. Franklin Frazier, the black sociologist, reported that, "In some cases, after the train crossed the Ohio River, the migrants signalized the event by kissing the ground and holding prayer services." The black population of Chicago grew from 44,000 in 1910 to 109,000 in 1920, and then to 234,000 in 1930. A local commission on race relations reported that 50,000 black people had moved to Chicago from the South in eighteen months during the war.

The South naturally wanted to stop the migration. Some towns levied heavy "licensing fees" on labor agents to prevent them from coming around. Some threatened to put the agents in jail. In some places the police would arrest black people for vagrancy if they were found in the vicinity of the train station, or even pull them off of trains and put them in jail. There was a great deal of local propagandizing against migration by planters, politicians, black preachers in the hire of whites, and the press. A headline of the time from the Memphis *Commercial Appeal*, the big-city paper most read in the Delta, said:

SOUTH IS BETTER FOR NEGRO, SAY MISSISSIPPIANS
COLORED PEOPLE FOUND PROSPEROUS AND HAPPY

None of these tactics seem to have worked, but it didn't matter. When the soldiers came home in 1918, the demand for labor in Chicago slackened immediately. Later, the Depression hit Chicago especially hard, and the effect in the South of the high unemployment rate in Chicago was to discourage migration; the black population of Chicago grew by just 44,000 in the 1930s.

Anyway, the planters of the Delta had, during and after World War I, created a significant, though unpublicized, black migration of their own, from the hills of northern and central Mississippi to the Delta. The most common family history among black families in the Delta is exactly like Ruby Daniels's: the family scratching out an existence in the mediocre soil of the hills; the Delta plantation manager painting his enticing picture of the bountiful cotton crop in the Delta and the economic promise of the sharecropper system; and then the move.

This inside-Mississippi migration almost always ended with the family feeling that it had been badly gulled, because it turned out to be nearly impossible to make any money sharecropping. The sharecropper's family would move, early in the year, to a rough two- or three-room cabin on a plantation. The plumbing consisted of, at most, a washbasin, and usually not even that. The only heat came from a woodburning stove. There was no electricity and no insulation. During the winter, cold air came rushing in through cracks in the walls and the floor. Usually the roof leaked. The families often slept two and three to a bed.

Every big plantation was a fiefdom; the small hamlets that dot the map of the Delta were mostly plantation headquarters rather than conventional towns. Sharecroppers traded at a plantation-owned commissary, often in scrip rather than money. (Martin Luther King, Jr., on a visit to an Alabama plantation in 1965, was amazed to meet sharecroppers who had never seen United States currency in their lives.) They prayed at plantation-owned Baptist churches. Their children walked, sometimes miles, to plantation-owned schools, usually one- or two-room buildings without heating or plumbing. Education ended with the eighth grade and was extremely casual until then. All the grades were taught together, and most of the students were far behind the normal grade level for their age. The textbooks were tattered hand-me-downs from the white schools.

The planter could and did shut down the schools whenever there was work to be done in the fields, so the school year for the children of sharecroppers usually amounted to only four or five months, frequently interrupted. Many former sharecroppers remember going to school only when it rained. In 1938 the average American teacher's salary was $1,374, and the average value of a school district's buildings and equipment per student was $274. For blacks in Mississippi, the figures were $144 and $11.

Each family had a plot of land to cultivate, varying in size from fifteen to forty acres depending on how many children there were to work and how generous the planter was. In March, the planter would begin to provide the family with a "furnish," a monthly stipend of anywhere from fifteen to fifty dollars that was supposed to cover their living expenses until the crop came in in the fall. The planter also provided "seed money" for cotton seed, and tools for cultivation. He split the cost of fertilizer with the sharecropper. Thus equipped, the sharecropper would plow his land behind a mule, plant the cotton, and cultivate a "garden spot" for vegetables. Between planting and harvest, the cotton had to be regularly "chopped" — that is, weeded with a hoe — to ensure that it would grow to full height. The standard of living provided by the furnish was extremely low — cheap homemade clothes and shoes, beans, bread, and tough, fatty cuts of pork — but nonetheless the money often ran out before the end of the month, in which case the family would have to "take up" (borrow) at the commissary.

The cotton was picked in October and November and then was taken to the plantation's gin, where it was separated from its seeds and then weighed. The planter packed it into bales and sold it. A couple of weeks would pass during which the planter would do his accounting for the year. Then, just before Christmas, each sharecropper would be summoned to the plantation office for what was called "the settle." The manager would hand him a piece of paper showing how much money he had cleared from his crop, and pay him his share.

For most sharecroppers, the settle was a moment of bitterly dashed hope, because usually the sharecropper would learn that he had cleared only a few dollars, or nothing at all, or that he owed the planter money. The planters explained this by saying that ever since the cotton crash of 1920 they hadn't made much money either; what every sharecropper believed was that they were cheating. There was one set of accounting practices in particular that the sharecroppers considered cheating and the planters didn't: a series of fees the planters levied on the sharecroppers over the course of the year. The goods sold at the commissary were usually marked up. Many planters charged exorbitant interest on credit at the commissary, and sometimes on the furnish as well — 20 per cent was a typical rate. When tractors came in during the 1930s, the planters would charge the sharecroppers for the use of them to plow the fields. None of these charges were spelled out clearly as they were made, and usually they appeared on the sharecropper's annual statement as a single unitemized line, "Plantation Expense."

Then there was indisputable cheating. There was no brake on dishonest behavior by a planter toward a sharecropper. For a sharecropper to sue a planter was unthinkable. Even to ask for a more detailed accounting was known to be an action with the potential to endanger your life. The most established plantations were literally above the law where black people were concerned. The sheriff would call the planter when a matter of criminal justice concerning one of his sharecroppers arose, and if the planter said he preferred to handle it on his own (meaning, often, that he would administer a beating himself), the sheriff would stay off the place. Some planters were allowed to sign their sharecroppers out of the county jail if it was time to plant or chop or pick, and pay the bond later on credit. (If a sharecropper committed a crime serious enough for him to be sent to the state penitentiary, in Parchman, he would pick cotton there too — it was a working plantation in the Delta.) If a planter chose to falsify a sharecropper's gin receipt, lowering the weight of cotton in his crop, there was nothing the sharecropper could do about it; in fact a sharecropper was not allowed to receive and sign for a gin receipt on his own. If a planter wanted to "soak" a sharecropper, by adding a lot of imaginary equipment repairs to the expense side of his statement, the sharecropper had no way of knowing about it. As one Clarksdale planter puts it, quoting a proverb his father used to quote to him, "When self the wavering balance holds, 'tis seldom well adjusted."

Everybody agrees that some planters cheated and some didn't. Numbers are understandably difficult to come by. Hortense Powdermaker, an anthropologist from Yale who spent a year in the 1930s studying the town of Indianola, Mississippi, sixty miles down the road from Clarksdale, estimated that only a quarter of the planters were honest in their accounting.

The end of every year presented a sharecropper who had come up short with not many good options. He could stay put, piling up debt at the commissary until the furnish started again in March, and hope that the next year he would make a good enough crop to clear his debt. He could move to town, live in an unheated shack there, and try working for wages as a field hand or a domestic. He could, finally, try sharecropping on another place, and this was the choice that most sharecroppers made sooner or later. Some of them would pack up and move, and some of them would "slip off" in the night, to escape a too-onerous debt or some other kind of bad trouble with white people. The great annual reshuffling of black families between plantations in the Delta during the time after the settle and before the furnish is in retrospect one of the most difficult aspects of the sharecropper system to understand. The relatively few plantations where the sharecroppers regularly cleared money rarely had openings, so the families that moved usually wound up at another dishonest place where they would end the year in debt. The constant churning of the labor force couldn't have been good business for the planters, either.

Many of the sharecroppers and planters obviously weren't thinking all that far ahead. The more marginal the planter, the more likely he was to cheat, so that he could see some money himself at the end of the year. The more he cheated, the more likely he was to lose his labor after the settle. The sharecropper's rationale for moving was, in part, some mix of optimism and disgust. John Dollard, the Yale psychologist who helped develop the theory that frustration leads to aggression, also spent time during the thirties in Indianola, Mississippi, and wrote the book *Caste and Class in a Southern Town* about it. Dollard explained sharecroppers' moving by saying, "It seems that one of the few aggressive responses that the Negroes may make ... is to leave a particular plantation ... it is exactly what they could not do in prewar days, and it probably represents a confused general distrust, resentment, and hope for betterment. ..."

The false-promise aspect of sharecropping, the constant assertion by planters that your poverty was your own fault—you and he were simply business partners, your loss was right there in cold type on the statement—made it especially painful. As a sharecropper, you found your life was organized in a way that bore some theoretical relation to that of a free American—and yet the reality was completely different. There were only two ways to explain it, and neither one led to contentment: either there was a conspiracy dedicated to keeping you down, or—the whites' explanation—you were inferior, incapable. Poverty and oppression are never anything but hard to bear, but when you add to them the imputation of failure, it multiplies the difficulty.

RUBY HOPKINS stayed on the plantation at Hill House for only two years. During that time, Ruby's mother, Ardell, met and married another sharecropper on the same place, a man named George Washington Stamps, known as G.W. In 1919 Ruby's grandparents quarreled and split up, and her grandmother, Letha Hopkins, moved the family — Ardell and G.W., Ruby, and Ruby's twin sister Ruth — down to a plantation in Anguilla, Mississippi, in the southern part of the Delta. In 1922, the plantation flooded; after the high water receded, the owner asked his sharecroppers to move to another plantation he owned, called Tallwood, which was outside Clarksdale on a rural highway that was known as New Africa Road because so many black sharecroppers lived there. The family moved.

In August 1924, Ruby's grandmother died; after the settle that year, Ardell and G.W. decided to move to another place on New Africa Road because they thought they could make more money. They made the crops of 1925 and 1926 there, but during 1926 G.W. ran off with another woman, stayed away for a while, then came back and asked Ardell for a reconciliation. She agreed, but in her heart she hadn't forgiven him for his transgression. After the crop she slipped off, taking Ruby and Ruth, and moved in with one of her sisters who lived on a pecan plantation that was on an island in the middle of Moon Lake, north of Clarksdale. They lived on the island during the great Mississippi River flood of 1927. Ardell remarried there, but immediately after the wedding her new husband became so jealous and possessive that while he was plowing the fields he would make her stand in the door of their shack so he could keep an eye on her. The first chance she got, Ardell arranged to leave the twins with an elderly minister and his wife on the island, slipped off during the night again, and went off to find a new life.

When Ardell was settled in with a new man — just housekeeping, not married — on a plantation in the nearby town of Lula, she sent for the twins. Ruby was baptized in Moon Lake in 1928. Ardell's romance broke up not long afterward; the twins were sent to live with their grandfather, George Hopkins, who by then was remarried and was a sharecropper on a plantation in Belen, northeast of Clarksdale. Twelve-year-old Ruby helped chop and pick the cotton crop of 1929 there.

In 1930 Ardell was married again, to a man named Sidney Burns, and she took the twins back. The family planted its crop on another plantation along New Africa Road. In August, Ardell took sick. Her body seemed to swell up, and she could barely move. For three months she stayed in bed, gradually getting sicker. Members of the family sat up with her in shifts. Nobody knew what was wrong; it was only years later that Ruby realized that it was hypertension, the same disease that had taken her grandmother a few years earlier. Lying in bed and living on a diet of very salty food was probably the worst thing Ardell could have done for her condition, but she didn't know that. On a Sunday evening, October 5, 1930, she died, at the age of thirty.

Ruby, Ruth, and Sidney Burns finished making the cotton crop, and then Ruby and Ruth started moving again: first to an aunt's place on another plantation, then to their grandfather's again. This was an especially hard time in Ruby's life. Despite Ardell's unsettled life and frequent absences, Ruby loved her without reservation and always felt the love was fully returned; now she missed her mother terribly. The Great Depression, or, as sharecroppers called it, "the panic crash," had begun, and times got harder. Ruby's grandfather always seemed to come out behind. One year at the settle he was told he had cleared fifteen cents, and he came home to his cabin, sat down at the table, and cried. After the settle in 1931, he owed money and decided to slip off, but the planter got wind of his plans and on a Sunday afternoon came to the family's cabin, took back the provisions they had just bought on credit at the commissary, kicked them out, and nailed the door shut behind them. At that point they were so poor that Ruby had no shoes; she had to walk barefoot ten miles down the road to an aunt's house and ask to be taken in.

Ruby's grandfather made a deal with a new white man and started sharecropping on his plantation. There Ruby and her step-grandmother began to quarrel. One day her step-grandmother hit her, and Ruby hit back; after that she left and stayed with some cousins on New Africa Road for a while. For the crop of 1933, Ruby's grandfather was on another plantation, and Ruby moved back with him. One day the planter, a white man named Tom Ware, sent for Ruby and her grandfather to come see him at his house. Ware called them into the living room — an unusual invitation, since a sharecropper almost never saw the inside of a white man's house — and asked George Hopkins whether he'd like to sit down and have some coffee. Then he said, "Uncle George" — white people called black people by their first names until late middle age, at which point the honorific "Uncle" or "Aunt" was applied — "Uncle George, I'd like your girl there." As Ruby sat silently, terrified, Ware complimented her grandfather on her beauty and maturity, and explained that if he agreed to this arrangement, he would clear money every year and never have to want for anything. George was noncommittal; that night the family slipped off.

Toward the end of 1933 things got a little better. Ruby's twin sister, Ruth, had already been married once very briefly and run off from her husband; now she met an older, settled man named Ernie Thigpen, and they decided to marry. Ruby's youngest aunt, Ceatrice, had gotten engaged too, to a man named Porter O'Neill. Ruth and Ceatrice had a double wedding in a cabin on a plantation on New Africa Road and formed a fairly stable extended family group. Ruby moved in with them. The group stayed together for the crop of 1934. After the settle, Ruby went to spend Christmas with her grandfather, who by then was a sharecropper on a big plantation outside the town of Marks, fifteen miles east of Clarksdale, that was owned (as were most things in the town of Marks) by a rich family named the Selfs. While she was there it rained for three days without stopping. Her grandfather's cabin was flooded, and so were all the roads; they camped out on a hill and waited for the water to recede.

George Hopkins had become friends with another sharecropper family on the Self place, called Daniels. The Daniels's son, W.D., used to come by and cut wood for George, and he and Ruby began to court. W.D. told Ruby he'd like to marry her. She told him he'd better do it soon, because as soon as the high water went down she was going back to Ruth and Ceatrice's place, and there was a young man there named Harold Brown who wanted to marry her too. On February 2, 1935, a Saturday, Ruby and W.D. were married by a preacher on the Self place. Looking back on it, Ruby didn't think she was really ever in love with W.D.; it was just that she was eighteen, and wanted to be grown.

Ruby and W.D. settled on the Self plantation and made crops there in 1935 and 1936. In 1937, W.D.'s father learned about a "Tenant Purchase Program" run by Franklin Roosevelt's Farm Security Administration that would lend sharecroppers money to buy land. He acquired forty acres in the woods, laboriously cleared it by hand, and began making a cotton crop of his own. Ruby and W.D. lived there too. That year the high water came again, and the place was full of snakes that rode in on the flood. Ruby's feelings about snakes were such that it was impossible for her to enjoy this new life of independent farming. She decided she wanted to move to town.

During that year, 1937, Ruby saw her father for the first time. After World War I, he had moved back to the hills, living here and there. Sometimes he would write letters to Ruby and Ruth in the Delta, or send them dresses. Now that they were grown, they decided to visit him. They traveled by train and bus to the town of Louisville, Mississippi, where they had arranged to meet him in front of a cotton gin. Their first glimpse of each other was a crystal-clear memory for Ruby into old age: "Oh, my children," he cried out, nearly overcome with emotion, and embraced them.

In 1938 Ruby found out that President Roosevelt had started another government program called the Works Progress Administration, which gave poor black people jobs doing manual labor for a dollar a day. She began trying to talk W.D. into taking one of those jobs in Clarksdale, and finally he agreed. After the crop they moved into town. Ruby's share-cropper days were over.

AMERICANS ARE imbued with the notion that social systems proceed from ideas, because that is what happened at the founding of our country. The relationship of society and ideas can work the other way around, though: people can create social systems first and then invent ideas that will fulfill their need to feel that the world as it exists makes sense. White people in the Delta responded to their need to believe in the system of economic and political subjugation of blacks as just, fair, and inevitable by embracing the idea of black inferiority, and for them the primary evidence of this was lives like Ruby's. To whites, the cause of the chaotic aspect of sharecropper society was not pain or deprivation, but incapacity. Black people were, in the words of William Alexander Percy, "simple and affectionate." David Cohn saw blacks as "emotionally unstable" and "childlike" people for whom "life is a long moral holiday."

The whites' capacity for rationalization was such that in their vision of Delta society, it was whites who were in a tough situation; being black was fun. Whites had to shoulder responsibilities, whereas the very concept of responsibility was foreign to blacks — the portion of the brain that contained it must have been missing in them. Whites had to make sure the work got done, because no black person would work unless forced to. The conscience was another faculty that blacks were born without; Cohn wrote that the lot of a black murderer "is softened because he is rarely a victim to the gnawing pains and terrors of remorse which so often make living a bitter unbearable reality to the white man who has killed a human being."

Most of the rules and customs that whites made for blacks to live by emerged from, or anyway were justified by, the whites' ideas about blacks' "nature." Scrupulous financial dealings with sharecroppers were pointless, since any money the sharecroppers cleared, they would only waste. There was nothing wrong with the planters' winking at all sorts of violations of the law by their sharecroppers, from moonshining to petty theft to polygamy to murder, because blacks had no moral life to begin with. The education of sharecroppers' children was haphazard as a convenience to the planters, but also by design, because, in David Cohn's words, "the Negro should be taught to work with his hands," and real schooling "tends to unbalance him mentally." The white ideal in the Delta was that a planter should be like a father and the sharecroppers like his children, dependent, carefree, and grateful. One of the big planters in Clarksdale, Roy Flowers, used to have his sharecroppers stand out in the fields at Christmas time while he proceeded down the turn rows with a pot of silver dollars, handing out (as another planter puts it) a little bit of the money he had stolen from them at the settle.

During the 1927 flood, William Alexander Percy was the head of the relief operation in Greenville, the largest town in the Delta, which is seventy miles south of Clarksdale. The Percys were probably the Delta's leading family and considered themselves to be devoted friends of the Negro. The family staunchly opposed the Ku Klux Klan for years; William Alexander Percy's father lost a seat he held briefly in the United States Senate to James K. Vardaman for being too liberal on "the Negro question." The flood put Greenville in a state of emergency that lasted for months; sixty thousand people, the great majority of them black, were in need of temporary housing. In working with the other town fathers to manage the situation, Percy wrote later, "Of course, none of us was influenced by what the Negroes themselves wanted: they had no capacity to plan for their own welfare; planning for them was another of our burdens."

The *Chicago Defender*, to Percy's utter shock, began to criticize him for his management of the emergency. He felt the *Defender*'s "campaign of vilification" against him had an "embittering influence" on blacks in

Greenville, and so helped cause a racial crisis that arose toward the end of the emergency. One day Percy lacked the hands to unload a Red Cross shipment of supplies, so he ordered the police to go to the black neighborhood and conscript some labor. One black man who resisted was shot and killed by a policeman. Soon, as Percy remembered it, "the Negroes had worked themselves into a state of wild excitement and resentment"; Percy called a meeting at a black church and insisted that no whites but him be present. There he delivered a speech blaming the murder on the blacks. As he recalled his words, he said: "Because of your sinful, shameful laziness, because you refused to work in your own behalf unless you were paid, one of your race has been killed. . . . That foolish young policeman is not the murderer. The murderer is you! Your hands are dripping with blood. . . . Down on your knees, murderers, and beg your God not to punish you as you deserve."

The black uprising that whites feared never materialized. The Red Cross agreed to begin paying people to unload supplies. The whole incident could be seen as an example of black commitment to nonviolent protest (against being forced to work without pay), even after a black man had been killed. The lesson whites drew from it was quite the opposite: blacks were cowards and would back down when confronted by the likes of William Alexander Percy; blacks were shirkers who, as David Cohn put it, "will discharge even the most rudimentary social obligations only under compulsion"; a social order based on blacks' being kept in a lower caste was the only answer for the Delta. There was a circularity to this logic. Blacks would be denied an opportunity — in this case, to express their views on the management of the emergency. They would respond in pretty much the way you'd expect. Their response would prove to whites that they'd been right not to trust the blacks in the first place. Education was a similar case: whites created a spectacularly poor school system for blacks that was designed to produce graduates who were only marginally literate; then whites would point to blacks' deficiencies in speaking and writing standard English as proof that blacks were ineducable.

All these childlike qualities that whites in the Delta read into sharecropper society were not really the heart of the matter, though. The heart of the matter was sex. Here is Cohn again: "The Negro . . . is sexually completely free and untrammeled. . . . To him the expressions and manifestations of sex are as simple and as natural as the manifestations of nature in the wind and the sun and the rain, in the cycles of the seasons and the rounds of the growing crops. Sexual desire is an imperative need, raw and crude and strong. It is to be satisfied when and wherever it arises." The idea that blacks possessed a powerful, uncontrolled sexuality was responsible for the rough edge of the white Delta ideal of benevolent paternalism: a certain harshness was necessary in order to protect white women from black men.

The civil rights movement in the South in the 1960s looms so large in the national memory today that the movement's great enemy, legal segregation, is remembered as the keystone of the caste system. But in the heyday of segregation, social segregation was more important to whites — social segregation built around absolutely preventing the possibility of a black man's impregnating a white woman. Gunnar Myrdal, in *An American Dilemma*, written just before segregation began to crumble, provided a ranking of the various aspects of segregation in their importance to white Southerners. Whether blacks voted was only fourth most important, and the denial of good jobs was sixth; first was "the bar against intermarriage and sexual intercourse involving white women." David Cohn wrote: "We do not give the Negro civic equality because we are fearful that this will lead in turn to demands for social equality. And social equality will tend toward what we will never grant — the right of equal marriage. As a corollary to these propositions we enforce racial separation and segregation." And: "It is the sexual factor . . . from which social and physical segregation grows."

In the panoply of white fears about blacks, this sexual one was not only the most important but also the most wholly misplaced. Whites were right that blacks, given the chance, would choose not to pick cotton any more, and would vote for black candidates for political office, but they were absolutely wrong in imagining that any relaxation of the social codes of segregation would lead to the dreaded result of amalgamation of the races. It is tempting to see the white conviction that mixing of the racial stocks was the ultimate danger as another aspect of the pose they had struck to justify the system they had set up, but if it was a pose, it was an unconscious one, a sincere self-delusion. Everything flowed from their idea that if blacks and whites were allowed to deal with each other as equals, sex would be the result. That was why blacks were always called by their first names and whites, from the age of ten or eleven, by "Mister" or "Miss." It was the reason a black person could not enter a white person's house by the front door, or sit next to a white person in a public place, or go to school with whites.

The family lives of sharecroppers were, for the white people of the Delta, Exhibit A in their case that segregation was a necessity because of the nature of black sexuality. The white interpretation of the sharecroppers' sex lives was that they were governed by the principle of absolute lack of inhibition: everybody was sleeping with everyone else whenever the impulse arose. Short-lived common-law couplings and illegitimate children were the inevitable (and, for many planters, the desired) result. Every aspect of the black social life on the plantations, as whites saw it, had a brazen sexual cast. At the Sunday church services there was wild shouting and singing, and women invariably "fell out" in swoons of not exactly religious ecstasy. The ministers were sleeping with their parishioners. In addition to religion, the sharecroppers practiced "hoodoo," hexing each other in the pursuit of their turbulent romantic lives. Young men played a game called "the dozens," in which they traded imaginatively worded sexual boasts and insults. On Saturday nights there were raucous parties on every plantation, in a shack known as a "tonk" or a "juke," or in a family's cabin. The sharecroppers shot craps, drank cripplingly impure moonshine whiskey, danced to loud, strange music, and got into fights. A standard Delta anecdote had a sharecropper approaching a planter with a sly smile and saying, "Boss, if you could be a nigger one Saturday night, you'd never want to be white again!"

A procession of professional observers from outside moved through the Delta and the rest of the sharecropper South during the 1930s, after the New Deal had brought a critique of the sharecropper system into the public debate. Probably the best-remembered of them today are James Agee and Walker Evans, the writer and photographer who collaborated on *Let Us Now Praise Famous Men*, which portrays the world of the small-scale white tenant farmer scratching out a living from the depleted soil of the Southern hills. The most detailed surviving accounts of the quite different plantation-based, all-black sharecropper system that prevailed in the Delta came not from journalists like Agee and Evans, but from professors; their work provides some evidence, from a source far more disinterested than the planters, about the nature of black sharecropper life. Hortense Powdermaker and John Dollard were both in Indianola in the 1930s. Charles S. Johnson, a sociologist trained at the University of Chicago (and later the first black president of Fisk University), published a study of black sharecroppers in rural Georgia, *Shadow of the Plantation*, in 1934. Arthur Raper's *Preface to Peasantry*, published in 1936, is a description of the same area in Georgia that

Johnson studied. Gunnar Myrdal traveled all over the South in the 1940s while he was working on *An American Dilemma*. All these writers rejected wholeheartedly the idea of black inferiority, but they agreed that family life among sharecroppers was different from the ordinary family life of the rest of the country.

Johnson surveyed 612 rural black families, most of them caught up in the sharecropper system. There were 181 illegitimate children in the survey; 152 of the families were headed by a single woman. Though most of the families were headed by a married couple (often the marriage was common-law), only 231 of the 612 families were headed by a couple both of whom were in their first marriage. "Sex, as such, appears to be a thing apart from marriage," Johnson wrote; in the county he studied, 35 per cent of blacks tested positive for syphilis. Raper, without citing statistics, wrote, ". . . there is more illegitimacy among the Negro group and consequently more children dependent on one parent."

Powdermaker wrote that "the typical Negro family throughout the South is matriarchal and elastic," and that the "personnel of these matriarchal families is variable and even casual," often including illegitimate children. Marriages were common-law in "the large majority of the households." Dollard wrote that "it is clear that social patterns governing sexual behavior are much less restrictive than they are among middle-class people . . . especially among poorer rural Negroes." Myrdal mentioned the "extremely high illegitimacy" among blacks in the South — 16 per cent of births to blacks were out of wedlock, a ratio eight times that of whites — and felt that the true figure for blacks was probably much higher because "The census information on the marital status of Negroes is especially inaccurate, since unmarried couples are inclined to report themselves as married, and women who have never married but who have children are inclined to report themselves as widowed."

In trying to account for what they found, these writers assumed they were seeing the continuation of a pattern of family life that began during slavery, when abduction from Africa, the brutal passage to America, and regular sales that split spouses apart and separated children from their families caused a mutation in the structure of the black family. Certainly the black sharecropper family as described by the scholars who observed it was quite different from families in traditional cultures, in Africa or anywhere else in the world, where marriage is an elaborately formal institution. The places in the world where marriage is regarded more casually are ones where people have been abruptly moved from a tradi-

tional culture to the fringes of an industrial one — like Venezuela or
Guinea-Bissau.

Today, a generation of historical scholarship — most notably Herbert
Gutman's *The Black Family in Slavery and Freedom* — stands in refutation
of the idea that slavery destroyed the black family. Gutman presents the
slave family as having been organized somewhat differently from most
American families (for example, there was no taboo against a woman's
having her first child before marriage), but on the whole, in his tableau,
the stable marriage was the dominant institution in African-American
family life during and immediately after slavery. The aim of his book is
to explode an exaggerated picture of black family life as having been
utterly and permanently incapacitated by slavery, and he does this convincingly. It isn't Gutman's aim, or that of other recent slave historians,
to tease out whatever differences there might have been between the
family structures of rural blacks and those of most other Americans.
Therefore the picture we have of black family life under the sharecropper
system essentially doesn't fit with the work that historians of the black
family under slavery have produced for the past quarter century. In particular, the available evidence about the sharecropper family indicates
that first marriages of lifelong duration were the exception, whereas in
the slave family, according to Gutman, they were the rule. Present-day
historians have not directed enough attention to the sharecropper system
to have worked out the differences between what we now know about
the slave family and the decades-old material we have about the sharecropper family. So it is somewhat mysterious where the structure of the
sharecropper family came from, if the observers of it described it accurately; but they do provide a few guesses besides the legacy of slavery.

Dollard more than the others bought the planters' idea of the lazy,
carefree sharecropper. "They are satisfied with a secure furnish, take it
easy, and let the white man worry," he wrote. He blamed this on the
planters. They had set up the system so as to inculcate a state of dependency in the sharecroppers: "The furnish system is a kind of permanent
dole which appeals to the pleasure principle and relieves the Negro of
responsibility and the necessity of forethought. . . . One can think of the
lower-class Negroes as bribed and drugged by this system." Powdermaker, on the other hand, didn't believe that sharecroppers were either
contented or absolutely free sexually. (If they were, she pointed out, then
jealousy wouldn't be the great cause of marital discord and violence that
it was.) She saw the caste system as pervasively denying respect to black

people, with the result in the lives of the black poor being not childlike enjoyment but grown-up pain: "Perhaps the most severe result of denying respect to an individual is the insidious effect on his self-esteem. Few can long resist self-doubt in the face of constant belittling and humiliation at the hands of others."

Powdermaker and Johnson both mentioned the relative economic independence of poor black women as a destabilizing influence on families, and both blamed the high rate of violent crime among sharecroppers on the custom by which white law enforcement officials regarded blacks as living (in Powdermaker's words) "outside the law." Johnson said that the sharecroppers' "extreme isolation from society" had allowed "unique moral codes" to develop, but he predicted that the closer the sharecroppers got to the mainstream of American society, the more disorganized their lives would become, at least in the short run. He wrote, prophetically for someone who had no idea how brief the run of the sharecropper system was going to turn out to be, "This group . . . has taken form . . . outside the dominant current of the American culture. . . . The very fact of this cultural difference presents the danger of social disorganization in any sudden attempt to introduce new modes of living and conceptions of values."

It is clear that whatever the cause of its differentness, black sharecropper society on the eve of the introduction of the mechanical cotton picker was the equivalent of big-city ghetto society today in many ways. It was the national center of illegitimate childbearing and of the female-headed family. It had the worst public education system in the country, the one whose students were most likely to leave school before finishing and most likely to be illiterate even if they did finish. It had an extremely high rate of violent crime: in 1933, the six states with the highest murder rates were all in the South, and most of the murders were black-on-black. Sexually transmitted disease and substance abuse were nationally known as special problems of the black rural South; home-brew whiskey was much more physically perilous than crack cocaine is today, if less addictive, and David Cohn reported that blacks were using cocaine in the towns of the Delta before World War II.

In the North, at the time, when problems of family disorganization appeared in black neighborhoods, they were routinely explained as a matter of recent migrants from the rural South bringing their old way of life with them to the city. W. E. B. DuBois, in *The Philadelphia Negro*, wrote, "Among the lowest class of recent immigrants and other unfortunates there is much sexual promiscuity and the absence of a real home life. . . . Cohabitation of a more or less permanent character is a direct offshoot of the plantation life and is practiced considerably. . . ." While researching the book, DuBois had spent a summer in rural Virginia because he wanted to learn about the area that many black Philadelphians had moved from; a few years later, in *The Souls of Black Folk*, he elaborated on the theme of troubled family life on the Southern plantation, saying, in a section about sharecropper life in rural Georgia, "The plague-spot in sexual relations is easy marriage and easy separation. . . . in too many cases family quarrels, a roving spirit, a rival suitor, or perhaps more frequently the hopeless battle to support a family, lead to separation, and a broken household is the result." E. Franklin Frazier, as a graduate student in sociology at the University of Chicago, studied the birth records at Cook County Hospital in the 1920s and found that between 10 and 15 per cent of the black mothers there weren't married. "Nearly four-fifths of these unmarried mothers were born in the South and over a half of them had been in Chicago less than five years," he reported. Frazier researched the unwed mothers' backgrounds and found that fewer than an eighth of them had grown up in the same home with both their parents; to his mind they were replicating the pattern they had known in the South.

Ruby Lee Daniels saw her early life on the plantations around Clarksdale a little differently from the way that either the planters or the experts saw it. Certainly the marital bond for sharecroppers was an extremely unstable one in her version. When she was in her seventies, she could think of only one longstanding happy marriage among the people she had known well, her aunt Addie Green's, and even Addie had had two marriages break up before she got into the good one. In the old days, as Ruby remembered them, marriage was an institution lightly entered and lightly left. Nobody had any money to put on a real wedding ceremony, and nobody bothered to get divorced, because they didn't have any possessions to divide. As she says, "People would get married on a plantation one week, and the next week one of them would be gone."

Ruby was well acquainted with the social scenery surrounding courtship and marriage — Saturday night, and so on. She went to parties on plantations practically every Saturday night when she was a young woman. They would usually take place in somebody's two-room shack, with all the furniture removed for the evening; there would be gambling in one room and dancing in the other, to the music of an acoustic guitar. At one party she remembered, a fight started, somebody fired a shot, and she and the other guests jumped off the porch of the shack and escaped through the cotton fields. Hoodoo was a theme in the life of Ruby's family all through the 1920s and 1930s. The deaths of her grandmother and of one of her aunts were attributed to their having been "fixed" by hoodoo doctors in the hire of their romantic rivals. The aunt who died had never recovered from the birth of a child; the theory was that another woman who was in love with her husband had sneaked into Ruby's aunt's house, stolen a lock of her hair, and had it fixed by a hoodoo man. Ruby's aunt Ceatrice was once involved with a man who mistreated her, but she wouldn't leave him. Ruby's grandfather became convinced that the man had had Ceatrice fixed, so he took Ceatrice to a hoodoo doctor to have the spell broken. The doctor instructed Ceatrice to go home, feel above the front door frame until she found a small bag, take it down, and throw it out the back door into the fields. Then Ceatrice had to walk out the back door, around the house, and back in the front door, and repeat this three times. She faithfully followed the doctor's instructions, and sure enough, she soon left the man.

All of this, though, had to do with the travails of courtship and marriage; in Ruby's mind, there was a great distinction between marriage and family. Marriage was a bitter disappointment. Everybody yearned for a happy marriage, but almost no one got one — as Ruby puts it, "there was no till death do you part." This was the most immediate and painful way in which the difference between the promise of American life and the reality of poor black life made itself felt. To Ruby, the best (but not wholly satisfactory) explanation for marriage not working out was the constant pressure of poverty and the no-goodness of most men, their drinking and violence and unreliability and infidelity.

Ruby's feelings about her blood relatives, on the other hand, were entirely positive. She loved both her parents, understood their failings, and harbored no resentments against them. Her circle of acquaintances outside her immediate family, especially her aunts, had been a crucial source of support when she was growing up. People with minimal resources of their own had taken her in, as if she were their own daughter, whenever she needed help. Underneath the disorganization that outsiders saw was an extended-family system that had real strength. The network of friends and relatives got one another through the constant round of crises that made up the sharecropper life, crises so severe that the accumulation of them caused many people Ruby knew simply to give up and lose themselves in fleeting pleasures. Ruby never gave up; as she puts it, she always found a way to scuffle and make it through. What enabled her to do that was a self-assurance that her family had somehow been able to create in the absence of any of the tokens of worth that are available to most people: "I know I don't have what other people have – money, cars – but I never felt lower than other people. My grandfather always taught me to feel equal to other people – the big-shot people who went to this and that college and have degrees. I can talk just as good as them. I know the words."

When Ruby and her husband moved to Clarksdale at the end of 1938, she got a job as a cook and housekeeper for a white lady, at $2.50 a week. Ruby's education was pretty good for someone of her generation – eighth grade, with some time spent in one of the country schools endowed by Julius Rosenwald, the Sears Roebuck tycoon in Chicago, which were much better than the ordinary plantation schools. Still, there weren't any careers open to her except the cotton fields and domestic work. The pay was so low that every respectable white family in the Delta – even schoolteachers' and mail carriers' families – had at least one full-time servant.

Ruby got by. In those days you could buy salt pork, or beans, or black-eyed peas, for five cents a pound. You could make a batch of biscuits with a nickel's worth of flour. A dress cost $1.98 at the shops on Issaqueena Street. When money ran short, people shared what little they had. Ruby could go out on the trucks and pick cotton on Saturdays if she needed to. Sometimes at work she used to think: "This white woman thinks I'm good enough to nurse her baby and to make the meals that her family eats. Why am I not good enough to go in her house by the front door?" But such thoughts were not to be given free rein, even in one's own mind. When Ruby was growing up, she was taught to look up to white people, not to hate them. White people ran everything. They lived well. If you were black, you had to get things from white people. Rebellion against segregation was fruitless, so it was for Ruby a subject dealt with in whispers and private feelings. She had only one childhood memory of a protest against the system, and it was a hidden protest: a group of old folks walking down a country road in the 1920s when there weren't any white people around, quietly singing the old folk song "We Shall Overcome."

Black people in Clarksdale passed around stories, which were gradually burnished into legend, about the worst excesses of the system – stories involving sex and bloodshed. One day a black boy in Clarksdale who was working in a white family's yard was called into the house by the white woman.

When he got inside, he saw that she had her blouse off. She asked him to fasten her in back. What could he do? Everybody knew that if a black man refused a white woman's advances, it was quite likely that she would accuse him of rape and he would be lynched. If he didn't refuse, and an affair began, and it was found out, an accusation of rape followed by a lynching was, again, the likely result. The woman could hardly afford to admit the truth, because if she did she would be banished from the community.

In this case there was no chance for the boy to make his decision, because the woman's husband walked in. She screamed, to indicate that she was being assaulted. The boy went on trial for rape, but the woman's husband had figured out the real story by then, and he stood up in court and said the boy should be set free. The freedom lasted only a few minutes. A gang of white boys waylaid the black boy as he was walking home from the courthouse, tied his feet to the back of a car, and drove all the way from Clarksdale to Marks with the black boy's crushed, bloody head bouncing along the roadbed.

Another story was about a crazy black man who got a gun, holed up in a cotton warehouse, and started firing shots out. The county sheriff, A. H. "Brick" Gotcher, arrived at the scene and went inside the warehouse to talk the black man into surrendering. The black man shot and killed Gotcher; Gotcher's deputies shot and killed the black man. In white memory, the story was completely nonracial because the black man had no grievance, and its lesson was that Gotcher was heroically brave. In black memory, the story was absolutely racial — the black man had probably been set up in some way, and after he was killed his body was dragged down the black commercial strip on Fourth Street in broad daylight to impress in the minds of the blacks of Clarksdale that nobody else ever better try anything like that again.

Black Clarksdale was full of rumors and secrets, because there was so much that couldn't be expressed openly or that blacks were in no position to investigate. Everybody black in Clarksdale knew, though there was no hard proof of it, that Bessie Smith, the great singer who died after a car accident outside Clarksdale in 1937, had been refused admission to the county hospital on grounds of her race, at a time when she could still have been saved. Shortly after that, the same hospital refused admission to the wife of one of Clarksdale's two or three most prominent black citizens, a dentist named P. W. Hill, when she was in severe distress during childbirth. She and her baby died on the road to Memphis, or so the story went; it was so shrouded in mystery that even Dr. Hill's son and namesake doesn't know what really happened, because he never dared to ask his father about it.

White society as a whole looked corrupt to black people, because the corrupt side of it was most of what black people (especially black men, who rarely entered white people's homes) saw. Black people knew things about white people's secret lives that weren't known in the white part of town. When a light-skinned baby was born in the black part of Clarksdale, gossip would circulate as to which respectable white citizen was the father. Sometimes a black family would live inexplicably well, and the reason was that a conscience-stricken white man was sending remittances for the support of his officially unacknowledged children. White men's cars would be seen parked in the black section, in front of the houses of prostitutes or mistresses or bootleggers. White policemen could chase women or gamble or beat people up in black neighborhoods without anyone in authority finding out about it. A lot went on in the county jail that never saw the light of day.

In addition to keeping white people's secrets, black people kept their own. In daily life, any resentment that blacks felt for whites was usually kept hidden under a mask of slightly uncomprehending servility that black people knew fit whites' basic picture of them. Involvement in a civil rights organization had to be kept quiet too, of course. At the time, most of the high school– and college-educated black people in Clarksdale were in teaching — "preach, teach, or farm" was the slogan that summarized the black career options — and the state required black teachers to sign an affidavit that they weren't members of the National Association for the Advancement of Colored People. The NAACP was a middle-class organization that without teachers on the rolls would barely have existed, so black teachers joined it secretly. Any black people who had managed to accumulate some money took pains not to put it on display, because it was easy enough for someone deemed a rich, uppity nigger to have his bank credit denied, to find his white clientele (if he did construction work, or hauled labor to the plantations) abruptly taking its business elsewhere, or to lose his land through a trumped-up title dispute. There was an old tradition in the Delta of blacks gaining some temporary advantage by informing on their own people, tipping off the white folks about an errant black person's inclinations and intentions — to slip off a plantation, say. The resentment of the snitches, the "white man's niggers," was so intense that keeping your mouth shut was considered not merely a matter of prudence with regard to whites, but also of honor within black society.

For the black middle class of Clarksdale — a group that made up about 15 per cent of the black population and was defined more by education and attitude than by money — the most important secret of all was not anything specific; it was the family life of the black poor. The catechism of the defenders of segregation ran this way: illegitimate childbearing, the short duration of romantic liaisons, and the constant domestic violence among the sharecroppers and poor blacks in town clearly demonstrated that blacks were sexually uncontrollable. This made social segregation a necessity. Social segregation led to legal segregation in education, government, and the economy. The main losers from legal segregation were not the black poor but the black middle class, whose members were educated enough to get good jobs but were denied them by law and by custom. The poor blacks' way of life, in other words, caused the middle-class blacks to suffer the humiliation and economic loss that went with second-class citizenship.

Outsiders who came down to study the South often mentioned how hard it was to get middle-class blacks to talk about the black lower class. "It is difficult to get the truth about the lower-class patterns from middle-class Negro people," John Dollard complained. There was a code of silence on the subject. A scene in Ralph Ellison's *Invisible Man* has the hero giving the rich white Northern benefactor of a black college in the South a tour of sharecropper cabins in the outlying rural area. They meet a share-cropper who tells the benefactor, in great detail, the story of how he impregnated his own daughter. The narrator reacts with horror: "How can he tell this to white men, I thought, when he knows they'll say that all Negroes do such things? I looked at the floor, a red mist of anguish before my eyes."

In Clarksdale, all blacks lived on the east side of the railroad tracks, and all whites on the west side, but there were distinct neighborhoods within the black area. Most of the poor blacks lived in an area called the Round-yard, which runs along the bank of the Sunflower River; all of the black middle class lived in the Brickyard, a little farther north. Families in the Brickyard went to the more middle-class churches, such as Friendship African Methodist Episcopal and First Baptist. Their social life revolved around church circles and associations like the Masons and the Knights and Daughters of Tabor, a venerable black mutual-aid society that operated a hospital in the all-black Delta town of Mound Bayou, twenty-five miles south of Clarksdale. Their children attended the county agricultural high school outside of town, which was the only secondary education available to blacks in Coahoma County, since Clarksdale didn't build a black high school until the 1950s. On Saturday night, most teenagers in the Brickyard were not allowed to go down to the clubs on Issaqueena Street, because they would be full of poor folks from the Roundyard and the plantations. If there was a shooting at the Red Top Inn, you were supposed to hear about it on the radio, not be an eyewitness. There were block clubs in the Brickyard; whenever a poor family, especially a poor family from the country, happened to move into the neighborhood, the block club quickly made contact and began the process of indoctrination into middle-class standards of household maintenance. The transition from plantation to town was supposed to be a step up in the world.

In 1940 Ruby's aunt Ceatrice left her husband and moved to the town of Massillon, Ohio, where some friends of the family were living. There she met a man from Mississippi named Ulysses Wilkes, and together they moved to Chicago. Ceatrice got a job with a company that did janitorial work in big office buildings at night. In her letters and on visits home she painted a rosy picture for Ruby of life in the North.

In 1941, Ruby's husband, W. D. Daniels, was inducted into the Army and left Clarksdale for what was sure to be a long time. Ruby met and fell in love with a married man named Kermit Butler. Kermit had a good job, driving an ambulance for the Century funeral home in Clarksdale. Funeral homes were the only substantial black businesses in Clarksdale. They existed because of the strength of two traditions: Southern racial custom made it unthinkable for a white funeral home to handle black corpses; and every black person in the Delta, no matter how desperately poor, was determined to receive a decent burial. All sharecroppers, knowing they would probably die penniless, carried burial insurance to pay for their funeral and interment. Hortense Powdermaker wrote, "In the dilapidated shacks of undernourished families, whose very subsistence depends upon government relief, the insurance envelope is almost invariably to be seen hanging on the wall." Burial insurance was provided by the funeral homes, and the steady trickle of premiums provided them with a secure economic base.

They all had ambulances, too, partly to function as hearses and partly because there were no municipal ambulances to take black people who were critically ill (and barred from the hospital in Clarksdale) to the Taborian hospital in Mound Bayou. The owner of the Century funeral home, T. J. Huddleston, the son of a slave, was reputed to be the richest black man in the Delta. (In the 1980s one of Huddleston's grandsons, Mike Espy, became Mississippi's first black congressman since Reconstruction, representing the Delta, and another, Henry Espy, was elected the first black mayor of Clarksdale, after defeating the scion of another black funeral-home dynasty.) Century at its peak had thirty branches; Bessie Smith's body was prepared for her funeral at the Century home in Clarksdale.

Even though he was married, Kermit Butler was able to give Ruby a nicer life than she had ever known. He bought her dresses. He took her with him in the Century ambulance when he rode around the countryside picking up bodies, a courting ritual that may sound grim but wasn't to Ruby, who had never had much chance to ride as a passenger in an automobile or to stay dressed in good clothes all day long. In another stroke of good fortune, Ruby got a job as a waitress in a cafe at the intersection of Highway 49 and Highway 61. Her shift was twelve hours long, from seven in the morning to seven at night, but she could make as much as $12.50 a week, fantastically more than she had been earning as a maid.

Ruby fell in love with Kermit in a way she never had with W. D. Daniels, whom she had married mainly as a way of making the passage to adulthood. In 1942 she became pregnant and decided to keep the baby. At twenty-five she was, by the standards of her friends and relatives, already well past the time to become a mother, and anyway she didn't believe in abortion. She knew quite a few girls who had died following the administration of quinine injections by older women, which was the standard abortion procedure in black Clarksdale, and, as she liked to say, you never knew whether that baby whose life you were taking might have grown up to be a preacher or even a doctor. She wrote W.D. a letter explaining the situation and offering him a divorce, an offer he took her up on when he came home on leave. Ruby gave birth to a son named George, after her grandfather, George Hopkins, and the next year she had another son named Kermit, after Kermit Butler.

At the end of 1944 Ruby's twin sister Ruth left her husband and moved to Massillon, Ohio, the same town where Ceatrice had gone before settling in Chicago. Ruth was not in good shape. She was pregnant and so was in no condition to be moving North by herself. Her health was poor, anyway. She lived a much faster life than Ruby—as Ruby puts it, "it was just party, party, dance and frolic." She drank too much, usually potent and impure home-brew corn liquor. In Massillon Ruth had a miscarriage and never recovered from it. She died in May 1945, at the age of twenty-eight.

At about the time of Ruth's death, a man from Clarksdale who had
been sick in a hospital in Memphis told Ruby that the man in the bed
next to his was her father, whom she hadn't seen since their meeting in
1937. Ruby went to Memphis to visit him. He told her he had left the
Mississippi hills and moved to Wardell, Missouri, where he was still a
sharecropper, with a new wife and children. After Ruby left Memphis,
she never saw or heard from him again.

The network of relatives that had sustained Ruby up through adulthood was pretty well gone now. George Hopkins had died in 1944. Her
closest kin now was Ceatrice, and Ceatrice was in Chicago. Kermit Butler, despite having had two children with Ruby, was showing no inclination to leave his wife, and that took a lot of the gloss off their romance,
to Ruby's way of thinking. Ruby began seriously to consider making the
move to Chicago herself.

THERE REALLY wasn't any young black person in Clarksdale who
wasn't thinking about Chicago. During the traditional family-
reunion periods, July Fourth and Christmas time, people who had made
the move would come home wearing dressy clothes and driving new cars.
The mere sight of a black person, dressed as a businessman, pulling up
to his family's sharecropper shack in an automobile — sometimes a Cadillac! — was stunning, a paradigm shift, instant dignity. Pay stubs were
passed around and admired. Then there was the talk. You could find a
job in Chicago in a matter of hours. Being black and from Mississippi
was the only credential you needed, because white people up there knew
that black folks from Mississippi were used to working hard; anyway,
because of the immigration restrictions passed in the 1920s, there wasn't
anybody else in Chicago who was willing to start out at the bottom. You
could make fifty dollars, a hundred dollars, a week. The migrants were
spoken of in awed whispers: "John's doing very well with General Motors." "Ben has a position with the Board of Education." In Chicago,
the migrants said, a black person could go anywhere, and could vote, and
was not required to step off the sidewalk so that whites could pass, and
was not called "boy," and did not have to sit in the back of the bus.
People who had spent time in Chicago seemed to have a whole new way
of carrying themselves — the police, who noticed it and didn't like it,
called it "The Attitude." The land of milk and honey had finally materialized for black folks, after all these hundreds of years in the wilderness.

The migrants were engaging in a good deal of gilding of the lily, of course. The new Cadillac was likely to be rented, or to have been bought on credit, and destined to be repossessed soon after the return to Chicago. The position with the Board of Ed might really involve holding a mop. White folks in Chicago, as everyone who moved North quickly found out, were not so completely different from white folks in Mississippi as was being advertised. Still, it was undeniable that the economic opportunity there was vastly greater; that moment in the black rural South was one of the few in American history when virtually every member of a large class of people was guaranteed an immediate quadrupling of income, at least, simply by relocating to a place that was only a long day's journey away.

The man who became the most famous son of black Clarksdale — McKinley Morganfield, better known by his nickname, Muddy Waters — was, at the outset of World War II, living in his grandmother's sharecropper cabin on the Stovall plantation, west of town. The Stovalls were one of the longest-established planter families in Clarksdale; Ruby Daniels had once made a crop on their place. Certainly they would never have dreamed — no white person in the Delta would ever have dreamed — that in the long run the blues music Muddy Waters played at jukes on Saturday nights would stand as the Delta's great contribution to American culture, while the writing of William Alexander Percy would be a near-forgotten artifact of a peculiar regional way of life. Carter Stovall, the young scion of the family, happened to pass by Morganfield's cabin one day in the early 1940s when he was home on vacation from prep school in the East, and was amazed when he saw that a white man with a bulky tape recorder — Alan Lomax, the folklorist from the Library of Congress in Washington — was sitting on the front porch recording his music.

In May 1943, Muddy Waters took the train from Clarksdale to Memphis and then caught the Illinois Central to Chicago, where he got a job on the loading dock of a paper factory. He came back often to visit, but he made his life and his music in Chicago.

A boy in Clarksdale named George Hicks, who was just entering his teens in those early years of the war, used to take special notice of the people coming back from Chicago in their cars and their clothes. George came from a family that was struggling to be upwardly mobile, so it was natural that the people from Chicago would make a strong impression on him. George's father, Oliver Hicks, grew up in a sharecropper cabin on a white man's plantation near the town of Bobo, just south of Clarksdale on Highway 61. In the early 1930s, when George was just a small child, Oliver Hicks moved into Clarksdale to try to find a way to support himself that didn't involve picking cotton. At one point he went to Memphis, leaving his family back in Clarksdale, and worked for a company that made fences. He ended up back in Clarksdale. He opened a fish market that failed. He opened a grocery store that failed. He became a minister and spent Sundays preaching. Finally, in the late 1930s, Oliver Hicks got a job as a burial-insurance agent for one of the funeral homes in town, Delta Burial. On Saturdays he would take George driving out in the country in a beat-up old black '37 Ford, going from plantation to plantation and from shack to shack on each plantation, collecting premiums from sharecroppers: fifty cents per person per month.

George couldn't remember his own years in a sharecropper cabin, but he saw and heard enough in the course of making rounds with his father to know what life was like on a plantation: the spotty education, the fishy charges at the settle, the big patched-together families. In the Brickyard, where the Hickses lived, things were better, though occasional humiliations occurred there too. Once George's father was driving through a poor white neighborhood when a child suddenly ran in front of his car and got hit. Oliver Hicks got out, took the kid in his arms, carried him to the hospital, and walked right in the front door, an unthinkable violation of the code of segregation. That night a gang of whites circled the Hicks house; Oliver stood on the porch and stared them down until they went away.

Another time, George was walking along Issaqueena Street with his uncle, on their way to the black movie theater. A white policeman was coming the other way on the sidewalk. The etiquette in such situations was that the black people were supposed to step off the sidewalk, assume expressions of deep deference and humility, and let the white man pass. George's uncle didn't do this. He kept on walking on the sidewalk, and, since the policeman kept walking too, they bumped into each other and the policeman fell down. George's uncle was taken to jail, where who knows what might have happened if a higher power hadn't intervened. The uncle was running day labor to plantations in trucks, so the planters needed him; one of them found out he was in jail, put in a call to the sheriff, and had him released.

Sometimes George, like any black kid growing up in Clarksdale, would be harassed by the police. Some of the policemen liked to keep black boys on their toes by creating hostile encounters. George might be standing on a corner, and a policeman would come up to him and say, "Boy, what are you doing?" The proper response was to avoid eye contact and say "yassuh" and "nossuh" a lot, in which case, after a while, the policeman would move on. If it ever happened that George passed a white woman on the street, he had to avert his eyes then, too. The municipal swimming pool in Clarksdale — white only — was at the edge of the white section of town, right next to the all-white Clarksdale High School. The high school's principal used to stand out next to the pool in warm weather and block the way of any black male who wanted to pass by — such as George, in the days when he was working as a delivery boy for a drugstore — so that he would not get a glimpse of white women in bathing suits. This business about white women was of the utmost seriousness. It wasn't too many years later that a boy named Emmett Till, back in the Delta on a visit from his family's new home in Chicago, was brutally murdered for supposedly saying "hey, baby" to a white woman — and the only thing that surprised George about the Till case was that the murderers were put on trial; the Till cases of his own teenage years never made it to a courtroom.

In March 1947, George Hicks went to Chicago for the first time with his father and one of his sisters. They got on the train at the Illinois Central station in Clarksdale at 3:15 in the afternoon. The ticket cost $11.50, one way — more than a week's pay for most black people. The train was packed. They got off in Memphis, boarded the Louisiane, and in the morning arrived at the Illinois Central station at Twelfth Street and Michigan Avenue, the Ellis Island of the black migration to Chicago, a vast towered pile of dark brown stone with a great oval waiting room. The station was south of downtown Chicago, only twenty-five blocks from the heart of the black belt on the South Side. The waiting room was full of people and baggage. Outside the station you might imagine, if you'd been told to expect it, that you could detect the pungent aroma of the stockyards, which were a few miles off to the southwest — the smell of abundant hard work that paid much better than picking cotton. If you looked to the north you could see the stolid office buildings of the Loop, and, to the south, the Chicago chiaroscuro of brick buildings, church steeples, and factory chimneys stretching for miles and miles through the thick hazy air as far as the eye could see; in George's words, "just a big raggedy smoky city."

They stayed for two weeks with an aunt of George's who had moved

⌐g. She showed them the sights of the South Side. They visited
ⁿeach along Lake Michigan and went to the movies on Forty-seventh
ₛtreet, the fabulous main commercial thoroughfare of black Chicago,
which was lined with department stores, theaters, nightclubs, and hotels.
There was no question but that they were going back home, though. By
that time the northward migration had so depleted the Mississippi countryside that the burial-insurance business had gone sour and Oliver Hicks
had lost his job, but the family's plans for George were still supposed to
be played out in Mississippi. George attended the county agricultural
high school for blacks, and after graduation he enrolled in Alcorn College, south of Vicksburg, the first member of his family to get past high
school. He played linebacker on the Alcorn football team—George
wasn't very big, but he had a strong bantam's head, shoulders, and chest.
The idea was that after graduation he would become a schoolteacher,
slowly move up the ladder to an administrator's job, and maybe operate
a little business or two on the side; bourgeois status, comfort, and security
was what he had in mind. He might have wound up trying to find it in
Mississippi (though that would have been a difficult proposition for someone of his generation), if he hadn't been always aware that there was
another route he could take: the route to Chicago.

Bennie Gooden, a younger friend of George Hicks's, more ambitious
than George, less comfortable, used to notice the people coming back
from Chicago too. Gooden's father had a good job, pressing clothes at
a laundry. His mother worked on and off as a domestic. With two parents
at home, both securely employed, Gooden felt lucky—but still he had to
pick cotton on weekends, and still he didn't know what kind of better
future he could make for himself. He knew he wasn't supposed to resent
white people. When his mother would bring home a bucket of chicken
backs and innards from the house where she worked, or when he would
be permitted to go over there and eat a plate of leftovers on the back
porch, there would be much talk in the family about how the people his
mother worked for were *good* white folks, *nice* white folks.

Because something bothered him about this attitude, he indulged himself in small acts of rebellion. Sometimes, chopping cotton, he would cut
off the roots of the plants with his hoe, just under the ground so no one
would notice, so that the man would lose some of his crop. Or, when he
was picking, he would weigh his sack twice to make more money. One
day when he was chopping on the Tallwood plantation out on New Africa
Road, a former home of Ruby Daniels's, the manager came over and

shouted, "If you niggers don't get the lead out of your asses, you won't get a nickel today." Gooden decided to get even. In the evening, when it was time to be paid, the manager sat in his truck and handed the money out the window to the black people as they filed past, not looking at them, as if to send the message that he considered them things and not people. Bennie went through the line, got paid, switched shirts with another boy, got back in line, and got paid again. He was paid four times that day without the manager's noticing, though afterward he felt a little ashamed and didn't tell his parents, knowing they would say he had dropped down to the white man's level.

Bennie Gooden went to school in Clarksdale, studying from white kids' discarded textbooks at white kids' discarded desks, and then to the agricultural high school and Jackson State, a black college. His intention was to become a teacher — what other ambition was available? He wanted to stay in Clarksdale, where his family was, but he hoped, desperately, that some way for him to become a big success would present itself.

Aaron Henry was born in 1922 on the Flowers plantation on Highway 49, the son of a sharecropper. When he was a small child, his father heard about Tuskegee Institute, the school Booker T. Washington, the former slave who was the most famous black man in turn-of-the-century America, had started in Alabama to teach blacks to become independent artisans in the segregated South. He brought the family to Tuskegee, took a course in shoe carpentry, and, on his return to Mississippi, opened a shoe store in the little town of Webb, twenty miles south of Clarksdale on Highway 49. When the store got established, the family moved into Clarksdale.

With the Henry family, half of Booker T. Washington's program for black America took, and half didn't: the family believed in becoming economically self-sufficient — especially because sharecropping was the alternative — but not in keeping quiet about segregation. Mattie Henry, Aaron's mother, was a member of the Women's Society of Christian Service, which was one of the few biracial organizations in Mississippi. White people, members of the society and their children, were occasionally in the Henry home. Aaron Henry had a white friend as a child. Once he asked his mother why he went to school only five months a year when the white boy went nine months. She said, "You're my boy, so you don't need but five." The whole routine of being called "boy" and "nigger" on the streets of Clarksdale always bothered him. Once, working in the same job that took George Hicks by the town swimming pool, bicycle delivery boy for a drugstore, Henry rode right past, and was caught and beaten by the police. When he was in the eleventh grade at the agricultural high school, he joined the NAACP — openly, thus severely curtailing his future career options.

Aaron Henry joined the Army in 1943 and served first in a segregated unit, then in an experimental integrated one in Hawaii, so that he experienced both the standard racial hypocrisy of the armed forces and a better alternative to it. He read *Native Son*, by Richard Wright (himself a product of the odyssey from a Mississippi plantation to the South Side of Chicago), and was influenced by its anger over the black plight. He became a protégé of Dr. T. R. M. Howard, an eminent figure who practiced surgery at the Taborian hospital in Mound Bayou and was a leader of the state chapter of the NAACP; they would talk about whether Henry should move North. Most of Henry's friends, two-thirds by his estimate, wound up leaving the Delta, usually for Chicago. But Dr. Howard urged him to stay in Clarksdale, arguing that he was one of a few black people who had a chance to work to change the system. If everybody like him left, life would be that much more difficult for the people who stayed behind.

Deciding to stay and work for civil rights wasn't purely an intellectual matter for Aaron Henry; also, he had a quality that doesn't come from books or conversations, courage. A solid, compact man, he appeared to be completely implacable, as if the risks entailed in fighting segregation simply had no place in his mind. During his years of working after school in a drugstore he decided to become a pharmacist. He got his degree at Xavier University, a black school in New Orleans, and came home to Clarksdale in 1950. By then he had already joined enough organizations and given enough speeches to church groups that, in his words, "There was the feeling that Mattie Henry's boy was a smart nigger." He went around to all the banks in Clarksdale to borrow money to start a drugstore, and all the banks turned him down. He scraped a little money together and started it anyway, without a loan, in a storefront on Fourth Street. At the same time, he became president of the Clarksdale chapter of the NAACP. He was convinced that sooner or later the Supreme Court was going to decide in favor of one of the school-desegregation cases that the NAACP's Legal Defense Fund had been filing for years, and that segregation would begin to crumble after that. The drugstore committed him to Clarksdale and gave him an independent base. He was ready for history to catch up to him.

Before World War II, the cotton planters of the Delta were absolutely opposed to black migration to the North. Hortense Powdermaker, enumerating the whites' "creed of racial relations" in 1939, wrote that one of its main tenets was, "Negroes are necessary to the South, and it is desirable that they should stay there and not migrate to the North." Whites kept the black school system in Mississippi inferior in part because they didn't want sharecroppers' children to have career options beyond sharecropping. Senator James K. Vardaman once said that educating the black man "simply renders him unfit for the work which the white man has prescribed, and which he will be forced to perform . . . the only effect is to spoil a good field hand and make an insolent cook." In the 1920s, Clarksdale was supposed to become the site of a new black college called Delta State, but the white planters succeeded in having it moved to the town of Cleveland, fifty miles away, because they didn't want new opportunities for blacks opening up in town. The relocation of Delta State was a well-remembered story in black Clarksdale, and there were lots of rumors about other enterprises the planters had kept out.

As late as the early 1940s, the owners of the King & Anderson plantation, an enormous spread of seventeen thousand acres just west of Clarksdale that was reputed to be the largest family plantation in Mississippi, sent two of their white managers to Chicago to see if they could get some of the sharecroppers who had left to come back home. The managers first met with John H. Jackson, the pastor of the magnificent yellow-brick Olivet Baptist Church, which was well on its way to becoming the largest black congregation in America. Jackson is probably best known now for having been the leading enemy of Martin Luther King within the black Baptist church; when the city of Chicago changed the name of South Parkway, the boulevard on which Olivet stands, to King Drive after King's death, Jackson changed the address of the church to Thirty-first Street so he wouldn't have to have King's name on his letterhead. In the 1940s Jackson was willing to entertain two white plantation managers, but he said he couldn't urge members of his flock to move back South until conditions for blacks improved there.

Then the managers held a long meeting with former King & Anderson sharecroppers in an apartment on the South Side. The managers announced that the plantation had undertaken a series of reforms, including

electrifying sharecropper cabins and providing sharecroppers with regular written statements of their accounts so they would not be surprised
at the settle. The former sharecroppers said they already knew all that,
along with all the other recent news from the plantation; the Mississippi-
Chicago grapevine was very active. They complained about having been
swindled on King & Anderson and other plantations, and about having
been abused, degraded, and beaten by plantation managers and policemen. They showed no interest in coming home.

When the managers got back to Clarksdale and told the owners of the
plantation what had happened, the owners arranged a meeting in Clarksdale to discuss the situation. After the meeting, the white leaders of
Clarksdale asked the black leaders of Clarksdale to draw up a list of
grievances, which they did. No good jobs. Cheating at the settle. Lynch-
ings. Being denied the courtesy titles of "Mister" and "Missus." Poor
schools. No hospitals. No sidewalks, gutters, or garbage collection in the
black neighborhoods. Confronted with all this, the whites did nothing;
the list of grievances could have been resubmitted virtually intact in the
early 1960s.

When word got around about the demonstration of the mechanical
cotton picker on the Hopson plantation, though, the attitude of the
whites toward black migration changed almost instantly. A plantation
didn't need hundreds of field hands any more; a handful would do. It
didn't matter if sharecroppers moved to Chicago. In fact, it helped to
solve the problem of where the sharecroppers would go after their jobs
were abolished.

Besides, the more far-sighted whites in the Delta had begun to detect
a slight crumbling in the citadel of segregation. The New Deal was a
generation old by now, and while politically it represented an accommodation between Northern liberals and Southern segregationists, the
Delta's planters perceived Franklin Roosevelt as a threatening figure.
During his reign, various critics of the sharecropper system who at least
raised segregation as an issue had emerged, and millions of Northern
blacks had been recruited into the Democratic coalition. World War II
had exposed thousands of young black men from the Delta to places
where segregation didn't exist, and, having fought for their country, they
seemed to feel entitled to things they didn't have in Mississippi. In
Greenville, just after the end of the war, four black veterans went to the
county courthouse and said they wanted to register to vote. The registrar

said they hadn't paid their poll tax for 1944. They came back with the money the next day, and the next, and the next, and every day they got a different excuse. Finally they filed a complaint with the FBI in Washington, and two agents came down to Greenville, interviewed the veterans, had them sign a complaint, and got them registered.

The implications of blacks voting were not happy ones for Mississippi whites, especially in the Delta, which was three-quarters black. In 1935, there were more black people living in Coahoma County alone than in the states of Montana, Idaho, Wyoming, Colorado, New Mexico, Arizona, Utah, and Nevada combined. Most middle-aged whites had been raised on their parents' and grandparents' horror stories about life during Reconstruction, when blacks were enfranchised. By the 1940s, the school-desegregation issue had reached the notice of white planters, as well as Aaron Henry. A few civil rights activities had started to pop up here and there. All in all, the idea of getting the numbers of blacks and whites in the Delta a little closer to equilibrium began to seem attractive to whites on political as well as economic grounds. The best, the only, means to that end was black migration to the North. As Aaron Henry puts it, "They wished we'd go back to Africa, but Chicago was close enough."

On the Hopson plantation, the idea of a looming civil rights crisis was very much on the mind of the Hopson family; it gave a new urgency to the long-running efforts to get the mechanical cotton picker ready for full-scale production. Howell Hopson's brother Richard, who ran the plantation office, wrote a long, impassioned letter to the local cotton-industry association in April 1944, a few months before the public demonstration of the picker, which makes clear the plantation's thinking on the picker's political implications. He wrote (via registered mail—an indication that he meant to make an important statement): "I am confident that you are aware of the acute shortage of labor which now exists in the Delta and the difficult problem which we expect to have in attempting to harvest a cotton crop this fall and for several years to come. I am confident that you are aware of the serious racial problem which confronts us at this time and which may become more serious as time passes." After a little more discussion, he arrived at the solution: "I strongly advocate the farmers of the Mississippi Delta changing as rapidly as possible from the old tenant or sharecropping system of farming to complete mechanized farming. . . . Mechanized farming will require only a fraction

of the amount of labor which is required by the share crop system thereby
tending to equalize the white and negro population which would automatically make our racial problem easier to handle."

Within a few years after the end of World War II, the mechanical
picker was coming into general use on the plantations, and the sharecropper system was ending. Usually a plantation would build up its stock
of machines until it had enough to harvest the whole crop, and then it
would announce to the sharecroppers that it was switching over to an
all-day-labor system to handle the chopping, which was still done by
hand. One by one the plantation commissaries were closed down. The
more established and paternalistic planters, such as King & Anderson
and the Stovalls in Clarksdale and the Percys in Greenville, allowed their
sharecroppers to stay in their cabins if they wanted to, but not to make
a crop of their own. A lucky few got salaried jobs as tractor drivers; the
rest who stayed had to work as day laborers, get jobs in town, or retire.
Some planters forced their sharecroppers out by informing them that the
garden spots they used for raising vegetables and keeping livestock would
now have to be plowed over and planted to cotton. The smaller and
rougher planters simply kicked out their sharecroppers and left them to
fend for themselves. Often, when a sharecropper family left, the planter
would bulldoze the cabin and grow cotton where it had stood. Sharecropper cabins were understandably not in demand as housing. If the
cabin wasn't on arable land, it usually just sat unoccupied, slowly sagging
and giving way to vines. The Delta today is dotted with nearly spectral
sharecropper cabins, their doors and windows gone, their interior walls
lined with newspapers from the 1930s and 1940s that once served as
insulation. They are humbler than what you'd ordinarily think of as the
ruins of a vanished civilization, but that is certainly what they are.

The sharecroppers who left the plantations sometimes moved directly
to Chicago. More often they settled first in the town of Clarksdale, either
in preparation for the second phase of their migration or to become day
laborers and continue to work in the cotton fields. Day labor as a large-
scale employment base was doomed in the long run, though, because in
the late 1950s the cotton planters embarked on a second phase of their
industrial revolution that was just as significant as the introduction of the
mechanical picker: the development of chemicals that killed the weeds
between cotton plants so reliably as to make hand chopping unnecessary.
Within ten years, virtually all the former sharecroppers had to find some
entirely new way to live.

The white people in the Delta were well aware that a massive displacement of people was under way, and that it would have enormous consequences — not necessarily for them, since the consequences would be played out largely in the North. Writing in 1947, David Cohn issued the following dire prediction, which, to say the least, did not rivet the attention of a nation that was consumed with resuming a normal life after the war and wasn't inclined in any case to pay much heed to jeremiads issued by an obscure Southern apologist:

> The coming problem of agricultural displacement in the Delta and the whole South is of huge proportions and must concern the entire nation. The time to prepare for it is now, but since we as a nation rarely act until catastrophe is upon us, it is likely we shall muddle along until it is too late. The country is upon the brink of a process of change as great as any that has occurred since the Industrial Revolution. . . . Five million people will be removed from the land within the next few years. They must go somewhere. But where? They must do something. But what? They must be housed. But where is the housing?
>
> Most of this group are farm Negroes totally unprepared for urban, industrial life. How will they be industrially absorbed? What will be the effect of throwing them upon the labor market? What will be their reception at the hands of white and Negro workers whose jobs and wages they threaten?
>
> There are other issues involved here of an even greater gravity. If tens of thousands of Southern Negroes descend upon communities totally unprepared for them psychologically and industrially, what will the effect be upon race relations in the United States? Will the Negro problem be transferred from the South to other parts of the nation who have hitherto been concerned with it only as carping critics of the South? Will the victims of farm mechanization become the victims of race conflict?
>
> There is an enormous tragedy in the making unless the United States acts, and acts promptly, upon a problem that affects millions of people and the whole social structure of the nation.

A few years earlier Richard Wright, who viewed the situation from the completely different perspective of a black man, a migrant to the North, and a Communist, sounded an uncannily similar, and similarly unheeded, warning:

> Perhaps never in history has a more utterly unprepared folk wanted to go to the city; we were barely born as a folk when we headed for the tall and sprawling centers of steel and stone. We, who were landless upon the land; we, who had barely managed to live in family groups; we, who needed the ritual and guidance of institutions to hold our atomized lives together in lines of purpose; we, who had known only relationships to people and not relationships to things; we, who had had our personalities blasted with two hundred years of slavery and had been turned loose to shift for ourselves — we were such a folk as this when we moved into a world that was destined to test all we were, that threw us into the scales of competition to weigh our mettle.

IN 1946 Ruby Daniels moved to Chicago. Her aunt Ceatrice had been living there for six years now, continuously reporting back that things were better in Chicago. Ruby's lover, Kermit Butler, was plainly never going to leave his wife. Older friends urged her to make the move. She gathered up her two sons, George and Kermit, and took the train to Memphis. She had friends there, a childless couple named A. C. and Frances Clark, who had been her neighbors in Clarksdale. Frances had often implored Ruby to give her a baby, since she couldn't have one of her own, and Ruby took the request seriously; the adoption of "gift children" by close friends was common among poor blacks in the South, a custom that involved generosity on both sides and usually helped get the child's natural mother through a hard time. Ruby felt that the difficulty of getting established in Chicago with two children in tow would be insuperable, so she left Kermit with the Clarks, bought an eleven-dollar ticket on the Illinois Central night train, and rode up to Chicago with George.

She moved in with Ceatrice at 3666 Indiana Avenue, in the heart of the poorest part of the black belt. (Bigger Thomas, the Mississippi migrant hero of *Native Son*, lived with his mother and his sister at the imaginary address of 3721 Indiana.) Ceatrice lived in what was known as a "kitchenette" apartment — an apartment in a building that had been chopped up into one- or two-room flats each outfitted with an icebox and a hot plate. All the residents of the five or six apartments on each floor shared a common bathroom. Established middle-class black Chicagoans regarded the kitchenettes with something close to horror, as breeding grounds for immorality and ruiners of good neighborhoods. St. Clair Drake and Horace Cayton, in *Black Metropolis*, an authoritative tour of "Bronzeville" (as they called black Chicago) published the year before Ruby moved there, wrote, "Into these kitchenettes drifting lower-class families moved, bringing a few clothes and buying a little furniture on time. . . . Thus once stable middle-class areas gradually become spotted with kitchenettes. . . . Middle-class neighborhoods in Bronzeville thus became the beach upon which broke the human flotsam which was tossed into the city streets by successive waves of migration from the South."

To Ruby, Ceatrice's place was wonderful. The rent was only ten dollars a week, the people were friendly, and there was always somebody around to look after George when she was out. Ceatrice was working nights as a janitor at the Montgomery Ward building, an imposing structure just to the west of downtown Chicago. Ruby immediately got a job doing janitorial work at Ward's too, making over forty dollars a week. She worked there for a little more than a year.

Then, back home, Kermit Butler's wife died. Kermit called Ruby and told her he would marry her if she would move to Clarksdale. He had gotten a good new job: Charles Stringer, a top employee of the Century funeral home, had left to start his own mortuary and brought Kermit along as the ambulance driver. Because Stringer wanted Kermit to be able to respond quickly to emergency calls, he let him live rent-free in a room at the funeral home. Ruby wouldn't have moved back just for the accommodations, but she was still in love with Kermit, and his new situation made marrying him seem prudent as well as alluring. She brought George back to Clarksdale and moved into the Stringer building on Fourth Street.

It didn't work out. Within a month, Ruby discovered that now that she was Kermit's wife, he was treating her the way he had treated his first wife — that is, running around with other women. At the end of 1948, she took the train back to Chicago, this time, she expected, for good.

ULESS CARTER was born in 1916, the same year as Ruby Daniels. He was the tenth of twelve children. He grew up on plantations all over the Delta, watching his father live out the sharecropper cycle of hope in the spring, anger and disappointment after the settle in December, and the road in January. Uless's parents stayed married and so were able to set their sights higher than Ruby's family. Miles Carter, Uless's father, several times became a renter, which put him in the upper class of the sharecropper world; renters supplied their own mules and farming equipment and got a three-fourths share of the crop, whereas sharecroppers, with no possessions at all, got only half. Miles Carter worked his children hard to ensure that he would have a good crop, and dealt with any hint of recalcitrance by getting out his old leather razor strop. During picking time, he woke the family before dawn, they picked all day, and if there was a moon, they picked into the night. They wore clothes made from old cotton sacks dyed with hickory bark, and greased their legs in the winter to stay warm. Often they had no shoes. Uless left school in the second grade so that he could begin working full time in the fields.

Because the Carter family was trying so assiduously to get ahead, the unfairness of the system went down especially hard for them. Industrious renters they might be, but the planter still kept the books, and if at the end of the year he said the family owed him money, there was nothing they could do about it. One year the planter called Miles Carter in and said he couldn't pay him because he had to send his son to college; Uless remembers his father coming home from that meeting crying. The family kept moving. They made a few crops outside the town of Sledge, northeast of Clarksdale, came out behind, and moved to a place in Indianola (the town Hortense Powdermaker and John Dollard studied) when Uless was ten. There the planter told Miles Carter he wanted the girls in the family to come up and work in his house. Miles, suspecting that the planter had more in mind for his daughters than housework, refused. At the settle the family didn't clear anything, and when they moved away, the planter came after them and took away their mule team to settle the debt. Miles went to the owner of the new place, told him what had happened, and said he wanted to hire a lawyer to get his mules back. The planter said, "Carter, you can always get another mule team, but you can't get another life." He didn't hire a lawyer. He did get another mule team, but after three years he was behind again, and lost his mules again in settlement of an unitemized debt.

In 1931, the Carters moved to the King & Anderson plantation outside Clarksdale. By this time Miles Carter was becoming less involved in farming. He had developed kidney trouble and was unable to work in the field much. Also, back in Sledge he had gotten the call to become a minister, and by now he was traveling widely to preach. Uless's older brothers left, one by one, as soon as they got to their late teens. It was as if the whole family was losing its will to keep trying to use the cultivation of cotton as an avenue of upward mobility. When Uless was seventeen, tall and bony, his father told him to "stand head of the crop" — that is, supervise the family's business affairs.

The manager of the section of King & Anderson where the Carters lived was a young, handsome, rough white man named Broughton. Broughton would ride around the place on a horse and stand over the black people who were picking cotton, sneering at them for being too slow. He and Uless took a dislike to each other. One Friday afternoon, Broughton came to the Carters' cabin and asked one of Uless's sisters why she wasn't out working in the fields. This infuriated Uless. He knew that most of the other families on King & Anderson used little tricks to fool Broughton. They'd chop just the ends of the rows and leave the weeds in the middle, then tell Broughton they were done chopping and do day work for cash. At picking time, they'd "pull" the cotton rather than picking it — that is, break off the cotton boll at the stem instead of separating it, which meant faster picking and a heavier sack, but dirtier and less valuable cotton — and, again, go off to do day work. They assumed they wouldn't clear anything from sharecropping, so they did a sloppy job at it, fooled the white people, and tried to make as much money as they could on wages.

This ethic was known as "getting over," meaning, specifically, getting your own crop over with so you could do something else; more generally, it meant running some kind of a hustle, especially on white people, in hopes of coming out ahead in a game you couldn't possibly win by following the rules. The Carters were not trying to get over, but this won them no points with Broughton. Uless confronted Broughton, saying that he stood for the crop and any complaints Broughton had should be taken up with him, not his sister.

Broughton had it in for Uless after that. Uless brought in a good crop, but when December came, it seemed to take forever for Broughton to settle. Uless went to the plantation office one evening and saw Broughton and the other managers through the window, laughing, eating, and playing cards. He knocked on the door and asked when the settle was going to be; the men told him to go away and come back in a day or two, because they were still working on it. Finally Broughton announced that the Carters had come out behind — so far behind that he would have to take their mules and equipment to settle the debt. He broke into their barn, took everything, and plowed up their garden spot for good measure. As Uless saw it, Broughton, in addition to being gratuitously cruel, was trying to bully the family into staying on the place as sharecroppers rather than renters; with no possessions left, with a debt hanging over them, and with a naive seventeen-year-old standing head of the crop, they wouldn't have much choice.

Uless and his father decided to call Broughton's bluff and leave King & Anderson — in fact to leave farming entirely, and move into Clarksdale. First Uless took the audacious step of going to see the head of the entire plantation, Edgar Lee Anderson, known among black people as "Mr. Edgar Lee," and telling him what had happened. Edgar Lee Anderson, a shy, quiet man, was a figure of awe in Clarksdale. He was the son of one of the two men who had started the plantation in 1873, and he ran it from the late nineteenth century until his death in the 1950s, supervising its expansion into a vast empire. The Andersons — Edgar Lee, his two sons, and their families — were the rare Delta planters who lived in something approximating what is thought of as the plantation style, in elegant white-columned houses furnished with French antiques purchased on Royal Street in New Orleans.

Uless went to the "big store," the main King & Anderson commissary, and asked to see Mr. Edgar Lee. He was ushered in and told his story. He said he was quitting. Mr. Edgar Lee seemed surprised. He said he knew the Carters were good farmers and had made a good crop. He had expected them to clear money. If they were determined to leave now, though, he would wipe out any indebtedness that they had on the plantation's books. He said this was the only case he knew of where a black family had been mistreated at King & Anderson.

Hearing this left Uless with a feeling that Mr. Edgar Lee might be a good man, a man of God, but there was a lot he didn't know about what went on at King & Anderson. He kept quiet, though, believing that the Lord would rectify the situation in his own way one day. Sure enough, ten years later, Broughton suffered his downfall. He had picked out a sharecropper's wife who appealed to him and decided to make her his mistress. Every so often, he would stop by their cabin and order the sharecropper to do some repair work in a faraway corner of the plantation. When he was sure the man was gone, Broughton would come back to the cabin and take advantage of his wife. One day the sharecropper happened to come back from his work early, and he saw through the window that Broughton and his wife were in bed together. He tied up his mules, got down his double-barreled shotgun, went into the house, and blew Broughton's head off.

The sharecropper went to Broughton's house, told Broughton's wife what had happened, and took off. He was captured several weeks later in Arkansas, but he was never put on trial or punished outside the law, partly because the Anderson family did not want the matter pressed. What Broughton had done was not consistent with Edgar Lee Anderson's view of what life was like on his plantation, and what the sharecropper had done was not a real violation of the code of segregation, since there was no white woman involved. To Uless, Broughton's violent end and ignominious burial without a head was the rare case of a white man's being punished for his mistreatment of black people.

The Carter family settled in the Roundyard, the poor section of black Clarksdale. Uless worked for a white family, then got a job at a restaurant, then worked for a white family again. His parents went out to the plantations on trucks to chop and pick cotton. The most money Uless ever made was six dollars a week.

He began to think more and more about the evils of segregation. The system seemed all-encompassing: it stretched back through as much history as Uless knew about and forward as far into the future as he could see. It permeated every aspect of his existence. Uless knew a little about his family's life under slavery, because his father's father had come to stay with them on a plantation during his final illness and had told Uless some things about it. He said the family got its name when some white people in Georgia named Carter (forebears of President Jimmy Carter, Uless later heard) bought a great-great-aunt of Uless's, just as you'd buy a horse or a cow. Slaves had to eat out of troughs as if they were livestock, Uless's grandfather told him. If you didn't pick fast enough to satisfy the white man, he'd whip you or kick you. If you wanted to pray or sing, you had to put your head inside a pot so you wouldn't be heard. The white man would put strong young men and women together and breed them, even if they were brother and sister.

In Clarksdale in the late 1930s and early 1940s, the indignities were not so severe, but they were constant and debilitating. Uless had to hurry home in the evenings because there was a town curfew for blacks (though not for whites). When he was working at white people's houses, he had to sit out on the back porch to eat the food he had cooked. He saw terrible things happen to people he knew. One boy was kicked by the police for walking past the swimming pool. Another, back from Chicago for a visit, had his new car's windows all smashed by a white policeman who didn't like his attitude. Another was hanged before a substantial audience (which included Uless) for having been a witness to the murder of a white shopkeeper by two black boys; Uless had no connection to the incident, but the day it happened, when a white mob went looking for suspects, he was afraid he might be rounded up and killed. His parents would tell him to respond to such risks by being inconspicuous and staying away from places where he wasn't wanted, and while he knew this was good advice, he found it unbearable to imagine living by it forever. By now Uless was in his twenties, an erect, dignified, gentle, square-jawed man with the bearing of a real personage, but he felt that as long as he stayed in Clarksdale he was consigned to being treated like a child.

Of course Uless had heard all about Chicago from other black people, and seen the suits and the cars at July Fourth and Christmas. One of his sisters had moved to Chicago and gotten a job as a maid at a black hotel. Some of the children of white people he worked for had urged him to go North. The daughter of one white family told Uless she had gone to a school in New York where white and black sat in the same classrooms; another family's daughter said she had colored friends at the college she went to in Chicago, and even lived on the same campus with black students. Uless found himself thinking about Chicago more and more, and finally he decided he had to go up and see it for himself.

In 1942, when he was twenty-five years old, Uless arranged to visit his sister in Chicago. On the day of the trip he went to the Clarksdale bus station to buy his ticket. When he got to the window, he handed his money to the clerk and called out his destination in a loud, nervous voice: "Chicago, Chicago" — a voice whose timbre came from the expectation and disbelief he felt over the prospect of traveling far beyond the borders of the state of Mississippi. The clerk, a young white lady, wouldn't look at him. Some white people came up to the window, and she sold them their tickets before Uless. Then another group of white people came in and bought tickets. Uless began to wonder whether the clerk was going to sell him a ticket at all. Finally she said, in a simpering, disgusted tone, "Chicago, Chicago," as if to show Uless that he might be able to take a bus to the North, but, in her opinion, he was just another nigger. Still not looking at Uless, she offhandedly tossed him the ticket, and he hurried to the back of the bus.

CHICAGO

As an old man, living alone, Uless Carter keeps a row of old photographs on top of the bookshelf in the spare, neat room where he stays. The first one shows a group of black people in a bare plowed cotton field, assembled for a picture. Men, women, and children, some quite small, they are dressed in rags, and they look solemnly at the camera. Behind them are two white men in khakis, wearing fedoras, mounted on horses. When he shows someone the picture, Uless calls attention to the way the white men would stand over you, high up on their horses while you were bent down in the rows, driving you almost as if you were livestock instead of people.

The second photograph is of Uless at twenty-five, shortly after he got to Chicago in 1942. He is wearing a natty wool suit, a tie, and a pocket square. He is sitting on a couch in a William Powell–like pose of suave relaxation, his legs casually crossed, his hands folded in his lap, his head turned as if he is listening to a sparkling conversation across the room. There is a confident smile on his face. The suit he is wearing in the picture is the first one he ever owned, and the couch is in a room in the basement of a kitchenette apartment building on the South Side—the kind of basement room that moved St. Clair Drake and Horace Cayton to write, "The poorest and most unstable elements often inhabited the basements of kitchenette buildings, where rents were lowest."

In the third photograph, Uless is forty years old. He is dressed in a minister's collar and black suit. He is wearing glasses. He looks serious and reverent. There is a circular zone of light around his head, the result of a printing trick the studio photographer who took the picture used to keep Uless's face from appearing too dark. When the photographer showed Uless the proofs of the picture, he said he could make the circle disappear in the final printing, but Uless told him to leave it just the way it was, because it showed how deep in the spirit he was at the time.

The bus that took Uless to Chicago left Clarksdale on a Saturday afternoon. When it reached the town of Cairo, at the southern tip of Illinois, he was permitted to move from the back to the front — though that part of the country, the boot heel of Missouri and the "Egypt" section of Illinois, was well known to be inhospitable to blacks; in fact there wasn't much friendly territory on the bus route before Chicago itself. Uless rode all night. As the light of dawn was breaking, the driver called out, "Chicago Heights." Uless walked to the door, but the driver explained to him that Chicago Heights was a small town south of Chicago; he should wait for the stop called Chicago Loop. When he got off at the bus station, which was at Twelfth Street and Indiana Avenue, just a block from the Illinois Central station, he looked around for his sister, but she wasn't there; the telegram he had sent informing her of his arrival time must not have made it. Looking around the station, he spotted a man he knew from Clarksdale. The man said that he had come to the station to pick up a bag, and that he would take Uless to his sister's apartment — he lived right next door. They took the streetcar down to Forty-ninth Street.

Uless's sister lived in a kitchenette building full of people whom Uless began to meet the minute he walked in the door. One of the women in the building told him her boyfriend had a good job in a restaurant that was looking for more help. She called her boyfriend over and made him phone the restaurant right then and there; the man handed the phone over to Uless, who found himself being offered a job as a dishwasher by the owner. He had come to Chicago only for a brief holiday; he had been in his sister's building for less than an hour. Now the owner of the restaurant was telling him he could come to work on Monday morning and make twenty-five dollars a week. His job in Clarksdale paid less than a quarter of that. Kitchenettes in the building rented for only seven or eight dollars a week, so he would come out far ahead if he took the restaurant job. Without hesitation he told the owner he would be there Monday, and now he was a resident of Chicago instead of a visitor.

The landlord of Uless's sister's building fixed up a room for him in the basement. After he had been working at the restaurant for six months, he heard that Armour & Company, the packing house that was famous for using every part of the pig but the squeal, was hiring. Uless went down to the stockyards — that enormous South Side enclosure where every day thousands of head of livestock arrived alive by train and left dead in boxes and refrigerated trucks — and got a job cutting meat to be sent to the soldiers fighting in Europe and the Pacific. The stockyards were hopping during the war. The work was hard, but you could make lots of hours, and every year there was a raise; the stockyards were such a familiar part of the iconography of black Chicago in those years that the blues singer Howlin' Wolf, in one of his best-known songs, accused a faithless woman of putting him on the killing floor.

After Uless had been working at Armour's for a few months, he met a young woman in church named Letha Mae Johnson, a migrant from Millsboro, Kentucky, who had a job at a small factory. Letha had two out-of-wedlock children who were back in Kentucky with her parents. She and Uless began keeping company, and after six months they were married. Their income was such that they were able to move to a better neighborhood, which, on the South Side of Chicago, meant going farther south.

The South Side is a long sweep of neighborhoods roughly in the shape of an isosceles triangle. The sharp northern point of the triangle is at Twelfth Street, where the bus and train stations were, and the two long sides extend southward for nearly fifteen miles until they reach the southern border of the city. The traditional black belt was at the northern end of the South Side. As migrants from the South crowded into the black belt, landlords converted more and more apartment buildings into kitchenettes to accommodate them. The neighborhoods became poorer and denser, and the black middle class became discontented and tried to get away from the slums by expanding the black belt southward into previously white neighborhoods — a difficult process, because nearly all of the white neighborhoods were segregated by fiercely maintained custom and, in many cases, also by force of law, through "restrictive covenants" that barred blacks from buying houses and were then perfectly legal.

Uless and Letha moved from Forty-ninth Street down to Sixty-first Street, on the fringes of a neighborhood called Woodlawn, a lower-middle-class area that during World War II was just beginning to change from white to black. Woodlawn had two lively commercial strips, one running north-south along Cottage Grove Avenue, the other running east-west under the elevated train tracks on Sixty-third Street, both lined with shops and restaurants. Uless loved Chicago in those days; living in Woodlawn so soon after leaving the Delta gave him a feeling of pure amazement and liberation. By that time, nearly a generation after the fading of the Harlem Renaissance, the South Side had become the capital of black America. It was (and still is) the largest contiguous settlement of African-Americans. It was home to the heavyweight boxing champion of the world (and the most famous black man in America), Joe Louis; the only black member of Congress, William Dawson; the most prominent black newspaper, the *Defender*; the largest black congregation, J. H. Jackson's Olivet Baptist Church; the greatest black singer, Mahalia Jackson; and a host of lesser-known prosperous people whose presence was proof that Chicago was a city where a black person could be somebody.

In the mid-1930s Elijah Muhammad (born Elijah Poole on a Georgia farm) moved his organization, the Lost-Found Nation of Islam, better known as the Black Muslims, from Detroit to the South Side. Elijah preached a home-brew Islamic religion he had learned from the mysterious Wallace D. Fard, his mentor in Detroit, according to whose teachings black people were destined to reinherit the earth after overthrowing a race of white devils that had been bred six thousand years ago on the island of Patmos by an evil scientist named Yacub. The Nation of Islam began attracting thousands of recruits, especially from the ranks of poor men who had recently arrived in Chicago from the rural South; Elijah, who required his followers to observe a strict code of dress, diet, and behavior and to contribute heavily to the church, used his money to buy up South Side real estate and start small businesses. By the 1940s Chicago had supplanted Harlem as the center of black nationalism in the United States.

The South Side had half a dozen shopping districts (Forty-seventh Street was the grandest), containing department stores, banks, nightclubs, movie houses, and such nationally known black institutions as the Regal Theater, the Savoy Ballroom, and the Hotel Grand. It had several wide boulevards lined with substantial homes; a large, elegant new apartment complex built around a courtyard, Michigan Boulevard Garden Apartments, that had been constructed by the Sears tycoon Julius Rosenwald; and a brand-new brick housing project for the lower middle class, the Ida B. Wells Homes. It had a spacious public park and a beach along Lake Michigan, where Uless in his early days in town would sometimes sleep on especially hot nights during the summer. Once he got established, which took very little time, Uless, who so recently had been barred by law from being out of the house at night and had no money to spend on entertainment anyway, was patronizing clubs that had big bands playing inside, and bouncers at the door to keep out the riffraff.

In addition to all its wonders, the South Side had more than its share of slums. Besides the kitchenette apartments, there were rickety three-story tenements all up and down State Street from Twenty-second Street down to Fifty-first Street, with heating, plumbing, and insulation that were rudimentary at best and often completely nonfunctional. The fine nightclubs were outnumbered by little taverns where the music was provided by nickelodeons or three-piece blues bands and where Saturday night shootings and stabbings were a regular occurrence. Prostitution was a minor industry, and gambling, in the form of substantial numbers games called "policy wheels," a major one, probably the biggest independent business in black Chicago. Law enforcement was casual because the Chicago police didn't consider black-on-black crime to be a problem worth solving. Black people were regularly charged more rent and paid lower wages than white people, and they were barred entirely from many good jobs. There were no black drivers of yellow cabs, no black sales clerks at the great department stores in the Loop, no black linemen at Illinois Bell, no black bus drivers, no black policemen or firemen except at the stations in the black belt, and no blacks in the building-trades unions. The sexual mores of the poor, and the concomitant problem of out-of-wedlock childbearing, were by the 1940s already a well-established subject of concern among the forces of respectability on the South Side.

What made the South Side look so good to Uless, and to most of the other migrants moving there, was the comparison to the South: money and dignity were indisputably in greater supply in Chicago than in the Delta. That didn't mean success would be automatic there, though. In migrant folklore, every poor person who moved North had one great advantage and one great disadvantage: the advantage was that there were plenty of jobs for people who knew how to work hard, which all the migrants did; the disadvantage was the constant temptation to fall into the wild life that was there on the South Side for those who wanted it. It was ever thus for country people coming to Chicago—pretty much the same situation confronted the heroine of *Sister Carrie* when she moved there in 1889. For black Southerners, the old ethic of getting over could easily be transferred to Chicago, where opportunities for extra-legal hustling and the accumulation of debt were far more extensive than they had been in the cotton fields back home. As E. Franklin Frazier put it, "In the urban environment the migrant is liberated from the control that the church and other forms of association exercised in the rural South."

To Uless the solution to this problem in the North was exactly what it had been in the South—religion—but plenty of other forces within the South Side were also at work to combat social disorganization. The world whose center was Forty-seventh Street was one in which the poor lived in close proximity to a large middle class that had a strong interest in maintaining order and safety. There was an overall sense of optimism. Uless, like most people familiar with the South Side in the years after World War II, knew that a lot was wrong there but believed without hesitation that on the whole it was a community on the way up.

Uless and Letha had their troubles; every time they got into an argument, she would go home to her parents' place in Kentucky for a while. They had no children. Their situation never had a chance to be resolved, because three and a half years into their marriage, during one of their separations, Letha, still in her mid-twenties, died of cancer in Kentucky.

A couple of years passed, and then Uless fell in love again—with another woman he met in church, a widow named Geraldine Avery, who also was a migrant from Kentucky. They were married in 1948 and moved into a new apartment in a better neighborhood—that is, one farther south.

One Sunday morning in 1949, Uless was sitting in a Baptist church at Forty-seventh and Indiana, a small place where he was a deacon. Someone he didn't know walked in, a light-skinned young man dressed in such fancy clothes that Uless assumed he was a pimp. The young man went to the lectern—visitors were often allowed to preach in the smaller black churches—and gave an eloquent sermon. Uless was listening raptly, thinking how wonderful it was that this man was preaching instead of pimping, when suddenly he heard the voice of the Lord telling him that He was sending for Uless to become a preacher himself. In his mind, Uless argued with the Lord. He said he had no education and no voice. The Lord told Uless he was qualified simply by virtue of his faith. Tears streaming down his face, Uless sat through the rest of the sermon. Then he went outside, intending to walk up to another church at Fortieth and Indiana where he was supposed to sing in the choir behind Mahalia Jackson. The Lord spoke to him again, saying it was time for Uless to accept the call. Uless walked back inside the church and announced to the congregation that he had decided to preach the Gospel. The minister told him he could have the pulpit to deliver his trial sermon on Wednesday night.

Uless chose as the text for his trial sermon a passage from the Book of John about the availability of salvation to all who believe: "And as Moses lifted up the serpent in the wilderness, even so must the son of man be lifted up: That whosoever believeth in Him should not perish, but have eternal life. For God so loved the world, that he gave up his only begotten son, that whosoever believeth in Him should not perish, but have everlasting life." He reminded the people in the church that they all were accustomed to spreading good news around to all their friends when it involved earthly things, such as the appearance of some nice produce in the market; so too should they spread the news of heavenly things. The sermon was a great success, so much so that Uless memorized it and delivered it once a year for the rest of his life. Afterward, the minister gave Uless a preacher's license. He was Reverend Carter now.

WHEN RUBY DANIELS got back to Chicago in 1948, she moved in again with her aunt Ceatrice and got her old job back doing janitorial work in the Montgomery Ward building. Soon she switched to a job at a laundry that paid seventy-five cents an hour, a sum that in Mississippi had been closer to a day's pay than an hour's. One night when Ruby was on her way home from work, she decided to stop in at a corner tavern to get a cup of coffee. She was standing in the doorway when a white lady inside saw her and quickly put a sign up in the window that said "Members Only." Ruby decided to take the hint and forgo the cup of coffee. She was beginning to realize that the stories that had circulated in Mississippi about how you could go anywhere in Chicago were nowhere near true, but she reminded herself that she had moved North to make money, not to be around white people. The money was no myth, and the kitchenette apartment building where she and Ceatrice were living was convivial. She didn't have any second thoughts about being in Chicago.

Ruby met a young man named Alvin Wilkes, also recently arrived from Mississippi, who was rooming with his sister just upstairs from her in the building and working in a factory. There was a connection between them: Alvin's brother Ulysses and Ruby's aunt Ceatrice had met and become a couple in Ohio in 1940. Ruby and Alvin became involved, and Ruby got pregnant. She quit her job and applied for public aid. This meant going downtown to a big office and being interviewed by a social worker. The social worker asked Ruby if she knew who the father of the baby she was carrying was, as if she thought Ruby, who had been a one-man woman for all of her life, was so promiscuous that the paternity might be a mystery to her. Ruby did get approved, but the social worker told her that if she came back pregnant again, her baby would be taken away from her and put in a home, because she would have demonstrated that she was an unfit mother. In the future, Ruby would go to great lengths to avoid having to deal with the public-aid department again.

On January 7, 1950, Ruby gave birth to her third son, named Larry. She expected that Alvin would marry her, but their romance had begun to turn sour during her pregnancy. Not long after Larry was born, Alvin married another woman. For a while he and Ruby kept up a great show of remaining friends. Ruby and Ceatrice would often go over to Alvin's apartment to play cards. Then, on one night when Ruby was there, Alvin's wife said she'd like to speak to him in private. They went behind a closed door, and sounds of scuffling and shouting emerged. Ruby could hear Alvin's wife loudly describing the kinds of physical harm she'd like to inflict on her. She left, and after that she stayed clear of Alvin's apartment.

Ceatrice heard about a large apartment — six rooms — that had become available in a poor but decent neighborhood off Forty-seventh Street, and she and Ruby moved there, taking in boarders from time to time to help with the rent. Now that they were in a spacious place, they began to give house parties on weekends that were the urban version of the old Saturday nights at the jukes on the plantations. They would eat dinner, play records, dance, and gamble. Lots of people were in and out of the apartment in those days — it sometimes seemed to Ruby as if everyone she had ever known in her life was in Chicago now. Alvin Wilkes would sneak away from home and make an appearance every now and then, and his sister and brothers came sometimes too. Another frequent guest was Harold Brown, who back in 1934 had been Ruby's teenage sweetheart on a plantation outside Clarksdale, just before she married W. D. Daniels. Ruby and Harold started going together, and soon she was pregnant again, once more without a real prospect of a wedding. In 1952 her fourth son, Terrell, was born.

The tenor of Ruby's life in Chicago was beginning to change for the worse. Instead of working, she was on public aid, which paid much less. She had been naive, to say the least, about marriage and contraception. The woman in Memphis who had been looking after her second son, Kermit, took sick, so Ruby had to bring him up to Chicago. With more children in the house she was eligible for an increase in her aid payment, but she couldn't bring herself to apply for it. She did apply for public housing, and was told that unwed mothers could not be given apartments in housing projects in Chicago.

Ruby had a family friend in Massillon, Ohio, the woman Ruth had moved up from Mississippi to live with years ago. She was childless, and for years she had begged Ruby to give her a child to raise. When Terrell was born, the woman renewed her entreaties, and Ruby decided she'd rather send him to Ohio, where he'd be sure to be well looked after, than go to the public-aid office again. Shortly after Terrell's first birthday, the woman from Ohio came to Chicago and got him.

Ruby and Ceatrice had a boarder named Mamie Brown. One evening Mamie brought a friend home, a Mississippi sharecropper turned Chicago factory worker named Luther Haynes. Luther, a wiry, sharp-featured man, was the child of sharecroppers who had lived on ten different plantations in the vicinity of Clarksdale during the time he was growing up; his parents separated once but got back together after a couple of years. He married young and made a few crops with his wife, but after four years she left him and moved to St. Louis. They had a few talks about a reconciliation, which foundered because she refused to move back to a cotton plantation. In order to get her back, Luther moved, in 1949, to Chicago, where two of his seven brothers were living, and got a job as a janitor. His wife did join him there, but they couldn't get along, and within a year they were divorced. After some knocking around in the labor market, Luther got a decent-paying, stable job in an awning factory in 1952, the year before he met Ruby.

As soon as Luther walked in the door of the apartment and saw Ruby, he said, "Look here, here's somebody I ain't seen in years. Ain't that Ruth?" Ruby explained that Ruth had passed away a few years back and that she was Ruth's twin sister. They got to talking, and hit it off immediately. Ruby had met the most important man in her life.

Ruby and Luther started going together. In 1954 they had a child, another son, named Johnnie. In November of that year, Ceatrice, who had high blood pressure, took sick and had to stay home from work for a while. On the day she was ready to go back to her job, she decided to take a nap in the afternoon, and asked Ruby to wake her at seven in the evening. At seven, Ruby went into Ceatrice's room and found that she couldn't wake her up. She called the police, and they took Ceatrice to Cook County Hospital. She died there at midnight, the victim of a stroke. A little while later, Luther Haynes moved into the apartment, and he and Ruby set up housekeeping.

D**URING THE 1940s**, the black population of Chicago increased by 77 per cent, from 278,000 to 492,000. In the 1950s, it grew by another 65 per cent, to 813,000; at one point 2,200 black people were moving to Chicago every week. By 1960, Chicago had more than half a million more black residents than it had had twenty years earlier, and black migrants from the South were still coming in tremendous numbers. The mechanical cotton picker was now in use everywhere in the South, and the sharecropper system had been phased out on most plantations. In demography, there is an important distinction between migrations driven by "push" and "pull" factors; the latter kind goes more smoothly. The attractions of Chicago still constituted a pull northward for many Southern blacks, but now that plantation life had simply ceased to be an option back home, Chicago began to attract people who had been pushed there, too. In black Chicago in the fifties, the slackening off of the demand for unskilled labor had become obvious; blues songs of the era, like J. B. Lenoir's "Eisenhower Blues" and John Brim's "Tough Times," attest to the change. But the number of migrants kept rising — where else was there for displaced sharecroppers to go?

Interested parties — reporters, academics, reformers, and liberal clergymen — would occasionally make field trips to the Illinois Central station and look out in wonder at the sea of humanity in the waiting room. The Roman Catholic Archbishop of Chicago himself, Samuel Cardinal Stritch, who was arguably the most powerful person in a city that was 40 per cent Roman Catholic, went there. It was a scene that stayed imprinted on the mind, because it dramatically illustrated the truth of David Cohn's assertion that race relations were inevitably going to become not just an issue but *the* issue in the North. In the South, the Civil War, Emancipation, and Reconstruction led to the creation of an all-encompassing new political and social system to deal with race — a tragic order, as it turned out. The migration from the South put Chicago in the same position of having to respond to the issue of race in a comprehensive way that would affect the whole fabric of life there — and again, the result was tragic.

In December 1946, the Chicago Housing Authority moved a few black families into a new housing project called Airport Homes, which was in a white neighborhood on the Southwest Side. Race was already well known to be an explosive issue in Chicago. On a Sunday afternoon in the summer of 1919, at the height of the first great migration of blacks from the South, a black boy drowned at a beach on the South Side after having been attacked by a gang of whites — an incident that set off a week of severe rioting that left twenty-three blacks and fifteen whites dead and hundreds injured, and stayed in the city's consciousness for decades as an example of the way that racial tension could induce Chicago simply to go out of control. Toward the end of World War II, with the black belt swelled to the bursting point by the migration from the South, constant small-scale incidents of racial violence occurred, usually involving whites fire-bombing the home of a black family who had moved into their neighborhood.

The housing authority therefore proceeded with some care in integrating Airport Homes. It obtained the blessing of the mayor of Chicago, Edward Kelly, who had since 1933 sat at the head of the Chicago Democratic machine. It carefully screened the black families to make sure they were all stable, with peaceful marriages and a reliable source of income, so that whites in the neighborhood could not raise the standard complaint about not wanting slum dwellers — people like Ruby Daniels — to move in. To minimize the risk of violence, the housing authority arranged for the black families to move in during working hours, when the men in the neighborhood would be away.

When word of the housing authority's plans reached the Southwest Side, a group of white squatters moved into the apartments at Airport Homes that were being held for black families. After they were evicted and the first two black families arrived, a riot began. More than a thousand whites gathered around Airport Homes, shoving, shouting, and throwing rocks. "It was little old ladies in babushkas using language I hadn't heard in the Navy," says Kale Williams, a Chicago activist for integration who as a young veteran helped one of the black families move in. Mayor Kelly publicly condemned the rioters, and sent four hundred policemen to maintain order, but the riot continued; after two weeks, the black families moved out of Airport Homes.

Shortly after the Airport Homes riot, Mayor Kelly announced his retirement — in other words, he was dumped by the machine. Kelly had become irritating to the downtown business establishment in Chicago because he accommodated gambling and other forms of corruption and so allowed Chicago's national image as a crooked, wide-open town to persist. Besides that, though, there were rumors that his conduct during the riot had been deemed too pro-black by the dukes of the Cook County Democratic Central Committee.

Kelly was certainly not a zealot on the subject of integration. His adviser on Negro affairs, Robert Weaver (later the first black Cabinet secretary), resigned in protest when Kelly wouldn't release a report he had written on housing segregation in Chicago. Still, Kelly had appointed a black man, Robert Taylor, the former manager of the Michigan Boulevard Garden Apartments, as chairman of the Chicago Housing Authority, and a crusading white liberal reformer, Elizabeth Wood, as the housing authority's executive director. Taylor's and Wood's decision to integrate public housing in Chicago was quite daring. The federal agency involved in public housing operated under a longstanding rule promulgated by the secretary of the interior, Harold Ickes, that required federally funded housing projects to reflect the racial composition of the neighborhood where they were located; that even as outspoken and powerful a liberal as Ickes wouldn't attempt to enforce residential integration shows how unpopular a cause it was at the time. The real estate trade association's code of ethics actually forbade realtors to move blacks into white neighborhoods. It would have been easy for Kelly to object when Taylor and Wood told him they planned to suspend the Ickes Rule in Chicago, but he didn't.

The man the machine picked to succeed Kelly as mayor, Martin Kennelly, a relatively nonpolitical businessman who was committed to cleaning up Chicago, kept his distance from Taylor and Wood, and would not publicly support their goal of integration. In August 1947, a few months into Kennelly's term, the housing authority opened Fernwood Park Homes, another new housing project in a white neighborhood on the Southwest Side. It was supposed to be 8 per cent black. On opening day, a crowd of five thousand angry whites appeared, and it took a thousand policemen two weeks to get the rioting under control. In 1948, the United States Supreme Court made racial restrictive covenants unenforceable in its decision in the case of *Shelley* v. *Kraemer*; in Chicago, the decision only increased the level of panic in white neighborhoods that now had no legal means of preventing integration. In July 1949, when a black family moved into a house in Park Manor, a neighborhood just south of Woodlawn, a mob of two thousand whites gathered outside and stayed all night, throwing rocks and fire-bombs. Also in 1949, a riot started in another South Side neighborhood, Englewood, merely because black people were seen entering a white family's house to attend a union meeting.

The Federal Housing Act of 1949, an ambitious piece of legislation that established the urban renewal program and provided funds for more than 800,000 new units of public housing, precipitated Robert Taylor's final crisis at the Chicago housing authority. In 1948, the Illinois legislature had passed a bill giving the Chicago City Council the power to approve the housing authority's construction sites. After the Housing Act passed, Taylor gave Mayor Kennelly a list of the sites where the housing authority planned to build first. Most of the sites were on vacant land in white neighborhoods. Kennelly passed Taylor's list to the council without comment, white neighborhood associations on the South Side mobilized, and for most of 1950 a raucous controversy over the sites dominated Chicago politics. It ended with the council's approving a plan to put almost all the new public housing inside the black belt, on land that would be made available by the tearing down of existing slums; meanwhile the federal government's urban renewal funds, in Chicago as elsewhere, were being spent to buy up some of the more promisingly located poor neighborhoods and turn them over to private companies at bargain prices for demolition and commercial redevelopment, while the former residents were forced to move to different slums or into the projects.

In November 1950, Taylor resigned. From then on, Chicago was firmly committed to using most of its bonanza from the federal government to build all-black housing projects inside already black (and usually also poor) neighborhoods. The Chicago Housing Authority's role in responding to the great migration from the South would be to try to keep as many of the migrants as possible apart from white Chicago.

The ugly racial incidents continued. Every white neighborhood on the South Side had an "improvement association" whose main purpose was to keep blacks out. Nearly every white tavern put up a lock and a buzzer on its door. For reasons of basic physical safety, black people had to watch where they walked, even in broad daylight. In the summer of 1951, a black family moved into an apartment building in Cicero, a white working-class town that borders Chicago and has a reputation among black Chicagoans as being the most prejudiced of all the prejudiced white communities in the area, the place where a black person standing on the sidewalk is in the most danger. A mob of whites numbering in the thousands attacked the building for several nights running; the National Guard had to be called in to end the riot.

In the summer of 1953, a single black family moved into the all-white Trumbull Park Homes, a Chicago Housing Authority project on the far South Side. The housing authority had made no preparations for an orderly integration because the black family that moved in was so light-skinned that the clerk who admitted them to Trumbull Park had mistaken them for white. Again a riot began, involving the usual bricks, stones, and bombs; the rioters also attacked blacks who happened to be passing through the neighborhood. After spending nine months as the constant target of violence, the black family moved out. Elizabeth Wood won the battle of Trumbull Park by succeeding in persuading the housing authority to respond by moving twenty new black families into the project and using enough police — at times, a thousand men — to ensure that they would be allowed to stay. But she lost the war: shortly after Trumbull Park quieted down, the housing authority essentially gave her job to another person, and she resigned. Just as Taylor's resignation represented the end of discussions of building new projects in white neighborhoods, Wood's represented the end of attempts to integrate the existing projects on a large scale.

All through Robert Taylor's long, bloody fight with the City Council, a deafening silence emanated from the leading black politician in Chicago, Congressman William Dawson. Dawson was a physically unprepossessing man with a wooden leg who was extremely adept at the art of machine politics. The South Side's first black congressman, Oscar DePriest, a Republican elected in 1928, was an imposing, fiery "race man" beloved by black Chicagoans for his outspokenness on civil rights. Dawson, who started out as a Republican protégé of DePriest's, switched to the Democratic Party during the New Deal, and held his seat in Congress from 1942 until 1970, concentrated his energies on making deals. He absolutely controlled first three, and then, as the migrants kept coming, four, and finally five of Chicago's fifty wards, turning out reliably enormous margins for the machine's candidate in every election. He had strong ties to the most prominent black ministers, to the *Defender* (for which he helped arrange a line of credit), to the local chapter of the NAACP (whose convention he once packed with his precinct captains in order to replace the president with a man more to his liking), to the policy kings of the South Side (whom he represented in his legal practice, and who contributed money to his organization), and to the mostly Southern leadership of the United States House of Representatives, where he operated in exactly the opposite fashion from the second black member of Congress, the militant Adam Clayton Powell, of Harlem.

In all these relationships, Dawson's governing principle was to keep quiet and to maintain as much control as possible over what went on in his kingdom. As late as the 1960 presidential campaign, Dawson, the country's most powerful black official, was advising John F. Kennedy's staff not to let Kennedy use the phrase "civil rights" in his speeches, because it might hurt the feelings of Dawson's Southern friends in Congress — friends who had given Dawson control over many jobs in federal agencies. In the case of the Chicago Housing Authority's building sites, Robert Taylor, an old ally of Dawson's, had violated two of Dawson's cardinal rules: he had come out for integration publicly, which Dawson believed would only create opposition and impede the steady progress of the race; and he had tried to locate significant numbers of black voters outside the wards that Dawson controlled. Dawson, and therefore the whole black political apparatus of Chicago, was entirely happy to keep the migrants who were streaming into Chicago inside the black belt, where their presence would automatically increase his power.

Like many Chicago politicians, Dawson looked better up close than he did from a distance. Even professional reformers usually didn't dislike him if they had the opportunity to get to know him. Privately he was not at all the frightened Uncle Tom that he sometimes seemed to be in public, and he did deliver for his people. He believed that his work was the centerpiece of the life of the South Side; one former protégé of his says, "Dawson used to say you live and die in politics. When you're born, a politician signs your birth certificate, and when you die, a politician signs your death certificate, and everything in between is government." At least in the early stages of the migration, people who moved into his wards would receive a visit from a precinct captain who would inquire as to their needs (while demanding absolute loyalty on election day). For those who served the machine well, Dawson was a munificent source of jobs — jobs with the city, with the county, with the state, with the Post Office, and even with the many private companies that used the machine as an employment agency in return for favorable treatment from City Hall. He could also obtain city contracts and redirect the flow of gov-

ernment services; the policy kings were eternally grateful to him for
having arranged the transfer of policemen controlled by The Outfit, as
the white organized-crime syndicate in Chicago was known, out of the
South Side so that they couldn't harass the numbers salesmen there.

For Dawson to accomplish his good works, the ability to make deals
in private was essential. Just to state the most obvious example, if he
didn't control his ward committeemen, he wouldn't have a machine; the
only way to control the ward committeemen was by financing them; and
the only way to finance them was to get money from the policy kings
and other business people with a strong interest in the activities of government. This could hardly be done out in the open, even though, in
Dawson's view, the results of it were entirely in the best interests of the
South Side; he once said, with some prescience, "If we don't have political
organizations, then we will have control by radio and television." The
section of the Kennedy presidential campaign where Dawson worked had
as its office an entire floor of a building in Washington, set up as an
enormous room without partitions. Dawson announced that he couldn't
work there because he needed a closed office. As someone who worked
with Dawson in the campaign remembers it, "So they built a little
wooden closed office in the middle of this open space. It really looked
like a little shack right in the middle. It was a very, very funny thing."

Although Dawson had no quarrel with Mayor Kennelly's quiescence
about the Chicago Housing Authority's choice of construction sites, he
quickly fell out with Kennelly. The reason was that Kennelly, whose
charter was to clean up Chicago, began sending policemen from downtown to raid the South Side policy wheels. Dawson asked Kennelly to
call off the raids. Kennelly refused. When it came time for the Cook
County Democratic Central Committee to reanoint Kennelly as its candidate in the 1951 mayor's race, Dawson sent word from Washington
that he found Kennelly unacceptable. As Mike Royko tells the story in
his book *Boss*:

They pleaded with him until he consented to come back to Chicago for a secret meeting with Kennelly to iron out their differences.
The meeting took place a few days later in a hotel conference room.
Kennelly sat behind a long table with some of the top ward leaders
on either side. He sat a long time, flushed but silent, while Dawson
limped back and forth on his artificial leg, cursing and shouting,

blistering him for his coolness to the political chiefs in general, and his arrogance to Dawson in particular.

"Who do you think you are? I bring in the votes. I elect you. You are not needed, but the votes are needed. I deliver the votes to you, but you won't talk to me?"

When he finished, and Kennelly was humiliated, the others took him aside and [Al] Horan, an old friend [and the Democratic Committeeman from the Twenty-ninth Ward], said: "Okay, you kicked his ass good. But we don't have another candidate." Dawson, who knew that in the beginning, agreed that Kennelly would get one more term, but only one.

When the 1955 mayoral election came around, the committee nominated its chairman, Richard J. Daley, a fifty-three-year-old career machine politician who then held the job of county clerk, as the Democratic candidate. For the rest of his life, Daley drove a car with a license plate reading 708-222 to commemorate the number of votes (many of them delivered by Dawson) he got in the 1955 election, which began his long reign as mayor. Race at that point may not yet have been an overt issue in the loftiest realms of Chicago mayoral politics, but already it had been crucial behind the scenes. The race issue had contributed to the downfall of Mayor Kelly, and, in a different way, of Mayor Kennelly too; the black wards of Chicago gave Daley a plurality of nearly 100,000 votes, and so formed his political base. It was certainly not the expectation of Mayor Daley that his time in office would be dominated by the consequences of the black migration to Chicago—but it was.

I N 1951, a couple of years after becoming a minister, Uless Carter organized his own congregation, called the Full Gospel Baptist Church. He rented a small space at 4637 South State Street, in the heart of the black belt, and began to offer services. Uless was what was known as a storefront, or "jack-leg," preacher, and as such he belonged to a group that had a poor reputation on the South Side. Middle-class blacks thought there were far too many black preachers in Chicago (there were many more preachers than congregations), and that storefront preachers represented the excess. Their churches were, as the name implies, rickety two-room buildings or former small retail establishments that opened directly onto the sidewalk, with crude hand-lettered signs out front; inside, the preachers, as Richard Wright put it, were "still able to perform their religious rituals on the fervid levels of the plantation revival." Storefront preachers had no formal ministerial training, and their motives for donning the cloth were suspect: many of them were in it for the collection-plate money, or at the very least merely for the chance to occupy a position of authority, and they were notorious for extracting sexual as well as financial favors from their mostly female parishioners.

Uless was prepared to admit that many storefront preachers fit the stereotype, but he thought he was being made to suffer for their sins. This was especially a problem in his marriage. His wife was a beautiful and well-turned-out woman, and she expected to be squired around town more than Uless had time to do. She seldom attended his Sunday services. On the frequent occasions when a parishioner would call in the evening and ask him to come over and help with a problem, she became upset and jealous and would accuse him of going off to have love affairs. One Saturday, after an especially bad argument, Uless moved out of their apartment — and on Sunday, he soon found out, a younger man moved in. Uless resolved never to marry again.

There were difficulties at work, too. At one time Uless was working at the Armour packing house days and at Swift's nights, and making very good money. As his congregation got established, there were times when he had to be away during working hours to attend to unexpected ministerial duties, such as presiding at funerals. Armour's wouldn't let him go. He decided that he had to put preaching first, so after eight years in the stockyards he quit and began working as a household servant in a wealthy white suburb called Hinsdale. Rather than taking a salaried job, he did day work for different families, which meant that his schedule was more flexible and his income substantially lower. Uless spent the rest of his working life in Chicago there, and this meant that the rapid upward economic progress of his first decade in the North came to a halt. The days of his moving to better neighborhoods were over.

The Full Gospel Baptist Church relocated a lot. A storefront preacher's parishioners were poor folks, so his church had to be near a concentration of kitchenette apartments. If the urban renewal program selected the neighborhood where the church was for upgrading, the church had to move, and in every new location Uless had to generate a new congregation, because kitchenette people rarely followed their minister loyally from place to place. Often there were problems with the city. The church would be found in violation of the zoning laws for some reason, such as being situated too close to a tavern or being poorly wired. There would be difficulties with parking permits. The established preachers in Chicago, led by J. H. Jackson of Olivet Baptist, had close ties to the Dawson machine—elaborate exchanges of money, votes, and jobs went on, and they never seemed to have these problems. By committing his life to the solitary pursuit of his ministry, Uless had taken himself out of the mainstream of black Chicago and staked out a permanent place on the fringes. This was not, however, the completely world-renouncing decision that it might appear to be from this distance of years: what Uless had always wanted most in life was to occupy a position of honor and dignity, and being a minister, even a struggling minister, brought him closer to that than being a meatpacker did.

I N THE same year that Richard Daley was elected mayor, Ruby Daniels and Luther Haynes had another baby—Robert, Ruby's sixth son in a row. The financial pressures on Ruby were such that it was imprudent for her to keep avoiding a visit to the public-aid office to apply for an increase in her grant, no matter how unpleasant it might be for her. Now that Ceatrice was dead and Ruby and Luther were living together, however, there was a new reason not to apply: if the public-aid office found out about Luther's presence in her apartment, Ruby would be kicked off the rolls, because it was a strict rule that a welfare mother was not allowed to have a man in the house.

The federal welfare program, Aid to Dependent Children, had been established in 1935 as part of the law that created the Social Security system. The law as a whole was aimed at giving money to people who were presumed to be unable to go out and earn a living, a category that in the minds of government officials in 1935 included the aged, the disabled, widows, and the temporarily unemployed. Aid to Dependent Children was for widows. It codified and supplemented an existing network of widows' pensions provided by most states. The life that everyone Ruby knew was living in 1935—a life in which it was commonplace for women to have children out of wedlock, or to break up with their husbands—was not something the planners of the program knew about. They certainly never dreamed that the American public would over the years become convinced that Aid to Dependent Children was mainly a support system for black women and their illegitimate babies.

The man-in-the-house rule was a serious matter; social workers were allowed to pay surprise visits to welfare mothers and search their apartments for evidence of the presence of a wage-earning male. Instead of taking that risk, Ruby decided to go off public aid voluntarily and get a job. Luther found a place for her at the awning factory where he was working. On her second day there, Ruby noticed that she had been given a much bigger awning to sew than her white co-worker at the next table over. "How come the white girl got a little awning and I got a big one?" she asked Luther loudly. Luther was horrified—that was, in his words, "*racial* talk," and although he might privately agree with it, he was sure it would get them both fired. Instead he got Ruby fired, and resented her for having, through her stubborn and unthinking frankness, consigned the family to the humiliation of poverty. Ruby got another, much less well-paying, job as a barmaid at a place called the Four Aces, at Forty-third Street and Indiana Avenue, just a few blocks from the first place she had lived in Chicago. Luther got a part-time night job at the Four Aces to supplement their income further. Ruby's oldest son, George, was twelve years old by now, and he was left in charge of the younger children at night while Ruby and Luther were at work.

Ruby and Luther moved to a place on Forty-third Street, near the bar. The neighborhood was a poor and somewhat rough part of the South Side, but it was lively. By now almost all of the prominent blues musicians of the Mississippi Delta were living in Chicago and had abandoned folk blues, which was played with an acoustic guitar and no drums, for the louder, faster, electrified urban blues style; the headquarters of the Chicago blues was the section of the South Side between Thirty-first Street and Forty-third Street. Muddy Waters, who had quickly established himself as the king of the Chicago blues, usually played in the neighborhood; Leonard and Philip Chess, the Polish immigrants who had the most important blues record company, started out as nightclub owners there. The Four Aces was a small place with no live band, but in her spare time Ruby often went to the bigger blues clubs to listen to music, dance, and see her many friends from Mississippi. She heard Muddy Waters play, and B. B. King, and Little Milton—just about everybody.

The bad side of all the time spent in taverns was that Luther began to drink too much. When he drank he got mean, and he and Ruby would get into ferocious quarrels. He was still working, but he wasn't always bringing his paycheck home. Ruby left the Four Aces and got a better-paying job as a maid at the Palmer House, one of the grand hotels in the

Loop. Now she was working days, which meant she had to get neighbors to watch her younger children until the older ones got home from school; usually she had to pay for this service. It got harder to make the rent. Feeling pressed, Ruby sent her third son, Larry, who was six years old, down to Clarksdale to live with a childless relative. In 1957, Ruby and Luther moved again, to a neighborhood called Lawndale on the West Side of Chicago.

In black Chicago, the West Side had an entirely different image from the South Side. The South Side had plenty of slums — the worst slums in Chicago, physically — but it was the seat of civilization, the home of all the great black institutions and of the middle class. Like Harlem, it was a place whose name connoted pride and the possibility of success all over black America. The West Side, for blacks, was always predominantly poor, with a weak institutional structure, and it had an especially depressing history.

Until 1950 the West Side was mostly white and represented the remarkable progress made by the children of poor immigrants from Eastern Europe. Families who had first settled in Chicago in the slums just to the west of the Loop — the area where Jane Addams founded Hull House, and where the famous Maxwell Street Jewish ghetto was located — moved a couple of miles farther west and found themselves in a neighborhood of solid two- and three-story brick and stone houses decorated with columns and filigrees that conveyed a sense of solid membership in the lower middle class. The West Side had three large parks — Douglas, Humboldt, and Garfield. It had imposing brick high schools that were renowned as engines of upward mobility. It had thousands of good blue-collar jobs. The enormous red-brick headquarters of Sears Roebuck, which took up five full city blocks, was there, and so were large factories operated by Western Electric and International Harvester, the company that developed the mechanical cotton picker. There were hundreds of smaller employers, and substantial shopping districts along Roosevelt Road and Madison Street. The West Side was a legendary incubator of Jewish success; Saul Bellow, William Paley, Benny Goodman, and thousands of lesser-known Jewish big shots grew up there.

During the 1950s, the West Side changed from white to black and from stable to poor with eerie rapidity. Lawndale, the neighborhood where Ruby moved, was 13 per cent black in 1950, and 91 per cent black in 1960. The sad drama of neighborhood transition played out faster there than anywhere else in Chicago. Sleazy realtors known locally as "panic-peddlers" would move a black family into a neighborhood, often subjecting it to the familiar terrifying round of fire-bombings and snarling crowds. They would go around to the white families and warn them that they'd better move out before it was too late, thereby obtaining their houses at rock-bottom prices. Then they would rush in new black residents, gouging them in the process. Apartment buildings were cut up into overpriced and undermaintained kitchenettes. Houses were sold "on contract," meaning that if the owner, who had been lured in with an unrealistically low down payment, fell behind on the substantial monthly payments, the realtor could kick him out, repossess the house, and sell it on contract to someone else. The West Side quickly became overcrowded (while Lawndale was changing from white to black, its population was also growing by 25 per cent), and it began to become physically dilapidated.

A sociologist seeking to understand the roots of black-Jewish tension in America could find no better case study than Lawndale in the 1950s. Many of the panic-peddlers, landlords, usurious furniture renters, and purveyors of inferior produce in the area were Jewish. Blacks who moved in usually found that their Jewish neighbors looked at them with contempt, and then quickly moved out, to more affluent neighborhoods and suburbs to the north of Lawndale. Jews who had left Lawndale saw how quickly it became a slum in its black incarnation and wondered what was wrong with those people, who couldn't possibly have had it any harder than their own pogrom-fleeing parents and grandparents from Poland and Russia.

Politically, Lawndale was the Twenty-fourth Ward, which for many years was a strong contender for the distinction of being the single most machine-dominated urban political jurisdiction in America. Franklin Roosevelt called the Twenty-fourth "the best Democratic ward in the country" after it gave him a majority of 24,000 to 700 in the 1936 presidential election. Another election result in the same year gives an even better sense of the extent of the machine's control: the overwhelmingly Jewish Twenty-fourth voted overwhelmingly against the first Jewish governor of Illinois, Henry Horner, in his campaign for reelection, because Colonel Jacob Arvey, the redoubtable boss of the ward, was angry at Horner for having vetoed a bill that would have allowed Chicago to license bookmakers. Arvey became chairman of the Cook County Democratic Central Committee after World War II, and from that post arranged the dumping of Mayor Kelly in favor of Mayor Kennelly. Kennelly understandably was made nervous by Arvey's power, and helped arrange for the dumping of Arvey as boss of the Twenty-fourth Ward — but Arvey's successors were Jewish, even though the ward had become black.

The moral justification for the machine was that it would use its absolute power to help its constituents, but in the Twenty-fourth Ward in the 1950s the machine didn't keep up its end of the bargain. The men who controlled the ward didn't live there. The quality of city services — police, fire, sanitation, education — deteriorated. The supply of government jobs for residents of the Twenty-fourth was unusually meager. In 1958, the Central Committee finally permitted the election of a black alderman in the Twenty-fourth, Benjamin Lewis, but only on the condition that Lewis sign an agreement not to get into the real estate or insurance business. This was like making an Olympic star promise not to do endorsements — politically connected insurance and real estate were the essence of the appeal of an alderman's job, since the salary itself was quite low. Lewis violated the agreement and also, according to rumor, started an independent numbers lottery in Lawndale, thus earning the enmity of both the machine and the South Side policy kings.

On February 26, 1963, Lewis was found in his headquarters handcuffed to a chair, dead from a gunshot wound to the back of the head. Another subject of rumors was the subsequent rise of Lewis's former bodyguard and factotum, George Collins, to the position of Twenty-fourth Ward committeeman, alderman, and, eventually, United States congressman from the West Side. Some said Collins had arranged not to be at Lewis's side the night Lewis was killed and had gotten his posts as a reward for his absence. After Collins died in a plane crash in 1972, his estranged wife, Cardiss, then living on the South Side, persuaded the Central Committee to nominate her as his successor. She has represented the West Side in Congress ever since, and with more distinction than her husband; she chaired the Congressional Black Caucus for a term.

There had been a brief period in the late 1940s and early 1950s during which upwardly mobile black families bought two- and three-flat buildings in the changing neighborhoods of the West Side. By the time Ruby Daniels moved to Lawndale in 1957, those days were over; only poor folks relocated there. The shops and hotels and blues clubs on the West Side tended to be dingier than the ones on the South Side. Musically, the South Side was ruled by the dapper, mustachioed, pomaded Muddy Waters, the West Side by the raw, overwhelming, enormous Howlin' Wolf, also a son of the Mississippi Delta. Most of the upwardly mobile families were on their way out — today, black people on the West Side who are blue collar on the way to white collar are confined to just a few small enclaves. The South Side looked down on the West Side, and thought of it as made up wholly of rural people from Mississippi who had proceeded directly there from the Illinois Central station. South Side families did not approve of romances between their children and young West Siders; children on the West Side dreamed of moving to the South Side when they grew up. A family who moved from the South Side to the West Side, like Ruby's, usually did so because it was down on its luck, and usually it hoped to get back to the South Side one day.

Ruby got pregnant again. She began to find that when she answered the phone, the person on the other end of the line would often hang up; from this, and from Luther's frequent absences from their apartment, she deduced that he had started seeing another woman. One Friday morning, Luther went off to work. In the afternoon Ruby began to have labor pains. She went to the hospital and spent the night there, but it turned out that she was in false labor, so on Saturday she went home. Luther wasn't there; he had picked up his paycheck on Friday and taken off somewhere, probably his girlfriend's place. He didn't come home Saturday night. He didn't come home Sunday. On Sunday night, Ruby went into labor again, real labor this time, and had a neighbor take her back to the hospital. At ten minutes before midnight on March 31, 1958, she delivered her first daughter, Juanita. On Monday morning, Luther went straight to work from wherever he had spent the weekend, and he didn't find out he was a father again until Monday night, when he finally came home.

Ruby got a job in a laundry way out on the South Side, but she found it was more than she could handle to do that and take care of the kids. She went down and applied for public aid. When the social worker asked her who her new baby's father was, Ruby, dreading the prospect of having to drag Luther into court for a child support proceeding and knowing that social workers would believe anything about the promiscuity of black women, said she didn't know.

A FEW BLOCKS away from Ruby in Lawndale, a future daughter-in-law and dear friend of hers, Constance Henry, was growing up. Connie was the daughter of one of the rare black migrant families on the West Side that were on their way down from the middle class, rather than up from peasantry. Her mother, Lillian Henry, had been raised somewhere in North Carolina in circumstances substantial enough that she had had two years of college; Connie's father, Charles Henry, was the product of a stable marriage, and when Connie was two or three years old he joined the Coast Guard, which was quite a prestigious employer for a black man to have at the time. Somewhere along the line, though, things had turned sour for the Henrys. Connie never learned exactly what happened, because by the time she was old enough to inquire about the family's history, her mother wouldn't tell her. She never heard anything about the old days in North Carolina; in fact, she was never able to find out where her mother came from there. After her father joined the Coast Guard, he didn't come home any more — again, no explanation given. He died in Boston, of what cause Connie didn't know, in 1957.

There were a few hints and clues. Lillian Henry had come to Chicago in 1948 and then had a son, named James. When she met Charles, she was a single mother, and his parents disapproved of her for that reason. She became pregnant with Connie before she and Charles were married. For a period they were apart and the issue of marriage was unresolved. Then they did get married, and settled in Chicago. Connie has a letter her mother wrote her father during the pregnancy, in which she is trying to persuade him to marry her. "Listen, baby, if you dare stop writing, when I get you down here the first thing I do would be to take you in my arms and kiss you like you never been kissed before," Lillian Henry wrote. "Baby, I can't get mad at you. You and Jimmy and (Boy or Girl?) are all I have." In another part of the letter, she seems to address the possibility that her unclear marital status was the snag in her relationship with Charles: "Baby, I would never give divorce or separation a second thought if I were you. You are what I want; if I can get it, I'll try and keep it."

Connie was born on the day after Christmas in 1950, and her parents had another daughter, Charlene, in 1952. After her father left, her mother took a turn for the worse. She went on public aid for a few years and then got a job as a crossing guard for the Chicago Board of Education. She began to drink. She became moody. Often she was bullying with the children, or depressed, or simply absent. At a certain point she stopped cooking dinner every night. If someone would call and ask her over for a drink, she would accept the invitation and leave the children to fend for themselves. One oft-repeated scene that Connie remembers is her mother, in the middle of the morning, sitting on a crate in the kitchen and crying. The children would ask her what was wrong, and she wouldn't say. Then she would get dressed and say, "I'm going out, and don't come looking for me," and be gone until that night, or even the

next morning. Sometimes Connie would go to the window of their apartment as her mother left, and watch her disappear into the tavern across
the street.

Lillian Henry kept a notebook in which she would occasionally write
poems, songs, letters not intended for the mail, and random thoughts.
The notebook makes it clear that she was lonely and lovelorn to the point
of desperation; as Connie says, she wanted to *belong* to something. The
object of her affection during those years, the late 1950s, was a factory
worker named Ferris Luckett. A few of Lillian's entries in her notebook—
written in handwriting that had become much shakier in the years since
her letter to Charles—convey the sad course of the romance:

> April 1, 1956—10:30 p.m. Letter to lover.
> Life is difficult for you, torn between two loves, one that can give
> you what money can buy, and one that can only give you love and
> most of all understanding ... you must stand firm and make your
> decision. If it's yes or no for me, I must know. . . . I met you in Sept.
> 1953. Since that time I have really known hurt, heartache, and trou-
> bles, but I don't think I could change now if I wanted to. It seems
> I can hardly wait to hear you bound up the stairs (2) two at a time
> and knock at my door. I must see you.

> April 7, 1956
> I hope you soon get over your confusion, and I can get over mine.
> We need each other so much but don't know how to explain to each
> other of our needs. I wish it were me with your child so close to my
> heart. I must have a child for you. That is what I want more than
> life itself. I can love the child even more than I do you. It is born
> so sweet and helpless. Please hurry and come back to me. I need
> you so very much more than you know. Darling, please love me half
> as much as I do you.

> April 8
> Well here it is three o'clock in the morning and I haven't slept a
> wink tonight. Lonesome for my baby wondering where in the world
> he can be. I called him yesterday and I called again today hoping
> and wishing I could just hear his voice. The place I called said no
> one was there by that name. Oh, my love, where can you be? . . . If
> I don't hear from you soon, I think I am going to crack up. . . . I

hope your leaving is not for good. If I lose you, I just don't want to go on living and putting my bitter pieces of this miserable life together again.

April 16, 1956

My dearest darling came over to see me and stayed about 40 min. and that little time was one of the happiest times since I let myself fall in love with him. He seems more attractive now that I have competition. . . . I realize I am being unfair being jealous but when you know what is happening between a woman and the man you love, you can't be no other way. Please come back to me.

And there is a letter, dated May 3, 1957, that Lillian wrote Ferris after a fight between them that became so violent that he ended up in the hospital:

This bed is so lonesome with nobody in it but me, and don't you worry, there is nobody in it but me, and won't be until you get here. . . .

Yours forever,

Lillian Luckett

(I hope)

P.S. . . . . I am enclosing a dollar for you. Connie said to come on and get well with us at home.

The Henry family lived in a one-room apartment on the Near West Side, in a poor area on the fringe between the Loop and the residential sections of the West Side that was dotted with flop houses, day-labor agencies, and small industrial storage facilities. Because the Near West Side was originally home to the Italian slums, the Greek slums, and the Jewish slums, it was that great rarity in Chicago, an integrated neighborhood. Connie had white and Mexican neighbors. Her grade-school class pictures show her, a smiling broad-faced girl, in multiracial groups.

As Lillian Henry grew more bitter, she would talk to Connie about how prejudiced America was. She said that white people called people like them niggers or black motherfuckers; but nobody ever called Connie those names except her mother, when she was drunk and angry. To Connie's mind, being black meant not being the object of any prejudice you could actually see, but instead being inexplicably consigned to a life of misery. When she would go to the home of a friend who was white, or Asian, or Mexican—or, for that matter, to the home of a black friend whose parents were together and both had jobs—there would be no rats or roaches around, no sense that life was a succession of disasters. Connie couldn't understand what the reason for the difference was; she some-times wished she were another color because it would mean that she wouldn't have to live the way she did, but being black was better than nothing, and she had to accept it. In 1959 Lillian Henry moved out to Lawndale because she could get a bigger apartment there for the same rent. From then on Connie had virtually no contact with white people.

Lillian and Ferris were back together. They would sleep in the apart-ment's one bedroom, and the three kids would sleep in the living room. On the nights when Lillian and Ferris had a quarrel, he would sleep in the living room, too, on a roll-out bed.

When Connie got to be ten or eleven years old, Ferris began, on some of the nights when he had been put out of Lillian's bed, to come over to where Connie was sleeping in the living room, put his hand under the covers, and run it along her body. This filled her with revulsion and fear. She told her mother about it, but Lillian didn't believe her.

One Saturday night, Lillian and Ferris had a long, loud argument that lasted almost until dawn and ended with Ferris being sent out to the living room to sleep. Late Sunday morning, Lillian came out of her bedroom and actually saw Ferris doing to Connie what Connie had been saying he did. She ran back into the bedroom and came out with a gun in her hand. She pointed it at Ferris's head and pulled the trigger.

The bullet struck Ferris in the jaw; he was alive, but bloody and badly wounded. The apartment was filled with a sick, rotting smell. When it registered with Lillian what she had done, she burst into tears and pleaded with Ferris to forgive her, because she hadn't really meant to shoot him.

Lillian was afraid to take Ferris to the hospital because she thought it might land her in jail. Instead, for the next month she kept him at home and nursed him back to health. He was holding a grudge, though; as soon as he got well enough to go out, he told the police what Lillian had done. They came to the apartment and led Lillian away in handcuffs, while the children, sobbing, begged them not to take their mother. As Lillian was leaving she told the children to go to Ferris's mother's place, which was around the corner on Madison Street and a safe berth because Ferris's mother took Lillian's side in her domestic quarrels. Connie and her brother and sister stayed there for two months, until their mother got out of jail and took them back home. She didn't see Ferris again until five or six years later, when he appeared one day in front of their building. Lillian went downstairs. Connie watched them through the window: they had a brief, heated conversation, and then he walked away. A little while later, Connie heard that he had died.

R ICHARD DALEY was, in a way, a political-boss version of that 1950s archetype, the Organization Man. Personally, he was nothing like the oft-transferred corporate employees for whom the term was coined — his world was the working-class Irish neighborhood of Bridgeport, where he lived all his life — but he had the same total belief in the system. In his case the system was the Chicago Democratic machine. The more complete the machine's control, the better off Chicago would be, in Daley's view. No good could come from conflict and disorder. There should be no random outcomes. Every person with political ambitions should play them out in the form of a long, slow climb through the ranks, of the kind that Daley himself had made. Problems could be solved quietly and efficiently so long as the machine, currently in Daley's stewardship, was in power and everyone was willing to abide by its rules.

The machine in its mid-twentieth-century incarnation was the brainchild of Anton Cermak, a Bohemian who was a Chicago boss in the 1920s, and was elected mayor in 1931. His great insight was that a political organization could be devised that would include all of Chicago's ethnic groups, rather than pitting one (the Irish) against the others. Daley believed in Cermak's vision, and that was why the black migration to Chicago did not alarm him. Blacks were, by Daley's time, reliably Democratic voters — in fact the black wards of the South and West sides were the core of Daley's support in the 1950s. More blacks in Chicago meant more good Democrats in Chicago. The machine would take them in. They would move up, extremely slowly of course, by participating in the system.

During his first term as mayor, Daley began to consolidate his position. Having seen the last two mayors toppled by powerful dukes, Jake Arvey on the West Side and Bill Dawson on the South Side, Daley, who had himself benefited from the topplings, made sure nothing like that would ever happen to him. Arvey, already out of power, wasn't even permitted by Daley to be a delegate to the Democratic National Conventions after

1956. Dawson was in a much stronger position: Daley was in debt to him, and with Arvey gone Dawson could justifiably try to get the West Side under his control, since it was now black. Daley wouldn't let him; instead he began to chip away at Dawson's power. He took away Dawson's right to appoint the committeemen in his wards, and instead had the Central Committee appoint them (in other words, Daley did it himself). This meant that the final say on the distribution of patronage in Dawson's wards rested with Daley rather than Dawson. Within a few years, Daley had arranged matters so that he personally approved everyone added to the city payroll (he could greet by name perhaps half of the city work force of forty thousand people); matters as trivial as requests to cut down a tree or fill a pothole came directly to his office for disposition.

For a long time Daley's system appeared, to Daley himself and to the outside world, to be a brilliant success. The tight control Daley established did not have the coloration of self-aggrandizement, because he led a modest existence. He lived in a workingman's house in Bridgeport, went to mass every morning, didn't run around with women, and did not participate in the glossy social life of the rich. He was absolutely provincial; Chicago, ordinary-people Chicago, was his whole world. He regularly turned down high-level job opportunities in Washington. He educated his children at Catholic institutions in Chicago. His one conspicuous luxury, custom-made suits, was more a tribute to the grandeur of his office than an example of his own taste for the finer things in life, which was otherwise undetectable.

That Daley's maneuverings had a larger public purpose was obvious. He made Chicago work, and he built things (O'Hare Airport, an expressway system, a convention center, skyscrapers in the Loop, hospitals, schools), tearing down slums to make room for them when it suited his purpose. The machine nurtured the careers not only of comically folkloric ward hacks, but of high-toned liberal intellectuals, such as Governor Adlai Stevenson and Senator Paul Douglas, both of whom rose to national prominence under its aegis. Daley got a reputation as the liberals' favorite boss. In 1957 Isaac Rosenfeld praised Daley in the pages of *Commentary*, then still a liberal magazine. The Kennedy brothers maintained warm relations with Daley well into their conversion to liberalism.

As far as blacks were concerned, Daley prided himself on having dealt them in to an extent unusual by the standards of big-city bosses. Didn't he have black aldermen and committeemen and state legislators and po-

lice captains numbering in the dozens? He would tell associates
envisioned a course for blacks in Chicago like that of the Irish: a long
slow climb from immigrant poverty to middle-class stability, engineered
through the steadily increasing provision of municipal jobs and contracts
in exchange for loyalty to the machine at the polls.

There were a couple of provisos. Blacks had to be patient and non-
confrontational. It is indicative of the nature of Daley's notion of black
progress that when Jesse Jackson came to call on him, shortly after moving to Chicago in the 1960s, Daley offered him a job as a toll-taker on
the Illinois Tollway. Also, segregation had to be maintained. Neighborhood racial transition was the only powerful force at work in the city
that posed a real threat to the machine. Ward bosses were the essential
actors in the system, because they, through their precinct captains, delivered the votes that were the machine's life blood. If a ward went from
white to black, it created havoc. The boss's loyal constituents became
angry, and moved to another jurisdiction. The constituents who replaced
them might be restless under the rule of the boss they had inherited.
The boss's cozy real estate and insurance business would inevitably become more difficult to operate, with so much property changing hands.
Eventually, hundreds of thousands of good machine voters would be lost
to the suburbs.

Leaving aside the morality of segregation, Daley's main practical mis-
take in dealing with the great black migration to Chicago was that, uncharacteristically, he didn't think big enough. It is obvious in retrospect
that the established black neighborhoods were far too small to hold all
the black people coming to Chicago, but Daley's efforts were directed at
finding ways to maintain the color line. His school superintendent, Ben
Willis, a respectable figure from the East who had been brought in to
clean up a scandal (the previous superintendent had his employees writing
textbooks under his name, which the Board of Education would then
order for the Chicago schools), was immediately faced with the problem
of severe overcrowding in the black schools. Instead of integrating the
adjacent and usually half-empty white schools, Willis put the black
schools on double shifts, eight to noon and noon to four, and installed
"Willis Wagons" — trailers converted into temporary classrooms — in
their playgrounds, thereby creating an urban equivalent of the inferior
rural black school systems of the South. Ruby Daniels's younger children
were educated half days in Willis Wagons. Daley did not object, and
when others objected, the ruler of all Chicago would point out that

the Board of Ed was an independent agency and there was nothing he
could do.

The Chicago Housing Authority was flush with federal money during
the early years of Daley's reign. In 1956, Daley's first full year in office,
the housing authority embarked on a massive building program: more
than 15,000 new housing units in a little over a decade. Nearly all of
them were in high-rise buildings designed for large families and built in
poor black neighborhoods. One reason for building high rises was that
the city, having decided not to build on vacant land in not-yet-black
areas, had fairly high land-acquisition costs and so had to fit many units
into limited spaces. Another was that everyone believed in high rises.
Elizabeth Wood was a great champion of high rises, and so were most
other liberals in Chicago. They were taking their cue from the leading
modern architects, notably Le Corbusier, who decreed in *The Radiant
City* that housing developments should be tall in order to leave room for
large empty adjoining tracts of land that the residents would use as parks.
The machine politicians liked high rises for a completely different reason,
which was that, because of the relatively complicated construction techniques they required, they were especially rich in the potential for
patronage.

The new housing projects were completed with characteristic Daley
efficiency. In 1957, the housing authority opened Henry Horner Homes
on the Near West Side, seven buildings of seven stories and two of fifteen
stories, with seven more tall buildings added four years later. In 1958,
Stateway Gardens opened: two buildings of ten stories and six of seventeen stories running in a narrow vertical strip through the heart of the
old South Side black belt. In two stages, the first in 1958 and the second
in 1962, Cabrini-Green opened: twenty-three more tall buildings on an
isolated tract of land on the Near North Side. Finally, in 1962, came the
crowning achievement, Robert Taylor Homes, the largest public-housing
project in the world, twenty-eight identical (except that some were covered with red brick and some with yellow) sixteen-story buildings. The
Taylor Homes represented a southward extension of the narrow strip
that contained Stateway Gardens, so that in sum an area one-quarter
mile wide and two miles long, from Thirty-fifth Street all the way down
to Fifty-fourth Street, became home to nearly 40,000 poor black people.
Parallel to this strip and just one block to the west, Daley built the Dan
Ryan Expressway, a new highway that coincided exactly with what was
then one of the boundaries of the black part of Chicago. The various

elements of Daley's vision are quite plain to anyone who sees the striking row of buildings marching in single file alongside the Dan Ryan: the faith in tangible accomplishment; the bountiful creation of jobs for loyal Democratic contractors and construction unions; the provision by the machine of a substantial benefit to blacks, namely cheap decent housing; and, no need to be subtle or concealing about it, segregation.

The Chicago political system, which was built on the principle that inclusion would always forestall the building up of the enmities that could destroy it, was now party to exclusion on a grand scale. Naturally, this created weaknesses in the system. A black case against Daley began to take form. No matter how pronounced Daley's efforts to maintain neighborhood segregation were, the magnitude of the black migration into the city was such that the destructive process of panicked, violent neighborhood transition was guaranteed to continue for a generation. In education and law enforcement, the machine had begun seriously to abdicate its traditional role as acculturation agency for poor newcomers to the city by allowing the public schools in black neighborhoods to deteriorate badly and crime to go unpunished. The black middle class, now sitting at the head of the largest ethnic group in Chicago, was becoming restless at the slow pace Daley had established for black political progress.

There was a sense that blacks were not really in on the intricate system of deals by which Chicago operated. When a white baby was born — to borrow a fable from a black Chicago politician named Richard Newhouse — certain things were guaranteed. The minute the priest sprinkled the water on his head at his baptism, it was as if three powerful interlocking institutions had lined up on his side: the Roman Catholic Church, the Cook County Democratic Central Committee, and the AFL-CIO Building Trades Council. He was in. He had a future. (Was it an accident that an unusually high proportion of the blacks who were truly wired into the machine were converts to Catholicism?) In grammar school, the priests would check the kid out and decide what track to put him on. If he was smart and ambitious, it would be Loyola or DePaul law school, the state's attorney's office, and then a partnership at one of the big law firms on LaSalle Street. If he wasn't so smart and ambitious, there was Washburn Technical Institute (which the unions controlled), a plumber's or electrician's license (the unions controlled the city licensing agencies, too), and a relatively undemanding billet with a municipal department like Streets and Sanitation or Public Works (again, hiring controlled by the unions in conjunction with the Central Committee). The kid might even achieve the Chicago Dream—a job with the city *and* a job with the county, running concurrently—or, failing that, he could at least supplement his salary with a little moonlighting on (union-controlled) private contracting jobs. Neither route, the one to the state's attorney's office or the one to Streets and San, was open to a black kid.

An organized black antimachine political movement started stirring. In 1959, a new organization called the League of Negro Voters ran an independent candidate for city clerk who got more than 50,000 votes. In 1960, an independent black candidate ran for the state senate from a South Side district. In 1962, Dawson himself attracted a black challenger who, amazingly, carried a couple of wards. In 1963, an organization called the Independent Aldermanic Alliance ran six candidates for alderman in black wards, one of whom won (and was quickly co-opted by the machine). The votes for all these efforts came from the middle-class neighborhoods at the expanding southern fringe of the South Side; the poor, housed in the old slums and the new projects at the South Side's eternally black northern end, were absolutely loyal to Dawson and to the machine. Ruby Daniels, who was recruited into the machine as a foot soldier in the late 1950s, stood out on street corners handing out Daley campaign literature whenever the mayor was running for reelection.

The most prominent middle-class black organization in the country, the NAACP, held its national convention in Chicago in 1963. Daley, confident of a friendly reception—his monumental new housing projects for blacks had just been completed, and, more specifically, he and Dawson had installed reliable allies at the head of the NAACP's Chicago chapter—told the press as the convention was opening, "there are no ghettos in Chicago." When he appeared before the convention he was, to his utter shock and dismay, booed off the stage.

Daley was canny enough to see that his support among blacks had begun to erode; on the other hand, his support among whites, many of whom perceived him as being too pro-black, had eroded much more severely and dangerously. In Daley's third campaign for mayor, in 1963, running against a white-ethnic Republican, he dropped below 700,000 votes for the only time in his mayoralty, and actually lost the white vote. A less adept politician than Daley might have drawn from 1963 the lesson that Dawson, who had greatly helped him once again by turning out big margins in his wards, was the key to his future. Daley saw instead that his black base might become precarious, and that he had better begin to shore up his support among whites. Doing this required only subtle shifts in his course, since none of his policies were actually objectionable to whites in the way that Mayor Kelly's policies had been. There was no need for him to abandon the system he had in place for the political management of black Chicago. To his mind it was still working pretty well, and, as a man of his generation, he saw it as perfectly natural and right, a local application of the ideas by which the country and the world were run in the post–World War II era: consensus, order, containment.

For a time, in the late 1950s and early 1960s, it seemed as if the whole black society of Clarksdale and the Mississippi Delta had transferred itself to Chicago. Everybody was either living in Chicago, or back and forth from Chicago, or occasionally visiting Chicago. Certain venues in Chicago were known to be gathering places for Clarksdalians — taverns on the South Side, kitchenette apartment buildings, weekly-rate residential hotels on the Near West Side. Children would be sent up for the summer to stay with relatives and get jobs that paid much better than chopping cotton on the plantations back home. People just graduating from high school or college would come up to seek their fortunes. Husbands would come hoping to get established enough to send for their families. Elderly people would come to help take care of their children's children. The parties to marital breakups would come to start over.

The organized white resistance to integration in Mississippi by then was actively encouraging black migration to the North, especially for anyone involved in civil rights activity. The Citizens Council, which was the leading respectable (that is, nonterrorist) segregationist organization, made a great show of promoting migration, through such means as standing offers of free one-way transport to the North. Dr. T. R. M. Howard, the civil rights pioneer who was Aaron Henry's mentor, wound up in Chicago Heights, having been subjected to some kind of pressure back in Mississippi that was intense enough to induce him to leave. A strange character in Jackson who called himself The Eagle Eye and published an angry one-page black-nationalist paper that went around on the samizdat circuit in black Mississippi could be seen on the streets of the South Side in the 1960s, hawking the same paper; the story went that a black Masonic organization had spirited him out of Mississippi in a casket, one step ahead of white vigilantes. Also displaced from Mississippi to Chicago because of segregation, in a sense, was a black woman the father of whose children, she said, was Theodore Bilbo, the racist, demagogic United

States senator from Mississippi, who had died in 1947 but who even while alive would not have been in a position to carry out his paternal responsibilities. The woman lived with her children on the West Side in an apartment with a picture of Bilbo hanging in the living room; Uless Carter knew them because they lived next door to his sister and sometimes attended services at one of his storefront churches.

George Hicks, the burial insurance agent's son and would-be member of the middle class, was settled in Clarksdale in the mid-1950s, but he was increasingly eager to leave. Since enrolling at Alcorn, he had been outside the South on a few more occasions, and he liked what he saw. The Alcorn football team used to travel to Ohio to play against Wilberforce College, a venerable black school named after the British politician who was the father of abolitionism in the West Indies. George left Alcorn to join the Army, serving in the Eighty-second Airborne Division and traveling some more, and came back and got his degree in 1955. He returned to Clarksdale and took a job as a junior high school teacher in a rural black school, making $250 a month. He married a woman he had met at Alcorn, who also became a schoolteacher. They had two daughters, Oliphia and Samara, born in 1956 and 1959; also George had two "outside children" by two poorer women with whom he had affairs.

What George really wanted was to be an independent businessman. He opened a saloon, called the Twilight Lounge, and a service station. He felt that other blacks resented him for his ambitions. One Saturday in 1958 the police came into the Twilight Lounge — on a tip from black folks, he later heard — and discovered that he was serving liquor there, which was a violation of the code of conduct for schoolteachers. On Monday morning he was summoned to the office of the superintendent of the rural black schools and relieved of his job.

George moved up to Chicago by himself and got a job at a service station on the South Side. At Christmas time he came back to Clarksdale for the holidays, and while he was there he persuaded the superintendent of the black school system in town to give him a job teaching at an elementary school in Clarksdale. He moved back home, but by that time he was completely disenchanted with Mississippi. He was making $300 a month. At the age of thirty-two, he felt like a failure, and thought he would never get another chance to make something of himself as long as he stayed in the Delta.

In May 1960, he left Clarksdale again, staying briefly in Detroit, where one of his sisters lived, and then moving on to Chicago. He got a night job as a clerk in the Post Office and a day job as an elementary school teacher in Lawndale. The teaching job alone paid $5,000 a year, which was more than the black superintendents were making in Clarksdale. His wife and daughters came up. They settled into an apartment in Wood-lawn, and then, after a year, bought a house in Englewood, a neighborhood to the southwest that had recently changed over from white to black and had a large cohort of middle-class homeowners. It was not George's intention that the story of his progress end there. He didn't want to spend his whole career as either a postal clerk or a grade school teacher. He kept an eye out for a better opportunity, not knowing quite what it would be — business, he assumed, but if anything else came along that offered him a chance to keep moving up, he planned to grab it.

O NE OF the few important white people in Chicago who were deeply interested in finding a way to integrate the black migrants into the economic and social life of the city was Saul Alinsky, the intellectual turned labor organizer turned neighborhood activist who ran the Industrial Areas Foundation. Alinsky was very close to Cardinal Stritch, who was a Southerner by upbringing and understood as most Northerners then didn't the extent to which racial prejudice could come to dominate the texture of a city's life. The Archdiocese of Chicago was Alinsky's main ally among the institutions that ran Chicago. It helped fund his operations, and it provided organizational support through a network of sympathetic parish priests.

Until the late 1950s, Alinsky had operated only in working-class white neighborhoods. Now he began to think about using his organizing techniques to create a racially integrated neighborhood in Chicago. His idea was that this could be done without having to undertake the fool's errand of trying to persuade people to move to a racial utopia. So many neighborhoods on the South Side were in flux racially anyway that you could pick one in the process of transition and try to stabilize it by persuading everyone there to abide by a racial quota system. The key to making it work was to pick exactly the right neighborhood, one in which the whites could be reassured that they wouldn't be surrounded by blacks for miles in every direction and that their black neighbors were stable people with families, houses, and good jobs. Alinsky settled on Englewood, the neighborhood where George Hicks moved from Woodlawn, which was bordered on three sides by white areas (one of them already home to a thriving Alinsky organization) and had a critical mass of middle-class blacks.

There was one insuperable problem: Cardinal Stritch wanted the project to be in Woodlawn instead of Englewood. The diocese had several substantial parishes in Woodlawn whose priests were struggling desperately to stay afloat as their white parishioners left and kitchenette apartments proliferated. The Woodlawn priests succeeded in convincing Stritch that he had to do something to stabilize the neighborhood, and he decided that the best solution was to bring in Alinsky. He told Alinsky that there would be no diocesan funds available for organizing in Englewood, but that he would contribute $150,000 toward the establishment of a new community organization in Woodlawn. The Woodlawn parishes would put in money too. Alinsky didn't have much choice; Woodlawn it was.

Alinsky's protégé and chief organizer was a young man named Nicholas Von Hoffman, a big strapping fellow with a shock of brown hair and wild blue eyes that communicated a sense of perpetual cosmic hilarity. Von Hoffman was all set to get started in Englewood, and he knew that Woodlawn was not a good choice for an Alinsky operation because it was too poor and unsettled. "Saul called me and said, 'We're gonna do Woodlawn,'" he says. "I said, *'What?'* He said, 'Just do it.'"

In late 1960, Von Hoffman hired a young black organizer named Robert Squires and got to work. On their very first night in Woodlawn, they got an omen of sorts, a sign both of what bad shape the neighborhood was in and of how much determination was there for them to draw on. A fire broke out in an apartment building on Sixty-third Street, and Von Hoffman and Squires were helping to evacuate the people. In the confusion, one woman left her newborn baby outside in the bitter cold. When she ran back to get the baby, it was nearly dead, and the ambulance was typically slow in arriving; then suddenly, to everyone's surprise, a drunken neighbor roused herself from her stupor and resuscitated the baby.

Von Hoffman and Squires instantly saw that the real problem in Woodlawn was going to be keeping it from turning into a hopeless slum like Lawndale. It was already headed in that direction. Their approach was to set up a political entity (The Woodlawn Organization), find a leadership figure to head it (the Reverend Arthur Brazier, a Pentecostal minister), and look for grievances around which protests could be organized that would galvanize the neighborhood and so create community spirit. The great villain they settled on was the University of Chicago, which was just north of Woodlawn and was buying up the northern end of the neighborhood, but there were other villains too: the Board of Education, because it was running overcrowded segregated schools; the department stores in the Loop, because they wouldn't hire blacks; the banks, which wouldn't make loans in Woodlawn; the landlords, who didn't keep up their buildings; and the city, because the quality of its services in Woodlawn was so poor.

The Woodlawn Organization began during an evanescent moment in American race relations. Black America had been through an enormous change, namely the shifting of its base from the rural South to the urban North, and attitudes were just beginning to adjust. The feeling that something entirely new in thousands of years of African-American history, a national culture not tied to agriculture, had come into being had not fully registered yet. Robert Moses, the great organizer for the Student Non-Violent Coordinating Committee during the civil rights struggle in the South, grew up in Harlem, but he remembers not really awakening to the idea that there was an urban black archipelago until he got a job in 1958 as private tutor to fourteen-year-old Frankie Lymon, the singer who recorded "Why Do Fools Fall In Love?" and traveled by bus to the black sections of dozens of different towns.

In all these places there was a heady sense of the coming into being of an established black presence, but at the same time it was plain that something was wrong. The poor sections were getting worse, the middle class felt stuck, and there was not a governing idea about what the problem was and what the reaction to it should be. Moses's father worked in an armory in New York and, for Moses, he exemplified the economic and emotional situation of many blacks in the cities: "It was a good job, but it didn't *go* anywhere. That ate away at him, and I think he himself never expressed that in terms of frustration at society as a whole. It was frustration that led to drinking that led to difficult times in the family. There was a lot of that middle-class frustration – a whole generation of people who were intelligent, rooted in family, and industrious, for whom there was just no opportunity. You'd always hear, 'It's gonna be different when *you* grow up.' So you had a slow buildup of frustration."

In Woodlawn, Von Hoffman found that it was still actually an advantage, in 1961 and 1962, to be a white man organizing a black neighborhood. He would dress up in flashy suits and be treated as a big shot. At meetings, when Brazier or Squires said something, every head in the room would turn toward Von Hoffman, because people wanted to know what the white man thought before they decided whether or not to believe Woodlawn's black leaders. On the other hand, Von Hoffman found that white Chicago had become so terrified by the enormous black presence there that he could bring any white institution to its knees merely by threatening to show up with a band of black protesters. One Saturday morning he chartered a fleet of buses to take people to City Hall to register to vote—and found it surrounded by policemen armed with machine guns.

Mayor Daley despised Alinsky, as he did anyone who tried to do things in Chicago without operating through the machine, but he had to maintain relations with The Woodlawn Organization because the Catholic Church was its patron. He tried in vain to loosen the diocese's connection to Alinsky. Once he took aside Father John Egan, the head of the diocese's office of urban affairs and another Alinsky protégé, and told him, in his customary tone of exaggerated politeness, "Father, I think you should be careful of your association with some of those people in community organizing. They're not your kind of people." Because such efforts proved unavailing, Von Hoffman found that he had the prerogative of getting in to see Daley whenever he needed to. On one occasion, Daley said to Von Hoffman, in an exasperated and resigned voice that implied that he had finally decided to cave in and do whatever Alinsky wanted, "Look, go see my guys, and we can work all this out. I'm sure we can."

Von Hoffman went to the Walnut Room of the Bismarck Hotel—the employee lounge of the machine, essentially—to meet with the head of the Cook County Board of Supervisors and the head of the Chicago Board of Realtors. They had lunch—as Von Hoffman remembers it, "an ice cream soda and three martinis." As the dishes were cleared away, the man from the Board of Realtors pulled out a large map of the South Side of Chicago and spread it out on the table. The head of the Cook County Board said to Von Hoffman, "Nick, draw the line. I don't care where you draw it, just draw it. And I'll stick to it as long as you promise that you and your people will stay on one side." Von Hoffman, a man rarely at a loss for words, stammered helplessly, thinking about the never-ending caravan of black migrants that he had often gone to see at the Illinois Central station. The head of the Cook County Board, as a signal of his good faith, offered to sign the map after Von Hoffman had drawn the line. Von Hoffman said he just couldn't deliver on this one.

Meanwhile, the mood in Woodlawn was changing. Back in the mid-1950s, after the murder of Emmett Till in Mississippi, Von Hoffman had gone to a rally in Washington Park, in the heart of the South Side, and seen only three hundred people there. Emmett Till was from Chicago! Now, in Woodlawn, a young man who had worked with The Woodlawn Organization went down South to participate in the Freedom Rides, the bus trips from Washington, D.C., to New Orleans that were being staged by the Congress of Racial Equality to dramatize the segregation of public facilities in the South. He ended up in a hospital bed in New Orleans, and he called Von Hoffman from there and asked whether he could bring some of the Freedom Riders up to speak in Woodlawn. Von Hoffman, remembering the disastrously ill-attended Emmett Till rally, agreed only reluctantly. He reserved the gymnasium at a parochial elementary school, and on the evening of the meeting he made sure the folding chairs were placed far apart so it wouldn't look too embarrassing when hardly anyone showed up.

By the time the meeting got under way, the gym was packed to the rafters, and loudspeakers had been set up in the street outside to handle the large overflow crowd. The evening ended with the Freedom Riders leading everyone in chorus after spirited chorus of "We Shall Overcome," which by now had become the anthem of the civil rights movement. After that, The Woodlawn Organization had the magic touch. It became fantastically easy to organize people by appealing to their racial pride. In the spring of 1962, the organization organized a one-day boycott of an overcrowded elementary school to protest the segregationist policies of Ben Willis, Daley's school superintendent; only 150 of 1,350 students came to school. There was no need even to have picket lines to shame people into staying away.

Professional organizers live for such moments but know they can't last long. What nagged at Von Hoffman was that he could see that despite his organizing victories, the tide was running out in Woodlawn. Working-class people with reliable jobs — the one absolute necessity for a long-running community organization, according to the Alinsky playbook — kept leaving for better neighborhoods to the south and west. Many of The Woodlawn Organization's own members left as soon as they were able to. The more ambitious commercial establishments along Sixty-third Street, such as the movie theaters, were beginning to close down. Street crime, which is the single most important force in driving employed people out of neighborhoods, was getting worse, not better.

An organized gang of teenage boys, called the Blackstone Rangers, appeared on the streets of Woodlawn. Von Hoffman has always claimed that Bob Squires, who could organize anybody to do anything, actually founded the Blackstone Rangers during one weekend when Von Hoffman was not around to remind him of Alinsky's dictum that adolescent males should never be organized because they will inevitably turn to crime. Squires has always denied it, and says Von Hoffman is confusing the Rangers with a group of *Chicago Tribune* newsboys in Woodlawn that he did organize. In any event, the Rangers were walking around on the streets carrying guns, their mere visible presence making life much less pleasant for law-abiding people in Woodlawn.

Von Hoffman's epiphany about where Woodlawn was heading came when The Woodlawn Organization staged its first rent strike, in 1962. After the strike got under way, Von Hoffman began a struggle to induce the landlord, who was white, to come to the building and hear his tenants' grievances — a struggle that he won by telling the landlord that if he wouldn't come, then the tenants would show up at his house and hold the discussion there. The landlord arrived with his lawyer. When they got into the lobby of the building, where Von Hoffman and the tenants were waiting, the landlord turned to the lawyer and said, "Well, tell them." The lawyer took a piece of paper out of his briefcase. He said it was the deed to the building, and if anyone in the lobby would give him a dollar, it was theirs.

"There was much whooping, but I felt we've got a real problem here," Von Hoffman says. "If the landlords are giving buildings away, that means they can't figure out how to keep them up. The income base isn't there. If you fixed it up, and took out the profit, people in Woodlawn still couldn't afford to pay for it. I remember calling Saul that night with a terrible feeling in the pit of my stomach that this was just insoluble."

It was naturally not the policy of The Woodlawn Organization to let the outside world in on such doubts. During this time, Woodlawn began to attract the interest of liberal journalists and foundation executives, who would be given what Von Hoffman calls "the Potemkin Village treatment" by The Woodlawn Organization and go home to write glowing accounts of the miracle on the South Side. The most important of these was by Charles Silberman, of *Fortune* magazine, who ended his book *Crisis in Black and White* (in all other respects an unerring prediction of racial disaster in the North) with a description of the salvation of Woodlawn by Alinsky. "In many ways the most impressive experiment affecting the Negro anywhere in the U.S. is going on now in Chicago's Woodlawn area," Silberman wrote in *Fortune* in 1962.

Woodlawn was in fact almost a perfect example of what was happening in black city slums all over the country: the messy racial transition, the overcrowding, the deterioration of education, law enforcement, and other essential institutions, and then the exodus of the black middle class and the descent into real disorganization. It was a problem the national leadership would have done well to think about. Instead, when Woodlawn became famous, it was for something that wasn't actually happening there, the transformation of a slum into a real functioning neighborhood through political confrontation. The official lesson of Woodlawn was that this could happen in other places too.

As Ruby Daniels's daughter Juanita emerged from infancy, Luther Haynes briefly turned over a new leaf. Ruby believed the reason was that Luther had always wanted a daughter without quite realizing it. He started spending more time around the apartment, bringing home more of his paycheck, and looking after the children, especially Juanita.

Ruby was a faithful churchgoer, though she switched from church to church a lot. Usually she stuck with the Baptist faith in which she had been raised, but sometimes she would go to a church operated by the Spiritualists, a denomination that used candles and incense and had an air of the supernatural about it. One Sunday she lit a candle at a Spiritualist church and prayed to get out of her apartment in Lawndale; and sure enough, soon a landlord with a seven-room apartment on the South Side, a man who had previously told her he didn't let children in his building, got back in touch and said she could rent the place after all.

After they moved into the new apartment, Luther began to drink more, and the quarreling started up again. It got to the point where he would go out on Friday evenings after picking up his paycheck, and Ruby would hope he wouldn't come home, because she knew he would be drunk. On the Friday nights when he did come home — over the years Ruby developed a devastating imitation of Luther, and could re-create the scene quite vividly — he would walk into the apartment, put on a record and turn up the volume, and saunter into their bedroom, a bottle in one hand and a cigarette in the other, in the mood for love. On one such night, Ruby's last child, Kevin, was conceived. Kevin always had something wrong with him — he was very moody, he was scrawny, and he had a severe speech impediment. Ruby was never able to find out exactly what the problem was, but she blamed it on Luther; all that alcohol must have gotten into his sperm, she said.

Having told her social worker that she was not currently involved with a man, Ruby was on public aid, getting $246 a month, but she had to worry about her relationship with Luther being discovered. She told him he ought to arrange to be out on Saturdays, when the social workers usually came around. He refused, saying (in accordance with his view that Ruby should go out and get a factory job like his, but without much logic) that *he* wasn't on public aid so he didn't have to dodge anybody. One Saturday, two social workers, a man and a woman, paid an unannounced visit to the apartment. Luther was sitting in the living room. They asked him who he was. He said he was James Mayfield. They asked to see some identification, and, of course, the name on the card he showed them was Luther Haynes — a name well known to the social workers, since he was listed on Ruby's aid application as the father of Johnnie and Robert. The male social worker went into the bathroom and saw that Luther's razor was there. When he came out, he said, as Ruby remembers it, "Luther Haynes, we've been looking for you. You have children to support. We could assess you for back payments, but we won't. Support your children from now on."

Ruby had been expecting an aid check on Tuesday, without which she wouldn't be able to pay the rent. Now she was cut off. She and Luther moved out of the apartment to a slummier place on Thirty-fifth Street, and she got a job cleaning office buildings in the Loop at night. Her hours were 6 p.m. to 2 a.m. Luther promised to stay home at night and watch the kids (now including Larry, who had come back from Mississippi because the relative who was taking care of him had taken sick), but it was a promise frequently broken. Many nights Ruby had to leave the kids alone because Luther hadn't shown up yet by the time she had to go to work. When she came home — a frightening trip at three in the morning, because by 1961 street crime had begun to get bad in that section of the South Side — she would often find the older children still awake, and when she would ask them if Luther had been there, the answer would be, "No, ma'am." One night Ruby got home, found that Luther wasn't there, and went to bed. She was lying awake when he came in, and she heard him pick up the phone, dial a number, and say, "Honey, I'm home." Ruby grabbed a high-heeled shoe, ran out, and hit Luther so hard that he had to be taken to the hospital.

Miraculously, a check for $246 arrived in the mail. It was Ruby's last public-aid payment, which she thought had been canceled but actually was already in the mail on the day she was cut off. It had bounced around to different addresses and finally made its way to her. In August 1961, with $200 of the money as the down payment, she bought a house on contract in Englewood. This was, by a wide margin, the best place she had ever lived. There was an upstairs with its own bathroom, and a downstairs parlor where nobody had to sleep. The wooden floors were polished to such a high shine that they looked wet. Ruby bought a new dinette set on the installment plan. The monthly payments on the house were steep, and making them required a careful husbanding of Ruby's and Luther's resources.

After only a few months, Luther ruined everything by going out and buying a brand-new 1961 Pontiac. It meant more to him than the house did, and when they couldn't make the house payment, he insisted on keeping the car. The contract-buying system meant that they had no rights to the house they had bought. They were kicked out unceremoniously; Ruby even had to leave the dinette set behind, because she had no place to bring it. She was so mad at Luther that she left him for a while. She moved with the kids into the attic of a house on the West Side, and he moved into a kitchenette in Woodlawn. The crime on the West Side was even worse than it was on Thirty-fifth Street, though, and soon Ruby moved back in with Luther, shoehorning the whole family into two rooms until she found a five-room place to move to. By now she was changing residences even more frequently than she had as a member of a sharecropper family in Mississippi back in the 1920s and 1930s.

It was getting on toward the end of the winter of 1962. Snow was still on the ground. The payments on Luther's Pontiac ate up most of his paycheck, so the family got into bad financial trouble again. The gas was cut off, and they were burning coal in the oven to keep warm. The kids had outgrown their coats and their shoes, and Ruby couldn't afford to buy new ones, so she had to keep them home from school. She knew that if she missed a single rent payment she would be evicted again, and it wasn't too long before she found herself completely out of money two days before the rent was due. Ruby and Luther both used to wonder sometimes in later years how they had ever gotten through times that hard.

Ruby took out her Bible and read a favorite psalm, the Twenty-fourth, which begins, "The earth is the Lord's and the fulness thereof, the world and those who dwell therein." She had always taken comfort from that line; to her it meant that even someone as poor and forgotten as she was could fairly hope for some of God's attention and life's bounty. She prayed to God to help her make the rent.

That night, Ruby dreamed that the front of her apartment building was consumed in fire. As soon as she woke up, she got out her "dream book," a pamphlet owned by most poor people on the South Side that matched dreams, names, and events to numbers on which bets could be placed at one of the policy wheels. The book said the number corresponding to fire was 6-46-69, so Ruby gave her son George two dollars and told him to run out and put it on that number. That night, Ruby found out she had won more than $400. She called her landlord and persuaded him to give her a day's grace, and when the payoff man came, she paid the rent and had money left over to buy clothes for her children.

Just a few blocks from where Ruby was living, the Robert Taylor Homes were going up. To Ruby they were a magnificent sight: tall, sturdily constructed buildings with elevators and balconies, fresh paint and central heating. The apartments there were said to be large and the rents quite low, less than $100 a month. Ruby had had an application on file at the Chicago Housing Authority ever since 1949, but she had never been admitted because the housing authority's usual policy was to screen out unwed mothers. Now that the Taylor Homes were almost finished, she decided to go down to the housing authority again and reapply. She drew a nice social worker there named Miss Coffee. Miss Coffee pulled out Ruby's file and asked her if she still went by the name of Ruby Daniels. Oh, no, Ruby said, I'm Ruby Haynes now. Miss Coffee asked Ruby who the father of her children was. Ruby said it was Luther Haynes, her husband. Miss Coffee told Ruby that if she would bring in her marriage license, she could have an apartment in the Taylor Homes.

Ruby and Luther went down to the courthouse and got married. The next day, Ruby brought her license back to the housing authority, and Miss Coffee stamped it: APPROVED.

The Robert Taylor Homes were built in four stages. By the time the last stage — the seven buildings at the southern end of the project, between Fifty-first Street and Fifty-fourth Street — was under way, the housing authority's tenant-screening procedures had begun to fray. The sheer volume of paperwork and interviewing required to fill more than 4,400 apartments was overwhelming, and toward the end the supply of tenants who were both poor and stable began to run short. In a show of Daley-era municipal puissance, the construction crews finished their work eleven months ahead of schedule, adding to the pressure on the tenant-screeners. Perhaps the need to get the place filled up, as well as her gullibility or kindness, explains why Miss Coffee was satisfied by Ruby's hastily executed marriage. The tenants in the three southernmost buildings in the project were, according to Robert Taylor folklore, barely screened at all, and those three buildings quickly acquired the enduring nickname of "The Hole," because they were so crime-ridden.

Ruby fixed her hopes on a specific building in the project, 5135 South Federal, one of a group of yellow-brick towers just to the north of the red-brick ones that comprised The Hole. She liked it because it was just a few steps away from the intersection of two bus lines, so it would be easy to get around town. Miss Coffee told her that if she could wait until October, she could get into 5135. Ruby instantly agreed, and on October 12, 1962, the family moved into Apartment 902 there.

It was a great day. There was a feeling of excitement and of festivity that went along with the inauguration of an impressive building, especially since the accommodations there were better than any of the tenants had ever had. Janitors were there to help everyone with their things. Workmen were grading the area around the building and planting grass. Everything was new and clean. The only odd note that day was that a Baptist church right across the street from 5135 burned down — but that could be taken as a sign of the momentousness of that spot, rather than a bad omen. The Haynes family chose to rejoice in their good fortune in becoming residents of the Robert Taylor Homes. As Ruby's son Larry, who was twelve years old at the time, says, "I thought that was the beautifullest place in the world."

WASHINGTON

I T REQUIRES a real leap of the imagination, a willed immersion in the mind of another time, to understand the attitude of the American establishment at the outset of the 1960s toward the issue of race in the big cities. The United States as a whole was in a kind of moral slumber about segregation in the South; white liberals were officially against it, but they held out little hope that it could be eliminated. The South was still an essential part of the Democratic Party's coalition in presidential politics—John F. Kennedy carried the old Confederacy in 1960. Southern Democrats held the highest leadership positions and controlled the most important committees in Congress. The white champions of civil rights were mostly people like Eleanor Roosevelt, religious leaders, and figures from the Congress of Industrial Organizations side of the labor movement, like Walter Reuther of the United Auto Workers—in other words, not members of the tough, pragmatic tendency within the Democratic Party. Kennedy, as a senator preparing to run for president, voted with his Southern colleagues to put an amendment into the Civil Rights Act of 1957 that guaranteed jury trials (that is, certain acquittal) to people accused of violating blacks' voting rights.

The development of the mechanical cotton picker had barely been noticed outside Southern agricultural circles. The epochal black migration to the North took place substantially without attention from the opinion-making classes. Conditions in the big-city black slums were an obsessive local issue that somehow did not rise to the level of national concern. The cities' successful assimilation of immigrant slum dwellers at the turn of the century was still fresh in people's minds, and there seemed to be no reason why it couldn't happen again. Simply by virtue of having left the South, blacks in the North were already on an upward trajectory. As late as 1964, *Business Week* wrote, "The basic cause of Negro poverty is discrimination—in education, jobs, access to medical care. Many Negroes have improved their lot by moving to the cities. But many others still live in the rural South." Slum clearance and the construction of decent housing for the poor—a cherished goal of reformers since the days of Jacob Riis—were proceeding on a far grander scale than ever before, without any noticeable bad results.

Kennedy's presidential campaign in 1960 operated on the assumption that blacks in the North were machine voters who could be reached through businesslike dealings with their political bosses—not people with special problems and a unique moral claim on the government's help. Kennedy staked out with some care a position on civil rights that was slightly less ardent than that of his main liberal rival for the Democratic nomination, Hubert Humphrey; when Roy Wilkins, the head of the NAACP, criticized Kennedy in the late 1950s, Kennedy responded not by making fiery speeches or adopting new positions, but by cultivating the publishers of black newspapers, who were powerful figures with no hesitance about getting directly involved in politics. After Kennedy got the Democratic nomination, the burning issue in the minorities section of his campaign was that the Democratic Party owed the black publishers $49,000 in unpaid bills for advertising space during the 1956 presidential campaign, and the publishers wouldn't get behind Kennedy unless he paid up. The feeling that money changing hands was a precondition of black support led the Kennedy campaign to offer to buy Simeon Booker's column in *Jet* magazine, meaning that the column would continue to appear under Booker's name but would be written by the Kennedy staff until November; Booker and his publisher refused.

The two leading black politicians in the country, Congressmen William Dawson of Chicago and Adam Clayton Powell of New York, were both regarded with some disdain by the Kennedy campaign—especially by the man running the campaign, Robert Kennedy. Bobby Kennedy disliked Dawson and Powell for different reasons—Dawson because he was an old-fashioned politician, and Powell because he was a rogue. Kennedy saw himself as a moral crusader, even in the days when he was a conservative Democrat whose favorite issues were crime-fighting and anticommunism. He didn't like rogues because they were impure. He didn't like politicians because they were talky, dilatory, and favor-oriented, and couldn't perceive issues in terms of right and wrong. In

1968, after a long meeting with the California boss Jesse Unruh, Kennedy said to one of his aides, "God, I hate that. I really don't like to sit around and bullshit with those guys. . . . We used to send Larry O'Brien [John Kennedy's emissary to the world of political patronage] to do that. . . . He could talk the balls off a brass monkey."

Both of these opinions shaped Kennedy's relations with the whole political world, not just blacks; for example, they help to explain his lack of respect for Lyndon Johnson, which created a tension that ran through nearly every aspect of domestic and foreign policy in the 1960s. Kennedy objected violently when his brother picked Johnson as his running mate in 1960. After Johnson had accepted, Robert Kennedy visited his hotel room and asked him to change his mind and turn the vice presidential nomination down. "I thought he'd burst into tears," Kennedy later remembered. ". . . He just shook, and tears came into his eyes. . . ." A show of weakness of that kind was a serious violation of Kennedy's standards of acceptable adult male behavior.

In the particular case of black politicians, Robert Kennedy said in 1964, with obvious contempt, "I think those running for office in the Democratic Party looked to just three or four people who would deliver the Negro vote. And you never had to say you were going to do anything on civil rights." In 1960, Kennedy at first refused to speak to Dawson, who was one of those three or four people. Louis Martin, a member of the inner circle of black newspaper publishers who was temporarily helping the Kennedy campaign, met Robert Kennedy for the first time at a meeting called for the purpose of Kennedy's chewing out the staff of the minorities section. Martin says, "Bobby jumped on us – he said we were not doing enough. I said, 'You don't know anything! You've got to meet with Dawson!' I didn't agree with Dawson, but he could deliver two hundred thousand votes. The Kennedys had never called him, and Dawson thought they were a little prejudiced. After the meeting, I went in and told Bobby to make sure the black political leaders were on board, including a personal meeting with Dawson. So I put Bill in a cab, brought him over, and left – Bill liked to *do business*. And after the meeting, Bill was still cool. He wouldn't say what happened, but he didn't like it."

Adam Clayton Powell presented himself to the world as a crusader, but Robert Kennedy didn't believe him. He once said that Powell "always exacts a price, a monetary price, for his support"; surely this explained Powell's endorsement of Dwight Eisenhower in the 1956 presidential campaign. Also, Kennedy saw Powell as lazy, and sloth was to his mind the deadliest sin. In 1960 Powell endorsed John Kennedy; knowing that there would be some expectation on the part of the campaign that he get out and speak for the candidate, Powell had a member of his staff call and magnanimously announce that the congressman was available for a multicity tour of the South. The last thing the Kennedy campaign wanted was Adam Clayton Powell's picture on the front page of every Southern newspaper, but Bobby Kennedy was so annoyed by Powell's gambit that he decided to call his bluff. He had an aide call Powell's office and say that a travel schedule was on the way; the call was not returned.

Both Martin Luther Kings, the prominent Atlanta minister and his son the young civil rights leader, were leaning toward Richard Nixon for president at the outset of the 1960 campaign. The elder King, who at one point formally endorsed Nixon, had, as his son later put it, "a feeling that a Catholic should not be President for religious reasons"; the younger King didn't share that prejudice, but he had other reasons to look kindly on Nixon. He told an interviewer in 1964, "I had known Nixon longer. He had been supposedly close to me, and he would call me frequently about things, getting, seeking my advice." What brought both Kings around to the Democratic ticket was John Kennedy's famous phone call to Coretta King in October 1960, when her husband was in jail in Georgia, but the call was made only after a great deal of maneuvering by the liberals on Kennedy's staff.

Sargent Shriver, Kennedy's brother-in-law and the head of the family's Merchandise Mart in Chicago, was in charge of the campaign's minorities section, but he was not a member of Kennedy's inner circle; he was considered too soft, too much the goody-goody, too close to the dreamy intellectual wing of the Catholic Church. In the words of one of his aides, Harris Wofford, "Shriver was the house communist." When Wofford first met John Kennedy's chief of staff, Theodore Sorensen, Sorensen, displaying the Kennedy family's suspicions about where Shriver's priorities lay, "said he wanted to make sure I knew the definition of good and bad: whatever helps the nomination of John Kennedy is good; whatever hinders it is bad." It was Wofford who suggested to Shriver that Kennedy call Coretta King. Shriver rushed to O'Hare Airport in Chicago, where Kennedy was waiting for a plane, to make the suggestion.

As Wofford remembered it later, "He got into the room and he looked around and he saw all the campaign aides and he concluded that if he brought it up in that crowd it would never happen. There would be a committee, and out of the committee would never come anything like this. So he waited, precariously because the plane was going to leave pretty soon. But Pierre [Salinger, the press secretary] went out to the press, and Ted [Kennedy] went to finish a speech, and finally Kenny O'Donnell [a close aide specializing in the tough side of politics] went into the john. Shriver put his foot against the door to keep it closed and said to John Kennedy, 'I know you can't issue a public statement, but Mrs. King is very upset and pregnant. What about just telephoning her?' And he said Kennedy looked up and said, 'That's a wonderful idea. Do you have her number?' Shriver did; put the call through."

When Robert Kennedy, whose overriding moral crusade at that moment was getting his brother elected president, heard about the call to Mrs. King, he was furious. He called Wofford and Louis Martin into his office and said, as Wofford recalled it, "'Now you bomb-throwers have done too much in this campaign,' or, 'This is the last thing you bomb-throwers are going to do in this campaign.' He was livid and angry, and I would have said perhaps frightened. In any case, he was pale, seemed so. And he told us about Southern states that were probably going to be lost because of this. He was very exercised." Kennedy gave Shriver a severe dressing-down too. But only a few hours later, Robert Kennedy called the Georgia judge who had put King in jail to demand his release — an incident that has gone down in history as an example of Kennedy's awakening racial conscience as well as of the impetuous, bullying streak in his character. In truth, though, as Kennedy himself admitted long afterward, he made the call at the request of the governor of Georgia, Ernest Vandiver, who thought that a long, well-publicized jail term for King would hurt John Kennedy's chances of carrying Georgia in November (which he did).

During his presidency, Kennedy's support for civil rights always came as the result of the black movement's prodding him into action. In civil rights leaders' discussions of him, words like "cautious" and "technical" come up again and again. "He didn't quite have the emotional commitment," King told one interviewer; "the moral passion is missing," he told Wofford. Kennedy's heart was in the great struggle with the Soviet Union, and he didn't conceive of race relations in the United States as a problem of similar magnitude and complexity. One day during the 1960 campaign, Harris Wofford was standing on a street corner in Washington waiting for a cab when John Kennedy, driving past in a red convertible, stopped and picked him up. "He was driving very fast and his left hand was tapping on the door of the car," Wofford remembered. "And he said, 'Now, in five minutes, tick off the ten things that a President ought to do to clean up this goddamn civil rights mess.'" After the election, Robert Kennedy rejected Wofford's candidacy for the job of assistant attorney general for civil rights because, as he said later, "Wofford was very emotionally involved in all of these matters and was rather in some areas a slight madman."

During the 1960 campaign, John Kennedy had promised to sign an executive order that would eliminate discrimination in housing "at the stroke of a pen." In office, he delayed the order until after the 1962 congressional elections, and Robert Kennedy issued it from the attorney general's office, after having made sure it was worded in a very limited way. In the spring of 1961, Robert Kennedy asked King to try to postpone the Freedom Rides (which were sure to lead to patently unjust arrests at the Southern bus stations where the riders stopped, and so to create bad international publicity for the United States at a crucial moment in the Cold War), and offered James Farmer, the head of the Congress of Racial Equality, tax breaks if CORE would stop demonstrating. As late as 1963, during a White House meeting to discuss the legislation that became the Civil Rights Act of 1964, John Kennedy's concern about the political perils of civil rights was obvious; Francis Keppel, commissioner of education, said later, "I had never seen President Kennedy so nervous as he was at that particular meeting. . . . I got a real sense of tension in him."

What made the Kennedys move over time toward a closer embrace of the civil rights cause was in part the series of atrocities visited on the civil rights movement's ground troops in the South, but it was also that the forces of segregation affronted them personally. Robert Kennedy's aide John Siegenthaler was beaten in Alabama in 1961. In 1962 Governor Ross Barnett of Mississippi fundamentally violated the Kennedy code by breaking his promise that he would allow the orderly integration of the University of Mississippi. Before that it was possible for the Kennedys to see the leading segregationist politicians as canny, practical men who possessed their most cherished virtue, toughness. (After the 1960 election, job-seekers would call the Kennedy transition office and announce, "I'm tough.") Afterward, Robert Kennedy dismissed Barnett with a withering one-word assessment: "Weak."

Among public-policy experts, the idea that an important national problem was brewing in the black slums of the Northern and Western cities was not at all a part of the conventional wisdom. In fact, the book in which the term "conventional wisdom" was introduced into the discourse—John Kenneth Galbraith's *The Affluent Society*, published in 1958—mentions race only once, as a mere aside in its sweeping vision of the form that liberalism should take in the years to come. Galbraith's idea was that the United States had largely conquered the problem of poverty during World War II and the postwar boom, and that now the country should address itself to the issue of "public squalor" by increasing the government's spending and the scope of its activities. John Kennedy's campaign slogan, "Let's get America moving again," echoed Galbraith; it was a politically attractive packaging for liberalism after Eisenhower, because it tapped into the impatient energy of the veterans of the war without contradicting the reigning idea that since the Depression, the United States had become a consensus society whose citizens could go forward all together, without bitter conflicts of class and region and ethnicity.

There were respectable liberals who disagreed with Galbraith, but they were well aware of being outside the mainstream of American thought. In particular, anyone working, during the late 1950s and early 1960s, on the assumption that a Northern racial crisis was on the way had ventured into daring, avant-garde intellectual territory. It wasn't just that among white intellectuals little was known about the urban black ghettos; the very notion that an enormous racial problem existed in the North caused the whole consensual vision of American society to crumble. Segregation in the South was a regional issue with deep historical roots. The civil rights movement was, obviously, the kind of bloody conflict that the country was supposed to have gotten over, but its end result would be the bringing of the South into the healthy, rational mode of operation of the nation as a whole. Deep-seated conflict in the North was another story—it wasn't supposed to exist. The realization of it popped up in a series of places on the fringes of the government-university-foundation nexus.

After *The Affluent Society* was published, Senator Paul Douglas of Illinois, a scholarly liberal of an older generation than Galbraith's and Kennedy's, commissioned a study of poverty in the United States to see whether it was really as insignificant a problem as Galbraith had said it was. Robert Lampman, an economist from the University of Wisconsin — an institution still imbued with the legacy of the great Wisconsin Progressive politician Robert M. LaFollette — published the study in 1959, and found that the rate of "exit from poverty" had already begun to slow considerably in the late fifties.

Harris Wofford, before going to work on the Kennedy campaign, was a law professor at the University of Notre Dame and a protégé of Notre Dame's president, Father Theodore Hesburgh. Hesburgh was a member of the United States Commission on Civil Rights, which undertook a major study of American race relations in the late 1950s. Wofford did some of the research for the study; when he traveled to Chicago, he was shocked to find that the conditions in which poor blacks lived there seemed to be even worse than they were in the South. The commission's report, also published in 1959, contains a mild warning about race relations in the North.

Nathan Glazer and Daniel Patrick Moynihan, two young social scientists, published a book called *Beyond the Melting Pot* in 1963. Glazer and Moynihan belonged to the first generation of city-bred white ethnics to rise to the highest level in American academic life; as such, they were far more street-wise than their elders, having actually grown up in the kinds of communities that the leading sociologists of the day knew only as researchers. They put forth the notion that ethnicity, supposedly a dissolving pill in the American body politic, was remarkably persistent as an organizing principle for urban society. The vision of *Beyond the Melting Pot* is of a pluralistic, quarrelsome society, especially on the subject of race.

Leonard Duhl, a psychologist at the National Institute of Mental Health, began in 1955 to assemble a loose group of experts to discuss cities. Duhl, a freewheeling character, was operating under an extremely generous interpretation of the charter of the NIMH, which directed it to look after "the mental health of the population of the United States." He was interested in creating a countervailing vision of urban life to the one that prevailed in the Eisenhower years. The urban renewal program was financing the demolition of older inner-city neighborhoods and the relocation of their (mostly black) residents, so that private developers could get rich building big, ugly new projects. The interstate highway program was encouraging the flight of the white middle class to the new, sterile, soulless suburbs, and helping another set of private developers —

homebuilders—to get rich. Nobody seemed to be objecting; Duhl wanted to marshal the intellectual opposition. His idea was, in the context of the time, not so much politically radical as it was weird; on the day that the Soviet satellite Sputnik was launched, in 1957, one of his experts said, "If they think *they're* out in space, they should see us," and thereafter Duhl's group was known as the Space Cadets.

Cadging money from here and there, Duhl began to finance a series of influential research projects: Herbert Gans's book *The Urban Villagers*, which attacked the urban renewal program for destroying a vibrant Italian-American neighborhood in Boston so that a luxury high-rise apartment complex could be built on its site (Gans wrote later that "the low-income population was in effect subsidizing its own removal for the benefit of the wealthy"); Elliot Liebow's *Tally's Corner*, a depiction of the drifting life lived by "street-corner men" in a black neighborhood in Washington; and *Behind Ghetto Walls*, by Lee Rainwater, which showed how frighteningly disorganized the all-black high-rise Pruitt-Igoe housing project in St. Louis had become only a few years after it was built.

Paul Ylvisaker was a mid-level official at the Ford Foundation, where he went to work after suffering a heart attack at the age of thirty-three and deciding he had better abandon for something more sedate his career as a fast-track aide to a United States senator. Ylvisaker lived in a suburb in New Jersey, and when he had to travel on Ford Foundation business, he would take a bus to the Newark airport that passed through Newark's black ghetto. "You could *see* the frustration," he says. "You could *read* it. You come to the North, where it's supposed to be better, and you find this!" Ylvisaker talked his superiors at Ford into letting him set up an organization called the Gray Areas Project to find ways to improve conditions in the ghettos. Gray Areas was a euphemism for black areas, necessary because the foundation's board was terrified of getting involved in anything that dealt explicitly with the subject of race. In 1954, a Ford Foundation subsidiary called the Fund for the Republic had made a $25,000 grant for a national study of housing segregation, and this set off a storm of protest; Ford automobile dealers in the South complained to Henry Ford II that they were afraid they might be boycotted. For years afterward, the foundation was willing to study racial issues only under some kind of cover.

One of the Gray Areas Project's first grants was to an organization in New Haven, Connecticut, run by a former regional director of the United Auto Workers named Mitchell Sviridoff. Sviridoff was close to the mayor of New Haven, Dick Lee; they both believed that something needed to be done to help the black migrants who had been streaming into New Haven from Georgia and the Carolinas. With abundant funding from the city and the Ford Foundation — $12 million a year — Sviridoff set up a series of programs to improve education and job training in the black slums. In early 1963, there was a great controversy in the New Haven Gray Areas Project: Jean Cahn, a lawyer working in the project's legal aid department, took on the case of a black man accused (and eventually convicted) of raping a white nurse. Sviridoff was caught between the mayor, who wanted him to dissociate himself from the case, and Paul Ylvisaker, who wanted him to support it. He decided to side with the mayor, and as a result the New Haven project maintained its good relations with the local political order, but Jean Cahn's program was made a separate entity from the Gray Areas Project.

Another important recipient of the Gray Areas Project's largesse was an organization on the Lower East Side of New York called Mobilization for Youth, which was the brainchild of two sociologists at the Columbia University School of Social Work, Lloyd Ohlin and Richard Cloward. Ohlin and Cloward were an unlikely-looking pair — Ohlin had the appearance of an apple-cheeked Midwestern uncle, while the younger Cloward played the part of the academic as urban hipster; their partnership represented the marriage of two great traditions in American sociology.

Ohlin's Ph.D. was from the University of Chicago, which was the Olympus of sociological research. The founding fathers of the Chicago sociology department, Robert Park and Ernest Burgess, encouraged their students to roam the streets of the city, especially the slums. Park, a former newspaper reporter, dispatched his students to the funerals of the victims in the St. Valentine's Day Massacre, because he thought they'd get good stuff there. Burgess, Park's drab and systematic partner, was Ohlin's thesis adviser (and also Saul Alinsky's, before Alinsky dropped out of academic life). There was a longstanding feud at the University of Chicago between the sociology department and the School of Social Service Administration. The social workers, strongly influenced by Freudian psychology, saw the slums as a mass of individual problems rooted in poor early-childhood development; to the sociologists, the slums were a part of a vast urban organism, and their problems were a natural part of the life of the city. Adherents of the Park-Burgess school liked to point out that certain Chicago neighborhoods always led the city in juvenile delinquency, no matter which ethnic group happened to be occupying them, because high delinquency was an unavoidable stage in each group's process of assimilation.

As a part of the cleanup campaign that followed the Chicago machine's dumping of Edward Kelly as mayor, a member of the Chicago sociology department named Joseph Lohman was made head of the Illinois Parole and Pardon Board. Lohman hired Ohlin, who spent nearly a decade as a parole official, using the job, of course, as an opportunity to do studies of criminals. In one of the studies, Ohlin looked at the records of juvenile delinquents who had been paroled to serve in World War II, and found that they usually served with distinction — proving that the social workers' idea that delinquents were psychologically crippled was wrong. Another defector from the Chicago sociology department to the parole board, Richard Boone, says, "We went through the inmate 'jacket,' or file. It was all there. Every goddamn case was in the mold of psychiatric social work. 'Breast-feeding ended early.' 'An Oedipal complex.' It went on and on. It was appalling. For parole, you could just *throw* the jacket and ask the other inmates."

Richard Cloward was a student of the leading theoretical sociologist of the day, Robert Merton of Columbia. Merton, who did his research at the library rather than on the streets, explained juvenile delinquency through the sociological concept of anomie: when teenage males in the success-obsessed American culture saw that it was not possible for them to achieve their goals through legitimate means, anomie set in, and they turned to the illegitimate means of crime. Cloward met Ohlin at a conference in the early 1950s, and in 1956 Ohlin left parole work to become a professor at the Columbia School of Social Work, where Cloward was teaching. Together they began working on a book that would synthesize Merton's theories with the Chicago school's field research, while also putting a slightly more positive spin on delinquency, which previously had been portrayed as an irrational and counterproductive response to difficult conditions. *Delinquency and Opportunity*, published in 1960, argued that society denies poor young men, especially blacks, any form of real opportunity, so that the ones who become delinquents are acting rationally, on the basis of a perceptive critique of society. Black delinquents did not even have the chance to get involved in profitable illegal activity, so their forays outside the law were more random and violent than those of white delinquents. It followed that if more real opportunity became available, there would be less delinquency.

Even before they finished the book, Ohlin and Cloward were in touch with the Gray Areas Project, which wanted to fund an organization in New York but was looking for, as Cloward puts it, "something a little more theoretically glitzy" than the traditional approach of the old-line settlement houses of the Lower East Side — hence the appeal of creating a social welfare agency on the basis of their new line of argument. The proposal that established Mobilization for Youth was an elaborate document that was years in the making — Mobilization didn't open its doors until 1962 — but the fierceness of the analytical back-and-forth among academic experts on the slums somewhat obscures the reality of Mobilization. For the most part, it was set up to do exactly what the settlement houses had been doing for years, and what the less theoretically glitzy Gray Areas Project in New Haven was doing: help speed up the assimilation process for poor migrants recently arrived in the city by providing them with special training in the ways of industrial society. What else could Mobilization do? It was founded on the concept that American society pervasively denied opportunity to the poor, but it is beyond the power of a neighborhood social service agency to solve that problem.

There was one crucial difference between the activities of Mobilization and the traditional forms of social work. Although Mobilization could hardly create more opportunity in the nation as a whole, it could at least try to create more opportunity on the Lower East Side by organizing the community to take political action. The theory here was a Marxian one: that poverty is more a political than an economic condition and that if the poor become politically "empowered," they will soon cease to be poor. Empowerment would give poor people a new spirit of community; they would run their own lives, and their neighborhoods, with renewed purposiveness and vigor, and they would learn to get things from the powers that be. As Leonard Cottrell, another Chicago-trained sociologist who was head of the Russell Sage Foundation and a close associate of Ohlin's, put it in 1960, speaking about black migrants from the South, "you get a community of people who have lost the competence to act in a community problem . . . the way to attack it would be to restore the community's confidence to act. . . ."

The history of The Woodlawn Organization in Chicago was a perfect demonstration of the shortcomings of the empowerment theory in the real world of a late-twentieth-century American city: no matter how well organized a poor community was, it could not become stable and not-poor so long as the people with good jobs kept moving out and the people left behind had very little income. This lesson was not yet clear in 1962, though: along with its education and job-training programs, Mobilization began to organize rent strikes and political protests on the Woodlawn model.

The Woodlawn Organization, funded as it was by a Cardinal who had absolute power over his dominion in Chicago, did not have to worry that its protests against Mayor Daley and the University of Chicago might imperil its financial base. The same was true of the civil rights groups organizing in the South: the order they were attacking had nothing to do with their sources of funds, which were church collection plates in the South and North, and Northern philanthropists. Mobilization was in quite a different situation, though nobody seems to have recognized that in 1962. It was founded by the still fairly cautious Ford Foundation, and early in the planning stages it began to seek financial support from the federal government. This meant that it did not have anything like total independence. Confrontational tactics could imperil its existence, because it was dependent on the largesse of the power structure it intended to confront. In the New Haven Gray Areas Project, Mitchell Sviridoff perceived this problem and decided to abandon confrontational tactics, focus on education and training, and retain the support of the mayor. Mobilization went in the other direction, and soon it would suffer the consequences.

To the extent that all these early tendrils of white liberal activity around the issue of blacks in the Northern cities came together, it was in an odd location: the office of the proud holder of the number-one job in the American law enforcement hierarchy, Robert Kennedy. Even more odd, the person most responsible for bringing the ghettos to Kennedy's attention was a complete stranger to the arcane byways of liberal intellectual life; he was Kennedy's best friend from prep school, David Hackett.

Hackett grew up in the proper Boston suburb of Dedham, the scion of an impeccably respectable (though not rich) family of Episcopalian naval officers. As an adolescent he was a golden figure, a superb athlete (he played on the U.S. Olympic hockey team) and a natural leader, the kind of boy who inspires the worshipful respect of other boys. As a student at Milton Academy, in Milton, Massachusetts, he was a legend — the character Phineas, the campus hero in John Knowles's novel *A Separate Peace*, is supposedly based on Hackett. Bobby Kennedy enrolled at

Milton in his junior year of high school, joining his class late after having already attended six different schools over the preceding ten years. Even if he had started at Milton when everyone else did, he would have been an outsider there: he was Irish in a school with no Irish, Catholic in a school with no Catholics, runty, shy, and the son of Joseph P. Kennedy, a hated figure in the Boston WASP culture that dominated the school.

Hackett, alone of all the students at Milton, reached out to Kennedy. They became close friends; Hackett brought Kennedy home for visits, over his parents' objections. The psychological grounding of their friendship contained an element of Hackett's reaching out to the oppressed and of Kennedy's feeling oppressed himself, though clearly Kennedy also touched some strain of the outsider that lay beneath Hackett's glittering exterior. "We were both, in a way, misfits," Hackett said later. Together they developed a mistrust of what Hackett calls, pejoratively, "normal behavior" — the kind of normal behavior that had led to Kennedy's ostracism at Milton.

In the years after Milton, Hackett appeared to be on his way to becoming an example of that common type, the glorious young student athlete whose magical aura evaporates after graduation and whose adult life is quite ordinary. The late 1950s found him in Montreal, working as the editor of an entertainment guide distributed free to hotel guests. When John Kennedy's presidential campaign began, Robert Kennedy brought Hackett on as a delegate-counter, and after the inauguration Hackett was installed in a small office adjoining Kennedy's at the Justice Department. In the array of law review editors, Rhodes scholars, and Pulitzer Prize winners with whom Kennedy surrounded himself at the Justice Department, Hackett stood out as exceptionally unexceptional. The Kennedy circle cultivated a laconic style, but Hackett was simply inarticulate — he would begin a sentence, get lost, and extricate himself by saying "et cetera," with a helpless wave of the hand. It is natural for the circle of advisers around a powerful man to be rivalrous; in Hackett's case, the natural tensions of the attorney general's suite were exacerbated by his fundamental difference from the other top aides to Kennedy, the bright, tough world-beaters. They didn't understand him. Some of them made cruel jokes about his having been hit by too many hockey pucks, or wondered out loud what exactly it was he did in the Justice Department, or spoke of him as belonging to the category of people the boss inexplicably adored, such as the singer Andy Williams.

Kennedy's sister Eunice Shriver, who had many years earlier assumed the informal role of family social worker (she was especially close to the retarded Kennedy sibling, Rosemary), was keenly interested in the issue of juvenile delinquency, and back in the late 1940s had worked on the staff of a government commission studying delinquency. She persuaded her brothers to set up a similar commission in the Kennedy administration. The President's Committee on Juvenile Delinquency was put under the purview of the Justice Department, and David Hackett was made its director—an assignment that did not enhance his status within the department, since the committee was seen as a pet project that had been created to placate Eunice, a world-class nagger. Such were the inauspicious beginnings of the American government's response to the consequences of the black migration.

Hackett began to travel around and meet the leading experts in the field. When some people at the Ford Foundation introduced him to Lloyd Ohlin, he instantly thought he had found the best way to attack delinquency—"it just made sense to me," he says, that, in his words, "barriers to people caused it." Ohlin became a consultant to the President's Committee on Juvenile Delinquency, and so did his old Chicago friend Leonard Cottrell of the Sage Foundation. Hackett hired Richard Boone, who had done parole research with Ohlin in Chicago and then gone to work at the Ford Foundation, as his full-time deputy. Boone looked the part of the Kennedy aide much more than Ohlin did. He was trim and compact, with crew-cut hair and a piercing gaze. In Chicago he had remained on Joseph Lohman's staff after the machine elevated Lohman from head of the state parole board to Cook County sheriff, which meant that Boone, though he was entirely a creature of the academic-foundation culture, eventually held the rank of captain on the Chicago police force—a wonderful credential for someone in the Kennedy Justice Department to have. Boone had the preferred Kennedy spirit: government was a cause for him, but it was also a game to be played with skill and daring.

Soon Hackett's office had formed an alliance with Leonard Duhl's Space Cadets, drawing on them for ideas and helping them get funding. (Already, Duhl was sending some NIMH money to Mobilization for Youth.) And it had relations with the Gray Areas Project, though Hackett had reservations about Ylvisaker, considering him too closely attuned to the established way of doing things. Hackett was also in touch with Daniel Patrick Moynihan. In effect, the President's Committee on Juvenile Delinquency became the government agency with the black-ghetto portfolio, which it was able to acquire largely because nobody else in the government was interested. Hackett and Robert Kennedy visited Harlem and other ghettos together.

The juvenile delinquency committee was the passageway that led Kennedy from his background as a conservative lawman into the political persona for which he is remembered, as the soulful champion of the downtrodden — it connected the two versions of himself. Delinquency was at first blush a law enforcement issue, so attending to it was consistent with the main thrust of Kennedy's career thus far; it didn't have the soft, abstract quality that he associated with most of the leading liberal issues and personalities. Unlike other criminals, though, delinquents were people he could identify with personally. They were troubled adolescents just as he had been — outsiders; the most common nickname for delinquents at the time, "young toughs," was a marriage of two words that carried the most positive possible connotations for Kennedy.

Kennedy liked to be out on, or even ahead of, the front lines. Once at a party at his house, a parlor game began in which everyone had to say what he would do if he could have a different life, and Kennedy said, "I'd be a paratrooper." At a time when no prominent figure in Washington was aware of the problems of young black men in the cities, for Kennedy to begin to comprehend the dimensions of the issue instantly put him in the vanguard of a great cause. Kennedy had never been a good student, and it was a part of his mystique that he wasn't scintillatingly intelligent in the way that his brother John was, as if that left room for simpler moral virtues to come to the fore. He was governed more by his heart than his head, more by his Catholicism than his Irishness; he was one of the rare politicians who see the world in terms of a battle between good and evil. His relationship with Hackett, another highly moral, not very clever man, was especially suffused with this idea. "The brightest people — that wouldn't include him," Hackett says of Kennedy. "But he had a quality. He went after the brightest people. Tremendous records. They were attracted to him because they saw a quality in him they didn't have — the guts, the ability to zero in and move in on issues."

Kennedy began to include black people in the wide circle of friends and advisers who were invited to his house on weekends. Burke Marshall, his assistant attorney general for civil rights, was also becoming concerned about racial problems in the North, and when the comedian Dick Gregory introduced him to James Baldwin, Marshall was so impressed that he invited Baldwin to have breakfast with Kennedy. Kennedy was impressed too; he asked Baldwin to set up a meeting in New York with people who could suggest ways to alleviate the urban racial crisis.

The meeting, held in May 1963, at the Kennedy family's New York apartment, was a famous disaster. Rather than gathering the group of policy experts whom Kennedy expected, Baldwin brought black intellectuals, activists, and performers who used the occasion to pour out their anger. One of the people there was a young CORE worker named Jerome Smith, whose initial commitment to nonviolence had been such that his nickname within the civil rights movement was Gandhi Two but who had lost that spirit in the course of receiving beatings in the South so severe that you could feel a soft spot on his skull. Smith told Kennedy that he would not fight for his country, a statement that Kennedy, who had lost a brother in World War II and had named one of his sons after General Maxwell Taylor, found profoundly shocking. Lorraine Hansberry, the author of *Raisin in the Sun*, the celebrated play about black family life in Chicago, said she would like to arm blacks so that they could start shooting white people in the streets. Kennedy was used to meetings that crisply followed an agenda and in which he was treated with respect; now these people, to whom he had reached out because he wanted to help them, were berating him without making any constructive suggestions.

As the experience sank in, though, it joined the list of Kennedy's redeeming trials by fire. There was a pattern in Kennedy's life in which he would have a hostile first meeting with someone, usually a person from a humbler background who thought of him as an arrogant rich boy, and then would become extremely close to the person, winning him over by proving his essential down-to-earthness. In the first encounter between Kennedy and John Siegenthaler, in 1957, Kennedy greeted Siegenthaler with "a veil over the eyes, tense lips, flared nostrils, his overcoat on with the collar turned up," Siegenthaler says; he immediately accused Siegenthaler of being late and stalked out. Within a year they were boon companions. Richard Harwood, of the *Washington Post*, one of Kennedy's closest journalistic friends and a veteran of many Marine landings during World War II, started out as a great Kennedy-hater but quickly came around. "Dick Harwood was a tough guy," says Hackett. "He had to find out if this guy was phony, and he found out he was real." The meeting with Baldwin's group — an early example of a much-repeated scene in the 1960s, in which an unsuspecting white liberal would be berated by blacks and, most of the time, leave feeling somewhat less liberal — was for Kennedy another opportunity to prove that someone's suspicions about him were wrong. It deepened his understanding and drew him emotionally closer to the slums; it was something nobody else at his level in Washington had been through.

It became explicit in Kennedy's mind that the President's Committee on Juvenile Delinquency was a program for the black ghettos. Hackett wrote to him in 1963, "Most of the programs in action or being developed will affect primarily minority youth — Negroes in almost every city." What the committee actually did was make grants to local organizations, many of which were already receiving help from the Gray Areas Project. Hackett had become convinced that the government's efforts in the ghettos had to have a from-the-bottom-up quality: the residents of the community should decide for themselves what their needs were, and then the government would try to provide it for them. The very process of formulating a plan would bring the community together and serve as a first step on the road out of poverty. Hackett believed that, as he says today, "the federal government is terrible" — rather an unusual conviction for someone to have then, when the federal government had had a thirty-year run of spectacular successes. Kennedy was sympathetic to Hackett's idea, because of his natural impatience with the slow, clumsy ways in which the post–New Deal consensus society moved. He believed in government as an instrument, but he preferred for it to operate through small, quick, anti-bureaucratic organizations. He admired the Green Berets, the elite corps of dashingly costumed anti-insurgency shock troops, much more than the infantry. It was no accident that the ghetto experts who were meeting regularly with Hackett began to call themselves "the guerrillas."

The organizations that received the monies of the President's Committee on Juvenile Delinquency were rarely true exemplars of Hackett's Zen-like notion of programs arising naturally from the people they were meant to serve. Usually they were run by social service professionals, albeit local ones. Even Mobilization for Youth, in its proposal, said it intended to provide delinquents with "opportunities for conformity." Hackett and Kennedy had no intention, either, of getting into battles with local politicians. In Harlem, the juvenile delinquency committee was funding an organization called HARYOU, which was run by Kenneth Clark, the black psychologist (Clark's classic book *Dark Ghetto* was funded by Hackett). When Adam Clayton Powell demanded a piece of the action, Kennedy, despite his personal feelings about Powell, assented, and Clark resigned in protest. In Chicago, when the director of the program began to attract the displeasure of Mayor Daley, Hackett wrote a memo reporting this to

Kennedy, and Kennedy wrote in the margin, "I would get rid of Shuler if he doesn't get along with Mayor." Kennedy's accommodationism is perfectly understandable: he may not have liked traditional politicians, but politics was his business. Neither he nor anyone else in his family had any thought of doing anything else.

Today it is possible to view the President's Committee on Juvenile Delinquency in the same spirit with which the hero of Delmore Schwartz's story "In Dreams Begin Responsibilities" looked at an imagined movie of his quarrelsome parents' courtship while shouting, "Don't do it!" Here was a Democratic administration, understandably heedless of the full consequences, embarking on the disastrous course of allowing itself to be identified with efforts to "understand" the urban street criminal, and helping to fund organizations that opened fissures in the urban political coalitions on which the Democratic Party completely depended. At the time none of this must have been apparent; Kennedy could not have seen that he was doing anything but strengthening the family political base by providing money and services and by developing his own powers of empathy toward a loyal and traditionally shortchanged Democratic constituency.

Lloyd Ohlin briefed both Kennedy brothers on his theory of juvenile delinquency, at different times. In May 1962, just before the ceremony at which the juvenile delinquency committee's generous grant to Mobilization for Youth was to be announced at the White House, Ohlin was brought into the Oval Office for ten minutes with the president. John Kennedy listened impassively, walked outside, delivered a flawless summary of the goals of the program, and then went on to the next item on his agenda with customary coolness. Robert Kennedy, who had invited Ohlin to breakfast on the day he was to testify in Congress in behalf of the authorization of funds for the juvenile delinquency committee, took much longer to get Ohlin's point. Finally, in the car riding to Capitol Hill, he said, "Oh, I see — if I had grown up in these circumstances, this could have happened to me."

WALTER HELLER, the head of President Kennedy's Council of Economic Advisers, was by virtue of his background and his training the kind of liberal who inhabits a clean, precise world of numbers and orderly concepts. Heller's father was a civil engineer in Milwaukee — "a good German," in his son's words. When he lost his job during the Depression, the family was rescued from destitution through the good offices of the Works Progress Administration, which gave him temporary employment and so won Walter Heller's undying gratitude to the New Deal and the federal government. The Hellers were devoted admirers of Robert La Follette; as a graduate student at the University of Wisconsin, Walter Heller toured the country by car, on a grant from the National Youth Administration, to do research for his Ph.D. thesis on the wonders of the state income tax.

He became an economics professor at the University of Minnesota, preaching to his students the gospel of Keynesianism and, because he was the kind of intellectual who was good at presenting his ideas crisply to busy people in the world of affairs, working on the side with liberal Minnesota politicians like Hubert Humphrey and Orville Freeman. In the 1950s Heller built a house in a neighborhood owned by the university, where professors were given vacant lots on the condition that they spend no more than $27,000 on their homes. Heller's was done up in the preferred academic style of the time — modern and unembellished, with picture windows, walls of exposed brick and wood, and Scandinavian furniture upholstered in honest nubbly fabrics, giving the overall impression that all frills and adornments had now been relegated to the dustbin of history.

Heller was not as wholehearted a believer as John Kenneth Galbraith in the tonic of increased federal spending, because he thought it would affect the economy too slowly. Increasing spending in the Kennedy administration was an elusive goal anyway, because the White House had a hard time getting the plumed dukes of Congress to pass new legislation. Heller began to focus on the possibility of pumping money out into the economy in another way, through an income tax cut. In March 1962, he began pushing the idea on Kennedy, and in January 1963, Kennedy finally agreed to it. Heller waited a couple of months and then suggested to Kennedy that the tax cut might come under attack for being a subsidy to the middle class and the rich unless the administration also did something for poor people, who didn't pay any taxes.

The White House was hardly a locus of intense interest in the problem of poverty. Michael Harrington's book *The Other America*, which claimed that one-third of the country was poor (and had one chapter on black city slums), had been published in 1962, but it attracted very little attention until one of the country's leading literary critics, Dwight Macdonald, rescued it from obscurity with a long review in *The New Yorker* (aptly titled "Our Invisible Poor") that appeared in January 1963. It is part of

John Kennedy's legend that *The Other America* spurred him into action against poverty, in the same way that Upton Sinclair's *The Jungle* had motivated Theodore Roosevelt to create the Food and Drug Administration, but the consensus among Kennedy's aides is that he read Macdonald's review, not the book itself. Certainly Macdonald's dry, witty, elegant essay was more up Kennedy's alley than Harrington's earnest, impassioned book would have been. Kennedy's one moving personal experience with poverty had been during his campaign in the 1960 West Virginia primary, when he saw Appalachia at first hand (and beat Hubert Humphrey, thus incurring a heavy political debt to West Virginia); as president his main antipoverty measure before 1963 was the creation of the Appalachian Regional Commission.

Kennedy told Heller to look into the idea of creating a new poverty program. Heller brought Robert Lampman, who was a former student of his at Wisconsin, onto the staff of the Council of Economic Advisers and asked him to condense the poverty research he had done for Paul Douglas into a memo. On May 1, 1963, Heller wrote Kennedy, "Bob Lampman, CEA's expert on poverty, has updated his 1957 data on this subject. The results are distressing. . . . Table 1-A shows the drastic slowdown in the rate at which the economy is taking people out of poverty." On June 3, Heller asked Lampman to write another memo that would answer the question, "Specifically, what lines of action might make up a practical Kennedy antipoverty program in 1964?"

Lampman considered himself much more the political realist than Heller, who had a practically unbounded faith in the influence of the Council of Economic Advisers; he thought any program explicitly aimed at doing something about poverty was doomed. His answer to Heller, dated June 10, 1963, is a subdued document that ends by saying, "Probably a politically acceptable program must avoid completely any use of the term 'inequality' or of the term '*redistribution* of income or wealth,'" although those were just the terms in which Lampman, as an economist, was accustomed to thinking about the problem. In August, Lampman returned to Wisconsin, convinced that the poverty initiative wasn't going to get anywhere.

Heller pressed on without much success. One day in that summer of 1963 he convened a lunch at the White House mess with Galbraith, Willard Wirtz, secretary of labor and an old Adlai Stevenson hand, and Wilbur Cohen, a first-generation New Deal social welfare planner who was deputy secretary (but the real power) at the Department of Health,

Education and Welfare, to sell them on the poverty idea. Heller had every reason to expect that they would be a sympathetic audience, but the lunch didn't go well. As Heller remembered it, "Galbraith sort of took the position he took in *The Affluent Society*. 'We even build our superhighways over them, on concrete stilts.' His position was, the poor were not a major element in the picture — not that it wasn't a problem, but that it was a problem the political system wasn't going to address. That disappointed me. Second, Wirtz, a friend since World War II, said, 'An attack on ignorance, on slums — fine. But on poverty? That's too diffuse.' He couldn't see it. That flabbergasted me. Then, I wanted a new agency. That's where I stepped on Wilbur Cohen's toes. He was interested in the objective but felt it should be done in HEW. I left that lunch crestfallen. I couldn't even get Lampman enthusiastic about it!"

Heller did not display his doubts to the president. On June 20, in a memo to Kennedy covering several points, he wrote, in blithe disregard of the spirit of what Lampman was telling him, "Poverty. I have asked Bob Lampman, CEA's poverty expert, to consider what might go into an Administration's 'assault on poverty' program in 1964." Heller also began to talk up poverty among the political people around Kennedy who would make the final decisions about the 1964 legislative program. He told them that a poverty program might help pull in votes — not from Northern blacks, who were going to vote Democratic anyway, but from good-hearted suburban Republican Protestant church women who might be wooed away from a moderate Republican presidential candidate like Nelson Rockefeller. The reaction of the political people, notably Theodore Sorensen, was that Heller should stick to economics. Yet another problem emerged when Heller, after Lampman's departure, had another one of his assistants, William Capron, take over the job of formulating a real program. Capron created an interagency task force — that most dreadedly slow-moving of all possible government entities — consisting of representatives from all the federal departments and agencies involved in social welfare issues. It was a miserable failure.

During the New Deal, Franklin Roosevelt had packed the federal bureaucracy with idealistic young reformers in their twenties and thirties. By the time of the Kennedy administration, most of them were still around, only now they were entrenched civil service lifers in their fifties and sixties. Every agency had a long list of programs that hadn't quite made the cut for the New Deal; now they were taken down from the shelf, dusted off, and presented to Capron, always with the proviso that only the agency suggesting the program was competent to run it. The Labor Department wanted jobs programs. HEW wanted education and welfare programs. Agriculture wanted farm programs. In October, after months of meetings, Capron, intending to demonstrate what a mess the agencies were making, presented Sorensen with a list of 150 separate programs for fighting poverty and got the reaction he was hoping for: Sorensen firmly told him to come back with something better.

Heller and Capron were badly in need of the public-policy equivalent of the cavalry riding to their rescue. Sure enough, one day that fall, they met David Hackett and Richard Boone and heard about the idea they had been developing at the President's Committee on Juvenile Delinquency, to which by now they had given the name "community action." There were three key elements to community action at that point: It would operate at the ground level; community action agencies would be located in poor neighborhoods, not downtown office buildings. It would coordinate a wide variety of social services in a single location, so that poor people wouldn't have to spend half their lives shuttling between the welfare office and the public housing office and the job placement office. Finally, it would plan its activities based on what the poor people actually wanted from government, rather than what bureaucrats in Washington thought they needed.

"Community action appealed to me immediately," Heller remembered. "The *moment* I heard about it, it became part of my thinking." Capron brought Paul Ylvisaker and Mitchell Sviridoff down to Washington to meet with Kermit Gordon, director of the Bureau of the Budget, and Ylvisaker's eloquently low-key sales pitch instantly made Gordon into another convert to community action. Finally the antipoverty idea had come into focus.

Community action had the excitement of a new idea; it seemed fresh and vigorous, and lent a groundbreaking spirit to the creaking antipoverty effort. Bureaucratically, it provided a wonderful rationale for doing what Heller and Capron wanted to do anyway, bypass the old-line departments and start an adventurous new government agency. Having originated in the financially constrained venues of a minor committee and a foundation, it was cheaper than the big Cabinet departments' ideas. It also struck the deep-seated chord of dissatisfaction with the New Deal approach to government that was floating around in the Kennedy administration. As Capron says now, a little ruefully, "I was an arrogant smart-assed economist, disdainful of the bureaucracy."

Heller was used to the idea of local governments' being the fount of public-sector innovation, because that was the tradition he had grown up with in Wisconsin. After World War II, he had worked for a time in Germany with E. F. Schumacher, later the author of *Small Is Beautiful*, and had become convinced of the merits of decentralizing power. During 1963, Heller had begun to develop a friendship with Robert Kennedy, whose connection to community action gave it the best possible patron that a new initiative could have in the Kennedy administration. One evening at a gathering at Arthur Schlesinger, Jr.'s house in Washington, George Kennan, the magisterially gloomy diplomat, said to Heller, "I hear you're working on the problem of the poor. The poor are always with you. If you lift up the poor, you'll just create more poor." Robert Kennedy, who was also there, immediately leaped to Heller's defense.

On October 21, 1963, Heller had an encouraging meeting with President Kennedy. According to Heller's notes, Kennedy said that an article on a poor white area of Kentucky by Homer Bigart in the previous day's *New York Times* had convinced him that "there was a tremendous problem to be met." The notes continue: "It's perfectly clear that he is aroused about this and if we could really produce a program to fit the bill, he would be inclined to run with it."

On November 20, Heller and six members of the Cabinet were going to leave Washington to attend a meeting in Japan. Heller decided he'd better check in with Kennedy about the poverty program before he left, so on November 19 he asked Kennedy's secretary, Evelyn Lincoln, for some time with the president. She told him she would squeeze him in at seven in the evening. When Heller arrived, he found John Kennedy, Jr., waiting for his father outside the Oval Office. The president told his son he'd be out in a minute and ushered Heller in. "We had ten minutes and covered enough things that it took me half an hour to write a memo to the staff on what he'd said," Heller remembered. "I popped the question: 'Mr. President, I have Bill Capron working on poverty, but I'm not sure after talking to Sorensen that you're willing to commit.'" Heller's notes record a response notably more lukewarm than Kennedy had given him a month earlier: "His attitude was, 'No, I'm still very much in favor of doing something on the poverty theme if we can get a good program, but I also think it's important to make clear that we're doing something for the middle-income man in the suburbs, etc. But the two are not at all inconsistent with one another. So go right ahead with your work on it.'"

Evidently political considerations had caused Kennedy's enthusiasm for the poverty program to cool. Sorensen later remembered, "He was a little shaken ... by a political strategy meeting we held on the 1964 campaign shortly before he died in which, during a discussion of issues, census director [Richard] Scammon talked about the number of people who did not feel they could identify with federal programs, and the President mentioned a poverty proposal. Scammon pointed out that most people did not consider themselves impoverished, and those were not the people we were trying to reach, and so on. But in a subsequent conversation the President told Walter Heller that while he would include other programs in his 1964 message, he still recognized the importance of going ahead on poverty." Capron describes the final signal from Kennedy as "an amber light tinted green." Everyone close to Kennedy agrees that he certainly did not have any kind of major effort in mind.

Heller was on the way back from Japan in a military plane, preparing to take a swim during a refueling stop at Wake Island, when the news came that President Kennedy had been killed. The plane stopped instead in Hawaii, so that the Cabinet members could receive a military briefing on the situation in Dallas, and then flew on to Washington. During that long trip, Heller remembered, "all we talked about was, what kind of man is Lyndon Johnson?" On the day Heller got home, Saturday, November 23, he got a chance to find out: he was called in to brief the new president.

LYNDON JOHNSON came to the presidency possessing intense feelings about liberals, especially liberal intellectuals. He considered himself a liberal, essentially — a practical liberal from a conservative state, not a dreamer or an idealist. His political roots were in the New Deal. He was uncomfortably aware, though, that liberals disliked and mistrusted him. One reason for this, Johnson felt, was that the leading liberals didn't understand the complexities of his own position or the nature of the real world of politics, in which nothing ever got done without compromises being made. As long ago as the 1930s, when Johnson was a loyal follower of Franklin Roosevelt, he fell out with his liberal friends when he refused to join in a fight against the poll tax. Johnson was planning his unsuccessful 1941 campaign for the Senate at the time, and all through the years when he knew that establishing a statewide constituency in Texas was a prerequisite to his realizing his ambitions, he kept his liberalism well hidden. In his 1948 Senate campaign, he supported the antilabor Taft-Hartley Act, and opposed Harry Truman's civil rights bill (which he called "an effort to set up a police state in the guise of liberty") and the establishment of the Fair Employment Practices Commission.

Johnson was a man with enormous insecurity and capacity for self-pity, and for years he told friends that no matter what he did, Eastern liberals wouldn't like him simply because he was a not-very-well-educated Southerner. "He used to tell me that even back in the 1930s, when he was meeting people from the East, he loved to be in their company, but they'd taunt him," says Johnson's longtime aide Horace Busby. "He said they said, 'What's a hick like you know about this stuff?' I don't know if they really did, but he said they did. He said his comeback to them was, 'If you're so close to Roosevelt, how come you can't get things done?' But I think he was inventing some of this."

The sense of being excluded from a charmed circle was painful enough on its own, but also, Johnson felt, the liberal wing of the Democratic Party could effectively block him from becoming president. Liberals' suspicions about Southerners were centered around the race issue, and Johnson knew well from personal experience how careful a Southern politician with national ambitions had to be about race. He had always considered himself to be a friend of civil rights at heart. As Texas state director of the National Youth Administration in the 1930s, he had befriended Mary McLeod Bethune, the great black educator, and funneled money to black colleges over the objections of the governor of Texas.

The very day that Horace Busby went to work for Johnson, in the late 1940s, Johnson out of the blue gave him a peroration about race relations, saying, as Busby remembers it, "The Negro fought in the war, and now that he's back here with his family he's not gonna keep taking the shit we're dishing out. We're in a race with time. If we don't act, we're gonna have blood in the streets." Johnson made the same speech to David Ginsburg, one of his New Deal friends in Washington. "I remember him always making the point over and over of the need to avert a crisis," Ginsburg says. "The issue had to be obliterated from our society. Blacks had fought in the war. They'd manned the factories. You couldn't treat them as second-class citizens." Johnson was never one for quixotic stands on issues, but even during his publicly segregationist days he would sometimes let nobler feelings about race show if he was sure the cost wouldn't be high. In 1948, at a campaign stop in the out-of-the-way town of Cleveland, Texas, which his opponent was sure to carry, he announced that he wouldn't start talking until the blacks in the audience crossed over and stood on the same side of the railroad tracks as the whites. Afterward in his hotel room, Busby says, "He called me in: 'Buzz, Buzz.' Beaming. He said, 'How many votes you think I'll get here?' I held up both hands: ten votes. He said, 'Oh, no,' and held up two fingers."

In the late 1950s, as Johnson began to think in terms of making himself attractive to a national constituency, his public position on civil rights began to change. His great triumph as Senate majority leader was pushing through the Civil Rights Act of 1957. Because he had accepted the jury-trial amendment, though, the liberals still mistrusted him, which wounded him. Why were the Galbraiths and Schlesingers willing to sign on with John Kennedy, who had agreed to the same amendment but done nothing to help the bill pass? Why did they love Senator J. William Fulbright of Arkansas, who had signed the Southern Manifesto, the congressional resolution condemning the Supreme Court decision in 1954 that struck down segregation in local public schools — as Johnson hadn't?

Still, he stayed interested in civil rights, out of some combination of sincere belief, a desire to redeem himself for his long silence on the subject, and ambition for the presidency. He would occasionally lecture his aides on the subject of great Southern politicians who had thrown away their chance to be national figures because of segregation. Once Johnson told Bill Moyers, his closest aide in the early 1960s, that the one senator from history he'd like to meet was Pitchfork Ben Tillman of South Carolina, because, as Moyers recalled the conversation, "He might have been president. I'd like to sit down with him and ask how it was to throw it away for the sake of hating." Another time, after Johnson as president had finished a meeting with his old friend Richard Russell, the senator from Georgia, he told Moyers, "God damn it. Jim Crow put a collar on more smart men as sure as if they were sentenced to a chain gang in Georgia. If Dick Russell hadn't had to wear Jim Crow's collar, Dick Russell would be sitting here now instead of me." The idea that his renunciation of segregation had enabled him to break the barrier keeping Southerners from the presidency was so important to Johnson that he once asked Moyers to commission a study from the Library of Congress proving that Woodrow Wilson wasn't really from the South.

When Johnson was vice president, there was a certain amount of ill will between him and the Kennedy brothers on civil rights issues. It wasn't something that attracted any public notice, but it was there. The

Kennedys, especially Robert Kennedy, thought that Johnson wanted to apply the brakes where civil rights were involved; Johnson thought the Kennedys were developing the habit for which he held liberals in contempt—choosing to take the position that would make them look good rather than doing what was necessary to achieve something substantive. President Kennedy made Johnson chairman of the President's Committee on Equal Employment Opportunity, which was supposed to promote the hiring of blacks as federal employees and contractors. Robert Kennedy also served on the committee, and several times during its meetings he and Johnson quarreled in a way that went far beyond the bounds of usual behavior in government. "I saw Bobby Kennedy treat Johnson in a most vicious manner. He'd ridicule him, imply he was insincere," says Robert Weaver; "I'd shudder at the way those two men would cut each other up in meetings," says Willard Wirtz.

Johnson removed the original executive director of the committee, a Kennedy appointee, and set up a program called Plans for Progress, which tried to get government contractors to hire more blacks voluntarily, nudged along by Johnson-style persuasion. Kennedy, who was worried about how the administration's hiring record would look in the 1964 campaign, favored a tougher (but in Johnson's view, less effective) approach, and considered Johnson's vice chairman, a black man, to be an Uncle Tom. At one meeting, Kennedy walked in late, sat down, and immediately began attacking Plans for Progress. He tore into James Webb, the director of the National Aeronautics and Space Administration (a favorite agency of Johnson's), for not doing enough, then got up and left. As one man who was at the meeting remembered it, "It was a pretty brutal business, very sharp. It brought tensions between Johnson and Kennedy right out on the table and very hard. Everyone was sweating under the armpits and so on."

The enmity was visible outside the confines of the equal opportunity committee, too. Once President Kennedy was called away from a White House meeting with civil rights leaders, and asked Johnson to carry on as chairman. Louis Martin, who had stayed on in Washington after the 1960 election as an official of the Democratic National Committee and was close to both Johnson and Robert Kennedy, was at the meeting. He remembered: "At one point Bobby looked up at me and motioned me to come over. . . . So I went over, and he whispered in my ear, he said, 'I've got a date, and I've got to get on this boat in a few minutes. Can you tell the vice president to cut it short?' So knowing something of the relationship of Bobby and the vice president at the time, I was absolutely thunderstruck. So I went back to my former position and did nothing. Then he motioned again. I went back over there and he said, 'Didn't I tell you to tell the vice president to shut up?' And Bobby was—I can't explain and describe adequately how he could talk to you. But anyway I was in such a dilemma I had to do something. The vice president was going full steam. I went around the table and got close to him, and he saw me. I whispered in his ear, 'Bobby has got to go, and he wants to close it up.' He glared at me, and didn't stop for a moment. He just kept going. I thought surely this was the faux pas of the year, as far as I was concerned, but I didn't really know what to do. I knew that the vice president, once he was aroused, was a pretty tough gentleman, and I was really sick. Fortunately, the meeting lasted only another ten or fifteen minutes."

When President Kennedy was formulating the civil rights bill, in the spring of 1963, Johnson was full of doubts. A tape recording was made of a remarkable long telephone call between Johnson, in his office at the Capitol, and Theodore Sorensen, at the White House, in which Johnson, one of the great monopolists of conversations, expresses his worries about the bill at great length without any response from Sorensen beyond the occasional terse, perfunctory, and somewhat patronizing expression of sympathy and agreement. Johnson's position was that before proposing the bill (which Kennedy did a week after the conversation occurred), Kennedy should soften up the Congress, and also stake some of his presidential prestige by giving speeches on its behalf in the South. It's obvious that Johnson had some grasp of the function the civil rights bill would serve in black America—it would be an important signal and a symbolic victory, but it would hardly solve the problem of the exclusion of most blacks from the mainstream of American society. He wanted Kennedy to propose education programs and to create government jobs for blacks along with the civil rights bill. One typical exchange will convey the flavor of the conversation:

> JOHNSON: I know these risks are great and it might cost us the South, but those sorts of states may be lost anyway. The difference is if your President just enforces court decrees the South will feel it's yielded to force. But if he goes down there and looks them in the eye and states the moral issue and the Christian issue, and he does it face to face, these Southerners at least respect his courage.

They feel that they're on the losing side of an issue of conscience. Now, I think the Southern whites and the Negroes share one point of view that's identical. They're not certain that the government is on the side of the Negroes. The whites think we're just playing politics to carry New York. The Negroes feel . . . that we're just doing what we got to do. Until that's laid to rest I don't think you're going to have much of a solution. I don't think the Negroes' goals are going to be achieved through legislation. . . . I think the Negro leaders are aware of that. What Negroes are really seeking is moral force and be sure that we're on their side and make them all act like Americans, and until they receive that assurance, unless it's stated dramatically and convincingly, they're not going to pay much attention to executive orders and legislative recommendations. They're going to approach them with skepticism. So . . .

SORENSEN: I agree with that and I think that's very sound.

Robert Kennedy saw Johnson as simply vacillating and unhelpful, possibly even lacking in guts, about the civil rights bill. He said later, describing his brother's attitude but plainly speaking for himself as well, "The President was rather irritated with him at the time because he was opposed to these things—this and a good number of other measures—but did not come up with alternative suggestions." By the time of the assassination the civil rights bill had gotten nowhere in Congress, so both Johnson and Robert Kennedy would have had no cause to revise their opinions about each other's shortcomings as champions of civil rights.

WALTER HELLER'S meeting with Johnson on the day after the assassination was mostly devoted to a review of the broad range of economic policy-making, but Heller did make sure to bring up the subject of his antipoverty program, perhaps exaggerating somewhat the extent of its progress so far. In his notes, made just after the meeting and marked HIGHLY CONFIDENTIAL, Heller wrote:

Then I went over with him the *attack on poverty* work. I indicated that this was an important theme for the 1964 program that we were working on with the hope (a) that we could develop a good basic concept for it and (b) that we could develop a good program content, mindful of the budget constraints in the first year. I noted that the Departments were quite stirred up about it, that there was a good deal of enthusiasm for it, though we did not yet know whether we had the final answer to an attractive program. I told him about my last talk with President Kennedy, about the fact that while he was interested in doing something for the middle income groups and suburbanites — or at least pointing out what we had done — he had also strongly urged me to move ahead on the poverty theme in the hope that we can make it an important part of the 1964 program. The new President expressed his interest in it, his sympathy for it, and in answer to a point-blank question, said we should push ahead full-tilt on this project.

Years later, Heller remembered Johnson also saying, "That's my kind of program."

The meeting took place late in the day, after seven o'clock in the evening. Johnson and Heller were both overwhelmed and exhausted, and when he had finished with his business Heller made ready to leave Johnson alone. According to his notes,

Just as I was about to go out of his office and had opened the door, the President gently pushed it shut and drew me back in and said, "Now, I want to say something about all this talk that I'm a conservative who is likely to go back to the Eisenhower ways or give in to the economy bloc in Congress. It's not so, and I want you to tell your friends — Arthur Schlesinger, Galbraith and other liberals — that it is not so. I'm no budget slasher. I understand the expenditures have to keep rising to keep pace with the population and help the economy. If you looked at my record, you would know that I am a Roosevelt New Dealer. As a matter of fact, to tell the truth, John F. Kennedy was a little too conservative to suit my taste."

In the weeks following the assassination, however, John F. Kennedy, as his associates went to work burnishing his reputation, began to become more liberal — in particular, more liberal than Lyndon Johnson. Caution and pragmatism do not make an easy foundation on which to build an argument for historical greatness, and they were not stressed in the memorialization of Kennedy. In early December 1963, in a eulogy that appeared in *The Saturday Evening Post*, Arthur Schlesinger, Jr., wrote, "In one of the last talks I had with him, he was musing about the legislative program for next January, and said, 'The time has come to organize a national assault on the causes of poverty, a comprehensive program, across the board.'" The severely grieving Robert Kennedy found a piece of note paper on which his brother, during the last Cabinet meeting he had conducted, had scribbled the word "poverty" several times and circled it; he framed it and kept it on display in his office at the Justice Department. Theodore Sorensen, who had been so skeptical about the antipoverty program before the assassination, now became an enthusiastic champion of it. Walter Heller was not averse to letting it be known that fighting poverty had been President Kennedy's last wish.

Johnson was certain that he could accomplish much more as President than Kennedy had, and he saw the poverty program as the most immediately available way to prove it. A week after the assassination, he invited two old liberal-bureaucrat friends from the New Deal days, Arthur Goldschmidt and his wife Elizabeth Wickenden, to Sunday dinner at his house in Washington, where he and his family were still living while Jacqueline Kennedy prepared to leave the White House. "Johnson talked very freely at that Sunday dinner," Wickenden says. "He said, 'I have a very difficult problem. I feel a moral obligation to finish the things that JFK proposed. But I also have to find issues I can take on as my own.' So he came to this poverty program — making it nationwide. He didn't go into what it would do specifically. He said, 'I have to get reelected in a year and a half, so I have to have something of my own.'" Very quickly, however, Johnson realized that the Kennedy people had succeeded in changing the stakes of the poverty program: the question, instead of being whether Johnson could take over what had been a small, stagnating Kennedy idea and make it his first major initiative without appearing to be one-upping the dead President, became whether Johnson could possibly be as fully committed to fighting poverty as Kennedy had been. He was suddenly at risk of bringing another hail of sophisticated liberal contempt down on his head if he made a misstep.

Before he had been President two weeks, Johnson wrote (and made public) a letter to the American Public Welfare Association promising, in words identical to those Schlesinger had ascribed to Kennedy, "a national assault on the causes of poverty." At that point Johnson had no idea what the assault would consist of. What few signals he had given to Heller indicated that he envisioned something along the lines of the National Youth Administration, in which young people would be taken out into the clean air and put to work creating visible accomplishments. Heller remembered, "He had this sort of *concrete* idea. Bulldozers. Tractors. People operating heavy machinery." Meanwhile, Heller's staff was moving full steam ahead on community action, which, since it had originated in the Justice Department, had begun to look like the one way of fighting poverty that was most faithful to the Kennedy legacy.

The idea of community action was still so new that it was completely unclear whether it did in fact work as a way of reducing poverty. Most of the projects being funded by the President's Committee on Juvenile Delinquency were barely more than a year old. David Hackett believed that the new antipoverty program should be tiny and hesitant, in recognition of how little the people running the government knew about community action: he suggested that it be funded at the level of $1 million a year, with the money going to small, closely watched experimental projects in just six cities. Walter Heller wasn't going to have any of that: he knew that he had the first chance in the generation since the sputtering out of the New Deal to get a big new federal social welfare program enacted, and he didn't intend to let it slip past him; anyway, Heller knew that Johnson wanted something big. On December 20, 1963, Heller sent a memo to Sorensen, who was still running the White House staff, laying out his idea for the poverty program. It would have community action as its centerpiece, and, true to the Hackett spirit, it would concentrate on "a *limited* number of demonstration areas—our current thinking is a total of about 10. . . ." But the budget would be nearly half a billion dollars a year, and in addition to community action, Wilbur Cohen of HEW (who was an old friend of Johnson's) would be given more than a dozen small new programs to run himself.

Heller's next task was to sell Johnson on community action. Over the Christmas holidays, he and Kermit Gordon of the Budget Bureau flew down to Johnson's ranch in Texas, where they laid out the idea. Apparently Johnson didn't like it. William Cannon, who was the member of Gordon's staff assigned to the poverty program, says, "Kermit told me he and Heller presented it to Johnson, but he was scared. He killed the community action part of it. But the next day they persuaded him, so they came back to Washington with it in." It isn't difficult to see what Johnson's reservations about community action would have been. It had a vague, tentative quality that was exactly what he didn't like in a government program; there was no guarantee that it would do the things Johnson instinctively believed in, teach children and put adults to work.

As a limited demonstration program, it would seem unimportant, and it would be difficult to pass because it didn't funnel money into many congressional districts. To the extent that it set up local agencies that were independent of mayors, governors, and members of Congress, it would attract political opposition. On the other hand, community action had already become a cause for the Kennedy people, so that if Johnson rejected it, he might be portrayed as having betrayed the legacy. "The idea didn't come from him. But these things get momentum," says Busby, who was the lone dissenter in the staff discussions of community action at the ranch that Christmas. "The forces of learning and light said it's the way to go. If he'd said no to it, people would've said, 'Oh, he's not really sincere, he's just a Southern racist.'"

On December 30, 1963, Busby stayed up late in Johnson's office at the ranch, writing Johnson a memo that urged him to watch out for the poverty program. "There is no workable program yet conceived," Busby wrote; he suggested (as Richard Scammon had suggested to Kennedy a few weeks earlier) that Johnson take care to show that he was paying attention to "the American in the middle." The memo went on: "People know instinctively these are your kind of folks—not the extremes. The politics of the extremes is what the typical American expects you to break away from. If you can do so, you can broaden the Democratic Party base as it has not been broadened in two decades."

Another doubter was Elizabeth Wickenden. On January 4, 1964, she wrote to Sorensen's deputy, Myer Feldman, objecting to community action on the grounds that it was too narrow in its focus and too politically perilous: "The problems of poverty are only in limited instances localized in character. They are for the most part widely distributed, related to economic and social factors that operate nationwide, and would require more than local action for solution." Also, community action could "be subject to severe political attack" because "a federal agency would be short-circuiting the normal channels of relationship to states and localities in their own areas of responsibility." In response, Wickenden received a brief, patronizing note from Sorensen's deputy's deputy. "Obviously, you have given careful consideration to the points you have raised and they are set forth in a concise and orderly fashion," it said. The die was cast; as Busby says, "If *they* thought it up, that was it."

On January 8, 1964, in his first State of the Union address, President Johnson said, "This Administration today, here and now, declares unconditional war on poverty in America." Sorensen was the primary author of the address; "war on poverty" was a phrase first used by John Kennedy in a speech delivered in 1960 on the occasion of the twenty-fifth anniversary of the Social Security Act. A research study Johnson ordered up after the State of the Union showed that it had been interrupted by applause more times than any other State of the Union address since 1933. He was a liberal hero at last.

IMMEDIATELY after Johnson declared war on poverty, Walter Heller issued the annual Economic Report of the President in Johnson's name, and in it promised that the war on poverty would spend "over $1 billion of new funds in the first year." Having secured Johnson's support of a new poverty program based on community action, at a far greater level of spending and of rhetorical commitment than he ever could have extracted from President Kennedy, Heller left center stage. Now it was up to Johnson to get the program up and running.

On February 1, Johnson announced the appointment of Sargent Shriver as head of the war on poverty. Johnson always devoted a great deal of care and cleverness to appointments, even when the most minor jobs were involved; in this case the stakes were especially high, and his choice was especially shrewd.

To all outward appearances, Johnson was putting a Kennedy family member in charge of the war on poverty and thus demonstrating that the program would be conducted in a manner faithful to the martyred president's conception of it. One of the reigning ideas in Washington was that the Kennedys were all eternally bonded to one another. The family itself had so much invested in its image of magical clannishness that by appointing Shriver, Johnson neatly headed off the possibility of Robert Kennedy's publicly criticizing the poverty program.

In truth, though, there was a palpable distance between Shriver and Robert Kennedy, and Johnson knew it. The Kennedys had made Shriver feel that he would be forever limited to supporting roles in the family drama, partly because he was only a brother-in-law and partly because they found him lacking in the essential quality of toughness. Shriver was noticeably rankled by the way he was treated. Through Eunice, he had been concerned with the issue of juvenile delinquency long before Robert Kennedy had been. In 1960 he had seen Robert Kennedy consistently try to cut back on the campaign's commitment to civil rights. The Kennedys were supposed to be aristocratic, handsome, and heroic, but Shriver was more aristocratic (coming from an old Maryland family), more hand-some (conventionally, anyway, with his barrel chest and resolute chin and jaw), and more heroic (he had a distinguished though unpublicized war record, having served four years in the Navy in the South Pacific). He was also more seriously Catholic and, unlike the Kennedys, had much deeper roots in the socially concerned branch of the church, having been a member of the Society of St. Vincent de Paul at a time when Robert Kennedy's Catholic heroes were Pope Pius XII, Cardinal Spellman, and Joseph McCarthy. In the Kennedy administration Shriver had been put in charge of a small, somewhat bleeding-heart program, the Peace Corps, and had turned it into the most successful new agency in Washington.

Shriver had signaled Johnson that he wasn't so blindly loyal to Robert Kennedy that he couldn't devote himself fully to serving the new presi-dent. A few days after the assassination, Horace Busby came upon John-son in the Oval Office studying a note-card headed "What Bobby Thinks," which contained a list of Robert Kennedy's complaints about Johnson's conduct since the death of his brother. Johnson had kept Jac-queline Kennedy waiting on the ground for two and a half hours inside Air Force One in Dallas so that he could be sworn in as President; he had been too quick to clear President Kennedy's things out of the Oval Office. These were not rational complaints—in fact, it was somewhat embarrassing to Robert Kennedy to have them circulated—but it was useful to Johnson to know about them. Who told you this? Busby asked him. Sargent Shriver, Johnson said.

During the Kennedy administration, Shriver's deputy at the Peace Corps had been Bill Moyers, Johnson's right-hand man. The two men became close friends, which gave Shriver an only slightly indirect line to Johnson; it was Moyers who persuaded Johnson to give Shriver the pov-erty job, hoping to open up the directorship of the Peace Corps for himself. (Instead, Johnson kept Shriver in both jobs simultaneously.) In the weeks before Shriver was appointed, some people in the administra-tion had the impression that Robert Kennedy wanted to be asked to run the war on poverty himself, so by accepting the job Shriver was muscling his brother-in-law aside. Also, Bobby Kennedy was known to harbor the ambition of being Johnson's running mate in the 1964 presidential cam-paign—and Shriver had the same ambition, which was another violation of the family rule that he should never compete directly with a Kennedy. In appointing Shriver, Johnson was doing something he knew would annoy Kennedy, and for him that was always an attractive proposition.

Shriver had other qualities that Johnson liked. He was hardworking and buoyant, and he shared Johnson's taste for the unembarrassedly grandiose approach to government. Shriver loved the application of the war metaphor to poverty—the idea of himself as the general in charge of managing, if not an actual military operation, at least something that belonged on the honor roll of large successful American efforts. "I said, 'Where's poverty? Where's the enemy?' " he remembers. He used to tell one of his department chiefs to think of himself as running the Chevrolet division of General Motors. When he was being briefed on what would become the Foster Grandparents program, a small part of the war on poverty, Shriver broke in impatiently, "It's not big enough! Not big enough!" He was a salesman, not an administrator; he naturally thought in terms of what would play well in Congress and in the press, and he liked to operate by charging ahead. Once during a weekend at the Kennedy compound in Hyannis Port, Shriver was playing in the customary afternoon touch football game. His side was losing, and one by one the relatives who were his teammates began to drift away and trudge back to the house. Shriver stayed on the field; in a tone of wounded pride, he said to one of his aides who was also playing, "See? The Kennedys know when to quit."

Johnson announced Shriver's appointment on a Saturday. It was characteristic of Shriver that by Sunday he was already hard at work. In his office at the Peace Corps, he convened a meeting of the people who had already been working on the poverty program, along with a couple of his own assistants. Johnson had told Shriver only vaguely that, as Shriver remembers it, "the White House has a plan and I'll have it sent over"; now Shriver heard about community action for the first time, and discovered that the people from the Council of Economic Advisers and the Budget Bureau expected him to build the whole poverty program around it. As Johnson had been at the ranch, he was immediately wary. During a break in the meeting, Shriver found himself alone in the men's room with Adam Yarmolinsky, whom he had in mind as his deputy in the war on poverty. Yarmolinsky was a small, tightly wound man who wore tiny bow ties and a bristling crew cut and, as an assistant to Robert McNamara at the Pentagon, had gotten a reputation as one of the most brilliant of all the brilliant young men in the Kennedy administration—someone who worked ceaselessly and got things done. Shriver said to Yarmolinsky, "It'll never fly."

ONE SIMILARITY between Shriver and Robert Kennedy was that they both loved to surround themselves with a group of scintillating people and debate the great problems of the world. In Chicago in the 1950s the Shrivers' living room had been the scene of frequent gatherings of politicians, artists, writers, and Catholic intellectuals; out of this kind of relentless, energetic cross-fertilization of the talented, a higher understanding was supposed to emerge. Harris Wofford met Shriver for the first time when he gave a speech in Chicago about his work on the civil rights commission and Shriver, who knew from Wofford's introduction that he had spent time in India, rose from the audience and asked how Gandhi's methods could be used to solve the racial difficulties of the Chicago school system.

The planning sessions for the war on poverty quickly turned into a typical Shriver seminar, a loose group of ebullient characters from inside and outside government. Frank Mankiewicz, a Peace Corps official in Latin America who happened to be in town, was brought into the meetings by Shriver; he mentioned the work of Michael Harrington, and Shriver immediately said, "Who's that? Get him in." The freewheeling nature of the proceedings served to obscure how much was at stake: this was, as it turned out, the one chance that the American government would have to create a paradigm by which the federal government made an intensive effort to deal with the difficulties of the black ghettos. As Daniel Patrick Moynihan, another participant, later put it, "a *big* bet was being made."

It is easy to see how unclear this must have been at the time. The country was finally beginning to seem reliably liberal in its political mood for the first time since the Depression, and it looked like this liberal heyday would be better than the last one. In 1964, the economy was prosperous — eternally so, it seemed, because of the success of Walter Heller's Keynesian techniques — and the house of liberalism was in much better order than it had been in the 1930s because there weren't any destructive internal battles with communists this time around. Surely whatever Shriver's group came up with would be merely an opening salvo; Johnson would be president until 1972, so there would be many years in which to fine-tune and expand the program. The idea that the federal government might have trouble solving a large problem was completely foreign to Shriver and his associates, whose formative experiences were watching Roosevelt defeat the Depression and then the Nazis. Because all the key participants in the meetings were white and from the North, they didn't have that ingrained awareness of the tragic potential of the national enterprise that virtually all African-Americans, and many white Southerners, possessed; to them, America almost by definition couldn't fail at anything. "For the proponents of social legislation, this was our Camelot," Adam Yarmolinsky says.

One person who wasn't at Shriver's meetings was Robert Kennedy, though he did let it be known that he was a strong supporter of community action. "We went to see him early on," Mankiewicz says. "Sarge and I, maybe Harrington, Moynihan, Dave Hackett, and Dick Boone. He looked awful. He just sort of sat there. He was still in shock. He asked if what we were doing was what President Kennedy had in mind, and Hackett and Boone assured him it was. He said, 'Fine.'" On the staff of the President's Committee on Juvenile Delinquency, there was a sense of reservation about the Shriver operation, a feeling that community action was going to be ruined by being made too big too fast. Hackett went to some of Shriver's meetings, but he didn't say much, and his disapproval was obvious. Lloyd Ohlin had his doubts. The one exception to the rule was Boone, who perceived that the war on poverty was his big chance: "You had to be pragmatic — where was the power, and what could be done with it?" Ohlin says. "Boone told me, 'Look, let's take advantage of the opportunity we've got now. Let's get the money out there.' It was a *war*. The notion of moving slowly was simply not appealing." When Paul Ylvisaker was summoned to Washington and asked to draw up a budget for community action, he came up with a grand total of $30 million; he was told to add another zero.

Of all the people at Shriver's meetings, Boone was the one whose ideas about the war on poverty departed most sharply from the liberal orthodoxy of the time, because he had in mind the politicization of the poor — not in the Bill Dawson join-the-machine sense, but with the goal of their becoming an opposing force to the establishment. There were several different strains in liberal thought about poverty in the early 1960s, but that wasn't one of them.

Most economists, and economics-oriented liberals, believed that the real cure for poverty was income redistribution, but that was not an option for the war on poverty, because Lyndon Johnson was unalterably opposed to it. "You tell Shriver, no doles," he told Moyers; on Johnson's instructions, Lester Thurow, then a junior member of the staff of the

Council of Economic Advisers, was given the task of going through the Economic Report of the President removing anything that could be construed as a reference to putting cash in the hands of poor people. There had to be *programs* to end poverty.

The need for programs meshed nicely with the reigning belief of liberal sociologists, anthropologists, and social welfare experts about poverty among the able-bodied, which was that it was caused by a "culture of poverty." The concept of "culture" as a shaper of behavior was invented by early-twentieth-century anthropologists with the intention that it would refute the idea that people who did not live in bourgeois societies were innately inferior in some way. In *The Affluent Society*, Galbraith divided poverty into two categories, "case," which was "related to some characteristic of the individuals so afflicted," and "insular," which "manifests itself as an 'island' of poverty." Insular poverty was cultural in nature, the product of group folkways rather than individual failures; in the early 1960s, the term "poverty pockets" entered the language as a mutation of Galbraith's notion. The term "culture of poverty" had been invented in 1959 by a popular anthropologist named Oscar Lewis, who described it as "a way of life which is passed down from generation to generation" and produces people who "are not psychologically geared to take full advantage of changing conditions or increased opportunities which may occur in their lifetime."

The culture of poverty was an attractive notion for liberals because the obvious cure for it was for the government to act as an agent of acculturation. If poor people did not train their children well for school, the government could train them; if poor people did not eat properly, the government could give them nutritious food; if they did not have good work habits, the government could teach that, too. The urban ghettos were a perfect place to try all this, because black sharecroppers who had migrated to the cities seemed to fit Lewis's paradigm perfectly; as he wrote, "The most likely candidates for the culture of poverty are the people who come from the lower strata of a rapidly changing society and are already partially alienated from it. Thus landless rural workers who migrate to the cities can be expected to develop a culture of poverty. . . ." Much of the promising work then going on in black ghettos, such as the Gray Areas Project in New Haven, appeared to be precisely aimed at breaking the culture of poverty through the use of special programs.

Oscar Lewis, a man who liked to move in nonacademic circles, turned up at Shriver's planning meetings. Michael Harrington, who was probably America's most famous socialist, was then an avid purveyor of the culture of poverty idea and had used the phrase "culture of poverty" repeatedly in *The Other America*. Shriver immediately became engaged in converting the concept into politically salable slogans for the war on poverty, such as "a hand up, not a handout." Almost all the programs that Shriver's group was considering fit under the rubric of acculturating poor people into the folkways of the middle class. Community action could be thought of that way. Head Start, the preschool program that has been the war on poverty's most enduring success, would prepare poor children for school better than they'd be prepared at home. Legal Services would help naive poor people master the art of not being constantly gouged. The Job Corps, Shriver's favorite antipoverty program, would do for teenagers what Head Start did for toddlers, get them ready for a successful entry into the job market by taking them out of their poverty pockets and putting them in healthy rural camps for a period of intensive job-skills training.

Dick Boone's conception of the way to end poverty was substantially different: people were poor because they lacked political power, and the way for them to escape poverty was to get political power—through the war on poverty, for example. The best instrument at hand for achieving this goal was the community action program, and the best way to ensure that community action would be a means of empowerment for the poor was to guarantee poor people "maximum feasible participation" in the local community action agencies.

Boone prided himself on being a master operator in the respectable not-for-profit sector, a mole of sorts. He describes his technique as "persistence and infiltration." At Shriver's meetings, he was playing a very tricky game. His hole card was his link to Robert Kennedy, through the juvenile delinquency committee, so he had to conceal the juvenile delinquency crowd's skepticism about the war on poverty and present himself as the attorney general's man on Shriver's team. At the same time, he took pains not to make his own view of community action crystal clear to his overwhelmingly acculturation-oriented colleagues. As one participant remembered it, "Dick Boone was careful not to raise with Shriver issues in which he felt that he would get the wrong answer from Shriver."

This wasn't so difficult as it might sound. Community action could be made to sound like an updated, streamlined version of what settlement houses did, with the cumbersome, overlapping federal bureaucracies neatly sliced away; indeed, when Ylvisaker or Sviridoff (who was also at Shriver's meetings) described it, it did sound that way. Boone's disdain for social workers played well, too, with his vigorous male audience. The term "ladies bountiful" began to be bandied about as the derisive name for a type who would have no place in the war on poverty. Frank Mankiewicz was an enthusiastic proponent of community action because it reminded him of a community-organizing effort the Peace Corps had launched in Latin America (not entirely successfully, the Peace Corps' own internal evaluation department thought). Boone liked to present himself as a protégé of Saul Alinsky — Alinsky's portrait hung on his office wall — and he could point to The Woodlawn Organization in Chicago as a success that the war on poverty could copy.

The practical selling point of maximum feasible participation was that it would be useful in the South, as a way of circumventing segregationist politicians' attempts to set up all-white poverty programs. Most of the people at Shriver's meetings had no inkling that it might be unpopular with politicians in the North. Shriver himself, during his Chicago days, had become close to Mayor Daley, and wouldn't have dreamed of doing anything to offend him. No one could ever be quite certain exactly what Boone had in mind, anyway. That was part of his technique; as Capron puts it, "People wondered — is Boone crazy?"

Boone didn't know exactly how maximum feasible participation would work when it was put into practice, and the uncertainty was part of the appeal. He liked to think of himself as a light-spirited, adventurous government official — liked, as he puts it, "just shaking things up." The highest accolade he can bestow on something he has done is to say, "That was fun." Pushing maximum feasible participation was fun. It might mean simply soliciting poor people as to their needs. It might be a way of funneling the social service jobs the poverty program would create to poor people instead of civil servants and social workers. It might, in the Chicago reform spirit, be a way of wresting control of a government entity from the machine. It might create some action in local elective politics. As Boone says, "It might lead somewhere, but we didn't know where."

Shriver's initial resistance to community action began to melt away. He had tremendous faith in experts, and nearly all of the experts he had gathered around him believed strongly that community action was the way to go. There was a theory going around that Bobby Kennedy got hold of Shriver early on and prevailed on him to include community action in the war on poverty, but Shriver categorically denies this. To his mind, he had the same instructions from a higher power, President Johnson — "the only thing he gave me was community action," he says. Community action was cheap, relative to every other idea being bandied about. It was the best way to make the war on poverty appear massive on a billion-dollar budget. There were myriad other issues to be resolved quickly. Instead of fighting it, Shriver focused his energies on getting other programs into the war on poverty, and on making community action more politically enticing to the Congress, which he did by departing completely from the concept of it as an experimental demonstration program. Community action went from Hackett's six cities, to Heller's ten, to fifty in Shriver's meetings, to two hundred and fifty in its first year in operation, to a thousand cities by 1967.

Boone's concept of maximum feasible participation sounded like a minor point not worth arguing over at length. On Tuesday, February 4, the third day of the meetings, as Yarmolinsky remembered it, "Dick Boone kept bringing up the idea of maximum feasible participation. Whether he used those words then I don't recall. I said to Dick, 'You've brought that idea up several times,' and he said, 'Yes, I have. How many more times do I have to bring it up before it gets into the program?' And I said, 'Oh, two or three.' He did and it did." Like supply-side economics in the 1980s, maximum feasible participation was a new and untested idea that, because it happened to hit Washington at a propitious moment, overnight became a sweeping national policy.

IT WAS a sign of Boone's cleverness that he was able to push relentlessly for community action without making Shriver and the others feel that they were fighting with him. The great bureaucratic battle of the planning sessions for the war on poverty was with someone else entirely: Willard Wirtz, the secretary of labor. Wirtz rubbed Shriver and his people the wrong way. He was a big, ponderous, humorless man who lacked the informal spirit that pervaded their meetings. He was intensely aware of being the head of the smallest of the Cabinet departments, and saw himself as having to be constantly on guard against humiliating slights. "Wirtz had to be seen to be believed," says Yarmolinsky. "One time he came to a meeting with McNamara at the Pentagon on a Saturday, in his limo. The security guard asked him for identification. Wirtz said, 'I'm the Secretary of Labor!' and got back in his car and drove off. He was that kind of person — terribly insecure. I met with him once, in his paneled office, to discuss some minor bureaucratic struggle. He said, 'I'd never have thought this of you, Adam.' Everything was a moral issue with him." Some years later, when Wirtz's son married a woman who worked in the Budget Bureau, he solemnly told one of the Budget Bureau officials who came through the receiving line that this union meant that the infighting between the Labor Department and the poverty program could now end.

Wirtz overplayed his hand badly by proposing that the war on poverty include a massive jobs program to be operated solely by the Labor Department, with a budget in the $3 billion to $5 billion range — much more than President Johnson was willing to spend on the entire poverty program. Besides the problem of the money, everybody knew that the AFL-CIO, which as the most powerful Democratic interest group was an organization whose support of the war on poverty was essential, disliked government jobs programs, believing that they took work away from union members. There was one jobs program that Shriver was interested in above all other aspects of the poverty program, the Job Corps, but he wanted to run it himself rather than ceding it to Wirtz. Wirtz made the disastrous tactical error of going over Shriver's head to Johnson with a proposal for a new federal tax on cigarettes to finance his jobs program. At a Cabinet meeting on February 18, Wirtz delivered an impassioned pitch for his idea, and Johnson made his unenthusiasm clear by reaching over, picking up the telephone that was always at his side, and, while Wirtz was still talking, placing a few calls.

Since it was beneath Wirtz's dignity to attend Shriver's meetings himself, he sent a representative to look out for his interests: Pat Moynihan, who was his assistant secretary for policy. Moynihan had practically invented the role of the social welfare intellectual in government — his job had no operating responsibilities, so he could devote all his energies to generating new ideas. As a thinker, he was not so much profoundly original as he was nimble. He had extraordinary radar that enabled him to pluck significant bits of information out of government reports or scholarly journals, and an ability to dramatize his findings in a way that would get the attention of high government officials. Like Wirtz, Moynihan was a great believer in government jobs programs, but the Labor Department had a difficult time making the need for them clear, because the unemployment rate was low, and dropping. Much earlier than the rest of federal officialdom, Moynihan realized that unemployment, especially among young men, was a big problem in the black ghettos, and he saw that this might provide the justification Wirtz needed for his jobs programs.

In 1963, Moynihan spotted a tiny item in the *Washington Post* saying that the Selective Service was rejecting half of all potential draftees because they couldn't pass a standardized eighth-grade equivalency test, and that the rejectees were disproportionately black. He talked Wirtz into commissioning a national study of the rejectees, and wrote a report about them, called "One-Third of a Nation" to evoke the memory of Franklin Roosevelt's stirring reference in his second inaugural address to the Americans who were ill-fed, ill-clothed, and ill-housed. The report was published just at the time that Shriver was holding his meetings to plan the war on poverty — in fact, Moynihan missed the press conference at which his findings were announced because he was at Shriver's office. The Pentagon did start a special program for Selective Service rejectees, called Project 100,000, but Moynihan's report did not electrify Shriver's group. It seemed too much an instrument of Wirtz's bureaucratic interests, and FDR was not the war on poverty's patron saint, anyway.

Personally, Moynihan was not nearly so skillful a player of the game as Boone. Shriver's aides thought of him as an impractical intellectual and as a water-carrier for Wirtz; Moynihan was given the job of drafting the presidential message to accompany the war on poverty legislation, and, in the minds of Shriver's people, he bungled it by emphasizing jobs programs to the exclusion of practically everything else. Wirtz, on the other hand, thought Moynihan had been captured by Shriver's crowd. He was furious when he learned that the Labor Department would be in charge of only a small jobs program in the war on poverty, the Neighborhood Youth Corps, and not the Job Corps; he blamed Moynihan for having been insufficiently protective of the Labor Department's interests. The final form the war on poverty took was a clear loss for Labor and a win for community action. Jobs would be created, but they would be jobs in the community action agencies — meaning that they would be social service jobs in the ghettos, locally controlled and subject to whatever political winds buffeted the community action program, rather than muscular, Washington-controlled construction jobs of the Works Progress Administration variety. It was a distinction that would make an enormous difference in the life of black America.

As the war on poverty took shape, Shriver began to focus on passing the law authorizing it, a daunting task at a time when Congress hadn't enacted a major piece of social legislation for a generation. One key point was not to make it look like a program for the black ghettos, although that was what most of its founders thought it really was. By 1964 there was beginning to be talk in Washington about the racial problems that would remain after the long fight against legal segregation in the South was finally won. In 1963, there had been a summer race riot in Rochester, New York, and James Baldwin had published *The Fire Next Time*, an eloquently bitter screed about conditions in the ghettos. Like the staff of the juvenile delinquency committee before them, the poverty warriors thought of themselves as an advance guard worrying about the racial issues that lay over the next hill (whose true dimensions even they severely underestimated), while most of the government was still focused on the Civil Rights Act. Of course all this had to be concealed; Congress was still an institution with a pronounced Southern flavor. As Yarmolinsky says, "We were busy telling people it *wasn't* just racial because we thought it'd be easier to sell that way, and we thought it was less racial than it turned out to be."

Although the heart of the war on poverty, to Shriver, was community action and the Job Corps, the legislation, announced by Johnson on March 16, contained ten new programs, including three aimed exclusively at rural areas. Shriver persuaded a Southern congressman, Phil Landrum of Georgia, to be the legislation's chief sponsor. There would be a new community action agency in a majority of the congressional districts. Job Corps centers were to be distributed all over the country, including places far from the homes of the ghetto teenagers they were meant to serve. The mantra of the people lobbying for the bill was that American poverty was mostly white and mostly nonurban. So when James Sunquist, the Agriculture Department's man on Shriver's team, was trying to talk the old-fashioned Texas congressman W. R. Poage into voting for the bill, he laid on thick the vague phraseology of "opportunity" and "coordinated service delivery." Poage looked back at him with blank uncomprehension. But finally, a light seemed to go on in Poage's head, and he smiled broadly and said, "Oh, I see! You're talkin' about the niggers!" Another man lobbying for the bill presented a document to Wilbur Mills of Arkansas, chairman of the House Ways and Means

Committee, that was supposed to answer Mills's objections; as he remembered it later, "He took that piece of paper and threw it across the room and said a few choice words about how he was not going to be involved in any program to help a bunch of niggers and threw me out of his office."

When more negotiable conservative objections to the poverty program came up, Shriver compromised. One idea that was bounced around was instituting Third World–style land reform in the Mississippi Delta and similar areas by breaking up the big plantations into family farms and turning them over to the sharecroppers — forty acres and a mule nearly a century late. When Jamie Whitten, the Mississippi congressman who was chairman of the House Appropriations Committee, made known his displeasure with the idea, it was dropped. A much more damaging compromise came when members of the North Carolina delegation, especially Congressman L. H. Fountain, demanded as the price of their vote the jettisoning of Yarmolinsky as deputy director of the war on poverty: he was Jewish, from a liberal-activist background in New York, and, in his Defense Department days, had helped to force the integration of public places near military bases in North Carolina. Yarmolinsky was convinced that Shriver would stand behind him; instead, as he remembered it, "it took me completely by surprise when Shriver, coming back from the Hill quite late one evening, stumbled into the room between our two offices and announced: 'We've just thrown you to the wolves, and this is the worst day of my life.'" Yarmolinsky and Shriver had made a good team, the manager and the salesman. Shriver never again found someone he fully trusted to run the poverty program while he attended to its reputation.

President Johnson signed the Economic Opportunity Act into law on August 20, 1964, thus creating a new government agency, the Office of Economic Opportunity, with Sargent Shriver as director. It was a great triumph — President Kennedy's hesitant effort brought to fruition as a major program — but it isn't entirely clear that Johnson, focused on the win as he was, fully understood the implications of what he was signing. The act had actually been drafted in a place that should have immediately raised Johnson's suspicions: an office in Robert Kennedy's Justice Department, with Dick Boone present to ensure that the language of maximum feasible participation of the poor in the community action program got into it. While Shriver was engaged in lobbying, Johnson's friend Elizabeth Wickenden got in touch with a veteran member of Johnson's staff, Walter Jenkins, to raise again her fears about the political problems that community action might create. As director of the Peace Corps, Shriver had gotten a reputation as a master of politics; he had supposedly called personally on all 535 members of Congress. What he hadn't learned, Wickenden felt, was that politicians always want to maintain control over government programs operating in their districts, so that the community action agencies would either have to knuckle under or would create powerful enemies. "I feel this is a very real political problem for which Mr. Shriver's experience has not prepared him," Wickenden wrote Jenkins. "(As I said to you on the telephone, it is quite a different problem from the Peace Corps since Nigeria does not have a delegation in Congress.)"

Very late in the game, after the bill had passed, Yarmolinsky was amazed to hear from Bill Moyers, "the President thinks that community action will be a publicly managed program like the old National Youth Administration he administered in Texas in the 1930s." There is some evidence, though, that Wickenden's warning got through to Johnson, even if he didn't do anything about it. Years later, Abe Fortas, the Supreme Court justice who was another member of Johnson's old New Deal crowd, told her that Johnson had said to him, "I should have listened to Wicky."

I NSIDE the civil rights movement, too, the question was being raised of what to do after segregation in the South was defeated. Of course, there had been civil rights activity outside the South for many years. The NAACP and the Urban League, both Northern-based organizations, dated back to the first decade of the twentieth century. CORE was staging demonstrations against housing segregation in Chicago and other cities as long ago as the 1940s. Only as the Southern struggle gained momentum did it absorb nearly all the movement's energies. CORE moved south with the Freedom Rides, in 1961. The two newest major civil rights organizations, the Southern Christian Leadership Conference and the Student Non-Violent Coordinating Committee, were active only in the South. During the early 1960s, it became an uphill struggle to focus attention on the problems arising from the black migration to the North.

Bayard Rustin, a socialist, pacifist labor intellectual who as protégé to A. Philip Randolph of the Brotherhood of Sleeping Car Porters was the chief organizer of the March on Washington in 1963, conceived of the march as the great event that would signal the broadening of the movement's attention beyond the borders of the South. The march's official name was "A March for Jobs and Freedom," which signified Rustin's conviction that the main long-range issues in black America were economic ones. Rustin had always regarded Martin Luther King a little patronizingly, in roughly the way a television producer views his on-the-air talent. He felt he had had to instruct King in the merits of non-violence, and he liked to think that he had to provide the conceptual direction for the use of King's awesome oratorical talents. "What are we going to do with Martin next?" Rustin used to ask his friends in the movement. After the March on Washington, Rustin was annoyed that King's overwhelmingly powerful "I Have a Dream" speech, in which he painted for a huge, rapt crowd a gorgeous picture of life under racial equality, had gotten most of the attention; in focusing on civil rights, King had departed from Rustin's carefully prepared script, and for years afterward Rustin would tell people that the real milestone speech delivered that day was the barely noticed one by Rabbi Joachim Prinz, which stuck to the theme of economic justice.

Another aspect of the March on Washington that annoyed Rustin was the behavior of the members of SNCC — "the kids," as Rustin called them. They had set up a chant, "Pass the bill, pass the bill," that had made the march look like a gigantic lobbying effort for Kennedy's Civil Rights Act, when to Rustin's mind it was really an effort to address a different and more important set of issues. John Lewis, head of SNCC, had almost caused tremendous trouble for the march by writing a speech that called for a black version of Sherman's march through Georgia; cooler heads read the text and prevailed on Lewis to take that line out, but he didn't give in until only a few moments before he took the podium.

Lewis himself was already becoming known as the voice of moderation within SNCC, which was undergoing an internal split. On one side were the original members, most of whom, like Lewis, came from poor, religious Southern backgrounds and would probably have gone into the ministry if the movement hadn't come along. On the other side was the "Howard contingent," so named because most of its members were students at America's most prestigious black university. They came from Northern, urban, middle-class backgrounds. The leader of the Howard contingent was Stokely Carmichael, who had grown up in the Bronx, the son of Trinidadian immigrants, and as a teenager had often listened to the black-nationalist oratory of street-corner speakers in Harlem, the most eloquent of whom was Elijah Muhammad's man in New York, Malcolm X; Lewis's father was an Alabama sharecropper who had saved up enough money to buy his own small farm. Carmichael was tall, slim, handsome, and spectacularly eloquent; Lewis was short and plain-looking, and he mumbled. Carmichael was deeply interested in the African independence movement and in the black-liberation theories of Frantz Fanon; Lewis's whole world was the rural South.

Lewis had been to the North only a couple of times. In 1951 he was brought to Buffalo, New York, to visit relatives who had made the migration North, and it looked to him like a paradise, in which blacks sat next to whites in restaurants and held down solid blue-collar jobs. In 1963 he made his first trip to New York City, to attend a planning meeting for the March on Washington, and he was shocked by the difference. "I saw a crowd of people on the street corner in Harlem chanting and raving about what they were going to do to whitey," he says. "The boarded-up buildings, the chains, the grates on store windows—it was very different from what I'd seen in Alabama or Nashville. It was despair." Carmichael wanted SNCC to mount operations in the North. A friend of his, Bill Strickland, ran a SNCC affiliate called the Northern Student Movement, and prevailed upon Carmichael to spend half of the summers of 1962 and 1963 in Harlem. But Lewis insisted on SNCC's confining itself to the South, and saw the Northern Student Movement as a supply and fundraising operation for the Southern struggle.

The Howard contingent was much more interested than the Southerners in the issue of black consciousness. In the 1950s Howard had been, like other elite ethnic-group institutions of the time, permeated by an ethic of extreme assimilationism which led to a cutting off of the students' grounding in black culture and history in a way that would have been impossible for ordinary black people in the South. Harris Wofford, who taught part-time at Howard Law School then, was surprised to find that the prevailing style among his students was an especially pronounced version of the conformity of white students of the Silent Generation. All the men wore ties to class, and all the women dresses; the students called each other "Mister" and "Miss." E. Franklin Frazier, who was teaching at Howard also, told Wofford that every year he asked whether anyone in his class was the descendant of slaves, and never a hand was raised. Howard was always firmly allied with the struggle for civil rights, but there was an undercurrent of rejection of blackness there, and therefore of rejection both of self and of the black masses. Carmichael sensed this and began to speak out against it. As Roger Wilkins, a young lawyer in the Johnson administration who, like many prominent blacks of his generation, had been touched by Carmichael's message, later wrote, "Stokely and the other young intellectuals in the movement knew what they were doing. They were purging themselves of all of that self-hate, asserting a human validity that did not derive from whites and pointing out that the black experience on this continent and in Africa was profound, honorable, and a source of pride." For the Howard contingent, the civil rights struggle in the South was a point of access to the main African-American experience and therefore to self-discovery.

In the summer of 1964, when the Civil Rights Act and the Economic Opportunity Act passed, the civil rights movement appeared to outsiders to be unified and, finally, fully in command of events, but inside the movement there were strong tensions. Hundreds of white college students from the North were going South for Freedom Summer, a protracted civil rights event that was covered ecstatically in the national press. The operations of Freedom Summer were not so pacific as they looked. Within the consortium of civil rights organizations that sponsored it, there was some ill will between the NAACP and SNCC, which always wanted to be more confrontational and often relied on the NAACP for bed, board, and bail money.

Within SNCC, there was a note of racial hostility. The interracial romances that naturally developed during Freedom Summer usually seemed to involve a black man and a white woman, which left the black women, especially, feeling angry and rejected. The press coverage created further ill will, because it seemed to focus on the nobility of the white johnny-come-latelies instead of the blacks who had been risking their lives in the South for years. The whites had a tendency to want to take over. "Up to the summer of '64, SNCC was busy developing local leadership," says Bob Zellner, a white Southerner who was a veteran member of SNCC. "Things like typing, stenciling, mimeographing—we were always teaching young local black people these things. Press releases. TV. Radio. Fundraising. How to run a meeting. All these things middle-class white kids just *know*. So here we had kids that were blossoming, bright kids—this is the chance of a lifetime for them. Suddenly, in an instant, in our town are five or six brightly scrubbed white kids from the North. Here's Jesse laboriously doing the stencil. Sally from Rutgers comes along and says, 'Here, I type 120 words per minute, let me do it.'"

Toward the end of the summer, the top civil rights leaders traveled to the Democratic Convention in Atlantic City to push for the seating of the integrated delegation of the Mississippi Freedom Democratic Party instead of the all-white official Mississippi delegation. President Johnson, who finally had the chance to be the emperor of a Democratic convention, was extremely eager that everything go smoothly, and by dangling the vice-presidential nomination before Hubert Humphrey, he was able to induce Humphrey and the whole liberal wing of the party to work out a compromise under which two members of the Freedom Democratic Party (one of whom was Aaron Henry, from Clarksdale) were seated. The SNCC leadership believed that the liberals and the more centrist civil rights people had sold them out, and they left the convention bitterly disillusioned. Bob Moses, SNCC's ace organizer, resolved to leave the country. In October, SNCC held a retreat at Waveland, Mississippi, at which, for the first time, the issue of limiting the white role in the organization was raised. The overall level of commitment to such apparent conceptual bulwarks of the civil rights movement as integration, nonviolence, and cooperating with the federal government was palpably beginning to fade.

Perhaps they weren't really bulwarks, anyway. The civil rights movement in the South had brilliantly practiced media politics, and its historic victories were immensely aided by the presence of easily identifiable heroes (like King) and villains (like Governors Ross Barnett and George Wallace, and Sheriff Jim Clark of Selma, Alabama), dramatic scenes of courage and oppression that could be broadcast on television (like black children in Birmingham being attacked by police dogs and fire hoses), and a clear overall goal whose moral righteousness was plain. Nonviolence and integrationism were crucial to the movement's public reputation, but they were never unshakable tenets in black America, especially given the brutal nature of the white resistance to civil rights all over the country. Medgar Evers, the Mississippi field secretary of the NAACP, owned a gun. In the 1950s, Bayard Rustin, on a visit to King at his home in Montgomery, Alabama, found a gun lying on an armchair in the living room. Kenneth Clark, a symbol of integrationism, was a friend of Malcolm X, who was becoming the country's best-known separatist; Clark arranged for King and Malcolm to meet one another.

Malcolm, more than anyone else, illustrates the difference between white and black perceptions of the civil rights movement. As the head of the Nation of Islam in New York and a street-corner orator of great eloquency, Malcolm became a minor national figure in the early 1960s. The white press portrayed him as a black racist, a hate-monger in the service of a bizarre cult whose success in the ghettos was a sign of how twisted black society had become after so many decades of oppression. But to young well-educated blacks he was a galvanizing figure, perhaps even more so than King: the only black leader who seemed absolutely focused on the problems of the ghettos, the only one who spoke directly about the issue of black self-denial, and the only one who could simultaneously stir poor street-corner people in Harlem and students at Howard. He was a black nationalist who was neither a cosseted intellectual — he hadn't finished school, and had served a long stretch in prison — nor a folkish figure like Elijah; there were few references to the evil Yacub and the island of Patmos in his speeches. To whites Malcolm looked like a divisive figure who was the antithesis of King; to blacks he looked like a generator of pride and self-reliance who belonged right next to King in the pantheon of black heroes.

The civil rights movement's relations with the federal government were another area where things weren't quite the way they seemed from the outside. Newspaper readers regularly saw pictures of high government officials and movement leaders shaking hands at bill-signing ceremonies, but as everyone in government and the movement knew, the truth was that there was a great deal of friction and mutual suspicion. James Baldwin told Clark in the mid-1960s that he was convinced his famous meeting with Robert Kennedy had been secretly taped, and that Kennedy had later turned the transcript over to President Johnson to help him plan the Great Society. In the Johnson administration, the officials who negotiated with leaders of the movement over the Civil Rights Act felt themselves to have been subjected to humiliating abuse just when they were putting everything on the line for the black cause. There certainly wasn't a clear agreement in the movement about how to put pressure on the government after the demise of Jim Crow. Camera-ready segregation did not exist in the North. The ghettos were not hotbeds of the spirit of nonviolent resistance to white power. There was no obvious organizing principle. In December 1964, after King received the Nobel Prize in Stockholm, he flew directly to New York; but when he got there, Louis Martin says, "Martin was the toast of the world, and he couldn't think of what to say in Harlem." It was anything but plain what the movement's next step would be.

Into this breach came the war on poverty. It had been conceived without the participation of the civil rights people, but there was some hope in Shriver's group that through the community action program, the war on poverty might serve as an enabling device for the movement in its next phase. Many local civil rights leaders were supposed to emerge to help run the community action agencies in the ghettos. What the planners of the war on poverty didn't realize was that these positions, partially protected as they were from elected officialdom, constituted an opening for the new black mood of mistrust of government and whites to be expressed. They were also naive to think that the community action program could serve as the incubator for something along the lines of the civil rights movement in the South. The leadership it would create was a diffuse and instantaneous one, with little chance to build strength and unity over time, and community action was wholly dependent on the good will of the federal government in a way that the movement in the South never had been. The Southern movement would have died out at a hundred points of controversy along the way if it hadn't been independent. Community action, if it offended mainstream American sensibilities, would be much more vulnerable — doomed, as it turned out.

From the perspective of the White House, the war on poverty was a problem program almost from the instant it started, and the main reason was Dick Boone's "maximum feasible participation" clause. Within a matter of days of Johnson's signing the Economic Opportunity Act, there was trouble at Mobilization for Youth in New York, one of the seedbeds of community action. Mobilization's relations with the police had been rocky for some time; it had even sued the New York Police Department. In the summer of 1964, a riot in Harlem followed the killing of a black teenager by a white policeman. Just before the riot, posters had appeared in Harlem saying WANTED FOR MURDER: GILLIGAN THE COP. The head of Mobilization for Youth publicly demanded the establishment of a civilian police review board, and the police suspected Mobilization of having generated the posters and therefore of fomenting the riot. On August 17, the New York *Daily News* carried a story by its police reporter with the banner headline YOUTH AGENCY EYED FOR REDS. All through the fall — campaign season for Johnson and for Robert Kennedy, who had left the Justice Department and was running for the Senate from New York — Mobilization was the subject of a controversy over the presence of several ex-communists on its staff. After election day, Johnson sent a couple of his Cabinet members up to New York to work out a compromise, but Mobilization's director resigned. It never got back on a good footing with the local political order.

In other cities, too, the community action agencies quickly ran into trouble with political officials. On January 20, 1965, not yet half a year into the life of the Office of Economic Opportunity, Johnson received a confidential letter from Theodore McKeldin, the Republican mayor of Baltimore, complaining that "your plans are being hindered at the federal level by individuals who insist on unrealistic requirements and who do not understand the problems and requirements of local governments" — a reference to the community action program. McKeldin said he spoke also for the mayors of St. Louis, Cleveland, and Philadelphia, who were Democrats. By the fall of 1965, the mayors had openly revolted. In September, Charles Schultze, who had taken over from Kermit Gordon as budget director, wrote to Johnson, "Many mayors assert that the CAP is setting up a *competing political organization* in their own backyards." He warned that "*we ought not to be in the business of organizing the poor politically.*" In December, Hubert Humphrey, who as vice president was Johnson's liaison to the mayors, reported that Richard Daley and several of his colleagues were planning to meet in Miami to share their complaints about the poverty program. "I see no conflict between full involvement of local government officials and 'maximum feasible participation' of the poor," Humphrey wrote Johnson. "What disturbs the Mayors is their belief that OEO is building and funding in the community action committees opposition elements to the city administration."

The best evidence that these complaints were not taken lightly is that on December 18, 1965, Johnson's aide Joseph Califano submitted to him a full-scale reorganization plan for the war on poverty in which the OEO (and Shriver's job) would be eliminated entirely, and its functions parceled out to the old-line departments and agencies that the planners of the war on poverty had wanted so badly to cut out of the action. Califano suggested putting the best face on it by making Shriver the first head of the new Department of Housing and Urban Development. He wrote: "My personal feeling is that the whole package — the reorganization of the War Against Poverty, the designation of Shriver as HUD Secretary (with a Negro as Under Secretary), the placing of the Community Action Program and Poverty coordination functions in the HUD, would be a typically dramatic Johnsonian move that would be received with applause across the board."

Mayor Daley was by far the most important enemy of community action. In Washington, he was regarded then as the essential Democratic mayor — not a crusader, to be sure, but a good guy, solid, reliable, and efficient. Shriver's people had expected to alienate some politicians — Southerners and Republicans — but the whole idea of the antipoverty program was that it would have the support of Northern white Democrats. Daley's respectability was backed up by his power, which, in national affairs, was at its peak then. Without his help, John Kennedy (and by extension, Lyndon Johnson) would never have become president. (Myer Feldman, an aide to Sorensen, later recounted the scene on election night, 1960, at the Kennedy compound in Hyannis Port in a way that makes it perfectly clear what Daley's role was: "I remember Steve Smith [another Kennedy brother-in-law] saying to me over the phone that, 'Well, we can always count on Mayor Daley. And if the ballot boxes down state aren't in, why, he'll hold out a few ballot boxes in Chicago too to equal them.' ")

Daley's clout extended far beyond the borders of his home state and the confines of the U.S. Conference of Mayors, because he controlled the largest bloc of votes in Congress that would reliably move on one person's orders. During the early machinations with Congress on the Civil Rights Act, when President Kennedy was still alive, one member of the Illinois congressional delegation, Roland Libonati, gave Daley his word that he would support the administration's position and then backed out at the last minute. When Daley heard about this, Robert Kennedy later remembered, he "reported back that Libonati wouldn't be running for Congress any more. And Libonati then retired from Congress, and they put a new man in." To Johnson, whose presidential ambitions lay largely in the area of passing legislation, someone who could manage a group of congressmen that tightly was a necessary ally whose wrath was not to be incurred.

As he had done when the President's Committee on Juvenile Delinquency began giving grants to cities, Daley moved quickly after the war on poverty began, and submitted a long, expensive plan for the program in Chicago, drawn up in such a way that he would control it absolutely. William Cannon of the Budget Bureau flew out to Chicago to have a talk with him about maximum feasible participation. It did not go well. "It was clear that there would be no poverty program without Daley running it," Cannon says. "He was explicit with me. I was explicit with him that there had to be local participation." The OEO began to push

Daley to loosen his grip on the program, and Daley began to call the White House to complain. "We had problems with Daley on *everything*, and he always went to the White House, and always won," says Frederick Hayes, who was the director of operations for the community action program. Bill Moyers received one of the first calls from Daley. As he remembered it, Daley said, "What in the hell are you people doing? Does the President know he's putting M-O-N-E-Y in the hands of subversives? To poor people that aren't a part of the organization? Didn't the President know they'd take that money to bring him down?" When Moyers told Johnson about the call, Johnson immediately returned it, though before doing so he instructed Moyers to leave the room. "The clearest picture Johnson got of the bad image of the OEO was from Daley," Moyers says. "He really began to rage at Johnson. That began to form a dark cloud in Johnson's mind."

Sargent Shriver was thus on the defensive almost from the start. He was surrounded by enemies. Kenneth O'Donnell, the old Kennedy political hand who stayed on for a while in the Johnson White House, didn't like him, and fed Daley's suspicions about the OEO. (After the vice presidency went to Humphrey in 1964, Shriver began to toy with the idea of running for the Senate from Illinois, and this made him especially eager not to incur Daley's displeasure, because he knew that the Senate race was an opportunity Daley could eliminate with a wave of the hand.) Johnson's old friend John Connally, governor of Texas, was another frequent caller to the White House with complaints about the OEO. An important liberal Democratic member of Congress, Edith Green of Oregon, had been suspicious of community action ever since its emergence in the juvenile delinquency committee days, and was a persistent critic of the OEO from the beginning.

The Cabinet departments, predictably, despised the OEO. "All these agencies at the time were run by people who were just as liberal as OEO, and just as committed," says Joseph Doherty, who was the Agriculture Department's liaison with the war on poverty. "They felt they'd been there first, and now OEO was shoving them aside and getting the money and glory." Wilbur Cohen annually tried to get Johnson to transfer most of the OEO's functions to HEW. In January 1965, Moynihan went to see Kermit Gordon to lobby against community action. "If you're an assistant secretary of a small department, you can one time ask to see the budget director on a point of personal privilege," he says. "I used my one time. I said, 'I know you've thought of community action as a way of coordinating services at the local level, but another view is, they could raise a lot of hell.' But there was no point in going on because it was clear Kermit Gordon thought I was *out of my mind.*" The tenor of Willard Wirtz's behavior toward the OEO can be adduced from the contents of a confidential handwritten note from Lloyd Cutler, a prominent Washington lawyer, to Shriver, which was passed on to Moyers: "Sarge: The strongest critic of the unit costs of the Job Corps is Willard Wirtz. Competition is good at this stage, but the Republicans get their best arguments from inside the Administration – the N.Y.C. [Wirtz's National Youth Corps] saying it does better than the Job Corps, etc."

Every accommodation Shriver made to the politicians who wanted the doctrine of maximum feasible participation toned down brought him criticism from the left. Dick Boone left the OEO in 1965 and started an organization called Citizens' Crusade Against Poverty, whose purpose was to make sure that the community action program didn't sell out. Adam Clayton Powell, who was chairman of the House committee that authorized the OEO's funds, was a constant thorn in Shriver's side; at one point he banned all OEO employees from his committee's offices. Certain offices inside the OEO – for example, the research division of the community action program, and the evaluation division – were openly more loyal to the spirit of maximum feasible participation than to Shriver. In April 1966, Shriver agreed to address a convention of Boone's organization in Washington, but he was, according to *The New York Times*, "booed, jostled, and almost hooted down" by the audience, and was spirited away, badly shaken, immediately after delivering his remarks.

Shriver's hope was that he could keep all the forces aligned against him at bay by producing well-publicized successes in the field. This was made difficult by the forced departure of his key administrator, Yarmolinsky, and, even more, by the way the war on poverty was set up. Almost by definition, a community action agency could not quickly be shown to be producing results; on the other hand, Shriver and Johnson had made the program so large that the risk of occasional horror stories emerging from the local community action agencies was very high. The community action office in Washington could, and did, labor long and hard to give its grants to reputable organizations and to create harmonious relations with mayors. Hundreds of the local agencies could, and did, go about their business with efficiency and dedication. By an iron law of journalism, however, the handful of messy situations got most of the coverage.

Head Start, from the very beginning the one major part of the war on poverty that was popular in Congress, was structured in such a way that its programs were run by local community action agencies; in fact, probably the main real activity of community action all over the country was operating Head Start programs. It was never possible fully to decouple Head Start's good image from community action's bad one.

It was impossible for Shriver to accept the inevitability of operational problems at the agency. In the words of one of his former aides, he wanted "to score a hundred on every test." He insisted that 10,000 kids be enrolled in Job Corps camps by the end of June 1965; his staff had them sleeping on the floors of gymnasiums to meet the quota. At the signing of the first batch of grants to community action agencies, Shriver picked out one, the agency in Albemarle County, North Carolina, and asked Fred Hayes, How do you know this one will work? It doesn't even have an executive director's name on the application. How do you know they won't pick someone incompetent? "I said, 'You don't know he won't be an incompetent,'" Hayes recalls today. "'He may well be. You can't control the grant recipients, and some of them are going to screw up.'"

Indeed, some of them did screw up. HARYOU, the agency Adam Clayton Powell controlled in Harlem, was under investigation for financial irregularities almost from the moment it received its first OEO grant, of $1.2 million, in June 1965. In Syracuse, New York, the community action program gave Syracuse University a grant to train community organizers in Alinsky's organizing techniques, thereby infuriating the mayor. Even in Chicago, an internal OEO report circulated in May 1965 showed that no books were being kept, that a subcontractor was working without a written contract, and that there was a one-to-one ratio of clerical to professional employees.

At the Job Corps camps several embarrassing incidents of violence occurred. At Camp Atterbury, in Indiana, one trainee was sodomized by several others. At Camp Gary, in Texas, five trainees held up and shot two enlisted men from a nearby Air Force base, and another trainee was stabbed to death outside a dance at the YMCA. At Camp Breckinridge, in Kentucky, a recruit shot a woman and then, while awaiting trial, managed to steal a car and ran into a family of four on the highway, killing them all. Probably incidents like these could have been avoided if the Job Corps had proceeded with great care from the start, rigorously screening its applicants, limiting the size of its camps, and providing very strict supervision of the enrollees — but Shriver wanted a big program right away, and he was under constant pressure from the left to minimize the program's rules and restrictions. It became a joke among the OEO's lobbyists in Congress that they should tell every recalcitrant member that if he didn't vote right on OEO bills they would put a Job Corps center in his district.

Shriver reacted to the problems of the OEO more by emphasizing his strength, salesmanship, than by correcting his weaknesses, conception and administration. He invented citizens' support groups, such as Athletes Against Poverty. He tried to hire Al Capp, the creator of the comic strip "Li'l Abner," to produce a comic book advertising the Job Corps. He barraged President Johnson with memos, written with the specificity and enthusiasm of a professional publicist, claiming that the image of the OEO was turning around. In a typical passage he wrote, "I can't remember hitting five major American newspapers simultaneously on any program in recent years. An eight-column head in the *Cleveland Plain Dealer* certainly marks some sort of high point."

By midsummer 1965, when he was beginning to prepare his first regular budget, Shriver had become converted, mainly through the efforts of the liberal economist James Tobin, to the idea of a guaranteed annual income as the best solution to the problem of poverty. He decided to ask Johnson for a very large budget increase — from the planned-upon $1.75 billion a year to, eventually, $10 billion — under which the OEO would become a much bigger and more comprehensive agency, presumably with community action becoming a less audible section in the symphony of antipoverty programs. "I said, 'Mr. President, we can actually eliminate poverty in the United States,'" Shriver says. "He said, 'Well, Sarge, we can't spend that kind of money.' I said, 'Well, if you want to wage war on poverty, this is how to do it.' He said, 'Congressional elections are coming up. After that we'll be out of this Vietnam thing, and I'll give you the money.' I knew the jig was up." Shriver threatened to resign, and backed down only when Johnson, playing to his sense of duty, told him, "if you quit, we'll just quit," meaning that he would follow Califano's suggestion and abolish the OEO. The agency, and Shriver, soldiered on.

T HE LAST glorious event of the Southern civil rights movement was the Selma-to-Montgomery march, in March 1965. SNCC had been trying unsuccessfully to register voters in Selma, Alabama, since 1963; in

January 1965, King arrived in Selma and announced that he would wage a campaign against the town's voter registration policies as a way of drawing national attention to the issue of black disenfranchisement in the South. Over the course of the weeks of rallies and marches, two civil rights people were murdered. Malcolm X came to town and criticized King's commitment to nonviolence. The dramatic climax of the campaign came in a series of marches across the Edmund Pettus Bridge. In the first one, a column led by John Lewis was repulsed by Alabama state troopers who used tear gas, horses, police dogs, and clubs to turn back the movement's foot soldiers. In the second, two days later, King, who had been frantically trying to maintain relations with the administration on the one hand and SNCC on the other, led the marchers up to the point where the state troopers were waiting, and then ordered a retreat. Finally, armed with a court order and protected by federal troops, a brigade of four thousand people, with King at the head, crossed the bridge and marched to the state capitol in Montgomery, where King delivered one of his greatest addresses. The movement had held, and triumphed; Jim Crow had finally received its mortal wound.

King and his lieutenants were talking about moving North all during their months in Selma, and immediately after the march, the Big Six, leaders of the major civil rights organizations, met to discuss the North. A few weeks later, one of King's best organizers, James Bevel, moved to Chicago to explore the possibilities for a civil rights campaign there.

Just before the Selma march got under way, President Johnson used the phrase "we shall overcome" in an address to a joint session of Congress, and proposed the Voting Rights Act. In June, Johnson moved rhetorically North himself, delivering a commencement speech at Howard in which he called for "not just equality as a right and a theory, but equality as a fact and equality as a result," and promised to hold a White House conference in the fall on what the government's new racial agenda should be. Johnson and the civil rights movement were hardly in perfect harmony, but it did appear that the time for everyone involved with civil rights to turn the spotlight onto the racial problems of the cities had finally arrived.

Just at that moment, the summer of 1965, the 1960s turned as if on a hinge. In July, Johnson announced the commitment of 100,000 additional American ground troops to the war in Vietnam. In August, five days after the signing of the Voting Rights Act into law, an ordinary incident in which a white policeman pulled over a black driver in a black neighborhood in Los Angeles mysteriously escalated into a riot in the section of town called Watts, which lasted for five days and left thirty-four people dead and more than a thousand injured. Watts instantly convinced the whole country that there was a severe crisis in the black slums, and so, ironically, gave the mission of the war on poverty a force and immediacy that it had lacked up to then; the ghettos moved in the blink of an eye from being an issue only among a small coterie to being a national obsession.

At the same time, Watts and the escalation of American involvement in Vietnam destroyed the mood of triumphant liberal comity that was supposed to be the foundation on which the solution to the crisis would be built. The first sign that something had gone profoundly wrong came in the weeks following Watts, when the White House released a report by Moynihan called "The Negro Family: The Case for National Action."

The Moynihan Report was the product of two of its author's distinguishing traits: his ability to spot trends in intellectual life, and his thirst for more attention than intellectuals were accustomed to getting. The roots of the report lay in a book called *Slavery*, published in 1959 by a young historian named Stanley Elkins. During the years after World War II, historians were only just beginning to portray slavery as brutal, rather than benign and paternalistic. Elkins, working in the long shadow of the seminal work in this line, Kenneth Stampp's *The Peculiar Institution*, wanted to darken the picture of slavery even further by showing that it had so devastated African-Americans as to have reduced them to a state of dependency. His evidence was that slaveholders among the Founding Fathers, such as Thomas Jefferson and James Madison, had portrayed slaves as being childlike, but he didn't really try to prove this assertion, only to offer an explanation supporting it; even the most liberal white historians of the day believed that there had been no such thing as a genuine, strong African-American slave culture. Elkins compared the effect of slavery on blacks to the infantilization that Bruno Bettelheim had noted in the Jewish inmates of Nazi concentration camps.

When *Slavery* was published, it got respectable reviews and sold at a rate of four hundred copies a year. After four years, it abruptly started to catch on. Nathan Glazer, Moynihan's friend and co-author, reviewed *Slavery* in *Commentary* and then gave Moynihan a copy; it became one of Moynihan's discoveries, and he began to pass it around Washington. Besides having the appeal that a dramatic new argument always had for Moynihan, *Slavery* served his political need to justify new social programs run by the Labor Department. "Why?" asks Elkins. "It provided a historical formula that was attractive to Northern liberals: ours was a particularly harsh form of slavery; we had a responsibility to correct it." It was especially important at that moment for liberals to drive home Elkins's point. All through the civil rights movement, liberals were able to argue that although they were supporting a lot of legislation aimed at helping blacks, the overall goal was simply to provide blacks with the same legal rights as everyone else; the second wave of racial reforms, aimed at the North—not just the war on poverty, but also affirmative action—had to be justified on the grounds that blacks deserved help from the government above and beyond what everyone else got.

Moynihan had already, with "One-Third of a Nation," written one sensational document based on what he knew about the problems of the ghettos, and it had failed to loose an avalanche of social programs. He needed new ammunition. Also, he was involved in complex career machinations that a stunning new report might serve. In the fall of 1964, he had campaigned for Robert Kennedy in New York, and Wirtz, still angry at him for having let the Job Corps slip away, had told Johnson, who had become predictably furious. Some masterstroke might repair Moynihan's relations with Wirtz and the White House. At the same time, though he hadn't told Wirtz about it, Moynihan was contemplating a run for the presidency of the New York City Council in the fall of 1965; being known as the author of a great liberal call to arms might help his chances there.

During the Christmas season of 1964, Moynihan called in his chief assistant, Paul Barton, one morning. "Pat said, 'We just have to do something,'" Barton says. "'We have to be different. We're not going to get attention to this problem because of the low unemployment rate. We're going to do a report.'" Moynihan told Barton he wanted to concentrate on the parlous state of the black family. Black out-of-wedlock childbearing had always been very high, and now it appeared to be rising even higher: nearly a quarter of all black children were now born to single mothers. The standard explanation of this, laid out most convincingly by E. Franklin Frazier and now given additional punch by Elkins, was that slavery had loosened the family bonds of African-Americans. More recently, high unemployment among black men, and the welfare system's provision of benefits only to single mothers, were making the male economically irrelevant to the poor black family, and more illegitimacy was the result. In *Dark Ghetto*, Kenneth Clark had a gloomy chapter on the deteriorating family structure and social fabric in the black slums, called "The Pathology of the Ghetto"; Moynihan picked up on this, too, and had a chapter in his report called "The Tangle of Pathology."

The work on the report was an all-consuming task in Moynihan's office. All through January and February 1965, Barton and Ellen Broderick, another of Moynihan's assistants, were in the office seven days a week, meeting at the end of every day with Moynihan to apprise him of their progress. Toward the end of the job, they came across a statistic that seemed to encapsulate their theory perfectly: the unemployment rate and the number of new welfare cases, which previously had moved up and down in perfect lockstep, had begun to "disaggregate": unemployment was falling, but welfare cases were rising. (Moynihan, a great reviser of his own history, now says it was the discovery of this statistic that prompted the report — "the numbers went blooey on me," as he puts it.) Finally Moynihan took a detailed outline from his assistants, wrote the report himself, and brought it to Wirtz.

"I remember the almost physical excitement of reading it," Wirtz says. "I said, 'Pat, let's not use this until we can suggest what to do about it.' It was very long on detail about the problem and very short on what to do. He was reluctant — impatient with my suggestions. He wanted to get it out." Moynihan had ideas about how to solve the problems of the black family — for example, instituting twice-a-day mail delivery and thereby creating thousands of new jobs for men at the Post Office, that bastion of black working-class employment. He convinced Wirtz, though, that proposing any specific policies in the report would only diffuse its impact.

A hundred numbered copies of the report were printed and distributed on a confidential basis around the upper reaches of the government. Richard Goodwin, a bright young man of the Kennedy administration who had stayed on after the assassination and become a speechwriter for Johnson, read it and included a passage about the black family in Johnson's commencement address at Howard; Martin Luther King, Roy Wilkins, and Whitney Young of the Urban League read the address and conferred their blessings on it before it was delivered. Moynihan insists that the report's general release, after Watts, came completely on the initiative of the White House, which needed to satisfy a press corps that was clamoring for some explanation of the riot. But everyone else involved in the report sees the fine hand of Moynihan in its becoming public. More than most government officials, he had a pride of authorship and of intellectual discovery that would have made it painful for him to know that he was not getting full credit for an important breakthrough; he speaks today with great feeling about how unjust it was that everyone simply adopted John Dollard's idea that frustration leads to aggression without attributing it to Dollard. Just as Johnson needed to pass legislation to prove his own worth, Moynihan needed to be known as an original thinker. Because he was too impatient for the grind of academic research, his oeuvre at that point was quite thin; his chapter on the Irish in *Beyond the Melting Pot* was by far his best-known work, and the report on the black family was the kind of major statement that could establish his place in the first rank of American intellectuals.

Well before the release of the Moynihan Report, a lengthy, respectful description of it, obviously written with a copy in hand, appeared in *The New York Times*, the publication most widely circulated in the audience that mattered to Moynihan. Also before Watts, Wirtz's mentor and former law partner Adlai Stevenson died, and while Wirtz was in Illinois for the funeral Moynihan called him to say he was going to run for office in New York. "And it was shortly after that that I began to hear there had been a 'suppressing' of the Moynihan Report, which upset me greatly," says Wirtz. "*I* didn't release it — I think he did." The idea of suppression came from a syndicated newspaper column by Rowland Evans and Robert Novak that helped put pressure on the White House to release the report. Goodwin's memory of how the report was released is that "someone came into my office and said there are press requests for the report, and I said, 'I don't care, call Pat, and if he wants it out, let it out.'"

The press coverage of the Moynihan Report was, in general, exactly what Moynihan had in mind. He was suddenly famous as a racial seer — almost the predictor of the Watts riot. It wasn't until October that it became clear that in black America the report was regarded as a grave insult. The notion of weakness in the black family struck familiar and uncomfortable chords: it brought to mind all the white Southern mythology about unrestrained black sexuality. Because Moynihan had left out the solutions, and because the press had concentrated on the parts of the report that dealt with out-of-wedlock childbearing and ignored the parts about unemployment, it was possible to perceive it as a brief for doing nothing to help the black poor, rather than as a "case for national action," because the straits they were in were of their own devising. That was exactly the perception of William Ryan, a white psychologist and civil rights activist in Boston, who after reading an article in *Newsweek* wrote a critique of the report that he circulated within the movement.

Ryan hit upon a brilliant slogan to sum up what he saw Moynihan as doing: "blaming the victim." His actual argument, later expanded into a book called *Blaming the Victim*, was something less than finely tuned — for example, he said that out-of-wedlock childbearing merely looked like a black problem because white illegitimacy was underreported — but the slogan was tremendously influential. It recast the whole long-emerging issue of the social ills of the ghettos as a question of whose fault it was, poor blacks' or white society's. If it was white society's fault, then efforts to acculturate black migrants were beside the point, and offensive; Ryan devoted a chapter of his book to attacking the idea of the culture of poverty for being just another form of blaming the victim. In a matter of weeks after the release of the Moynihan Report, it was impossible to convene a meeting of the leading liberal thinkers on the ghettos that would have the friendly tone of Shriver's meetings at the beginning of 1964. The subtle differences between liberals and left-liberals became, because of the Moynihan Report and the escalation in Vietnam, a bitter split.

It was still some months before the SNCC leaders Willie Ricks and Stokely Carmichael, on a march through the Mississippi Delta, electrified audiences by leading them in the chant, "We want black power!" In black America, especially among civil rights activists and intellectuals, the Moynihan Report helped to set the stage for that resonant moment. Moynihan, following Elkins, seemed to be denying blacks a usable past. Just at the time when the black privileged classes were struggling to rid themselves of their traditional distaste for the black poor (and by extension for their own blackness), Moynihan was encouraging the public to think of poor blacks as a breed apart. Some civil rights leaders, such as King, responded to the Moynihan Report in muted tones, but most were furious — even such members of the old guard as Bayard Rustin, and James Farmer of CORE.

Young academics, black and white, set to work producing answers to Moynihan. Historians rewrote the history of slavery to emphasize the strengths of the slaves' families, and sociologists described the female-headed ghetto family as a logical adaptation to conditions there. Black intellectuals used the Moynihan Report as the take-off point for attacking the values of white society in general and of white social scientists and policymakers in particular. Joyce Ladner, a SNCC veteran who had joined the faculty at Howard, wrote in *tomorrow's tomorrow*, "Conceivably there will be no 'illegitimate' children and 'promiscuous' women in ten years if there are enough middle-class white women who decide that they are going to disavow the societal canons regarding childbirth and pre-marital sexual behavior." Andrew Billingsley, also of Howard, wrote, "The family is a creature of the society. And the greatest problems facing black families are problems which emanate from the white racist, militarist, ma-terialistic society which places higher priority on putting white men on the moon than putting black men on their feet on this earth"; and he wrote, "All the major institutions of society should abandon the single standard of excellence based on white European cultural norms."

Today the Moynihan Report stands as probably the most refuted doc-ument in American history (though of course its dire predictions about the poor black family all came true). Attacks on it are still being published. The practical effect of the controversy over it was exactly the opposite of what Moynihan intended — all public discussions in mainstream liberal circles of issues like the state of the black family and the culture of poverty simply ceased. At a planning session for the White House conference on race that Johnson had promised in his Howard speech, the man running the conference, Berl Bernhard, announced, "I want you to know that I have been reliably informed that no such person as Daniel Patrick Moy-nihan exists." The subject of the black family was stricken from the agenda of the conference itself, and the Moynihan Report was never mentioned during the proceedings.

Race relations inside the movement and in the social sciences — sup-posedly the two main sources of ideas for the new racial initiatives di-rected at the North — continued to worsen. In May 1966, at a meeting in Kingston Springs, Tennessee, Stokely Carmichael ran against John Lewis for the chairmanship of SNCC and won by one vote. Later that year, during a SNCC retreat at a resort in upstate New York owned by a black entertainer named Pegleg Bates, the leadership of the organiza-tion debated the question of asking the whites who held staff positions to resign. After that, all the white members of SNCC except Bob Zellner drifted away. Zellner hung on until a meeting in Atlanta in 1967, where he was planning to propose a new organizing campaign. "I was in one room, and the executive committee was in another," he says. "They offered me a compromise: you can do the project, but you can't come to meetings. I wouldn't accept that because SNCC never required second-class citizenship of anyone. Then they said, Okay, you can come to meet-

ings, but you can't vote. I said no. They finally said, Okay, good luck."
James Farmer left CORE, an institution with a quarter-century of interracial history behind it, and his successor, Floyd McKissick, made it a
SNCC-like, nationalist, all-black organization. The emergence of an
openly antiwhite strain in the civil rights movement — and, in particular,
of an openly anti-Semitic strain in the black-power movement — severely
curtailed the movement's ability to exert a moral claim on the nation.

At the elite universities that provided a supply of ideas about the domestic operations of the federal government, the acrimony over race was
probably even more intense and longer-lasting than it was inside the
movement. The extreme example was the experience of Edward Banfield,
a tall, thin, bespectacled stork of a man who was a professor of government at Harvard. Banfield had spent most of his early career at the
University of Chicago, writing about the Democratic Party machine
there and, especially, its reaction to the black migration. In 1968 he wrote
a book about black ghettos called *The Unheavenly City*. Banfield's stance
was that of the emotionless, infinitely reasonable, eternally skeptical conservative who calmly picks apart the meliorist liberal pieties of the day.
He presented his own views in a dolorous tone that implied that he would
have much preferred to come to some more hopeful conclusion but was
prevented from doing so by his commitment to remorseless logic. *The
Unheavenly City* actually said all the things that Moynihan had been accused of secretly believing: that the poverty of the black lower class was
self-generated, the product of its irredeemable "present-orientedness";
that antipoverty programs couldn't work; that racism was not the cause
of the problems in the ghettos.

At Harvard, Students for a Democratic Society, the leading white student radical group, held regular anti-Banfield demonstrations. He left
for a job at the University of Pennsylvania, and the leader of the Harvard
protests followed him there and enrolled in graduate school. One day
she led a group into his class to present him with a "Racist of the Year"
award. When the university didn't kick her out of school, Banfield returned to Harvard. A guest lecture on Adam Smith that he was invited
to give at the University of Toronto had to be delivered under police
protection, and a seminar scheduled for the following day was canceled
for security reasons. Demonstrators prevented him from delivering a
lecture at the University of Chicago; it was rescheduled for the next day,
but with a by-invitation-only audience of faculty members and a heavy
police guard. A seminar on *The Unheavenly City* at a British university

had to be canceled when it was discovered that all the copies of the book on reserve at the library had been vandalized—by faculty members, Banfield says. Banfield was hardly the typical academic policy intellectual, but nearly all discussions of the ghettos at universities took place in a charged atmosphere that, as his case demonstrated, could turn ugly. The atmosphere of easy, comfortable interaction on the subject of the ghettos between social scientists and the practical-minded men at the top of the government perceptibly dissipated.

The one government program most directly affected by the new mood was community action—it was the federal agency that seemed able to address the altered state of race relations. After Watts, Shriver began to make the case for community action as a riot-preventer; "Would they have preferred a Watts?" he said after the scandal at HARYOU broke. The logic of the attacks on the Moynihan Report led unerringly to community action as the one available cure for the ills of the ghettos; community action's rhetoric of empowerment fit perfectly with the idea that ghetto society was not in any way weak or flawed or in need of middle-class outsiders to take it by the hand. Unlike other government agencies, community action's local offices were usually physically in the ghettos, the most visible federal presence there. The maximum feasible participation clause offered the black-power movement a possible beachhead for organizational activities in the North, with the community action agencies providing a link between the new nationalist generation of movement leaders and their hoped-for constituency in the slums.

The possibility of blacks in the North achieving political power through the traditional means of winning elective office still seemed extremely remote, and that increased the allure of community action as the only available means for black people to control political institutions that affected their lives. "If you'd told people in 1966 that Africans would have three hundred mayors, they wouldn't have believed you," Stokely Carmichael, who has since changed his name to Kwame Ture, now says. The strongest advocate of the movement's engaging in elective politics was Bob Moses. "The tool for organizing in the Northern cities is political activity," he says. "Running people for office. But you couldn't get people to think like that. It was hard to get people to think about using the electoral process as an organizing tool. In the movement, the commitment was to leadership more than organizing—media leadership. You couldn't export sit-ins or voter registration to the North. Community action was a government-funded program, which is different from the

Mississippi Freedom Democratic Party, which was an independent political effort. The traditional route in the cities is through politics. That was not clearly articulated in the 1960s." Moses was not in a position to communicate his skepticism about community action, though, because he was living in Africa at the time, and feeling that his own efforts to become involved in politics had turned to dust at the 1964 Democratic Convention in Atlantic City.

In most of the North's big cities, the interplay between the black-power movement and the community action program was an essential part of the fabric of the war on poverty. Some of the officials of community action, such as Fred Hayes, go so far as to say that if there had been no black-power movement, maximum feasible participation would have turned out to be the insignificant bit of boilerplate Shriver expected it to be. Certainly all of the greatest controversies of the community action program had to do with the unbridgeable gap between the black-power movement and the political system. In Oakland, California, after the mayor refused to cooperate with the OEO, the community action grant went to a nationalist organization. The Black Panther Party — nationalists with guns and uniforms, who became the most famous black radical group of the period because of their gun battles with the police and their links to privileged white liberals — was actually founded in an Oakland community action office where the party's chairman, Bobby Seale, a former leader of the Soul Students Advisory Council at Merritt Junior College, had an administrative job with a poverty program. In New York, a HARYOU affiliate gave a grant to the poet and playwright LeRoi Jones to stage street theater; one of his plays had Rochester, the black valet on Jack Benny's popular radio and television shows, rising up and killing his white oppressors. Within a couple of years of its birth, community action had the reputation of being not only a black program — the perception that Shriver had wanted so badly to avoid — but a black radical program.

In Washington no less than in the field, black power became a source of tension for the OEO. Adam Clayton Powell publicly renounced the use of the words "Negro" and "integration," and called on Shriver to resign. Inside the OEO, supporters and critics of black power were constantly at odds; a substantial group wanted to give grants to nationalist-oriented projects and forge close ties with the black power movement, and it struggled constantly against Shriver's desire to keep the OEO politically respectable. Kwame Ture says he was once offered a $35,000-

a-year job with the OEO. The internal memo traffic, especially from the OEO evaluation division, is full of moral fervor about the rightness and efficacy of tilting the community action agencies toward the black-power movement and away from the mayors. The sudden death of the liberal consensus about race relations and social programs made it impossible for Shriver to steer the OEO toward the entrenched status that most government agencies quickly manage to achieve.

As for Moynihan, he lost his race in New York and withdrew to academia. He became understandably bitter over the way he had been treated. He, the high government official with the keenest understanding of the problems of the ghettos, the issuer of the direst warnings of the trouble to come; he, who had grown up in a poor fatherless home himself and knew the pain of it at first hand — he was now being portrayed as, in effect, the Sheriff Clark of the North. "If my head were sticking on a pike at the South West Gate to the White House grounds the impression would hardly be greater," he wrote in 1966 to Harry McPherson, his closest friend in the upper reaches of the Johnson White House.

Moynihan continued to present himself as the champion of a government policy to keep families together — he began calling for the establishment of a Western Europe–style "family allowance" under which every American family, regardless of need, would get a government grant — but he stopped mentioning the racial component of the family issue. As he wrote to McPherson, "obviously one can no longer address oneself to the subject of the Negro family as such." In a combative moment after his report was published, he contracted to write a book on the black family, but he dropped that project. He began to develop a new preoccupation besides social policy: the danger posed to the American polity by the left, as demonstrated by the reaction to his report. In 1967, he wrote an article for *Commentary* called "The President & the Negro: The Moment Lost," in which he blamed the attacks on the report for dissipating the political consensus for healing the ghettos that had built up by the summer of 1965; "The liberal Left can be as rigid and destructive as any force in American life," he wrote.

Ordinarily, when a government official leaves Washington in a hail of criticism, his inevitable sour musings afterward are interesting but not important. Moynihan's case was different. His bitterness mattered a great deal, because, unlike everyone he served with in the two Democratic administrations of the 1960s, he would be back in power.

Lyndon Johnson, according to his aides, never read the Moynihan Report. His attitude toward it was, in the words of Bill Moyers, "I don't know what was in there, but whatever it was, stay away from it." Fully as much as Moynihan, though, he was wounded by attacks from the left when they came his way, which they soon did.

There can be no doubt but that Johnson's consuming dream was to be a great — the greatest — liberal president. That he hadn't expected to get the job only invested him with the zealous appreciation of the chance he had been given that anyone who is granted an unanticipated reprieve has. Johnson had spent many years pursuing his voracious ambitions. He had a lot to atone for, and nothing left to achieve but redemption.

Johnson may have made the requisite remarks about living up to the standard set by John F. Kennedy, but his real mark was Franklin Roosevelt. Once, while strolling through the White House with Hugh Sidey of *Time* magazine, Johnson stopped at a bust of FDR and caressed it. "Look at the *strength* in that face!" he told Sidey. Roosevelt's achievements, and not Kennedy's, were of Johnsonian scale, and Johnson knew exactly what it was that Roosevelt hadn't been able to do: Establish free medical care for the poor. Get federal aid to education through Congress, so that students in poor school districts would have the same chance in life as everybody else. Guarantee blacks in the South the right to vote, and the other appurtenances of full citizenship. Break the hold of the Southern segregationists on the Congress and the Democratic Party. Heal, finally, the wounds left by the Civil War and Reconstruction and bring the country together. Nobody had been able to do that — not Washington or Jefferson, not Lincoln, not Roosevelt. Johnson thought that given his skills, his historical moment, and his roots in the South, he could.

The only real measures of presidential achievement for Johnson were tangible ones. No charisma, no tone-setting, no moral philosophizing for him — he would build a record. Johnson was a totally political man, a government provincial. He had no hobbies, read no books, and could barely sit through a movie. One of his Cabinet officers remembers going to see him on a Sunday at Camp David and finding him on the phone with a friend in Texas running down the results of local school board elections there — just to relax, as it were. He wanted to set world records in politics and government, as a star athlete would in sports. "Get those coonskins up on the wall," he would tell the people around him. He decided he wanted to desegregate four thousand Southern school districts by September 1965, and as the deadline approached he had an aide call the commissioner of education daily: How many more have you brought in? What's the count? (Johnson himself would wander into his aide's office periodically to say, "Get 'em! Get 'em! Get the last ones!") On the day before Congress went on its Easter recess in 1965, when Johnson's lobbyists were sweating to finish up the many bills they were working on already, he called one of them to say, "Well, can't you get another one or two yet this afternoon?"

Johnson did not expend his energies during his presidency with a politician's customary caution; he saw himself as something like a political version of Phidippides, the courier in ancient Greece who dropped dead after running all the way from Marathon to Athens (though the reference would have been lost on him), using up everything he had in order to produce a timeless feat. It was a point of pride with him that he was doing things that would hurt him politically. "Every day while I'm in office, I'm going to lose votes," he told one aide; "I will probably lose a million votes a month," he told another in the great days after the 1964 election. After the Civil Rights Act passed, he told aides, accurately, "I think we just gave the South to the Republicans." There was at times a recklessness to the way he spent his mandate. He first submitted the Fair Housing Act, the one piece of liberal legislation that most terrified members of Congress, a few months before the 1966 midterm elections.

In return for his sacrifices, Johnson wanted to be loved — not by the old Southern crocodiles on Capitol Hill, whom he knew he would alienate, and not by bosses like Mayor Daley, whose implacable air of control made him uncomfortable, but by all the people whose wholehearted admiration he had not been able to win before: the little people; the blacks and the Mexican-Americans; the college students; the liberals; the professors and writers. These were the people for whom Johnson was doing more than any president ever had. When he began to sense, in 1965, that they did not love him — that, in fact, their hero was Robert Kennedy, newly ensconced in the Senate — it tore him apart, brought his everpresent suspicion and insecurity more and more to the fore, and ensured that he and Kennedy, however similar their goals, would always work at cross-purposes.

By the summer of 1965, Johnson's obsession with Kennedy had already progressed so far that Harry McPherson wrote a memo pleading with him to stop worrying whether his Cabinet members were more loyal to the Kennedys or to him and to stop opposing good policies just because Kennedy was for them. McPherson was highly skilled in the art of handling Johnson, and he took pains in the memo to show that he fully understood Johnson's own view of Kennedy:

> He is trying to put himself into a position of leadership among liberal Senators, newspapermen, foundation executives, and the like. Most of these people mistrusted him in the past, believing him (rightly) to be a man of narrow sensibilities and totalitarian instincts. . . . as we know the intellectuals are as easy a lay as can be found. I can imagine them believing that, although Bobby is an absolutist with little sense of the subtle shadings of an argument, and little tolerance for those who cross him, they can still *use him* to get across radical ideas. . . . The Kennedys are handsome and dashing, they support fashionable artists, and they can pay for almost anything. They support a great many good causes. And to some people even their rudeness and ruthlessness is exciting.

It tormented Johnson that Kennedy, who was not even passing bills, who was merely a symbolic figure, was attracting such a following. He told Moyers once, in exasperation over the liberal world's failure to see through Kennedy, "That boy rode around this town in a maroon convertible! You can't win respect in this town doing that." Johnson was well aware that Kennedy and his circle didn't respect him either, and regarded as laughable his picture of himself as a strong, sophisticated man of affairs. For years Johnson had taken great pains with his grooming and clothes. He was a graceful ballroom dancer; he liked to think of himself as elegant. And yet John Kennedy was well known to have considered Johnson vain, ungainly, crude — almost a comic figure.

After the assassination of his brother, Robert Kennedy's contempt for Johnson turned into an obsessive hatred. He fastened on Johnson as the symbol of the end of Camelot, and refused to recognize his achievements. Well after the assassination, he customarily referred to his brother as "the President" and to Johnson as "Johnson." When the Civil Rights Act was signed, Kennedy sent his assistant John Doar a pen in a frame with a photograph of the signing ceremony (which shows Kennedy in the center of the front row of the audience, staring desolately into the middle distance); the inscription read, "Pen used to sign President Kennedy's civil rights bill."

The black ghettos were an area where Bobby Kennedy especially felt that his understanding surpassed Johnson's. Kennedy had been visiting ghettos for years, whereas to Johnson they were terra incognita. The Watts riots came as a complete surprise to Johnson, a betrayal by people who should have been grateful for all he had done for them. Kennedy knew about the explosive anger in the ghettos long before Watts, because of his meeting with James Baldwin. Johnson would never have had such a meeting; his own favorite story about the horrors of racism had to do with the time his servants, Helen and Gene Williams, transported his dog from Washington to Texas and were unable to stay in motels or eat in restaurants. He had a hard time treating the civil rights landmarks of his own administration with the dignity they deserved. He summoned Louis Martin to the White House for the announcement of the appointment of Robert Weaver as the first black Cabinet member — an appointment he had already delayed making for months on end, humiliating Weaver — by saying, "I was sitting in the toilet here and I got to thinking about you." A month before election day in 1964, Johnson made a speech in Louisiana in which he said about Southern voters, "All they ever hear at election time is nigger, nigger, nigger" — and yet, he never dropped his own lifelong habit of occasionally using the word "nigger" in private.

Johnson felt uncomfortable with civil rights leaders to the left of Roy Wilkins and Whitney Young, including Martin Luther King, whom Johnson considered to be vain, preachy, communist-influenced, and, when King began to oppose the Vietnam War, a man who cared more about posturing than helping his own people — "the crown prince of the Vietniks," as Harry McPherson wrote Johnson. In September 1966, Nicholas Katzenbach suggested to McPherson that the White House "informally and quietly" try to talk Wilkins, Young, and King into "establishing a militant but peaceful organization of young people which could successfully compete with SNCC." McPherson wrote Johnson that "there is no longer any need to have SNCC and CORE represented" at White House meetings on civil rights.

Kennedy, on the other hand, tried to maintain relations with new-generation black leaders, and made himself a champion of advanced notions for helping the ghettos, starting with community action. Johnson's conception of the road to black advancement after the vanquishing of segregation was entirely old-fashioned: "vote power" and better schools. "He didn't believe *anything* would work but politics," says Louis Martin. "He told me once, 'What the hell, you got an awful lot of warm bodies.' He felt politics was the only way to move blacks. He said Paul Douglas would vote like Jim Eastland [the segregationist senator from Mississippi] if he came from down there, and vice versa." Johnson told Elizabeth Wickenden, "If they give blacks the vote, ol' Strom Thurmond will be kissing every black ass in South Carolina." (After the Supreme Court decision in *Brown* v. *Board of Education* came down in 1954, Johnson had told Wickenden's husband, Arthur Goldschmidt, "It's too bad, they shouldn't have taken up schools, they should have done voting rights first.")

Johnson's relentlessly political approach to the presidency and to racial issues was itself a strike against him in Robert Kennedy's eyes. A few weeks after the assassination, Kennedy told Arthur Schlesinger, "My brother barely had a chance to get started — and there is so much now to be done — for the Negroes and the unemployed and the school kids and everyone else who is not getting a decent break in our society. . . . The new fellow doesn't get this. He knows all about politics and nothing about human beings." Everything seemed to be a game to Johnson; nothing was important enough to be immune from his addiction to scheming. On the very day Johnson was to appoint Henry Fowler as Secretary of the Treasury, with Fowler waiting to be introduced to the press, an aide to Kennedy who happened to be in Johnson's office watched in amazement as he called up a senator and floated another man's name for the job, *pour le sport*.

Johnson was especially galled that the intellectuals, into whose universities he had poured more money than any other president, couldn't appreciate his passion and his achievement in race relations. Robert Wood, his deputy secretary of housing and urban development, once got a telegram from Johnson asking him to count up the number of people in the administration with Ph.D.s from Harvard and MIT and then to see if there were more of them than Kennedy had had. Wood was put in charge of a task force on urban affairs by Johnson, which, because Johnson was fanatically secretive, operated out of unidentified offices at the United States Maritime Commission; then Johnson leaked a list of the task force's members to the press in order to prove that he had eggheads working for him.

In 1966, several of Johnson's aides began taking trips to leading universities to meet with groups of intellectuals and ask for suggestions about domestic policy. Quite often the response was that because of the war in Vietnam, they would not cooperate. "So long as the President persists in these policies, there is no hope at all for expanding the Great Society. . . . So count me out," William Leuchtenberg, then of Columbia University, wrote back. Robert Eisner, of Northwestern University, suggested additional spending on the ghettos of $50 billion a year (roughly half of the federal budget), but added, "I must stress, the war has contributed to a profound alienation from this Administration of intellectuals and social scientists whose efforts would be essential to the domestic revolution required."

Robert Kennedy, privately contemptuous of Johnson for years, began to position himself publicly as a critic of the administration — not just of its handling of the war but also of its insufficient response to the crisis in the ghettos. In the fall of 1965, Johnson opened up what was essentially a second front in the war on poverty, by pushing through the legislation that created the Department of Housing and Urban Development and, at the same time, instructing Robert Wood's secret task force to formulate an ambitious new program for the ghettos. The task force developed what became HUD's first great mission, the Model Cities program, which was supposed to spend billions to rehabilitate the ghettos physically and otherwise, atoning for the sins of urban renewal by fixing slums up rather than tearing them down. In the spring of 1966, after the plans for Model Cities had been made public, Kennedy arrived late at a small dinner attended by several administration officials and delivered a tirade against the new program. "He said, 'It's too little, it's nothing, we have to do twenty times as much,'" says Wood, who was there. During this period, a California real estate developer named Victor Palmieri was summoned to the White House to be offered a job with Model Cities. When he said no, he was ushered into the Oval Office. "Then, forty-five minutes of ridiculous browbeating," he says. "Johnson said, 'I know you, you're one of those Kennedy-lovers.'"

In 1967, Kennedy made a well-publicized trip through Mississippi to hold Senate hearings on hunger, helped to orchestrate hearings on the "urban crisis" (as the problems of the ghettos had become known) that were critical of the Johnson administration, and proposed bills to create two million new public service jobs and to channel government and private investment into rebuilding the housing stock and the employment base in the ghettos. Johnson had no respect for this kind of position-striking; he considered the real purpose of all Kennedy's activities to be the embarrassment of Lyndon Johnson. (He was also convinced that Kennedy would have attacked him from the right if he hadn't escalated the war.) He opposed Kennedy's jobs bill, his ghetto-development bill, and an expansion of the food stamps program that was proposed after the hunger hearings. When Kennedy, after much planning and private fundraising (and the expenditure of some of his family fortune), opened a model ghetto-development project in Bedford-Stuyvesant, a black neighborhood in Brooklyn, Johnson dispatched Robert Wood to the dedication ceremony, where, Wood says, "in my little talk I announced that we'll give them two million dollars, which is one million more than Kennedy's giving."

One theory about why Johnson decided not to run for reelection in 1968 is that he was afraid of losing to Kennedy in the primaries and going down in history as the man who presided over the interregnum between two Kennedy administrations. Certainly he kept a close eye on Kennedy's presidential plans. In January 1968, he asked a group of his advisers for memos assessing Kennedy's intentions in the presidential race; he got back a batch of sycophantic assurances that Kennedy wouldn't dare run, couldn't win if he did, and would endanger the republic if the impossible somehow happened. "Bobby is an emotional fellow. He is quite capable of jumping off the deep end," wrote James Rowe. "He is an arrogant little *schmuck*," wrote John Roche. Johnson's decision to retire, and even Kennedy's assassination, in June 1968, didn't take any of the edge off his hatred. Just before leaving office, he personally cut from the federal budget the funds for a memorial to Kennedy at Arlington Cemetery.

Johnson began to look upon the Office of Economic Opportunity as a nest of his liberal enemies. He would affect to be unable to remember its name, referring to it only as "Shriver's group." Harry McPherson mimicked a typical Johnson tirade against the OEO in a note to Joseph Califano about a letter from a small-town Ohio Jaycee complaining about the OEO: "If you and Sarge weren't in this thing and always working and humping for that program that never mentions anybody's name we wouldn't get into this kind of problem with these people here. Neither one of you ever ran for constable and you just can't sit still for wanting to talk about this program everybody says is just criminal and wrong." Califano tried to solve the problem of the OEO's not mentioning the president's name enough by suggesting that Johnson's signature appear on the diploma of every child who completed the Head Start program, because "If they were to bear your signature, I think you would begin to receive much more credit for the progress that is being made." Johnson agreed. Still, his touchiness on the subject of the OEO was such that Califano once felt compelled to write Johnson a memo asking permission to deliver a five-minute speech about the OEO to a gathering of reporters.

"They're not against poverty, they're for Kennedy," Johnson told Bill Moyers. After reading a newspaper clipping about Kennedy and Shriver, Johnson sent it on to his rough-playing, conservative appointments secretary, Marvin Watson, with a note that said, "Marvin: Start keeping a file on these two." He told Wilbur Cohen that he considered virtually everyone at the OEO to be disloyal and a troublemaker. Several times he refused to let Cohen appoint people who had worked at the OEO to positions at HEW, saying, as Cohen remembered it, "Well, I don't want to appoint that fellow. He's from OEO." In one case Johnson turned down the candidacy for the number-two job at HEW of a lifelong federal bureaucrat who had briefly served at the OEO, and instead put in a Texas crony of his who immediately got into a scandal and had to resign.

In his 1967 economic message, Johnson said about poverty, on which he had declared unconditional war only three years earlier, "There is no wonder drug which can suddenly conquer this ancient scourge of man." In his valedictory State of the Union address, in 1969, he gave an uncharacteristically muted assessment of the war on poverty ("The antipoverty program has had many achievements. It also has some failures"), and asked Congress "to improve the administration of the poverty program by reorganizing portions of it and transferring them to other agencies." (Even during his period of maximal disapproval of the OEO, though, Johnson did find room in his heart to have Job Corps trainees in Texas put to work on beautifying the commemorative park opposite his ranch.)

In the final stages of his presidency the idea of large-scale government programs for the ghettos had become so bound up in Johnson's mind with liberal opposition to him that he became positively hostile toward it. "I realize that currently your view is to make substantial cuts in Great Society programs," Califano wrote him in December 1967; in September 1968, Johnson ordered up a memo on who had thought up the idea of the Great Society, anyway, and was told that the culprits were Richard Goodwin and Bill Moyers, both long since departed from the White

House staff and deep in Johnson's bad graces. He was immensely suspicious of the Kerner Commission, which he had appointed after the terrible Detroit riot in July 1967 — 4,700 federal troops flown in from military bases to restore order, 43 deaths — to determine how future riots could be avoided. Johnson had been stunned by Watts, but after Detroit he was simply angry. Nothing bothered him more than seeing the country he had wanted to knit together spinning out of control instead. He was particularly haunted by the idea of the presidency being undermined by insidious forces; the exception to his aversion to movies was *Seven Days in May*, a thriller about a president being surprised and toppled by a military coup, which he watched over and over.

There were 164 race riots in the first nine months of 1967; it seemed at least possible that a full-scale national race war might break out. Johnson became convinced that the riots were being centrally orchestrated by someone, possibly the communists — a view much encouraged by J. Edgar Hoover of the FBI, who sent Johnson regular confidential reports on "Current Racial Developments" that quoted informers' predictions of mayhem in the ghettos and ended with the assurance that "the situation is being closely watched." "The FBI always knew when and where the next riot was going to take place and it had always taken place when and where they predicted," he told Katharine Graham, the publisher of the *Washington Post*. Shriver regularly had to reassure Johnson that OEO employees were not instigating some of the riots; in the fall of 1967 he reported that only sixteen OEO employees had been arrested for rioting during the previous summer, which could not have done much to lay Johnson's suspicions to rest.

Johnson's old friend David Ginsburg, who was the Kerner Commission's executive director, says that when Johnson called him in after his appointment, "he made it very clear that in his view it was simply not possible to have so many outbreaks at the same time without someone orchestrating it." As the commission began its work, Johnson quickly sensed that its dominant member was going to be John Lindsay, the sleek liberal Republican mayor of New York, rather than the chairman, Otto Kerner, the governor of Illinois. Johnson disliked Lindsay to begin with, and suspected him of wanting to turn the commission into a vehicle for his presidential ambitions. He began to insist that Charles Schultze, the budget director, cut back its funding, so Schultze had to slip the commission money in odd places in the federal budget that Johnson wouldn't notice. Sure enough, Lindsay preempted the report, which was lengthy and sober, by prevailing on the commission at the last minute to begin it with a dramatic executive summary written by his staff. It is the summary, not the report, that contains the famous warning about America's becoming "two societies, one black, one white — separate and unequal"; Ginsburg added the only other still-remembered line in the report, which blamed the condition of the ghettos on "white racism," and also arranged without Johnson's knowledge for the report to be published as an instant mass-market paperback a few days after its release.

Johnson was furious about the report, not least because it ruled out the possibility of a conspiracy behind the riots. He felt it put him in an impossible position — he couldn't respond to it in a way that matched the bits of angry language that had gotten the headlines, and he certainly couldn't get through Congress the billions of dollars' worth of new government programs for the ghettos that the report recommended. Despite the entreaties of his staff, he refused to comment publicly on the report, refused to allow the commission to present it to him, refused even to sign the form letters his staff drew up thanking the members for their work. "I just can't sign this group of letters," he told McPherson. "I'd be a hypocrite. And I don't even want it known that they got this far. . . . Otherwise somebody will leak that I wouldn't sign them. Just file them — or get rid of them."

On April 10, 1968, right after Martin Luther King was assassinated, with riots being quelled in Chicago, Baltimore, Washington, and other cities, Califano sent Johnson a long memo suggesting that he react to the crisis by making an address to a joint session of Congress, adding billions to antipoverty programs, and appointing well-known experts to look into a major reordering of the government's fiscal priorities. Johnson, who rarely wrote anything down, scrawled angry comments all over the memo. To Califano's reminder that he had promised to address a joint session of Congress, Johnson responded, "I promised nothing. I stated my intention only. Since changed by riots." To the suggestion that he ask the advice of "someone with a completely open mind," like McGeorge Bundy, the former hawkish national security adviser who was then the very visibly liberal head of the Ford Foundation, Johnson's answer was, "Ha! Ha!" At the end of the memo he wrote, "Forget it."

THE COMMUNITY action program was without doubt a political failure. In 1967, the OEO nearly died when Congress, angry about community action, missed the regular deadline to renew its appropriation. It survived only because Congresswoman Edith Green seized on the agency's troubles as an occasion to realize her long-cherished dream of defanging the maximum feasible participation clause, which she did by attaching an amendment to the appropriation bill giving elected officials control over one-third of the seats on the local community action boards. A few months later, Johnson appointed Shriver ambassador to France—a reward, Horace Busby says, for the "What Bobby Thinks" conversation back in 1963.

Practically, community action was not a success, either, at least in the way it was supposed to be. "I'd guess the performance, by numbers, was worse than the bureaucracy would have done," says Fred Hayes. There is no clear example of a community action agency in a poor neighborhood accomplishing either the original goal of reducing juvenile delinquency or the subsequent goal of reducing poverty. It was part of the official mythology of the OEO that one or another community action agency had helped "cool" a black ghetto where a riot might otherwise have broken out, but overall, street crime by teenagers became much more severe in the ghettos during the heyday of the war on poverty, for reasons having nothing to do with the OEO. Most of the ghettos became poorer, too, as their better-off residents continued to move out. Hundreds of the community action agencies have survived and even flourished long after the federal government's support for them evaporated, but most of them are in the traditional social service business that the community action program was supposed to be a rejection of.

Among the founding fathers of the war on poverty, the case made for the success of community action is that it trained a new generation of black leaders in the ghettos, many of whom went on to win elective office. "Parren Mitchell was on the street!" says Shriver, referring to the Baltimore community action official who later became a congressman. It is hard to believe, though, that these leaders wouldn't have emerged anyway; given the number of blacks the great migration brought to the cities, it was inevitable that black candidates would begin to win elections, whether or not the federal government provided them with leadership training. Parren Mitchell, to use Shriver's example, was the brother of

Clarence Mitchell, who as chief lobbyist for the NAACP was one of the most prominent black men in America. Probably a better argument for a positive legacy of the war on poverty is that it raised its general subject matter to the level of national concern, and so helped pave the way for successful programs like Medicare, Medicaid, and food stamps.

Still, community action did achieve an important victory of a kind: it helped to establish in Washington the idea that the ghettos could be transformed into stable, decent neighborhoods — that this would be the solution to all the troubles that followed in the wake of the great migration. Community action, originally an idea for delivering government social services in poor neighborhoods more efficiently and sympathetically, mutated over the course of the 1960s into the concept of community development, in which the government would turn poor neighborhoods into middle-class ones. The father of both ideas was Robert Kennedy.

Kennedy never thought of himself as a liberal politician. In 1964 he told an interviewer, "What my father said about businessmen applies to liberals. . . . They're sons of bitches. The people who are selfish are interested in their own singular course of action and do not take into consideration the needs or requirements of others or what can ultimately be accomplished. They're not very helpful, I think." Until the end of his life, his pantheon included men who were anathema to the left; his aide Peter Edelman remembered, "Kennedy was a great admirer of Herbert Hoover . . . and he was a great admirer of Douglas MacArthur." In his last campaign, in the 1968 California presidential primary, at a time when he was hero to much of the long-haired upper-middle-class youth of America, a bearded man wearing a turtleneck shirt stood up in the audience after a speech and asked Kennedy why he wouldn't publicly repudiate J. Edgar Hoover. "Because people like you are asking me to," Kennedy said.

Ever since his election to the Senate in 1964, though, Kennedy had been instinctively picking up the pace of his search for a political stance different from the hard-nosed pragmatism of his early years. He no longer had to be the fierce protector of his brother's political interests (especially against lost-cause-loving liberals). His right-wing father, to whom he was extremely close, had been incapacitated for several years because of a stroke and was not able to exert influence on him. His constituency was a liberal, sophisticated one long accustomed to being represented in the Senate by crusaders. His essential aides in the Senate,

Peter Edelman and Adam Walinsky, were both impassioned young liberals. Still Kennedy was not a creature of the New York *monde*. Homosexuals made him, in Edelman's words, "extremely uncomfortable." In 1967 he innocently asked Frank Mankiewicz, who was his press secretary by then, "What's a repertory company?" Politically, there was never a moment in his career as an elective officeholder when he didn't have an eye on the national electorate, which was much more conservative than New York's.

During his first year in the Senate, Kennedy concentrated on federal aid to education — one of Johnson's legislative triumphs in 1965, and a traditional liberal cause — as the key to helping the ghettos. Soon he decided it was insufficient. In January 1966, he signaled the broadening of his horizons by delivering speeches about the ghettos on three successive days in New York. He was still quite a ways from community development. The first speech was mainly integrationist: he condemned segregation in public housing, suggested enrolling ghetto children in suburban schools, and called for "ending the isolation of the ghettos" — pretty much the course of action being taken individually by millions of members of the black middle class. The second speech was about the need for government job-training and job-creation efforts; and the third was an attack on the welfare system for breaking up families. By May of the same year, though, he declared that he had a new "overriding theme and goal — the involvement of the community," and in December he announced his own project to rehabilitate Bedford-Stuyvesant, which was the most-publicized and best-connected community development program and so served as the model for many more around the country.

Many forces had been at work to push Kennedy in this direction. With any program for America's ghettos that required the passage of major legislation, he would inevitably run afoul of Johnson; but a single project in New York City, funded mainly by donations from corporations and foundations, was something he could get up and running on his own. All the other ideas he mentioned in his January speeches had become politically problematic. The welfare rolls had grown rapidly over the past few years, creating a great deal of antiwelfare sentiment in the white working class. By now liberals (including Edelman and Walinsky) were united behind the idea of a government-guaranteed minimum income, but it was politically unpopular and never sat right with the moralistic Kennedy anyway. (In Indiana during the presidential campaign of 1968, when the Kennedy entourage was riding in a bus on the way to a speech at Purdue

University, Edelman cornered Kennedy: "I said, 'Senator, we've prepared a position paper which would have you coming out for a guaranteed income.' He said, 'I'm against that.' I said, 'No, you're not. You've said this and this and this in the past.' He said, 'I know, but I'm against it.' Meaning he was not about to go out in a presidential campaign and say the words 'guaranteed income.' ")

Jobs programs, an enduring cause of Kennedy's and one he never backed away from, had the drawback of unlikelihood. Of the whole array of government antipoverty programs, job training and job creation are by far the most expensive — much more expensive even than giving every poor person enough cash every year to get above the poverty line. A fact oft quoted by opponents of the Job Corps was that it cost more to send a kid to a Job Corps camp than to Harvard for a year. The cost of jobs programs was one reason why they were never more than a minor element of the war on poverty. In January 1965, Kermit Gordon wrote a memo to Johnson outlining a $1.4 billion program to lower the national unemployment rate below 4.5 per cent and create 600,000 unskilled government jobs, "particularly in the big cities" (that is, for black migrants). The memo is heartbreaking to read retrospectively, because, far more than community action, the jobs program would have helped poor people in the ghettos, and it represents the road not taken. Gordon obviously wrote it at Johnson's request rather than on his own initiative, and he filled it with signals meant to allow Johnson to turn the idea down. He emphasized the cost, the "stigma of a 'new WPA,'" and the inevitability of "substantial problems (unions, city civil service, etc.) if this program were used to increase regular city payrolls." Johnson said no. Within a few months, the escalation of the war in Vietnam was constraining the federal budget, and of course the unions and the civil service continued to stand in the way of job-creation efforts unless they were confined to the performance of intangible tasks inside the ghettos.

Actual racial integration was even more politically perilous. Every elected politician who represented cities knew how intense white opposition was to integrated schools and housing. Local activism aimed at preventing the federal government from ordering busing as a way of integrating the public schools had already emerged in the Northern cities by the mid-1960s; there is actually an antibusing rider in the 1964 Civil Rights Act. In the 1966 congressional elections the Democrats lost forty-seven seats in the House. Paul Douglas, a staunch opponent of residential segregation, lost his Senate seat in Illinois. Ronald Reagan, in his first race for political office, took the California governorship away from Pat Brown, a liberal Catholic Democrat, by a substantial margin, in part thanks to his constant hammering on issues like welfare and riots; Brown told *The New York Times* afterward, "Whether we like it or not, people want separation of the races." Bill Moyers remembers Johnson telling him, after Reagan's election, "You see, these people aren't a flash in the pan. The very thing we're doing in the South, combined with what the blacks are doing to *us* in the North — it'll move beyond George Wallace and become respectable." After the local elections of 1967, Johnson's aide Ben Wattenberg wrote to him, "In Gary [Indiana], 90% of the whites, normally Democratic, voted Republican. In Cleveland, 80%. [The victorious Democratic candidates for mayor in Gary and Cleveland were black.] In Boston, about 50%, but Kevin White [the new Democratic mayor] is not a Negro. . . . In Gary, one block away from Croatian Hall, in a white ethnic precinct that was 68% Democratic in 1964, the count was 93% Republican."

Unelected federal officials felt the pressure too. Johnson passed the Elementary and Secondary Education Act, which finally put into law the long-deferred liberal goal of giving federal aid to local schools, in 1965. A week after the new money started to flow to school districts, Francis Keppel, the commissioner of education, sent a telegram to the Illinois state superintendent of education threatening to withhold funds from Chicago unless something was done about school segregation there. "Chicago was by far the best case in the North of de facto segregation," Keppel remembered. "And I felt a little gutless to be whacking away at the Southern districts. Let's move North; we had the money now. Well, the shit hit the fan. The state superintendent was a basketball coach. He just disappeared. Daley hit the ceiling."

As usual, Daley called Johnson. Keppel said Johnson later told him, "Frank, you know what Daley said to me? He said he could be difficult." Johnson summoned Wilbur Cohen to the White House and told him to go to Chicago and resolve the situation, saying, as Cohen remembered it, "Mayor Daley thinks there is a conspiracy in the federal government of people in the OEO, the Labor Department, and HEW to embarrass him." When Cohen and Daley met, Cohen said, "The general attitude of Daley was, 'You're taking away the funds from me without ever having consulted me. You never told me about the issue; you never consulted me or asked me what my views are; you never tried to get me to resolve it; all you do is you send a telegram and I read it in the newspaper.'"

Cohen worked out a toothless but face-saving agreement with the Chicago school board, and Keppel was soon relieved of his duties as commissioner of education and made, as he put it, "assistant secretary of HEW in charge of nothing." Keppel's successor as commissioner of education, Harold Howe, was stripped of his civil rights enforcement responsibilities in 1967 after having offended Judge Howard Smith of Virginia, chairman of the House Rules Committee, on the integration issue.

In the spring of 1966, Johnson's Model Cities bill ran into heavy weather in Congress, in large part because John Sparkman of Alabama, chairman of the housing subcommittee in the Senate, felt that, as Robert Weaver wrote Johnson, "There are overt and hidden implications of racial integration in the proposal." One of Johnson's lobbyists wrote, "I think you will have to overcome ... the race problem" before the enabling legislation for Model Cities could pass Congress. Over the summer the bill's requirement that new housing be integrated was dropped, and in the fall Model Cities passed.

Robert Kennedy moved steadily away from the ardent condemnation of the isolation of the ghettos that he had laid out at the beginning of 1966. To embrace the cause of integrating the North would have cost him dearly with his white constituency, and by 1968 the civil rights movement was no longer pushing integration either. In a debate during the 1968 California primary campaign, his opponent, Eugene McCarthy, called for ending big-city residential segregation; Kennedy accused him of wanting "to take ten thousand black people and move them into Orange County."

Kennedy's political dream was to put together a coalition that united blue-collar whites in the North with people of color. Specifically, right up to the end he was counting on the support of Mayor Daley. The strategic advantage of community development was that it was a way for Kennedy to demonstrate his genuine and deeply felt concern about the ghettos without raising the issue of integration at all. Community development would be a first step, a way of turning the ghettos into the kind of launching pads for immigrant upward mobility that the Irish neighborhoods of Boston had been for Kennedy's own forebears. It was the kind of bold, streamlined, concentrated assault on a problem that Kennedy liked. It put him ahead of the crowd on a big national issue, which was where he always wanted to be.

The greatest success of his project in Bedford-Stuyvesant, and of most other community development efforts that have worked, was that it shored up the housing stock and thus stabilized Bedford-Stuyvesant as a residential neighborhood—although, like all ghettos, it continued to lose population. The greatest failure was in the attempt to create jobs by inducing businesses to locate in Bedford-Stuyvesant. Kennedy enlisted the support of a blue-chip board of investment bankers, foundation executives, and corporate board chairmen for the job-creation effort, and he put John Doar, the former assistant attorney general for civil rights, in charge of it, but only one corporation put a significant new plant in Bedford-Stuyvesant. That was IBM, which had a Democratic chairman, Thomas Watson, and two members of Kennedy's inner circle, Burke Marshall and Nicholas Katzenbach, in the upper ranks of its management.

Johnson was making a grand gesture in the direction of community development himself with the Model Cities program, which was launched at the same time as Kennedy's project in Bedford-Stuyvesant. Model Cities was conceived of as an improvement on—perhaps eventually a replacement for—the community action program. "I feel that the Community Action Program in urban areas has been superseded by the Model Cities effort," one of Califano's aides wrote to him in 1968. Model Cities would be run by the manageable Department of Housing and Urban Development instead of the unruly OEO, it would engage in at least one tangible activity, building housing, and it had a "citizen participation" requirement that was a much watered down version of community action's, so that there was no question about the mayors' controlling it.

All these differences from community action obscured a basic similarity: both programs were attempts to heal the slums from within—to produce, in the slang of the time, a gilded ghetto. Like community action, Model Cities was originally supposed to be a very limited demonstration program operating in only a few cities until it could be determined what worked and what didn't. In fact its name was "Demonstration Cities" until a Georgia congressman objected because, as Robert Weaver reported to Johnson, "he feels it suggests the image of racial conflict in the South." As soon as the lobbying for Model Cities began, it was expanded to a hundred and fifty cities so that it would be in more congressional districts; there was never a chance to field-test it. Still, people in the Johnson administration who had given up on community action maintained high hopes for Model Cities, because they believed in the concept of community development. A young intellectual at HUD wrote a long confidential memo in the fall of 1967 laying out various scenarios for the future of the ghettos. One of the more hopeful ones predicted, "Many middle-class Negroes, who could move to the suburbs if they wanted to, are encouraged by the positive results of 'black power' ideology and the growing sense of community generated by the Model Cities program, and decide to stay on in the central city."

It was not then, and for that matter still isn't, clearly understood by policymakers in Washington that the pattern in the ghettos was exactly the opposite: everybody who could get out did. Not only that, community development programs actually encouraged the outmigration, because they created white-collar government jobs that put money in the pockets of many ghetto residents and enabled them to leave. Vernon Jordan, who became head of the Urban League after the death of Whitney Young in 1971, was working in the late 1960s at the Southern Regional Council in Atlanta, which mounted a community development effort in a neighborhood called Vine City. "We were trying to help the indigenes, not the middle-class blacks," he says. "So we hired a woman named Doris Reed, who was poorly dressed and walked with her head down. Then she got her first paycheck. She started to smile a little. Then the next one. After about six months I met her at the elevator balancing boxes. She said, 'Mr. Jordan, today is moving day. I'm moving out of Vine City.' I said, 'What about helping the community?' She said, 'All my life I've wanted to get out.'"

Part of the appeal of community development was that it had no enemies. Everyone from nationalists who wanted black self-determination to conservative Republicans who wanted to avoid large, centrally run government programs liked it. In its rise as an idea, something broader was going on, though. By now, America had abandoned the *beau idéal* of a consensus society and become more openly pluralistic. The idea of ethnic neighborhoods as quasi-independent entities, so daring only a few years earlier, was now a standard part of mainstream thinking.

The black migration to the North had a great deal to do with this change. The millions of blacks who migrated did so in order to have lives more like those of most other Americans. Their presence in the North made the rest of the country more aware of African-American culture than it had ever been before. The awareness produced a dual reaction. On one hand, the black influence on national life greatly increased. Most of the substantial changes in the folkways of the white middle class during and after the 1960s had their roots in black life. Rock-and-roll music was an outgrowth of the Mississippi blues; the Rolling Stones named themselves after a song by Muddy Waters. The white protest movements—antiwar, feminist, environmental, gay rights—were modeled on the civil rights movement. The founders of SDS learned their techniques in Mississippi. A seminal event in the feminist movement was a rebellion by the women in SNCC at the Waveland, Mississippi, meeting in the fall of 1964. (The women's rights movement in the United States began in the 1840s as a rebellion within the abolitionist movement, so the women in SNCC were repeating a time-honored pattern.) The general abandonment by white youth of pseudo-aristocracy as its preferred style, in favor of the mores denoted by the ghetto terms "cool" and "hip," represented a black-to-white cultural transmission. The edge of disappointment with which blacks viewed the national enterprise had made its way into white America.

On the other hand, the migration hardly created a harmonious, racially synthesized country. It was disruptive; it engendered hostility. The fabric of city life in the United States changed forever. Some of the bitterness of race relations leached into city politics. The ideal of high-quality universal public education began to disappear. Street crime became an obsessive concern for the first time in decades. The beginning of the modern rise of conservatism coincides exactly with the country's beginning to realize the true magnitude and consequences of the black migration, and the government's response to the migration provided the conservative movement with many of its issues. The idea that government programs don't work, and can't work, comes out of the Great Society, and particularly the war on poverty; all through his political career, one of Ronald Reagan's favorite sayings was, "In the 1960s we fought a war on poverty, and poverty won." So does the idea that most middle-class people are paying too much federal income tax to support harebrained social betterment schemes, which was central to Reagan's (and therefore also George Bush's) rise to the presidency. In intellectual life, the neo-conservative movement, whose influence on Republican policy-making has been enormous, was founded by former liberals who lost faith in large part over the issue of race in the North; in Irving Kristol's famous apothegm, "a neo-conservative is a liberal who has been mugged by reality," it's not difficult to guess what color the mugger was.

As Lyndon Johnson predicted, the Republican Party seized upon the political opportunity presented by the Democrats' embrace of civil rights, and induced the South to switch from Democratic to Republican in presidential elections. The great migration then delivered the coup de grace to the Democrats as a presidential party: it hastened the movement of millions of middle-class white voters to the Republican suburbs, and it caused millions more blue-collar voters who didn't move to stop voting for the Democratic candidate for president. Richard Nixon narrowly lost the presidency in 1960 and narrowly won it in 1968; the biggest states that moved into his column the second time around were all ones where white backlash was a significant force — Illinois, New Jersey, Missouri, and North Carolina. The only way the Democrats could have maintained their presidential majority without the South was by hanging on to the urban whites of the North, and in that sense the community action program, which heightened the differences between Northern blacks and the white-ethnic political structures instead of muting them, hurt politically. Consensus was the Democrats' ticket and Johnson's dream; but Johnson, by letting his insecurity triumph over his natural instincts during the first weeks of his presidency, had let pluralism into the tent.

For blacks in the North, the main direct effect of the works of Lyndon Johnson was the creation of a great many new jobs for blacks in government — not the kind of ghetto leadership positions that loomed large in the minds of the founders of the war on poverty, but ordinary public payroll jobs. The political scientists Michael K. Brown and Steven P. Erie estimated in 1981 that the Great Society generated two million new government jobs, most of them nominally on state and local payrolls but funded by new federal programs in education, health, housing, and other areas of the welfare state. A disproportionate share of these jobs went to blacks. Brown and Erie said that black employment in public social welfare programs increased by 850,000 from 1960 to 1976 (a period during which the black middle class tripled in size), and many new government jobs were also created for blacks outside the social welfare sphere, for example in local transportation authorities and law enforcement agencies. In 1970 government employed 57 per cent of black male college graduates and 72 per cent of black female college graduates.

At the same time, the jobs that had drawn blacks to the North in the first place dried up. From 1960 to 1964, manufacturing employment increased nationally by 3 per cent but fell in New York, Chicago, Los Angeles, Philadelphia, and Detroit, and later the drop in urban unskilled manufacturing jobs became more precipitous. The economic base of black America, which had switched from agriculture to unskilled industrial labor in the 1940s, switched again in the sixties, from unskilled labor to government; the industrial age for African-Americans lasted for not even a full generation. There was some awareness within the Johnson administration that the war on poverty and its successor programs were creating a lot of jobs for blacks — Charles Schultze, the budget director, several times wrote memos urging Johnson to think of the OEO as a jobs program — but on the whole, one of the great ironies of Johnson's response to the problems of the ghettos was that while repeatedly rejecting the idea of a big jobs program for poor and poorly educated urban blacks whose traditional form of employment was evaporating, he in effect created just that for blacks with a decent education, who used their new prosperity to leave the ghettos where they were now employed as social workers.

At the level of national debate, the dependence of blacks on government employment has been continually condemned by everyone from Stokely Carmichael (who in his book *Black Power* called it "welfare colonialism") to conservative Republicans, but it was the hand black America was dealt. It wasn't altogether a bad one, although it didn't provide much help for the poorest people in the cities, who only became more isolated from the rest of society, black and white. Very soon, though, the expansion of government services, in which blacks now had such a strong vested interest, came under attack, and from an unlikely source: the intellectual champion of employment as the solution to America's racial crisis, Daniel Patrick Moynihan.

Moynihan's wide range of contacts included many Republicans, and his writing and thinking after the furor over his report on the black family became markedly more conservative; when Richard Nixon's presidency began, he landed a job on the White House staff as chief adviser on urban affairs. Moynihan retained his membership in the Democratic Party, but he saw his future in it as bleak. "I have been an active Democrat, and if they allow me (which alas I doubt) I will be one again," he wrote to H. R. Haldeman, Nixon's chief of staff, in 1969. His service to Nixon was not, to his mind, a brief bipartisan interlude in his career, but a crucial opportunity to affect the direction of the government. Never before had he even approached the influence he came to have in the Nixon administration, when for a time he truly had the ear of the president. Even during his current career as a Democratic senator from New

York, he has had much less influence on policy-making than he did in
1969 and 1970.

It was on the surface an odd pairing, Moynihan and Nixon. Moynihan
was entirely preoccupied with the issue of race in the North — his service
in three successive administrations made him the one person most continuously involved in formulating the government's response to the black
migration. For Nixon, race was a side issue. The two civil rights leaders
he dealt with most were Vernon Jordan of the Urban League and James
Farmer, formerly of CORE, who briefly worked in his administration.
"He didn't care about the basic issue," says Jordan; "He had no strong
feelings on any social issues," says Farmer. "He was capable of doing
either good or bad with equal facility. He made decisions based on politics, not right or wrong."

During the 1968 Republican Convention in Miami Beach, a last-
minute run at Nixon by Ronald Reagan caused Nixon's delegate strength
in the South suddenly to begin crumbling. To shore it up, Nixon held a
series of meetings with Southern delegates in which he laid out a new
go-slow position on racial matters. The nomination held; after the election he brought onto the White House staff a protégé of Strom Thurmond, the old segregationist who was a senator from South Carolina,
and began to implement a "Southern strategy" meant to reassure the
white South that it would not be subjected to radical racial change. The
political calculations of the Nixon administration didn't include blacks,
whom Nixon had conceded to the Democrats. As Moynihan reminded
Nixon in March 1969, he attained the presidency having won probably
the smallest percentage of black votes of any president in American
history.

Very occasionally Nixon entertained wistful hopes about discovering
a contingent of blacks who would vote for him — "30% who are potentially on our side," he once scribbled on the margin of a memo — but on
the whole he was far too much the realist to believe that he would ever
have a significant black constituency, and he knew that some of his white
support came from people who were voting on the basis of their resentment of blacks. "There were subliminal racial messages in a lot of Nixon's
campaigning," says John Ehrlichman, Nixon's chief domestic policy adviser. "It was subtler than code words. It was, 'I am on your side. I am
going to deal with it in a way you'll approve of.' I know he saw Johnson's
embrace of blacks as an opportunity. He exploited it." Ehrlichman says

that on two occasions, Nixon told him that he considered blacks to be less intelligent than whites. "He thought, basically, blacks were genetically inferior," Ehrlichman says. "In his heart he was very skeptical about their ability to excel except in rare cases. He didn't feel this way about other groups. He'd say on civil rights things, 'Well, we'll do this, but it isn't going to do any good.' He did use the words 'genetically inferior.' He thought they couldn't achieve on a level with whites."

The real link between Moynihan and Nixon, the obsession they shared, was a deep dislike of the left-liberal political culture that had grown so dramatically in the past three or four years and reached its height of influence during Nixon's first years in office. Both men had been through, and been deeply wounded by, the experience of being reviled by the left. As early as 1966, Moynihan was writing to Harry McPherson, "I have the feeling that you fellows, being Southern populist types do not really understand the Northern Left," and since then his views on the subject had only grown more pronounced. It was easy for Moynihan to conjure up for Nixon a nightmarish picture of the legions of Nixon-haters (who were also no doubt Moynihan-haters): Ivy League professors, black-power advocates, social-change-promoting foundation executives, peace-marching Georgetown hostesses, affluent student revolutionaries, and to-the-barricades journalists. While reading a description by Moynihan of Leonard Bernstein's fundraising party for the Black Panthers in 1970, Nixon wrote a note to himself: "The complete decadence of the American upper class intellectual elite." There was a close connection between these people and racial issues: in domestic politics, race was the means they would use to heap abuse on Nixon.

Moynihan, probably more than Nixon, came to see the left as a threat not just to him personally but to the basic social peace of the country. Unlike Nixon, Moynihan viewed the United States from the vantage point of a position within the intellectual subculture, where the left was a far more significant force than it was in national life generally, and his natural tendency toward overdramatization made him quick to perceive crises anyway. From where he sat, the state of the nation in those days of Kent State and Cambodia and My Lai seemed extremely dire. In May 1970, he reported to Nixon that the SDS had threatened to burn down his house in Cambridge and that his family had gone into hiding. ("Even so, I'm sticking here," he wrote. "I am choosing the interests of the administration over the interests of my children.") Later that year Moynihan told Nixon that ten-year-old John Moynihan was afraid his father would be assassinated. Moynihan believed that the overarching purpose of the Nixon administration had to be the Lincolnesque one of preserving the union. He wrote to Nixon just before his inauguration: "Your task, then, is clear: to restore the authority of American institutions. Not, certainly, under that name, but with a clear sense that what is at issue is the continued acceptance by the great mass of people of the legitimacy and efficacy of the present arrangements of American society." This would necessarily be a matter of political self-preservation for Nixon, as well as statesmanship. As Moynihan wrote to Nixon the following year, "*To be blunt, the people who brought down Johnson want to bring down Nixon.*"

Other people in the administration shared some of Nixon's hurts and resentments, but Moynihan had a special influence. Like Henry Kissinger on the foreign policy side, he had the ability, rare among high government officials and prized by Nixon, to put the activities of the administration in a sweeping historical context. "He's so stimulating," Nixon told Ehrlichman once. Moynihan was brimming with ideas for grand initiatives (a constitutional convention in 1976, a Nixon architectural policy, a new federal Department of Higher Education and Research) and with interesting predictions (feminism as a major social force, a series of urban fiscal crises). He could explain to Nixon the similarities between his situation and that of other distinguished figures he knew Nixon admired: Lincoln, Roosevelt, Wilson, Churchill. Nixon could discuss with Moynihan, as he could not with Haldeman or Ehrlichman, his admiration for Disraeli, and for *War and Peace*. In the early days the relationship was suffused with praise; each man knew well what the other liked to hear. "It is reassuring to have a true intellectual in residence," Nixon wrote Moynihan in 1969, and a few months later he said, perhaps sensing Moynihan's restlessness with university life, "You belong in the exciting things." He reassured Moynihan that he wanted peace in Vietnam, and Moynihan usually expressed his opposition to the war as gently as possible. The memos that Moynihan often sent Nixon were filled with small bouquets: "your great Inaugural Address"; "your brilliant first year in office"; "What you have done for racial equality is without equal in American history"; "New Federalism . . . is generally held [in England, where Moynihan had just been] to be the most important domestic initiative since the New Deal."

Moynihan's flattery (and self-flattery: the presidential ideas he extolled were often the ones that he had thought of) had a higher purpose: he used it, successfully, to help coax Nixon into agreement with his vision of what the administration should do. Nearly all the great presidential initiatives he wrote to Nixon about were meant, in Moynihan's mind, to send a message — not to average voters or foreign leaders or any of the other standard objects of symbolic presidential actions, but to intellectuals. Actually bringing them around to a position of support for Nixon, which Nixon thought of as part of Moynihan's job, Moynihan realized was, in 1969 and 1970, impossible. But they could be neutralized, he thought, through a kind of one-upmanship: if Nixon built up a record of liberal accomplishment, it would become clear that the intellectuals' attacks on him were based not on any substantive objection to his policies, but on pure destructiveness. In the end they would be discredited, which was a necessary precondition of the moral restoration of the republic.

Nixon instinctively disliked the war on poverty. During the 1968 campaign, Patrick Buchanan, who was one of his speechwriters, sent him a memo on welfare on which Nixon wrote an exclamation point in the margin next to the statement that "a concerted effort has been made through the Community Action Programs of the War on Poverty to urge people to apply for welfare." He wrote back to Buchanan, "Good for a *tough* statement later? (Particularly the part about how welfare workers *urge* people to go on welfare.)" One of Nixon's minor campaign promises was that he would eliminate the Job Corps. Two months after taking office, he wrote Ehrlichman, "No increase in any poverty program until more evidence is in"; on another memo, which listed all the presidential appointees at the OEO, he wrote, "I want immediate action on all these characters." Moynihan might have been expected to urge Nixon to follow his inclination to put the OEO out of business; at the time, he was probably the best-known critic of the war on poverty in the country, having published in 1969 a book attacking community action called *Maximum Feasible Misunderstanding*. He sent Nixon a positive review of the book in January 1969, with a note saying "Wait till the OEO types get to me!" "Very intriguing — !" Nixon wrote back.

And yet Moynihan's position was exactly the opposite: in the first few months of the administration, he was responsible for convincing Nixon to spare the OEO — for strategic reasons, not because he considered it an effective government agency. Why give the left any ammunition? "Avoid, at whatever immediate costs . . . an enormous controversy over the 'war on poverty,'" he wrote Nixon a month after the inauguration, and in a new introduction to *Maximum Feasible Misunderstanding*, written in early 1970, he proudly reported that all suspicions that Nixon harbored ill will toward the poverty program had been shown to be nonsense. For the same reason, he pushed for budget increases for Model Cities, too, and distanced himself from his old Harvard friend Edward Banfield, who was the leading intellectual skeptic about the program; "Pat did not welcome my presence in Washington when I went there," Banfield says. "He did not want to be perceived as a conservative." Moynihan's entire record as an adviser to Nixon is one of always pushing him to make liberal gestures, great (like more government spending on social programs) and small (like restoring the funds that Johnson had cut for Robert Kennedy's memorial at Arlington, and granting a passport to the widow of W. E. B. DuBois), and always making the case for them primarily on the basis of the need to neutralize the intellectual left.

It helped Moynihan that the general tenor of the American establishment during the first Nixon administration was probably more liberal than it had ever been before and than it has been since. Conservatism of the variety that prevailed during Ronald Reagan's presidency was a fringe ideology in the early seventies, and Nixon would have had to wage all-out war against the Congress, the press, the universities, the foundations, and even most corporate leaders if he had wanted to reverse completely the rising tide of social welfare programs. His real area of interest was foreign policy, and he was not inclined to expend his political capital on trying to bring about a conservative counterrevolution in domestic affairs.

Among his advisers, the people who would qualify as conservative by today's standards consistently lost their battles with the forces of moderate Republicanism. As one of Nixon's aides, Richard Nathan, puts it, "We just didn't have a new conventional wisdom—we accepted the paradigm of the Great Society." During the transition period between Nixon's election and his inauguration, Nathan ran a task force on welfare policy that recommended eliminating the then-slender work requirements for welfare mothers on the grounds that they were "coercive," said "Model Cities is gaining momentum rapidly," praised community action for "building self-help capacities and citizen participation," and called for the establishment of a new "Agency for Community Development." In the course of Nixon's first term, HEW pushed forward with many school-desegregation cases in the South. Labor established the use of numerical goals in affirmative action plans. Under pressure from the Democratic Congress, Nixon signed into law a program to create temporary jobs in the ghettos, a subsidized housing program, revenue sharing and block grants for cities, increases in welfare payments, a major expansion of the food stamps program, and a new program under Social Security that made payments to disabled people. That period in the past, now so often mentioned in conservative political speeches, when we threw money at our problems, was really the first Nixon administration more than it was either of the Democratic administrations of the 1960s.

Aside from the reason that Moynihan favored all these programs, Nixon knew that government spending had political uses that Republicans tended to be blind to. It was a lesson he had learned the hard way during his unsuccessful first presidential race: "Very bad advice '60 to Ike—should have spent more," he told a group of aides a few months after taking office. Domestic expenditures could have a calming effect on the country—"He spent to keep the lid on," says Leonard Garment, who was Nixon's adviser on civil rights. On racial issues, the desire in the White House, not least on the part of Nixon himself, was to demonstrate a specifically Republican form of moral superiority that the nation had been deprived of during the 1960s. The Democrats were the messy, passionate, ultra-political party, and the exemplary Democrat was Lyndon Johnson, who always overheated the rhetoric, who cloaked calculation in talk of the public good, who had raised expectations too high and worked the country into a frenzied state. On January 20, 1969, Johnson's aides turned over to Nixon's a stack of blank executive orders declaring martial law—all you had to do was fill in the date and the name of the city. The Nixon administration would cool the country off, and it would help blacks even though there was not a single vote to be gained by doing so. Somehow this seemed purer than the racial concern of politicians like Johnson and Robert Kennedy, who expected the reward of black votes in return for their good deeds.

"Disgraceful in past 100 years both parties have demagogued the race issue," read Ehrlichman's notes of what Nixon said to a group of his aides during a meeting in 1971. "Used the issue. Haven't tried to solve it." Speaking on the telephone to Reagan in 1972 about the Democrats and blacks, he said, "They exploited them." Nixon constantly emphasized to the people around him the importance of keeping a low profile while carrying out civil rights policy. "Don't let the federal government be heroic," Ehrlichman's notes of the 1971 meeting continue. "Won't help blacks or the cause." In 1970 Haldeman wrote a memo summarizing Nixon's views on desegregation. It began, "All people concerned are to do only what the law requires and they are to do it quietly without bragging about it." He continued, "We have to do what's right, but we must separate that from politics and not be under the illusion that this is helping us politically." The memo that Moynihan wrote Nixon in January 1970, saying "The time may have come when the issue of race could benefit from a period of 'benign neglect'" — which caused another hail of criticism to descend on Moynihan when somebody leaked it to the press a couple of months later — was entirely consistent with the overall tone of the administration. Racial progress was supposed to continue, but very quietly.

The one liberal cause that Nixon took care to stay far away from was the integration of schools and neighborhoods in the North, because unlike all the others it could really damage him politically. The first Nixon administration coincided with the peak of the antibusing movement. Every year the House of Representatives voted on an antibusing measure; in 1969 and 1970 it failed, but in 1971 and 1972, following a Supreme Court decision upholding the legality of busing orders, it passed. Nixon frequently reminded his aides that he was against busing in the North. Members of the administration who were seen as advocating integration openly, such as Leon Panetta, the director of HEW's Office of Civil Rights, and James Allen, the commissioner of education, usually found themselves out of jobs. In 1970 Ehrlichman wrote Nixon about another problem official, George Romney, the former governor of Michigan who was now secretary of HUD: "Suburban Integration. This is a serious Romney problem which we will apparently have as long as he is there. There is no approved program as such, nor has the White House approved such a policy. But he keeps loudly talking about it in spite of our efforts to shut him up. . . . And he is beginning some administrative maneuvers in this direction." Nixon wrote back, "Stop this one." (During the 1972 campaign, the Republican National Committee worked up faked letters from private citizens to Democratic senators asking them what they thought of Romney's views on integration, evidently hoping to elicit favorable responses that could then be used against the senators in the campaign.) After Nixon's reelection, when he was reshuffling his Cabinet, he told James Lynn, Romney's successor at HUD, according to Ehrlichman's notes, "Black problem. Romney pandered."

Whenever the thought of simply becoming more openly conservative on racial issues across the board occurred to Nixon, he concluded that he shouldn't, because the course he had set — for the continued dismantling of legal segregation in the South, against trying to integrate the

North — was the most politically prudent one. Patrick Buchanan wrote
Nixon a memo in January 1970, suggesting that he was being unfair to
the South by desegregating the schools there and not in the North. Nixon
wrote in the margin, "Is de facto segregation OK in the North and not
in the South?" and "Why should we continue to kick the South and
hypocritically ignore the same problem in the North?" By March,
though, when Buchanan was fighting with the rest of the White House
staff over what position a presidential message on desegregation should
take, Ehrlichman's notes have Nixon telling him, "No good politics in
PB's extreme view: segregation forever. . . . Right: Believe should carry
out desegregation. Integration not wave of future. No massive program.
Lean: integration hasn't worked."

M OYNIHAN'S vision for the Nixon administration was far too ambitious for him to limit himself to ensuring that the government
simply float along on a liberal tide. He had an idea in mind that would
dramatically establish a new course for American social policy: a national
guaranteed-income program called the Family Assistance Plan.

For years Moynihan had been advocating some kind of new government income support for families, and more recently, the idea of a guaranteed income had moved steadily into the forefront of his opinions, and
the idea of full employment and jobs programs into the background.
During the Nixon administration, "Moynihan was not pushing strongly
for an employment solution," Ehrlichman says. The strategic advantages
of a guaranteed-income program, at that moment, were many. For a
substantial initiative, it was quite inexpensive. It would replace something
that nobody liked, the welfare system. It was easy to sell to Nixon: it was
an antipoverty program that did not require venturing into such perilous
territory as promoting integration or expanding the federal bureaucracy;
as Moynihan presented the idea, it would cost only $2 billion a year and
cut back on the size of government by consolidating the vast Democratic
hodgepodge of federal income-support programs.

Additional attractions of the Family Assistance Plan lay in areas that
could not be publicly discussed. The subject of black out-of-wedlock
childbearing was still strictly verboten — "You weren't supposed to talk
about that," says Richard Nathan — but the percentage of black children
born to single mothers was continuing to rise. If the welfare system was
to blame, then the Family Assistance Plan, which would give money to

intact families as well as female-headed ones, would reverse the trend. Another trend it might reverse was the black migration to the North. For several years it had occurred to government officials that the crisis in the ghettos might be solved by finding a way to keep rural Southern blacks from moving to the cities. Toward the end of his presidency, Johnson set up a secret Interagency Task Force on Rural-Urban Migration to look into this question, and in 1969 Moynihan set up a White House task force on "Internal Migration." At Moynihan's urging, Nixon said in his 1970 State of the Union address, "We must create a new rural environment which will not only stem the migration to urban centers but reverse it."

These efforts always foundered for the simple reason that upon investigation, it became clear that the great migration was already coming to an end. By the late 1960s, the dislocations caused by the mechanization of cotton cultivation in the South were substantially complete, and the word was out in the black South that the Northern ghettos had become short on unskilled jobs and long on street crime. To people in Washington, though, it appeared that the tremendous disparities in the level of welfare benefits from state to state — Illinois consistently paid from three to four times what Mississippi did — were inducing poor blacks to move North just to get on welfare there. The Family Assistance Plan would establish a national uniform benefit level and so remove that incentive. Although Moynihan now stoutly denies that he believed the Family Assistance Plan would stem the black migration, the original proposal for it said, "No more will poor persons be driven out of one section of the Nation by inadequate or even punitive welfare legislation, and forced into crowded and hostile cities." When Nixon made his first speech about the plan, he said the welfare system "has helped draw millions into the slums of our cities." In *The Politics of a Guaranteed Income*, Moynihan's book on the Family Assistance Plan, published in 1973, he approvingly quoted an article from *The Economist* that said, "A major requirement here is to get deserted welfare mothers and their large families out of the city centers instead of ridiculously saying that they can draw higher benefits only if they stay there."

Perhaps the most appealing of all the nonobvious features of the Family Assistance Plan was that it would cut out of the action the kind of social welfare employees who Moynihan and Nixon recognized were the left's main entering wedge into the government. In Moynihan's formulation, the Family Assistance Plan represented the administration's embracing an "income strategy" against poverty to replace Johnson's "services strategy." One member of the White House staff remembers that at the first big meeting where Moynihan proposed the plan, when he said that it would eliminate tens of thousands of social workers from the federal payroll, Nixon's eyes lit up. As Moynihan imagined his proposal playing out, the left would be inescapably trumped: it would of course be horrified by the Family Assistance Plan as a matter of self-interest, but to work actively for the defeat of the most sweeping liberal social initiative in years would appear hypocritical. This logic appealed to Nixon, too. On Christmas Eve, 1969, an assistant of Moynihan's named John Price had to pay a brief visit to the Oval Office, and he found Nixon in a voluble mood. Price says, "Nixon said, 'We as Republicans have to accept that the Democrats will always try to raise the payments from a guaranteed income and make us look mean. But the important thing is this:' — he pointed his finger at me — 'We established the principle!' "

The Family Assistance Plan was by no means universally popular within the White House. Arthur Burns, a conservative economist who was then a high-ranking aide to Nixon, mounted a ferocious attack on it that lasted for months, based on the argument that it would cost more than Moynihan was saying and would cause the welfare rolls to grow even faster than they were growing already. Even as Nixon's speech announcing the plan was in the final stages of preparation, Burns tried (unsuccessfully) to insert a passage in which Nixon categorically stated that the Family Assistance Plan was not a guaranteed income, because that was something he could never support. Moynihan never fully refuted Burns's objections, but for him fiscal prudence and shrinking welfare rolls were not the real goals of the Family Assistance Plan anyway. At that point he had Nixon's ear more than Burns did, partly because, as Burns's deputy, Martin Anderson, puts it, "Arthur treated Nixon like a child." In April 1969, Nixon wrote Ehrlichman, "In confidence I have decided to go ahead on this program."

The plan twice failed to pass in Congress. The opposition that sealed its fate came from conservative Southern Democrats, most importantly Senator Russell Long of Louisiana. To Moynihan's mind, though, the real villains of the piece were the left-wing organizations that, contrary to his expectations, decided to campaign actively against the plan, such as the Welfare Rights Organization. The defeat of the Family Assistance Plan deepened his conviction that the left had become the main obstacle to the achievement of liberal goals in America.

In 1973, when he was ambassador to India, Moynihan wrote to Melvin Laird, who had taken over his portfolio at the White House, to urge a third try for the Family Assistance Plan; his argument makes it clear how much more focused he was on the plan as an intellectual gambit than as a social program. It would not pass, he wrote, because "*A guaranteed income will never be enacted while President Nixon is in office.*" Still, the fight was worth it, because the plan was not "addressed to the poor" but "*addressed to the cultural strata*" — that is, it was meant to vitiate the arguments of intellectuals who liked to portray the Nixon administration as heedlessly right-wing. As to the objection of people like Burns and Long that the plan would encourage welfare dependency, Moynihan's attitude was, essentially, that they might be right, but so what? Reducing dependency wasn't the point. A large welfare-dependent class "will come to be accepted as the normal and manageable cost of doing urban business," he wrote Laird. "It is in ways a political subsidy, as irrational perhaps as those paid to owners of oil wells, wheat fields, or aerospace companies, but whoever said politics was rational? Not Melvin Laird!"

Moynihan was occasionally able to induce Nixon to get into the spirit of bitterness about the liberal opposition to the Family Assistance Plan. In 1970, he wrote to him, "Can you believe the Urban League would be against FAP? Talk about class interests. . . ."; this prompted a handwritten response from Nixon to Moynihan, Ehrlichman, and Haldeman, with each man getting a message custom-tailored to the nature of his relationship with the president:

Pat Good job! (However I'm not surprised at the Urban League getting "political" as November approaches.)

E I think this cooks Whitney Young. He is hopelessly partisan.

H — Can't some of our people who help finance the Urban League hit him? See if you can't get someone on this.

On the whole, though, Nixon was losing interest in the plan; as a politician in office, he could not afford to be so utterly consumed as Moynihan was with the thrust and parry of intellectual life. By the late summer of 1970, Ehrlichman's notes have Nixon telling him, "Just get something done. . . . Let it appear we've fought and come half way. . . . Avoid appearance of defeat." It was especially unfortunate for the Family Assistance Plan's standing with Nixon that the Democratic presidential nominee, George McGovern, whom Nixon regarded as a dreamy, ineffectual leftist, proposed a guaranteed income during his campaign in 1972. At one point, while discussing McGovern's plan with Ehrlichman, Nixon called in his faithful manservant, Manolo Sanchez. If McGovern won and implemented his plan, Sanchez said, according to Ehrlichman's notes, "I quit — go on welfare."

MOYNIHAN knew exactly what was going on in black America. He had seen for years that the black poor in the cities were in trouble — that their unemployment rate was rising alarmingly, that their family networks were becoming more unstable, that their likelihood of going on welfare was increasing, that crime in their neighborhoods was growing more and more severe. More recently, he had realized that the growth in government employment was a great boon to the black middle class, and that as more blacks began to do better, the poor people in the ghettos would be cut off. It would seem that somebody who saw all these trends taking place would conclude that the worst possible answer for the problems of black America at that moment was concentrating on higher welfare payments at the expense of programs: that would cut off the growth of the social service jobs that were giving blacks their main avenue of opportunity without giving any additional jobs, education, or training that might help the poorest people to get out of the ghettos. That Moynihan, knowing what he knew, put all his political chips on a guaranteed income is testament to the ability of his preoccupation with the left to distract him from what should have been the real point of his service in the White House.

In March 1969, just when he was beginning to promote the Family Assistance Plan, Moynihan wrote a long memo to Nixon, filled with urgent italicized warnings, on the state of race relations in America — a memo that would have gotten him in much more trouble than the "benign neglect" memo if it had ever been publicized. It demonstrates the line of reasoning that was pulling Moynihan away from the idea of giving blacks more government programs, and toward giving them more welfare instead.

Moynihan began the memo by stressing the need for "the integration into the larger society of what is now a sizable urban lower class which at the moment is experiencing more than its share of the bad habits and bad luck which through history have affected such groups and caused them to be seen as 'different' or undesirable by their more prudent and fortunate neighbors. . . . *The Negro lower class would appear to be unusually self-damaging, that is to say, more so than is normal for such groups.*" He went on to show how mixed his feelings were about the new black middle class, because of its political leanings:

> The Negro poor having become more openly violent — especially in the form of the rioting of the mid 1960's — they have given the black middle class an incomparable weapon with which to *threaten* white America. This has been for many an altogether intoxicating experience. "Do this or the cities will burn." And of course they have been greatly encouraged in this course by white rhetoric of the Kerner Commission variety. But most important of all, the existence of a large marginal, if not dependent, black urban lower class has at last given the black middle class an opportunity to establish a secure and rewarding power base in American society — as the provider of social services to the black lower class. . . . What building contracts and police graft were to the 19th-century urban Irish, the welfare department, Head Start, and Black Studies programs will be to the coming generation of Negroes. They are of course very wise in this respect. These are expanding areas of economic opportunity. By contrast, black business enterprise offers relatively little. In all this there will be the peculiar combination of weakness and strength that characterizes Negro Americans as a group at this time. . . . There is no true Negro intellectual or academic class at this moment. (Thirty years ago there was: somehow it died out.) Negro books are poor stuff for the most part. Black studies are by and large made up of the worst kind of ethnic longings-for-a-glorious-past. . . .

Helping the ghettos would, Moynihan continued, deprive "*the militant middle class*" of the ability to make an ongoing "*threat to the larger society, much as the desperate bank robber threatens to drop the vial of nitroglycerin.*" Hence the income strategy: a gesture toward the ghettos that would simultaneously take the play away from the militant middle class.

The relationship between the Family Assistance Plan and the income strategy is like the one between the community action program and the idea of community development: the specific program failed politically, but the general principle succeeded. The Nixon administration in effect did implement the income strategy by greatly increasing the payment levels of welfare, food stamps, Social Security, and disability pensions, while allowing government social welfare employment to level off. At the same time, the proportion of blacks in poverty, which decreased from 55 per cent in 1959 to 32 per cent in 1969, also leveled off and has stayed relatively level ever since, lacking a decisive nudge from either the manual-labor economy or the federal government. In his own fashion Moynihan had done exactly what he so often accused the left of doing: claiming to be motivated by concern for the poor, he had set a course whose real aim was to embarrass his enemies, one that was not in the best interest of the people he was supposed to be helping.

Another gesture arranged by Moynihan to demonstrate the genuineness of the Nixon administration's interest in the problem of black poverty was a meeting in the White House, on May 13, 1969, between representatives of the Poor People's Campaign and Nixon and several high-ranking members of the administration, including nearly half the Cabinet. The Poor People's Campaign was a legacy of the assassinations of 1968. The idea for it came from a conversation in the summer of 1967 between Robert Kennedy and Marian Wright Edelman, a younger-generation civil rights leader and the wife of Kennedy's aide Peter Edelman. As Peter Edelman remembered the conversation, Kennedy said to Marian Edelman, "I think what really has to happen is that you got to get an awful lot of them, you've got to get a whole lot of poor people who just come to Washington and say they're going to stay here until something happens and it gets really unpleasant and there are some arrests and it's just a very nasty business and Congress gets really embarrassed and they have to act." Marian Edelman passed Kennedy's suggestion on to Martin Luther King, who immediately embraced it. During King's final campaign, in Memphis, he visited Marks, Mississippi, the Delta town immediately east of Clarksdale, and, according to legend, burst into tears when he saw a muddy, unpaved, shack-lined road there called Cotton Street. He decided that the Poor People's Campaign should form a mule train in Marks and walk all the way to Washington.

After King was killed, in April 1968, his lieutenants carried out the plan. By 1969, decades after the introduction of the tractor, it was difficult to find mules in the Delta, but some were rounded up; in a twist that would have confirmed Moynihan's suspicions about poverty programs, the Poor People's Campaign used the Head Start center in Marks as its administrative headquarters. After making its long journey, the mule train set up a dispirited, muddy encampment on the Mall in the newly Re-

publican Washington; the group that came to the White House included
Marian Edelman, King's former second-in-command Ralph Abernathy,
Andrew Young, and Jesse Jackson. Its meeting with Nixon was a fiasco.

The delegation from the Poor People's Campaign arrived late. Abernathy opened the meeting by reading in its entirety a nine-page statement
outlining a sweeping, expensive new political program that would have
struck everyone in the White House as wildly unrealistic. After Abernathy had finished, Nixon replied in a friendly but guarded and unspecific
way, his arms folded in front of him. Then he looked at his watch and
said that an urgent matter concerning the Vietnam War had come up
and he could not stay for the rest of the meeting, though the group
should know that he wanted both to help poor people and to bring peace.
Abernathy asked Nixon not to go yet and replied at length. Everything
about Abernathy seemed wrong to the people from the administration —
his presumptuousness, his verbosity, the way he was dressed (in a gray
suit more elegant than what any of them were wearing, and gold cuff-
links), his way of speaking (he said that to the poor, the American promise
was "a cruel hoax," pronouncing it "hoe-axe"). One White House aide
described him in a memo as "a pompous, tired charlatan."

After Nixon finally managed to beat a retreat, Vice President Spiro
Agnew — a man who had been a liberal Republican as governor of Maryland until a similar meeting with black leaders in the late 1960s made
him so angry that he began to turn to the right — took over, and was
upbraided by several poor people Abernathy had brought with him. Then
Agnew excused himself, but the meeting continued. After it had gone on
for nearly three hours, Moynihan reported to the group that some poor
people who had come to the White House with Abernathy and were
waiting in another room were now threatening to stage a demonstration.
With that the meeting was adjourned. On leaving the White House,
Abernathy told television reporters that it had been "the most disap-
pointing and the most fruitless of all the meetings we have had up to
this time."

All this was far outside the accepted boundaries of White House meetings, and it was a blot on Moynihan's record. It was his meeting, he had
failed to control it, and he had also failed to rise to Nixon's defense.
Nixon "referred to that meeting for *four years* as the worst experience of
his presidency," Ehrlichman says. "When I'd bring up a meeting with
black leaders, he'd say, 'You want me to have another meeting like that
Moynihan meeting.'" It was fortunate for Moynihan that he had already

persuaded Nixon of the value of the Family Assistance Plan by then, because his influence in the White House began to decline. At the end of 1970 he returned to Harvard, though Nixon continued to like him personally and kept communicating with him.

Once Nixon was reelected in 1972, he no longer saw the need to outfox his critics by keeping the old poverty programs they had expected him to gut. "Model Cities — flush it," Ehrlichman's notes have Nixon saying a few days after the 1972 election. A couple of weeks later, during a series of meetings with Ehrlichman to plan his second administration, he elaborated on the theme. Ehrlichman's notes include several Nixon directives about the war on poverty: "OEO — legal services. Sally Payton [a black lawyer on the White House staff] — tell her to screw it up"; "Take the heat on OEO — it's the right thing to do. Be prepared to take it head on"; and, "Flush Model Cities and Great Society. It's failed. Do it, don't say it."

During Nixon's first term, the OEO had been run by a team of neutral, managerial, problem-solving Republicans, including three men who later became secretary of defense: Donald Rumsfeld, Frank Carlucci, and Dick Cheney. In January 1973, Nixon put a thirty-two-year-old product of the conservative youth movement, Howard Phillips, in charge of the OEO, with instructions to dismantle it, abolish community action, and transfer everything else to other departments. Because Watergate was consuming Nixon's energies, Phillips was never confirmed by Congress, and his plan was not carried out. In the fall of 1974, Gerald Ford put another moderate in charge of the OEO, changed its name to the Community Services Administration, and allowed community action to survive. The agency limped along until 1981, when it became the only government entity Ronald Reagan succeeded in eliminating entirely; the single biggest of Reagan's budget cuts was in the jobs programs run under the auspices of the Comprehensive Employment and Training Act, a 1973 law that consolidated all the work-related antipoverty programs and put them under the control of the Labor Department.

Even more than Nixon realized in the fall of 1972, a moment had passed in American history — or, to use the phrase Moynihan coined to describe the events that followed the publication of his report on the black family, a moment was lost. Race remained, and will remain, one of the obsessive themes of American life, but the period when it was the central domestic concern of the federal government seemed to be over. The presidential electorate had become essentially Republican. Within liberal circles, race now had to share the domestic liberal agenda with other causes, like environmentalism. The summer riots had tailed off, and therefore so had the idea that the condition of the ghettos threatened the country as a whole. After the OPEC oil embargo of 1973, the national sense that there was enough economic breathing space to allow for the contemplation of expensive social reforms evaporated.

Over time, the tenuous nature of the war on poverty faded from memory; it began to seem that the government had tried everything to help the ghettos, spending untold billions in the process, and that nothing had worked. David Stockman, driving William Greider of the *Washington Post* through the poor black section in his hometown of Benton Harbor, Michigan, just before taking charge of domestic policy in the Reagan administration, said, "I wouldn't be surprised if $100 million had been spent here in the last twenty years. Urban renewal, CETA, Model Cities, they've had everything. And the results? No impact whatever."

But we hadn't tried everything. We never tried making Head Start a universal program, or expanding it beyond the preschool years. We never tried the kind of major public-works program that the Labor Department pushed for in the 1960s. We never tried putting enough police on foot patrol in the ghettos to make a real dent in the disastrous level of crime there. We never replaced the welfare system with something designed to get poor people into the mainstream of society. Of the billions the federal government spent, by far the lion's share went to the elderly, the sick, the disabled, and the hungry, and in all those areas the problems it addressed were substantially solved. The black middle class grew faster during the Great Society period than at any other time in American history. One of the things we did try, community action, which used up most of the war on poverty's political capital, was an idea that couldn't possibly have accomplished what it was supposed to; all the federal efforts in the ghettos took place during a uniquely difficult time for liberal initiatives aimed at racial problems.

Nonetheless, the idea endures that anything the federal government might do for the black poor will surely fail, and it has become a powerful force in its own right; misapprehensions about the past have a way of determining the future.

AT THE same time that Nixon was trying to dismantle the war on poverty, Lyndon Johnson was preparing for a big symposium on civil rights at the new LBJ Library in Austin, a typically Johnsonian overblown marble block. Johnson was well aware that it was time for him to settle up his accounts. His heart had become very bad. Even in public he was constantly popping nitroglycerin pills to ease his angina pains. The civil rights symposium was planned in a spirit of comity indicating that Johnson's soul was far more at peace than it had been in his last years as president; movement figures who had been routinely barred from White House ceremonies, like Floyd McKissick of CORE, were now cordially invited. Johnson delivered a passionate speech. He said that of all his work as president, civil rights "holds the most of myself within it and holds for me the most intimate meanings," and that "the black problem remains what it has always been, the simple problem of being black in a white society."

A few weeks later, Walter Heller had a speaking engagement at Johnson's alma mater, Southwest Texas State University, and Johnson invited him to come out to the LBJ Ranch afterward and spend the night. The completely self-controlled Heller was amazed at how unwilling or unable Johnson was to change his habits in deference to his health. Dinner was fried shrimp. The customary telephone was still at Johnson's side at the table, and was still ringing constantly. A week later, Johnson was dead.

The main subject of Johnson's disquisition at dinner was how deeply he cared about civil rights — how strong his record was, how it was his real legacy. Like many of the people who worked for Johnson, Heller, while fond of him, was accustomed to wondering whether he really meant what he said or was just trying, in effect, to win a vote for that one last bill, the Lyndon Johnson Historical Greatness Act of 1973. Johnson was incapable of being anything but exaggerated, florid, calculating, vulgar. At one point in his review of his achievements he explained to Heller why he had appointed the black economist Andrew Brimmer to the Federal Reserve Board. "First I put Bob Weaver in the Cabinet," Heller remembered Johnson saying. "But they said, 'No, he's *smooth*-faced. We want somebody with'" — and here Johnson pressed the corners of his mouth together with his two index fingers — "'*fat lips*!' Well, nobody's got fatter lips than Andy."

Heller was repelled by this display, but he left the ranch convinced that Johnson had been speaking from the heart. Even though Johnson simply could not come across in private as the conventional version of a distinguished statesman, and even though everybody who knew him well knew that he was regularly capable of insincerity, nobody — not Heller, not the civil rights leaders he fought with, not even, in the long run, the

Robert Kennedy aides who maneuvered against him — doubted in the end that racial justice became a cause for him. As the years pass, it has become clear that Johnson, in whose own soul was lodged a measure of the fundamental white American ambivalence about blacks, was the only president in this century who was willing to put the American dilemma firmly at the center of his domestic agenda. He told Heller that night, "I've done more for blacks than any other President. That young hero I replaced may have done something. But I did more."

CHICAGO

In 1962, during the months before she moved into the Robert Taylor Homes, Ruby Haynes began having trouble with her second son, Kermit, who was a teenager by now. Sometimes in the late afternoons and early evenings he would come home at a dead run and lock the door behind him. Ruby would ask him what was the matter, and Kermit would always say it was nothing. On one of the days when he ran home, as soon as he got inside the house in Englewood where the family was then living he went upstairs and peered anxiously outside; a few minutes later, a brick came crashing through the living room window, and a shard of glass lodged in three-year-old Juanita's head.

The Hayneses arrived at the Robert Taylor Homes on October 12, the day their building opened, thinking this would be the last step in a long journey that had taken Ruby and her husband, Luther, from the sharecropper cabins of the Mississippi Delta, where they had both grown up, through fifteen years of scraping in the black slums of Chicago, to, finally, a world of material decency—even comfort. While their furniture was still in a pile in front of the elevator bank, waiting to be taken up by the janitors, Ruby saw a group of teenage boys, whose families were also waiting to move into their apartments in the building, come up to Kermit and greet him effusively. She heard one of them say, "Hey, man, we're gonna be together." In a matter of days, Kermit's suspicious behavior had started up again. There would be a knock at the door of the family's apartment, and Kermit would rush to answer it. He would open the door a crack and position himself so that nobody could see who was there. A hushed conversation would ensue, and then the door would be closed. What was that all about, Ruby would ask; nothing, Kermit would say.

The Hayneses' building, 5135 South Federal Street, quickly filled up, and at night Ruby began to hear ominous sounds — loud domestic squabbles, teenage fistfights, even gunfire. Pretty soon, as Ruby put it later, "I'd hear those blue lights," and then the police would arrive. One night, one of Ruby's neighbors came over and said she had just seen Kermit running away from the police down in the plaza in front of the building. Ruby rushed downstairs in time to see Kermit being put into a paddy wagon and hauled off to the police station. She went and got him out, but soon his tangles with the police became commonplace, and from time to time he would have to spend a week or two in jail. Once, while cleaning Kermit's room, Ruby lifted his mattress and discovered several bicycle chains and a set of homemade brass knuckles. When he came home she asked him about them, and he said he was just keeping them for another boy. When Kermit was eighteen, Ruby found him one evening lying on one of the housing project's baseball fields, bleeding profusely from a beating; she took him to the hospital, where the doctors, after fixing him up, told her that he had almost died.

Finally it dawned on Ruby what everybody else seemed to know already: that Kermit was in a gang. When she confronted him about it, he said he had been made to join by other boys, who had told him they would hurt his family if he didn't. This was the standard excuse given by gang members to their mothers, once it became impossible simply to deny everything, and Ruby half believed it. The truth was, though, that Kermit was not just a reluctant gang member, but a gang leader. Operating under the "street name" of DeMarco, he controlled two buildings in the project, 5135 and 5201 South Federal, on behalf of the Vice Lords, a gang mainly based on the West Side that saw the Robert Taylor Homes as a vast and enticing new turf.

Teenage gangs have always existed in the tough neighborhoods of Chicago; according to black Chicago folklore, Mayor Daley belonged to an Irish gang in Bridgeport and participated in beatings of blacks during the 1919 riot. Every ethnic group produced gangs once it got settled in the city, in accord with the University of Chicago sociology department's theory about delinquency as one of the inevitable stages in the assimilation process, and the immigrants' children were always more lawless than the immigrants themselves. Black gangs had existed in Chicago for years — Ruby heard talk about them from the moment she first arrived there, in 1946 — but they proliferated in the late 1950s and early 1960s, just after the peak years of the great black migration. Emerging as they did from the largest and poorest of all Chicago's immigrant groups, they became the roughest and most extensive gangs the city had ever known.

Over time the dozens of black gangs formed themselves into two broad, perpetually warring confederations, the People and the Folks. Every gang had its own symbols, but all the gangs associated with the People spray-painted the buildings in their territory with five-pointed stars, and all the Folks' gangs used six-pointed stars. People wore earrings in their left ear and pointed the bills of their caps to the left; Folks wore earrings in their right ear and pointed their caps to the right. The leading Folks gang was the Disciples, headquartered on the South Side; the leading People gangs were the Vice Lords, from the West Side, and the Blackstone Rangers, from Woodlawn.

Kermit's generation — young black men who had been born in the South during the 1940s and brought to Chicago in early childhood, and who were teenagers during the mid-1960s — produced most of the celebrities of the gang world, the people who masterminded the transformation of scattered groups of street fighters into large criminal organizations that were armed, murderous, prosperous from drug dealing and other illegal businesses, and firmly in control (after dark, at least) of Mayor Daley's new high-rise housing projects. The gang leader with the highest profile in the press was Jeff Fort, the head of the Blackstone Rangers (born in 1947 in Aberdeen, Mississippi), but every kid growing up in the projects was familiar with the identities and exploits of half a dozen other leaders whose names never appeared in the papers: the Disciples bosses "King" Hoover and David Barksdale, other Blackstone Rangers like the Harper brothers and Jerome "Pay Soldier" Cantwell, and the West Side Vice Lords chieftain known as "Peppilow."

Most of these people wound up either dead or in jail for life, though Kermit escaped both of those fates. For thousands and thousands of other black kids in Chicago, gang life was an interlude taking up all of the adolescence of the projects, which lasted from age eleven or twelve to sixteen or seventeen — years devoted to fighting, petty thievery, selling drugs, skipping school, and otherwise making life miserable for their neighbors and completely unpromising for themselves. The gangs were the main visible force responsible for the Robert Taylor Homes' changing from the oasis of decent housing for the black poor that they were intended to be, and that their initial occupants like Ruby and Luther

Haynes expected them to be, into a hellhole whose residents were ter-
rorized by constant violence.

The two side-by-side elevators that were the means of access to the
upper floors of the sixteen-story buildings in the project became, in many
cases, checkpoints controlled by the gangs; merely entering the secluded
alcove where the elevators opened on the ground floor could induce knots
in the stomach, because gang members might be there. Soon the open
breezeways on each floor had to be enclosed in a tight floor-to-ceiling
steel mesh, to prevent young criminals from throwing things at people
down in the plazas. The gangs became a major factor in the life of the
schools in the area. As the project's reputation got worse, families began
to leave, and the demand for their apartments was slack. The Chicago
Housing Authority's executive director, Charles Swibel, allowed the
screening process for new residents to wither away. Ruby and Luther
had hastily married in order to qualify for a place in the Robert Taylor
Homes, but very quickly most of the people moving in were down-on-
their-luck single mothers with large families, assigned there by the Chicago Housing Authority because the Taylor Homes consisted entirely of
multibedroom apartments. The architecture of the buildings made it
impossible for mothers to monitor their children once they had left the
family apartment. The relative lack of adult men meant that there
wasn't a physically strong countervailing force inside the project to the
boys in the gangs, and the gang members themselves, mostly teenagers
whose fathers didn't live at home, lacked any close-at-hand picture
of masculinity that identified it as being something other than sheer
aggressiveness.

The Vice Lords weren't a power in the Robert Taylor Homes for very
long. The main combatants in the war for control of the project were
the Vice Lords' allies, the Blackstone Rangers (along with several other
affiliated People gangs), and the Disciples. Today, a quarter century later,
most of the Robert Taylor Homes is Disciples territory.

Inside the Haynes home, the main effect of Kermit's gang activity was
to create tension between Ruby and Luther. Kermit was not Luther's
son, and he refused to recognize Luther's authority over the apartment;
soon Kermit and Luther were fighting regularly, and Luther was blaming
Ruby for not keeping Kermit in line and thus allowing his role in the
family to be eroded. At the same time, Luther had run into problems in
his work life. He lost the job in an awning factory that he had had for a
decade, and then bounced around a little. He lost jobs because of trans-

portation problems, because of layoffs, because of a bout of serious illness, because of his drinking, because he had a minor criminal record (having been in jail for disorderly conduct following a fight with Ruby), and because creditors were after him. He was feeling that he didn't occupy — and could never occupy, in his current family situation — a position of respect.

Luther took up his old habit of not returning from work on Fridays after he got his paycheck. One weekend in early 1965, when he didn't come home at all, Ruby went through his clothes and found a parking ticket. It had been made out early on a Sunday morning in front of a hotel at Fifty-fifth Street and Michigan Avenue, a few blocks away from the Robert Taylor Homes. By this time Luther's 1961 Pontiac had been repossessed, so Ruby called the motor-vehicle registry and asked who owned the car whose license plate was listed on the parking ticket. The answer was Dorothy Johnson — a name that was very familiar to Ruby, because until quite recently she and her children had lived just downstairs from the Hayneses, in Apartment 801 of 5135 South Federal. After leaving the project, Dorothy had moved to an apartment just around the corner from the hotel at Fifty-fifth and Michigan, and Ruby had seen her driving a car around the neighborhood. As Ruby thought about it, she recalled that during the years when Dorothy was still in the project, Luther had often announced that he was going out for a drink and walked out of the apartment, but when Ruby, annoyed and distrustful, would go to the window and look outside, there would be no sign of Luther leaving the building. Other times, Luther would say he had to go to the store, and Juanita, who adored him, would ask if she could go along; he would say no, and Ruby now realized that the reason was that his real destination was Apartment 801.

When Luther came home after work on Monday, Ruby began fussing at him about the ticket, but he insisted he didn't know anything about it — he said it had just somehow ended up among his things. Pretty soon the secret was out anyway. Ruby's children began reporting to her that their friends at school were saying, "I saw your father over at Miss Dorothy's house." Luther was not being particularly careful; he saw in Dorothy, who was younger than Ruby, who had three children compared to Ruby's eight, who had a job while Ruby was on public aid, the promise of an escape from the ghetto, and he was entranced. Finally Dorothy herself called Ruby and said, as Ruby remembered it, "I got him and there's nothing you can do about it." One Saturday evening, Ruby was

on the bus riding to her job as a hotel maid in the Loop when she saw
Luther and Dorothy walking down Michigan Avenue together, near the
hotel. She got off the bus at the next stop, in time to see Dorothy driving
away in her car; she noticed that the license plate number matched the
one on the parking ticket she had found. Luther was walking back toward
the project, alone. Ruby caught up with him at the corner of Fifty-first
Street, and they stood there yelling at each other. A small crowd of people
stopped and stared at them. Luther said he was going home. Ruby went
to a pay phone and called in sick to her job, and returned to the apartment
to continue the fight. As she tells the story, Luther told her, in a gruff,
belligerent voice, "I don't like no jealous woman"; in an almost out-of-
control rage, she replied that she had a razor blade in her purse and
intended to use it on Dorothy if she saw her again.

A few nights later, there was a knock on the door of the apartment.
Ruby opened up to see Dorothy standing in the hallway with two policemen. The police said that Dorothy had made out a complaint against
Ruby for threatening her. Ruby reached past them and grabbed Dorothy
and said, "Go away, or you'll *have* something to get me for." The police
pulled her away, and said they wanted to speak to Luther privately. Ruby
retreated, he went out into the hallway for a few minutes of hushed
conversation, and the police and Dorothy left.

The final drama came on the night of July 19, 1965. Two of Luther's
friends were over, playing records and drinking with him. The phone
rang. Ruby answered it. "Can I speak to Mister Luther?" a child's voice
said. "Who's calling?" said Ruby. The child — one of Dorothy's, Ruby
surmised — hung up. A few minutes later, the phone rang again. Luther
went back into the bedroom to answer it; Ruby picked up the extension
and listened in. She heard Dorothy say, "I thought you were coming
over tonight," and Luther reply, "I just got held up." At that point Ruby
broke into the conversation and started cursing Dorothy. Luther hung
up and came out to the living room. An especially bad fight began. Luther's friends hurried out. The smaller children started to cry. Kermit,
who was visiting a friend next door, heard the noise, ran over, and throt-
tled Luther. He said, as Ruby remembered it, "I've been living with this
all my life, and I'm a man now. You stop fighting with my mama!" He
was holding Luther's neck tightly with both hands, and he wouldn't let
go. Ruby called the police. When they arrived, they pried Kermit and
Luther apart and said that Luther had better leave before somebody got

killed. A couple of days later he came back with a suitcase, packed his things, and left for good.

Ruby was forty-eight years old. She never had a man living in her house again.

In the summer of 1964 George Hicks heard that the Chicago Housing Authority was giving out summer jobs to community- and tenant-relations workers in the projects. George was then just a few years into his second stint of living in Chicago. He had a wife and two daughters. After years of trying to escape the lower-middle-class billet in Clarksdale to which he seemed to have been assigned at birth, he still hadn't been able to do it. He had tried small business a couple of times but it didn't work out, so he was holding down, without much pleasure, the traditional job of the black Southern college graduate: public school teacher.

George applied for one of the jobs at the housing authority, and got it. He was assigned to Cabrini-Green, the large, isolated project tucked into an out-of-the-way corner of the white North Side, quite near the Loop. Cabrini-Green was built in phases. The first section, consisting of two-story brick row houses, opened during World War II and housed mostly white families whose breadwinners were working in the war industries. It replaced a notorious Italian-American slum, and had a reputation as a good place to live. In response to the great black migration, the housing authority added fifteen high-rise buildings to the project in 1958, and another eight high rises in 1962. By the time George got there, Cabrini-Green was almost entirely black, but it still had some aura of social improvement about it. New residents were screened. There were a lot of rules and regulations; even walking on the grass was an offense punishable by the payment of a fine. A family that wanted to move someone into its apartment had to get permission from the management office.

George's job theoretically made him the kind of government-funded community organizer that the people in Washington who planned social programs were beginning to be interested in placing in the ghettos, but in fact he was mainly a social worker. He counseled families moving in, and helped set up tenant councils in the high-rise buildings. He liked the work well enough, but the main attraction of the job was the chance it offered for him to obtain a berth in the Chicago Housing Authority bureaucracy, a civil service system with a multistep promotion ladder that, once you got a little way up in it, paid considerably better than teaching school. At the end of the summer, he managed to get a permanent job at Cabrini-Green, and he left the school system forever. His starting salary was $5,700 a year. A career as a government social service bureaucrat wasn't what he had originally had in mind, but he was thirty-five by then, and it was obvious that at that moment in his life, it was by far the best available way for him to achieve the comfortable life he had always dreamed of.

In October 1964, only a few months after getting on with the housing authority, George left the all-black neighborhood in Englewood where he had been living. For $22,000, he and his wife, Orlean, bought a handsome brick bungalow a dozen blocks to the south of his old house, in a neighborhood that was just beginning to change from white to black. He was the first black homeowner on his block, which looked out on the playing fields of Calumet High School. Miraculously, the racial transition on the block proceeded extremely smoothly and gradually; the last white family didn't move out until 1987, and there was never any harassment or bombing. The block looks today the way it looked when George moved in: a row of small, solid, well-kept detached houses with tiny neat lawns and flower boxes in their windows, through which can be glimpsed living rooms decorated with wall-to-wall carpeting, matched sets of furniture, and children's graduation pictures.

After a year at Cabrini-Green, George was promoted to the level of assistant manager, and he moved to a job at a smaller high-rise project, Rockwell Gardens, on the West Side. The people running the management offices of housing projects in Chicago were not especially powerful figures — they were building superintendents, essentially. Downtown, at the Chicago Housing Authority headquarters, was where the decisions were made and the political wheeling and dealing went on. Downtown set policy, assigned families to the projects, hired employees, and, most important, controlled the millions of dollars of contracts that, after intense consultation with the Democratic machine and the unions, were parceled out to construction and maintenance companies. People who wanted to use their careers with the housing authority as a way of wielding real power in Chicago found jobs downtown, not in the projects themselves. People at George's level merely met with tenants' councils, supervised minor repairs and routine operations, and listened to people's daily complaints, often responding that nothing could be done about them.

George soon began to witness the terrible decline of the projects, mainly as a helpless bystander. The screening got much less thorough. The American Civil Liberties Union took up the banner of housing project tenants' rights, and began filing suits to cut back on the rules and regulations and on what little screening there was. A manager had almost no control over who was admitted to a project as a tenant, or who worked on the office staff—downtown handled that. He could evict a trouble-some tenant only by going through a lengthy and complicated legal pro-cedure that was difficult to complete successfully. The gangs became better organized, more powerful, and more involved with guns and drugs; quite often, the managers of the projects would get to know the gang leaders and negotiate with them to maintain order. As the tenants changed from working families to single mothers on public aid, the need for repair work increased, but the money for it didn't seem to be forth-coming from downtown. The security function was taken away from the managers and transferred to downtown. Finally, toward the end of the 1960s, Senator Edward Brooke of Massachusetts got an amendment into a housing bill that set public-housing rents at a quarter of each tenant's income, which made living in the projects cheaper for people on aid but more expensive for the families with jobs who provided the social glue in the project, and many of them left.

In the summer of 1966, while George was working at Rockwell Gar-dens, a team of lawyers assembled by the ACLU sued the Chicago Hous-ing Authority, on behalf of a group of tenants and applicants, for violating the Fourteenth Amendment and the Civil Rights Act by building seg-regated housing projects. The Gautreaux case—named for its lead plain-tiff, Dorothy Gautreaux, a resident of the Altgeld Gardens project on the far South Side—was in the courts for nearly a decade, until the United States Supreme Court decided it in favor of Gautreaux, who had since died. The immediate effect of its being filed was to bring the hous-ing authority's high-rise construction program to a grinding halt. No more big projects were ever built in Chicago, and the ones that were already in place remained segregated and over the years became only more poor, more isolated, and more chaotic.

In 1967 Orlean Hicks died of a sudden heart attack at the age of thirty-five, leaving George alone with their two daughters. He induced his parents to move up to Chicago, and they brought George's mother's mother along with them. George's father got a job in a laundry. By that time all of George's siblings, four sisters and a brother, were living in

Chicago too. His career at the housing authority was going well. After a year and a half at Rockwell Gardens, he was transferred to the office that operates housing projects for the elderly, which were generally peaceful and, in some cases, integrated places. He had progressed to the point where he could realistically hope to be promoted to manager, but first he needed to complete a tour of duty somewhere at the upper reaches of the assistant manager level. In 1968 he became one of the two assistant managers of the Robert Taylor Homes, with authority over fourteen buildings, including the one where the Haynes family lived.

WHEN THE WAR on poverty began, Richard Daley started a community action agency called the Chicago Commission on Urban Opportunity, installed a reliably loyal black bureaucrat from the public-aid department named Deton Brooks as its director, and began to receive from Washington the kind of especially generous funding that befitted a politician of his stature. The commission opened a series of Urban Progress Centers on the South Side and the West Side that functioned as the neighborhood offices out of which the poverty programs were run. Daley didn't really believe that any special efforts beyond the ordinary good works of the Democratic machine were necessary to help the ghettos, but if Washington insisted, the Urban Progress Centers would certainly be sufficient to do the job.

The black political opposition to Daley, then and later, was concentrated in middle-class areas; to the extent that there was a countervailing force to him inside the slums, it consisted primarily of The Woodlawn Organization and the Coordinating Council of Community Organizations, an organization founded in 1962 by a wiry, intense black high school teacher named Al Raby to protest the segregationist policies of the Chicago school superintendent, Ben Willis. In the fall of 1963, after Daley reacted to the criticism of Willis by giving him a vote of confidence, the CCCO staged what was probably the single largest civil rights protest in the history of Chicago, a boycott in which 200,000 students stayed home from school for a day.

It was Raby's success (along with Adam Clayton Powell's hostility to the presence of out-of-town black leaders in New York) that persuaded Martin Luther King to choose Chicago as the city where he would launch the civil rights movement in the North. James Bevel, King's organizer and scout in Chicago, got to know Raby soon after moving there in the spring of 1965, and a few months later King visited Chicago himself, met Raby, and was impressed by him. Toward the end of the summer, when King officially announced to the press that the Southern Christian Leadership Council would be setting up shop in Chicago, he said he intended to focus on the issue of school integration.

King made plans to move to Chicago early in 1966. In the meantime, Bevel settled into an apartment on the West Side and set about conceiving a plan of action. Bevel, a small, moon-faced, hot-tempered man, was, like most gifted organizers, not a great believer in doing things by the book. His experience had taught him that the best way to proceed with a local civil rights effort was to arrive on the scene without a definite agenda, scope out the situation, listen, meet people, and then decide what to do. This technique had led him to come up with one of the civil rights movement's great strokes of tactical genius, the decision in 1963 to use children as demonstrators in Birmingham. The more time Bevel spent on the West Side, the more disenchanted he became with the idea of a movement based on opposition to Willis. Bevel felt that focusing on Willis's removal was inconsistent with the highest principles of nonviolent protest. "See, in the nonviolent movement you don't get rid of anybody," he says. "You have to get involved in a constitutional issue. Movements don't address getting rid of a person." At the same time, in keeping with his view that an organizer has to find his foot soldiers in unlikely places, Bevel began getting to know the gang members in the area, especially the Vice Lords, and he became convinced that they could be brought around to the path of righteousness and assistance to King. That was another reason to drop the Willis issue: it was never going to mobilize the gangs.

Seeing at first hand how rapidly the social fabric of the West Side was deteriorating, Bevel concluded that King needed to set a grand, nonspecific goal for the movement; "End Slums" became his working slogan, meaning that King should attack the problems of poverty, hunger, unemployment, poor schools, and inferior housing all at the same time. King's advisers, especially Bayard Rustin, were extremely doubtful about the workability of Bevel's idea. Ending slums was too vague a goal to provide the television news shows with a morally simple struggle of good against evil to report on, and invading Daley's turf was perilous. King's own thoughts, however, were increasingly turning to the broad problems of the black poor, which could not be solved by one specific victory in the political arena. Now that the Voting Rights Act had passed, he recognized that, in the whole panoply of racial problems in America, the urban ghettos stood out as exerting the greatest claim on his, and he hoped eventually the nation's, attention. All this made him receptive to Bevel's idea, and soon he had signed on to it.

On the evening of July 12, 1965, a fire truck rushed out of a station on the West Side to answer an alarm, absent the man whose job it was to steer its rear end. The driver of the truck, like everyone else who worked at the fire station, was white. The back of the truck went out of control and knocked over a light pole, which hit, and killed, Dessie Mae Williams, a twenty-three-year-old migrant from Clarksdale who had come to Chicago in 1959 and was working in a fishery. Two hundred people from the neighborhood quickly surrounded the firehouse and began throwing bricks and bottles, and soon Chicago's first all-black ghetto riot had begun. It lasted four days and left dozens of people injured.

The riot was profoundly shocking to Daley—the next month, Congressman Dan Rostenkowski, then a young protégé of Daley's, requested a personal meeting with President Johnson to express alarm about the mayor's state of mind, and to suggest that Daley be sent out of the country for a while on some pretext—and it gave Daley a specific reason to worry about King's presence in Chicago. Mayor Daley had no use for King to begin with. He believed that the crisis King was beginning to address in Chicago simply didn't exist, and by his lights no one who was not actually from Chicago had any business getting involved in Chicago's affairs. After the riot, he recognized that there was at least a danger that the thing he feared worst of all, a loss of order and control, might occur again in the ghettos, and he believed that King would stir up trouble there.

Daley had long since become accustomed to dealing with problems, when they arose, by making deals. He was much too clever anyway to provide King with the opportunity that so many white politicians in the South had by initially refusing to have anything to do with him and rejecting his whole program out of hand. King was planning a visit to Chicago two weeks after the riot; Daley sent him a telegram suggesting that they meet personally (King turned him down), and dispatched the director of the Chicago Commission on Human Relations, Edward Marciniak, to greet King when his plane landed at the airport.

In January 1966, King rented an apartment in Lawndale, and announced that he would live there three days a week for the duration of the Chicago campaign. In February, Daley announced a new program to clean up the slums. King's own program sputtered along. He seized a badly deteriorated apartment building a few blocks from where he was staying, but that didn't play well in the press. Bevel arranged for him to meet with Elijah Muhammad, who was then at the peak of his power, at Elijah's mansion on the South Side, but that produced nothing more than cordial encouragement from Elijah. Bevel generated more bad press by showing a film of the Watts riot to a group of Blackstone Rangers. Al Raby and Bevel were by now openly feuding. The winter and spring of 1966 passed without King's accomplishing anything important; the summer would be the make-or-break season for the Chicago campaign, because that was the only time of year when the civil rights movement could reliably turn out its people in large numbers. If the weather turned cold again without King's having done something, his momentum would be gone, and all his work in Chicago would be for naught.

King announced that he was going to hold a huge rally on July 10, a Sunday, at Soldier Field, the stadium where the Chicago Bears played. Afterward, he would lead a march to City Hall, where, just as his name-sake Martin Luther had tacked his ninety-five theses to the door of the church in Wittenberg in 1517, he would attach a list of demands to the front door. When the day came, King was under intense pressure from within the civil rights movement, because only a few weeks earlier, Stokely Carmichael had introduced the slogan "black power" in Missis-sippi, and the movement's commitment to integration and nonviolence was noticeably crumbling as a result. The Chicago rally was much more poorly attended than King had expected it to be, and the list of demands, produced by a committee, was long and overly complicated. The next day King met with Daley, who refused to accede to a single one of the demands and insisted that he was already doing everything for the slums that needed to be done.

After the meeting with Daley, King and his lieutenants abruptly changed course. They decided to stage a series of marches in white neigh-borhoods to protest housing segregation, which was still the maximally explosive issue in grassroots white Chicago. (In 1964, a sociology pro-fessor at the University of Chicago named Philip Hauser wrote a report attacking segregation in the city, and afterward had to be put under the kind of twenty-four-hour police guard that previously had been necessary only for black families who moved into white neighborhoods.) On July 30 they marched in Gage Park, on the South Side, and were greeted by whites throwing rocks and bottles. The next day they marched in Marquette Park, also on the South Side, and got the same reception; the white crowd there destroyed fifteen of the marchers' parked cars. Two days later they marched again, without incident. The next day they marched again. On August 5, King led another march in Marquette Park; Daley sent more than a thousand Chicago policemen to maintain order, but nevertheless King was hit by a rock just as the march began. Now King had created just the kind of situation that had brought him his great victories in the South: a dramatic confrontation between his nonviolent forces and brutal, hateful whites, over a single, morally clear-cut issue. Public support for the "End Slums" campaign had been flagging badly; as John McDermott, a white Chicago liberal who was working with King, puts it, "people woke up and literally *poured* into the movement" as soon as the focus shifted to housing.

Daley began to get entreaties from his white ward committeemen on the South Side to do something to stop King's marches. At the same time, he was becoming more and more worried about the situation in the West Side ghetto, which he felt King was making worse. In July, two days after King's rally in the stadium, a riot broke out on the Near West Side when police turned off a fire hydrant that kids in the neighborhood had opened to cool themselves off. There was looting, rock-throwing, and gunfire all over the West Side for four days, and 4,200 National Guardsmen had to be called in. Two blacks died, one of them a fourteen-year-old pregnant girl; two policemen were shot. Concern in Washington was high enough that John Doar and Roger Wilkins of the Justice Department were dispatched to Chicago on an Air Force plane; there they dropped in on King at his apartment in Lawndale and witnessed a remarkable nearly all-night meeting between him and a group of Vice Lords and members of other gangs, in which he labored to convince them that nonviolence was preferable to rioting. On the day of the march in which King was hit by a rock, Harry McPherson wrote President Johnson, ". . . the situation in Chicago is extremely bad. . . . Earlier this afternoon there were two telephone threats to King's life. A frequently unreliable informant told the FBI that he had been present at a meeting of the National States Rights Party where King's assassination was discussed."

King's forces turned up the heat on Daley to the highest possible level by threatening to hold a march in the notoriously prejudiced white suburb of Cicero — Cicero, which made Marquette Park look like a Quaker summer camp; Cicero, where only a few months earlier a black teenager had been beaten to death by four white kids. Daley agreed to hold a "summit meeting" on August 17 between the city's political and business establishment and the civil rights movement. The meeting went on all day and ended inconclusively with everyone agreeing to meet again on August 26. In the interim, Daley double-crossed King by getting a judge to issue an injunction against future marches; King retaliated by promising to march in Cicero on August 28 if the next meeting didn't produce an agreement.

At the second summit meeting, King promised to stop marching, and he and Daley signed a new open-housing plan for Chicago, which was immediately denounced as a sellout by the elements of the movement to the left of King. On August 31, Ben Willis resigned as school superintendent. In September, the local chapter of CORE marched through Cicero, without King. Nothing happened.

The dramatic byplay between King and Daley served to obscure part of the meaning of what was going on that summer: the chance for an effective mainstream civil rights movement in Chicago (indeed, in the North generally) that would focus on the problems of the ghettos essentially evaporated. Because of its timing, so soon after the riot, the summit agreement looked like a measure aimed in part at helping the West Side, but the truth was that the End Slums campaign hadn't caught on, and open housing was an issue only for blacks who had the money to buy houses—it was irrelevant to the life of a project dweller like Ruby Haynes. To the extent that the agreement had an effect, it was only to hasten the movement of blacks with jobs out of neighborhoods like Lawndale.

One other effort begun in 1965 by King's forces in Chicago lasted. Operation Breadbasket, an organization led by the young Jesse Jackson, by threatening to stage consumer boycotts induced businesses with substantial black clienteles to hire more black employees. It, too, mostly helped working-class and middle-class blacks with good employment histories, who then often used their new jobs as a way of leaving the ghettos. Also in 1965, Father John Egan, Saul Alinsky's friend in the Catholic archdiocese, helped to found an organization called the Contract Buyers' League, which organized protests against the system under which realtors would sell blacks houses "on contract" and repossess them if the monthly payments lagged. The Contract Buyers' League took off, too: it turned out hundreds of people at its weekly meetings for years, until, in 1970, the real estate industry agreed to reform its practices — another victory for blacks who wanted to establish themselves outside the slums.

The organizational legacy of the summit meeting is an agency created under King and Daley's agreement called the Leadership Council for Metropolitan Open Communities. Today the leadership council's main job is to run a program begun in 1976 as part of the settlement of Dorothy Gautreaux's lawsuit against the Chicago Housing Authority. The program places black families from the projects in integrated neighborhoods in the suburbs, one by one and quite successfully. On the days when the leadership council holds an open sign-up for people who want the program to move them, there is usually a mob scene at its office, with thousands of residents of the projects lined up to get their name on the list so they can get out.

Almost the instant that the summit agreement was signed and King gave up his apartment in Lawndale, the interracial, nonviolent civil rights movement in Chicago disappeared. The furtherance of black progress became essentially a black cause, pursued in a way that was quite similar (aside from the rhetoric of self-determination) to the standard Chicago ethnic-group staking of claims to a rightful share of the benefits of the political system. King was fully attuned to the problems of the ghettos, and he continued to search for the magic formula that would persuade the country as a whole to identify with poor blacks in the cities in the same way that it had identified with Rosa Parks in Montgomery, and the children in Birmingham, and the people marching across the Edmund Pettus Bridge in Montgomery — to see them as decent people who had been subjected to a wrong that could now be righted. He never found it, and nobody else did either.

AFTER Connie Henry's mother, Lillian, finished her jail term for shooting her lover and moved back into their small slum apartment in Lawndale, the life of the family never really got on track. Lillian had seen her marriage and then a serious romance fall apart, leaving her feeling lonely and bereft; also, the community life of the West Side ghetto where she was living with her three children was crumbling before her eyes. For reasons she didn't understand but that she suspected had to do with her race, she had been subjected to a long, steady descent from her middle-class background in North Carolina to this. She reacted by giving up. She stopped supervising her children very much, aside from yelling at them occasionally, and she drank. Through her elementary school years Connie had always been a good student, but when she became a teenager she adopted the practice of getting dressed for school in the mornings, leaving the apartment, meeting her friends, waiting until Lillian had gone off to her job as a school crossing guard, and returning home to spend the day just hanging out. One day when Connie was thirteen, her younger sister, Charlene, came home from a neighbor's apartment and told her that there was a boy sixteen or seventeen years old visiting there who had asked her if she had an older sister at home. That sounded interesting to Connie; she went over and met the boy, whose name was Ivy Hart, Jr., and soon they were dating.

Lillian Henry was delighted with Connie's new romance — so much so that Connie, reflecting on it later, felt that her mother had pushed her into something more serious than she had in mind. Ivy was a high school dropout from the West Side, but his mother was married, and he had a good job in a paint factory. The great point in his favor, to Lillian's mind, was that he was generous with Connie. He took her shopping for clothes at the stores along Roosevelt Road; virtually anything she asked him for, he would buy. He gave her money, too — usually fifty or sixty dollars a week, and sometimes as much as a hundred. He began to talk about marriage, and even bought Connie a ring.

In return for all these favors, Ivy expected Connie to sleep with him, and she did. "If you accept something from someone, you have to pay back too," she says now. "It was a duty — just something you had to do." Lillian had never told Connie anything about contraception, and Connie didn't use any. Only fourteen years old, she got pregnant. When she told Lillian that she had missed her period, Lillian went into a rage — "My mother said, 'You done give up your life now,'" Connie says. "She cussed me from a boot to a shoe." The teachers at school started asking her why she was putting on so much weight; in those days, a pregnant girl had to leave her neighborhood school and go to a special maternity school. Preferring to avoid that, Connie stopped going to school altogether. When she was fifteen, she gave birth to a daughter, Maxine.

Connie and Ivy's relationship went downhill. He lost his temper a lot; sometimes he slapped her. Before long they split up, but Connie was pregnant again. When she was sixteen, her second child, Marlo, was born. Her mother and her sister helped out with the babies, and Connie sporadically attended Farragut High School, a big brick structure on the West Side that was particularly suffering under the policies of Ben Willis:

it had 3,400 students, divided into two shifts, and there were twenty-one of the mobile classrooms known as Willis Wagons set up in its playground.

In 1965, the long arm of the war on poverty reached out to Connie. She saw a flyer describing a program to help kids get jobs — it was the National Youth Corps, the Labor Department's small piece of the antipoverty action. Connie went down to the Urban Progress Center on Roosevelt Road and put in an application, and two days later she had a job as a laboratory aide in a veterans' hospital, paying $1.45 an hour. She liked the work, but after a year and a half, all the National Youth Corps trainees at the hospital were told there had been a funding cutback in Washington and were laid off. After that, Connie never got back on the road to any kind of career. She got summer jobs with the city, took care of her children, and visited with her friends.

Now that the family included Connie's babies, the Henrys' three-room apartment in Lawndale was much too small, so Lillian found a bigger place a few blocks away, on Ogden Avenue, a wide shopping street that was rapidly deteriorating into a slum as its businesses closed down and its landlords abandoned their apartment buildings. The Vice Lords controlled the neighborhood. Connie's brother, James, joined a small gang called the Ogden Boys. The apartment where Dr. King had lived was just a stone's throw away; his visit to Chicago made a deep impression on Lillian Henry, and was one of the few things Connie remembers her mother ever holding up to her as a cause for feeling optimistic about the world they lived in.

On the night of April 5, 1968, the Henrys were at home watching television when a report came on that a riot had broken out on Roosevelt Road, seven blocks to the north of their apartment, in the wake of King's assassination in Memphis. Connie went out to have a look. She found a scene of complete chaos. Roosevelt Road was up in flames. The streets were full of people — kids from the neighborhood breaking windows, throwing fire-bombs, and ransacking stores, and police doing battle with the rioters. Overhead, unbeknownst to Connie, Mayor Daley was watching from a helicopter. A police detective called Connie a "black bitch." At one point she was caught in the middle of hand-to-hand combat between the police and the rioters and had to run full-speed down an alley to escape injury. After that she went back home; by the next morning, Roosevelt Road was a smoldering ruin. Daley gave a press conference where he made what Mike Royko called "the most famous utterance of his career":

> I have conferred with the superintendent of police this morning and I gave him the following instructions: I said to him very emphatically and very definitely that an order be issued by him immediately and under his signature to shoot to kill any arsonist or anyone with a molotov cocktail in his hand because they're potential murderers, and to issue a police order to shoot to maim or cripple anyone looting any stores in our city.

Any shred of hope that Lawndale had of being a decent neighborhod was now gone. More stores closed. Within a few years, the great factories run by Western Electric and International Harvester, and a host of small ones, were gone. Sears moved its headquarters to the Loop. Boarded-up buildings, and empty spaces where there used to be buildings before they were torched by hired arsonists, were everywhere; the address where King stayed is now a vacant lot. The residents left in droves, except for people like the Henrys, who didn't have the money to.

Connie began going with a young man named Charles Mays, a guitar player she had met at a little recording studio in Lawndale where she hung out sometimes. Charles played in little clubs on the West Side, but he wasn't really going anywhere as a musician: he lived with his grandfather, supported himself with a public-aid check (welfare is available to single men and women, as well as to unwed mothers, in Illinois), and drank too much wine. Early in 1969, Connie got pregnant again, and on March 14 of that year, at the age of eighteen, she got on public aid herself. On November 21, her third daughter, Melanie, was born. By that time Connie had long since broken up with Charles; although he never fought with her, he was always either drunk or just dull and torpid, and he seemed to offer her no hope of economic support or even lively companionship.

Back in the 1950s, when Ruby and Luther Haynes were living on the West Side, their apartment was on Ogden Avenue, quite near the building where Connie Henry and her family lived in the late 1960s. Ruby used to send her oldest son, George, over to a little neighborhood supermarket to pick up the family's groceries. When George got into his late teens, the owner of the store hired him and trained him to be a meatcutter. George got married, pursued his career, and stayed on the West Side when the rest of the Haynes family moved back to the South Side. Now he lived in the same building as Connie Henry, 3355 West Ogden, and Connie and George's wife became friends. George was still in close touch with his mother and his brothers. Sometimes when they ran out of food he would send groceries over, and there were regular visits back and forth. On Memorial Day, 1969, Connie and her sister dropped by George's apartment and found his younger brother Johnnie there — a tall, thin, handsome fifteen-year-old. Johnnie immediately became interested in Connie's sister, but she wasn't attracted to him, so he turned his attention to Connie. During the summer of 1969, when Connie was pregnant with Melanie, they became a couple.

One night in 1970, in a tavern on Ogden Avenue, Lillian Henry ran into a woman named Dorothy Jane Beard, who was her rival for the affections of a man. They got into an argument that kept escalating until Dorothy Beard pulled a gun out of her purse and shot and killed Lillian. When the police made inquiries, nobody who was at the tavern that night wanted to talk; Dorothy served a prison term of only 117 days. To Connie's mind, the tragedy was made worse by the sense that her mother had gotten to a place in life where it was as if she barely existed. Her murder went essentially unpunished. She left behind no money and few worldly possessions. Her children, going through her things after her death, couldn't even find a birth certificate.

Connie moved in with a friend in the neighborhood, and, when another apartment opened up in the same building, she took it. It was an awful place — rat-infested and regularly without gas or water. The landlord, a man Connie knew only by his Lawndale nickname, "the Jewman," was never around except when the rent was due. Connie was terribly lonely without her mother, and she began thinking seriously for the first time about getting married and somehow finding a real life for herself.

A T THE headquarters of the Office of Economic Opportunity in Washington, there was a great deal of ill will toward Mayor Daley and his Urban Progress Centers. It was bad enough that Daley considered the gospel of maximum feasible participation to be so lacking in merit that he chose to ignore it entirely, and even worse that he had enough power to be able to get away with such a radical departure from the spirit of the war on poverty. Sargent Shriver heard constant grumbling about Daley from his troops. "They do not permit any type of community organization," an official of the OEO's Office of Inspection wrote Shriver in 1966. "The problems of the Chicago program are sins not of commission, but of omission. We sensed a general hostility . . . to programs involving community organization or social action; in other words, hostility to programs which deal with the poor not as a collection of individuals with problems, but as a group sharing certain common difficulties." An internal memo of the Office of Inspection written a few months later sarcastically referred to the head of Daley's antipoverty agency as "our beloved Deton Brooks."

In 1967, a junior White House aide spent three days in the Chicago ghettos and reported back that "the poverty program does not reach the people and is controlled by the city government"; an OEO evaluation report written in the same year complained that "there is no real attempt . . . to involve the poor," and ended with this warning: "A peaceful city is not enough! Meaningful change is needed!" Daley's hostility was extended to agencies other than the OEO, too. When the Department of Health, Education and Welfare made a grant to Martin Luther King to run an adult literacy program in Chicago, Daley called the White House and had the grant rescinded; Wilbur Cohen, who was in Chicago on other business, tried to get an appointment to soothe him, but Daley refused to see him.

The riots lent a special urgency to the arguments of Daley's critics in Washington: maximum feasible participation was not just a good idea, but a necessity if the big explosion in Chicago that everybody feared was to be avoided. Deton Brooks kept the Urban Progress Centers open until midnight every night during the summer of 1967 to help prevent riots, but most of the people at the OEO headquarters in Washington didn't believe that that would do the job, because they thought Brooks's operation was out of touch with the real leadership of the ghettos. In looking for some organized force in the ghettos that seemed to be truly controlled by the poor, as Daley's machine wasn't, they began to turn in the same direction that James Bevel had a couple of years earlier — toward the gangs.

The Blackstone Rangers, Chicago's most famous gang, had always maintained some connections outside the criminal world. A radical white Presbyterian minister in Woodlawn named John Fry had adopted the Rangers as a kind of auxiliary organization of his church; he let them hold weekly meetings, and even store weapons, there. The Rangers also had longstanding ties to The Woodlawn Organization, which was now run by Arthur Brazier, the Pentecostal minister recruited by Saul Alinsky and Nicholas Von Hoffman back in the early 1960s. Jeff Fort, the head of the Rangers, had begun to use the rhetoric of black nationalism and to talk about turning his gang toward community-building efforts. Awestruck reports circulated about Fort's ability to get thousands of otherwise unmanageable kids to follow his orders, and to dissipate near-riots with a wave of his hand. Fort, an undersized, illiterate teenager, was a figure in black Chicago. Once he brought a delegation of Blackstone Rangers over to the offices of the *Chicago Defender*. Louis Martin, who had returned to Chicago from his service to Presidents Kennedy and Johnson and was running the paper, met with them. "I had seven or eight of them in," Martin says. "I didn't know what they were like. They talked and talked and I couldn't understand them. I couldn't understand what it was about Jeff Fort that inspired people so much. They were all very deferential to Fort. I told them if they wanted to make some money, they could sell the *Defender*, but when I broached this it was clear it was the last thing they had in mind."

What they did have in mind, in part, was playing a role in the war on poverty.

The Woodlawn Organization had received a few antipoverty grants, but never anything major, because of its opposition to the machine. Early in 1967, an OEO official named Jeremiah Bernstein approached Arthur Brazier with the idea of his putting together a program, involving real money, in which The Woodlawn Organization would work with the Rangers to fight poverty in Woodlawn. In the spring, Brazier submitted a detailed proposal to the OEO in Washington for a program that would have the Rangers, along with the Disciples, running a job-training program under the supervision of The Woodlawn Organization.

A strain of faith in the redeemability of teenage criminals had always existed in the OEO and, before there was an OEO, in the President's Committee on Juvenile Delinquency. In 1962, in a letter to Lloyd Ohlin about the Chicago gangs, a field representative of the juvenile delinquency committee had written, "While members of the group engage in constant social deviance, this is not an integral aspect of group life. The deviance is not carried out collectively, but by individuals in twos and threes, independent of the group." The idea that the gangs could be steered into productive activity if the opportunity for it were provided by Washington was part of the theoretical foundation on which the OEO rested, and besides, the Rangers appealed to the group at the OEO that most enthusiastically embraced the daring spirit of the late 1960s. "They were ballsy," says William Haddad, then the OEO's inspector general and one of its leading radical voices. For Shriver, making the grant to the Rangers was a way to demonstrate to his staff and to his many outside critics on the left that he had not completely forsaken the spirit of maximum feasible participation in Chicago out of deference to Daley. In June, the OEO announced that it would give The Woodlawn Organization and the gangs $927,000 to operate their program for a year.

Shriver was typically ebullient about the grant. "TWO will put the Blackstone Rangers and the East Side Disciples to work," he wrote Joseph Califano shortly after the announcement. "The City Police will see that armed fighting stops between the Rangers and the Disciples. . . . Finally, the grant was concluded without any exhortation from the Citizens Crusade Against Poverty, Walter Reuther, RFK, [Illinois Senator] Chuck Percy, Dick Boone, the Presbyterian ministers, Pat Moynihan, or other heavy thinkers." David Stahl, Daley's top assistant and later his deputy mayor, happened to run into Shriver in Washington at around that time; bursting with pride, Shriver told him about the Rangers grant, saying it was "for the city of Chicago." Stahl says, "I said, 'That's not for the city of Chicago, that's for the Blackstone Rangers.'"

Daley, outmaneuvered at last, was furious. He always believed that the real reason the grant had gone through was that a secret deal had been struck between The Woodlawn Organization and its old archenemy, the University of Chicago, under which TWO would lay off the university if the university would help TWO get more antipoverty money. The grant was announced with such fanfare that Daley couldn't do much to stop it, but he needn't have worried about its permanently eroding his authority. In the history of the OEO, there was no grant that was as complete a failure. The deadly war between the Rangers and the Disciples continued. Only seventy-six of the eight hundred participants in the program were actually placed in jobs. Accounting procedures were spotty. At the program's four training centers (one initially run by Jeff Fort, another by David Barksdale of the Disciples), "much time seemed to be spent . . . on gang-related business," according to an exhaustive report done later by the University of Chicago's School of Social Service Administration. One observer quoted in the report said, "For the most part, a walk through the classrooms presented a picture of bored and sullen youngsters. No one in authority interacted with them, and they interacted with each other minimally."

In the fall of 1967, just after the program began, Jeff Fort was arrested on murder charges. Eugene Hairston, then the number-two man in the Blackstone Rangers and a literacy instructor in the program, was also arrested for murder. Three Rangers who worked in the training center run by Fort were arrested for rape, and Brazier allowed them to keep their jobs in the program. On New Year's Eve, 1967, Henry Porter, another instructor in the program and a member of the Disciples, shot two Rangers who were students in the program, killing one of them. The *Chicago Tribune*, then still the leading voice of Midwestern Republicanism, took off after the program with great glee. A few headlines will convey the flavor of the *Tribune*'s coverage:

OEO AIDS FACE KILLING, RAPE TRIALS

NAPS, DICE, AND COMIC BOOKS:
POLICE TELL HOW OEO'S $972,000 IS SPENT

QUIT SCHOOL FOR EASY MONEY, GANG LEADERS URGE

John McClellan of Arkansas, chairman of the Senate Government Operations Committee, held outraged hearings about the grant, at which Fort appeared in response to a subpoena but refused to testify. President Johnson himself became concerned about the situation.

In May 1968, the OEO shut down the project. In June, Bertrand Harding, who had replaced Shriver as head of the OEO, reported to Johnson:

The present situation is that the project is closed down and we are considering an application for renewal which would materially change many of the controversial features. As I indicated to you on the phone, I have been delaying final action on this application in order to be sure that whatever I did was consistent with Mayor Daley's views. He has, however, refused to render an opinion. My best judgment at this time is that, in spite of the changes proposed in the project, we will not refund. Most of the evidence I have now indicates that the project was one of those experiences that just didn't work out.

Harding finally turned down The Woodlawn Organization's application for renewal.

Oddly enough, the liberal establishment maintained its illusions about the Blackstone Rangers. Fort's admirers said he deserved credit for preventing a riot on the South Side after King's assassination. Senator Percy brought two Rangers to one of the Nixon inaugural balls in 1969. The Ford Foundation gave the Rangers funding. Well into the late 1980s, Shriver said proudly, "I'd go into Chicago, and the Rangers would come up with a plan and if my people liked the plan, I'd give 'em a half million. You put the money where the problems are."

The Rangers themselves never made the hoped-for transition to respectable community leadership, to say the least. Fort changed their name to the Black P (for "prince," or "power") Stone Nation. In 1972 he was put on trial for defrauding the government of money during the Woodlawn program, convicted, and sent to prison; there he converted to Islam, changed his name to Malik, and changed the name of the gang again, to the El Rukns. The gang bought a defunct movie theater in the old South Side black belt, outfitted it with a thick steel door, and declared it to be its mosque; inside, in dark windowless rooms decorated with Islamic symbols, Fort's followers would reverently tell the visitors who sometimes happened by about the struggles of "our beloved Imam Malik, may the blessings of Allah be cast upon him," against religious persecution by the Chicago Police Department. Fort moved to Milwaukee, but he could occasionally be seen riding around the South Side in a chauffeured limousine. In 1981 dozens of El Rukns were indicted on charges of drug dealing. In 1987 the FBI charged Fort with sending two El Rukns to Libya to offer their services to Muammar Qaddafi as terrorists in the United States, for a fee of $2 million, and Fort was indicted for ordering the murder of a member of a rival gang. Today Fort is back in prison but is still supposed to be running the El Rukns, who have the reputation of being the most ruthless and violent of all the gangs in Chicago.

Daley no longer had much trouble with challenges, from the OEO or anybody else, to his absolute control over the poverty programs in Chicago. When the Model Cities program got under way, Daley brought into his office a young bureaucrat from the state employment service named Erwin France, worked out a plan, received his usual generous share of funding from Washington, and then, at the beginning of 1969, shifted Deton Brooks to another job and put France in charge of all Model Cities and OEO programs.

France, who was thirty years old at the time, belonged to a younger generation of ambitious college-educated blacks who gravitated to local administrative positions in the war on poverty because that was the best opportunity for advancement available to them. He grew up in St. Louis, the son of a janitor, and came to Chicago to go to George Williams College, a school that trained people to work in YMCAs. France was the only black member of his class. When he graduated he found that no YMCA in the country would have him, so he got a job as a neighborhood worker with the Chicago Commission on Youth Welfare. From there he went to the employment service, which set up offices in the Urban Progress Centers, and then to Daley's office. Although France had spent his whole career up to that point in the ghettos, he was a machine man at heart — "a bureaucrat with elbows," Louis Martin says — and he quickly demonstrated that he was more adept than Deton Brooks at helping Daley deflect the parries of the community action people in Washington. On one of the occasions when Washington was threatening to cut off Daley's funds because of his resistance to sharing control with neighborhood groups, France remembers, "Daley said, 'Talk to them.' I said, 'I already did.' He said, 'Did you get the fellas to go with you?' He meant the nine members of the Chicago congressional delegation. I called the regional director and said, 'I'd like to bring some concerned citizens to talk to you.' They believe in citizen participation, right? Well, when they saw who the nine citizens were, they nearly shit. The funds didn't get cut off."

The Model Cities program in Chicago focused its attentions on four neighborhoods: Lawndale, Woodlawn, an area around the Robert Taylor Homes known officially as Grand Boulevard, and a poor section of the North Side called Uptown. It mounted large special-education, community-relations, and health-care programs, and built some new housing. The only place where there was any dispute over Daley's control of the program was Woodlawn, because of the presence of The Woodlawn Organization, the control of which was by now passing from Arthur Brazier to Leon Finney, a young man of about France's age who was a grandson of T. J. Huddleston, the black funeral home king of the Mississippi Delta. Daley had very little trouble swatting aside The Woodlawn Organization's challenge this time around: he simply put a few of its members on the neighborhood Model Cities board, but not enough to prevent people he controlled from having a voting majority.

France had few illusions about the ability of the Model Cities program to clean up the ghettos. What it and the other poverty programs he ran were really about was jobs, starting with his own exalted position and moving down through thousands and thousands of humbler billets. At its peak, just before the reelection of Richard Nixon, France's empire had a budget of $200 million and employed 20,000 people — half as many as there were on the regular city payroll. In 1971, during the summertime (the season when antipoverty funds flowed most freely, because the government was still terrified about the possibility of more riots breaking out), France was sending checks to 70,000 people.

The net result of Model Cities in Chicago was an especially pronounced version of the same old story of community development efforts in the ghettos. The many people who got jobs in the program were helped enormously, while the neighborhoods that were supposedly being healed got worse, not least because many of their residents used their new government paychecks to finance their relocation to better areas. Grand Boulevard, the neighborhood around the Robert Taylor Homes, lost 32 per cent of its population between 1970 and 1980. Lawndale lost 35 per cent. Uptown, the North Side Model Cities neighborhood, lost 13 per cent. Woodlawn, which suffered an especially severe epidemic of arson as its landlords cut their losses — there were 1,600 fires a year there in 1970 and 1971 — lost 33 per cent of its population in the 1960s and another 32 per cent in the 1970s. A statistic that helps to demonstrate where all the people who left the ghettos were going is the rate of black population growth in the Chicago suburbs: 65 per cent in the 1960s, 80 per cent in the 1970s. Demographic change is usually incremental; these are unusually dramatic numbers. Since the residents who left the ghettos were the better-off ones, the ghettos became poorer as they were depopulated. In Grand Boulevard in 1970, 37 per cent of the residents were below the poverty line and 40 per cent were in female-headed families; in 1980, 51 per cent were poor, and 71 per cent lived in female-headed families.

Erwin France, and also Leon Finney, went on to become private consultants: affluent, well-turned-out (France in middle age could be seen around Chicago during the winter wearing a full-length mink coat), and well-connected men who knew what was what in the mayor's office, the school board, and the housing authority, and were often blessed with municipal contracts. They were only the most famous members of a large cadre of black Chicagoans who used the war on poverty as a launching pad into the upper reaches of local government. "It helped usher in a middle class that didn't exist," says Louis Martin. "The 'bureaucrats' who took all the money were blacks — college grads who would have been in the damn poverty line themselves. Go back and look at the resumes of the blacks that are around now and you'll find ninety per cent of them were tied into some screwball poverty thing. Each generation has to find their jobs." Aside from the poverty programs themselves, the settlement of antidiscrimination lawsuits against the police and fire departments produced hiring plans that created many new positions for blacks. A massive school-building program in the ghettos, undertaken by Daley to alleviate the overcrowding of the Ben Willis years without putting blacks in white schools, led to a large increase in the number of black teachers in the system. New community colleges were built in black areas, and they were staffed substantially by blacks. The Chicago Transit Authority hired many black drivers and motormen. In Chicago as in the rest of the country, government became the business of the black middle class.

Mayor Daley didn't like his city's being sued and otherwise prodded from outside the system, but the net result for Chicago of the Great Society and its aftershocks was not completely displeasing to him. The black migration was over, and the machine had held, while becoming much bigger and richer than it had been before the Democrats recaptured the White House in 1960. He was still in control; nobody had ever gotten the best of him, except perhaps for the case of the Blackstone Rangers grant, and that had plainly been a Pyrrhic victory for the OEO. Even the 1968 Democratic Convention, where the Chicago police's attacks on demonstrators created Daley's best-known public embarrassment, was free of racial turmoil, because, even though it was held only a few months after the worst riots of the decade, Daley had been in a strong enough position to cut a deal with black leaders to keep black protesters off the streets. He completely fended off such liberal Washington policies as requirements that new public housing for blacks be built outside the ghettos (Daley simply stopped building public housing altogether), and school busing orders; in the case of busing, the Department of Health, Education and Welfare contemplated moving against Chicago for years and finally decided it would be foolhardy even to try. Stanley Pottinger, who was assistant secretary of HEW for civil rights in the Nixon administration, says, "In Chicago, the people at HEW told me it's impossible. Have you ever been to the South Side? Do you know how many buses it would take? Sometimes there's a case where you just throw up your hands, and Chicago was it."

Daley did eventually begin to lose his political grip on black Chicago—never to the extent that his mayoralty was threatened, but enough to bother him. When he finally suffered a defeat that really mattered, though, it came not from the outsiders against whom he was constantly on guard, but from within his own organization.

ALL THROUGH the 1950s and 1960s, the Reverend Uless Carter was working as a servant for a group of white families in the rich suburb of Hinsdale, spending each day doing chores at a different house there. Uless had spent his first few years in Chicago following the typical trajectory of black migrants from the Mississippi Delta. Because he had grown up in a sharecropper family he lacked an education, so when he moved to Chicago he found unskilled employment, first in a restaurant, then in the stockyards. He married twice; he moved out of the poor kitchenette district to bigger apartments on the expanding frontier of the South Side black belt; but then some combination of circumstances—the breakup of his second marriage, the strength of his social idealism and his religious faith—led him to become a minister and embark on a low-paying career as a domestic so that he would have more time to tend to his flock. He lived a modest bachelor's life on the South Side, staying for the longest single stretch at a rooming house a few blocks away from Ruby Haynes's building in the Robert Taylor Homes. His real energies went into his duties at his congregation, the Full Gospel Baptist Church.

Eventually Uless built Full Gospel up to the point where it had nearly three hundred members, and many of them were elderly people, the most valued kind of parishioners for a storefront preacher because they attended church faithfully and tended not to move to different parts of the city as their economic fortunes changed. After several moves from its original location, Full Gospel was housed in a building in Woodlawn. Uless was alarmed by the presence of the Blackstone Rangers in the neighborhood—occasionally he would see members of the gang walking along Sixty-third Street carrying guns—but on the whole he felt the church was well situated and likely to keep growing. In fact, he was so busy by now that, after fifteen years of running Full Gospel all by himself, he began to feel the need for an assistant minister.

A group of young women joined Uless's congregation as gospel singers (even a small Baptist church needed a choir, as well as an electrified band and a few women in nurses' uniforms to assist parishioners who lost their composure during services), and they introduced Uless to a young man named Reverend Davis, who functioned as their manager. Uless liked him so much that he offered him the job of assistant minister, which Reverend Davis accepted with alacrity. Their partnership went along smoothly for a while. Then, one day, the local Democratic precinct organization asked Uless if it could hold a meeting at the Full Gospel church. He said no, because he didn't believe in mixing religion and politics, but when a Methodist minister down the street agreed to let his church be used, Uless offered to go over and lock the place up after the Democratic meeting was over. On the night of the Democratic meeting, a Bible class was scheduled at Full Gospel; Uless arranged for Reverend Davis to teach it so that he could look after the Methodist church.

While Uless was watching the political meeting wind up, another Baptist minister who was a friend of his happened by. "Reverend Carter, I didn't know you had a Moslem teaching your congregation," he said. Uless asked him what he meant by that; the minister said that he had stopped by Full Gospel and heard Reverend Davis saying things that were inconsistent with Baptist doctrine. Alarmed, Uless hurried back to Full Gospel as soon as the Democrats were done and stood quietly in the doorway. There he heard Reverend Davis say that Jesus had been a sinner like all other men, that he had risen from the dead only in the minds of his followers, rather than corporeally, and that he was not blessed with eternal life and therefore could never return to this world. Uless walked into the church so that everyone could see him and said, as he recalls it, "I think every one of you needs to be on the sinners' bench and be saved. Reverend Davis, from what I heard, you're no longer my assistant preacher. You can sit in the congregation. Baptists *believe* that Jesus rose from the grave and has eternal life. We *believe* in the Resurrection."

There was grumbling from some of the deacons, and no one rose to Uless's defense; obviously, there was some kind of insurrection going on. At the next meeting of Full Gospel, and the next, Uless wouldn't let Reverend Davis preach. Reverend Davis's allies responded by calling a meeting of the congregation for eight o'clock one evening. Uless announced that he would hold a meeting the same evening at seven. When he arrived, he had the church secretary read his letter of resignation.

As holder of Full Gospel's charter, Uless got to retain possession of the name, but he lost the building and, with it, his painstakingly built-up congregation. Judging the South Side to be so oversupplied with churches that he would never be able to build up a congregation again there, he started Full Gospel from scratch in an old house on the West Side. Reverend Davis prospered in Uless's old location for a few years, but then he left Chicago suddenly. Uless heard that a series of legal and personal troubles had befallen him, involving his being caught at misdeeds in various extracurricular economic and romantic undertakings he was engaged in. Uless saw this turn of fate as divine retribution for Reverend Davis's stealing his congregation, similar in kind if not in severity to the demise of Broughton, the plantation manager back in Clarksdale three decades earlier. But the Lord's meting out of justice didn't extend to the restoration of the Full Gospel Baptist Church to its former prosperity.

Full Gospel's new home was in the Twenty-fifth Ward, whose political boss was Vito Marzullo, one of the longest-lasting old bulls of the machine—he served as the Twenty-fifth's alderman from 1953 to 1984. Soon after Uless opened his church there, his precinct captain, a man who had a job in City Hall as Marzullo's private secretary, began paying him regular visits. One night there was a big revival meeting in a rented hall on the West Side at which a lot of black ministers, including Uless, spoke; the precinct captain was there listening.

The city had planted trees along the residential street where Full Gospel was located. Most of them were quickly torn down by gang members, but Uless put fences around the trees in front of his church and chased away the neighborhood boys when he saw them hanging around. In his speech at the revival meeting, he told the story of the trees. He said that when the city planted trees in a white neighborhood, you could go back a few years later and see that they were growing nicely; but in the black neighborhoods, folks would let the trees get torn down, and neglect their lawns, and throw garbage out on the sidewalks, and not keep a strict disciplinary eye on their children. Uless said that black folks had to realize that the mayor couldn't take care of their neighborhoods or raise their children; they had to put their own house in order. It wasn't what people wanted to hear, but he had to say it.

A few days later, the precinct captain came by the church to see Uless. "Reverend Carter," he said, "you really hit the nail on the head in that speech." He said he had told Alderman Marzullo about the speech, and the alderman had been impressed; not only that, Alderman Marzullo had told the mayor about it, and the mayor had been impressed. The precinct captain said that on behalf of the alderman and the mayor, he'd like to

make Uless an offer: he could have a good job with the city and a nice
building for his church. He didn't even have to say what he expected in
return, because Uless was well aware of the way the system worked.
Plenty of ministers he knew were on the city payroll in some capacity
that rarely required their presence at work. When a neighborhood
switched over from white to black, these ministers would be given the
opportunity to take over the most substantial newly vacated churches and
halls in the area, for little or no money, as the new homes for their
congregations. One minister he knew had recently been given a large
movie theater on Roosevelt Road. The ministers' side of the bargain was
simple: all they had to do was guarantee that all their parishioners would
vote with the machine.

Uless turned the precinct captain down. He still felt that politics and
religion shouldn't be joined together. The precinct captain accepted his
refusal graciously and remained friendly, but of course there would be
no job and no new church for Uless. Uless never regretted his decision.
In fact, he felt it had been vindicated (and his belief in the inevitability
of God's punishment of sinners borne out) when, a few years later, a
politically connected minister on the South Side named Edmond Blair
was found shot to death in his Lincoln Continental—obviously not by
street criminals, since his diamond ring and the wad of cash in his pocket
were left untouched. Full Gospel had to keep struggling, though. It
moved around to different places on the West Side, and then finally, in
1977, back to the poorest and most rapidly depopulating section of the
South Side, not far from its very first location in the early 1950s. It was
in a crummy building: water leaked from the ceiling in a spot directly
over the pulpit, and Uless's dwindling congregation was beginning to
grumble a lot. Uless found that he was unable to get in touch with his
landlord about fixing the leak, so he went down to City Hall to find out
what was going on. There he discovered that the building had been
repossessed by a bank. He decided it was time to give up, and he closed
Full Gospel down.

On his sixty-third birthday, Uless had to have surgery to remove a part
of his stomach. After that, he had trouble doing his work. He couldn't
reach above his head, and sometimes while he was picking up something
from the ground he would pass out. He moved out of his rooming house
into one of the Chicago Housing Authority's senior citizens' projects on
the West Side.

He was not feeling good about his life in Chicago. The main reason was that he had lost his church, but also the parts of the city that were in his ambit had greatly changed for the worse. Having lived all his life in ghettos, Uless had little sense of what forces in the outside world might be affecting them; once, in Hinsdale, he had fished a thrown-out Bible from the trash because he wanted to find out if white people had a different Scripture from black people. But the evidence of disaster in his neighborhood in Chicago was incontrovertible, even if the reasons for it were mysterious. Forty-seventh Street—the Forty-seventh Street that had so amazed him as a young man, with its stores and theaters and bustling street life—was gone; it had become a neighborhood of stores with steel grates on their windows, housing projects spray-painted with gang graffiti, and vacant lots where men stood around fires built in garbage cans and passed around wine bottles wrapped in brown paper bags. Sixty-third Street was gone. He had missed the train that carried people to better neighborhoods and better jobs; his best-paying employer in Hinsdale gave him forty dollars a day. Everybody he knew talked constantly about shootings and stabbings.

Uless had no wife and no children to keep him in Chicago, and he was old enough now to get on Social Security. He decided to retire, and, in 1979, he moved to Flint, Michigan, where one of his sisters was living.

THE CHILDREN of families living in the Robert Taylor Homes did not have to travel far to go to school. Mayor Daley built new elementary schools to handle the large increase in the number of children in the neighborhood brought on by the construction of the project. One of them, Beethoven, was on the grounds of the project; another, Farren, where Ruby Haynes's younger children went, was right across the street. Ruby's kids went to middle school at Parkman, which is on the other side of the Dan Ryan Expressway from 5135 South Federal, and to high school at DuSable, also just across the street from the Taylor Homes, at Forty-ninth and State.

DuSable long predated the project: it had opened its doors back in 1935 as Chicago's second black high school, and had a proud tradition as one of the essential institutions of black Chicago. It was named for Jean Baptiste Pointe du Sable, a black trader from the Caribbean who built a cabin on the Chicago River in the late 1700s and by the twentieth century was enshrined in civic lore as Chicago's first settler. During the glory years of Forty-seventh Street, a DuSable education helped propel many black Chicagoans into the middle class. John H. Johnson, the publisher of *Ebony* and *Jet* and the richest black man in Chicago, was in the first graduating class; Harold Washington, Chicago's first black mayor, graduated from DuSable too.

Within a few years of the opening of the Taylor Homes, having the schools so nearby had become a mixed blessing for parents. It was easy for students to drift in and out of school because of the proximity of their homes, which were often unoccupied during the daytime. The gangs had no trouble expanding their sphere of influence from the project to the schools. As middle-class families left the neighborhood, the schools' student populations became 100 per cent poor, and extracurricular programs that depend on the involvement of decently fixed parents began to dwindle. The DuSable PTA then for several years entirely ceased to exist. By the late 1960s, DuSable was changing from an incubator of upward mobility to a gang battleground. The Blackstone Rangers and later the Disciples made DuSable part of their turf. Students sometimes carried weapons to class. There were a couple of shootings inside the building.

Every morning, at the beginning of school, a contingent of gang members would be standing outside DuSable, encouraging the arriving students, especially the boys, not to go in and to spend the day hanging out instead. Ruby's sons often succumbed to the temptation. Kermit put his energies into being a gang leader and never finished DuSable. Larry, the next son and always the best-behaved of Ruby's boys, did graduate from DuSable, in 1968, and a few months later he joined the Army and was sent off to fight in the Vietnam War. Terrell grew up in Ohio, under the care of a friend of Ruby's. The next two boys, Johnnie and Robert, were only occasional students; many were the days when they would go off in the mornings carrying their books and, a few hours later, the DuSable truant officer would call Ruby to ask where they were.

In 1970, Johnnie enlisted in the Job Corps, which had a recruiting office in the neighborhood Urban Progress Center. He was sent to Camp Atterbury, in Indiana (a camp well known in the OEO headquarters in Washington to be "just horrible," in the words of the Job Corps' deputy director), for a two-year training program, but after a few months he quit, returned to Chicago, and began working at odd jobs in hotels and restaurants. His romance with Connie Henry continued; early in 1971, she became pregnant, and in August of that year she gave birth to her fourth daughter, Melissa. The apartment building on the West Side where she was living was condemned. The city cut off the gas and water.

Evidently the landlord had defaulted on the building, because he was nowhere to be found. There were rats all over the place. Connie put in an application with the Chicago Housing Authority, and, because the vacancy rates were growing in the high-rise projects by then, she was quickly assigned an apartment. In 1972 she and Johnnie and the children moved into one of the least desirable places in the Robert Taylor Homes: 5247 South Federal Street, Apartment 1608, on the top floor (meaning maximally at the mercy of the unreliable and often gang-controlled elevator system) of one of the buildings in the ill-screened south end of the project. Shortly after the move, Connie and Johnnie went down to City Hall and got married, with Ruby as their witness and sole wedding guest. A few months later, Johnnie enlisted in the Army and left Chicago again.

Robert, during his early teens, became a gang leader in 5135 South Federal, on a smaller scale than his brother Kermit had been. The Vice Lords were gone from the building by then. Robert's gang was the Cobra Stones, an ally of the Blackstone Rangers; the head of the Cobra Stones, Mickey Carwell, was married to a woman in 5135. Robert's best friend and co-head of the gang in the building was Thomas Chairs, a boy just his age who had been born on a cotton plantation in the Mississippi Delta, moved to New Orleans with his parents as a small child, and gone to Chicago with his mother after she and his father split up. In 1968, Thomas's mother moved her children into an apartment on the same floor of 5135 as Ruby Haynes's.

Robert and Thomas were not fully committed to the gang life. They went to a few meetings with Cobra Stones higher-ups, where the subject always seemed to be how to procure more guns, but for the most part they simply tried to hold on to a position of leadership in their own building. Their true concern was with somehow maintaining the essential quality most prized by young men growing up in the projects, which was a combination of bravery, toughness, street wisdom, ambition, sexual accomplishment, and precocious maturity—American male adolescence, in other words, as it played out in a place where male adults were probably less of a forceful presence, and where the ordinary workings of society were more distant and mysterious, than anywhere else in the country.

Robert lost his virginity at the age of nine, in the sixteenth-floor stairwell at 5135 South Federal, courtesy of a twelve-year-old girl in the building who initiated his brother Johnnie and another friend at the same time, each one taking his turn while the others held the stairwell doors shut. It was an experience that had more to do with attaining a certain status than with physical passion: "You were a *man* then," Robert says. "You *knew*." Every year or so Robert would have a similar experience to reestablish his bona fides, if not in a stairwell then in the elevator (which had an emergency stop button) or in the building's ground-floor laundry room. He got into the gang because he wanted to demonstrate that he was a leader. He and Thomas would talk about what kind of life they were going to live one day: they would get out of the projects; they would have sons named Robert Junior and Thomas Junior, to leave something behind in the world; they would start a funeral home; they would do things that were inconceivable to the other kids in the project, who thought only about short-term survival.

In 1971, Robert dropped out of DuSable and joined the Job Corps. Like Johnnie, he was sent to Camp Atterbury, where he signed up to study the trade of brick masonry. After a little more than six months, he was asked to leave because on several weekends when the recruits had passes to go to Indianapolis, he had missed the bus back to the camp. He came back to the project, tried school again, and then, as soon as he turned seventeen, enlisted in the Navy. That turned out the same way as the Job Corps — after nine months, on shore leave in Japan, he missed his ship's departure for Hong Kong and was kicked out of the service. In the way that parents have of pigeonholing their children, Ruby and Luther both considered Robert to be the smartest of their sons, but also the one most prone to muff opportunities, because he was hopelessly addicted to trying to outfox the system. His postmilitary career seemed to bear out their assessment. He attended a community college for a while, got a job running a mail-sorting machine at the Post Office, got fired, and settled into a drifting life: some time in Chicago, some time in Los Angeles (where he had served in the Navy), various low-level jobs, periodic stints in different schools, residence in one or another girlfriend's apartment, a little too much wine, and, always, some dream or scheme of something better.

One afternoon in 1970, before Robert joined the Job Corps, he and Thomas Chairs were walking down State Street in front of the project, on their way to a store, when a gang member Thomas had gotten in a fight with a couple of days earlier accosted them, pulled a gun, and shot Thomas point-blank. The bullet passed through Thomas's rib cage without hitting any organs or arteries; he spent five days in the hospital. The same year, Thomas was playing basketball in front of 5135 South Federal when a friend of his called "Skid-Row," whose family had recently left the project, drove up in a new car. Skid-Row lent Thomas the car to go get some beer. The police stopped him and discovered that the car was stolen, and Thomas spent thirty days in the county jail. Both incidents, in a way, had been brought on by an assertion of pride verging on bravado: the trouble that ended with his being shot had begun when he tried to avenge a beating that had been inflicted on his younger sister while she was walking home, through hostile gang turf, from the Parkman middle school; the stint in jail was the result of his wanting to have the heady experience of driving a nice car through the neighborhood. Like Robert Haynes, Thomas Chairs had hoped that the same sense of pride would carry him to something better than the Robert Taylor Homes one day, but in the short run, certainly, he was off the route to upward mobility. He dropped out of DuSable, worked summers for the National Youth Corps as a groundsman at Soldier Field, and otherwise supported himself by working as a day laborer through a manpower agency.

Thomas began dating Robert's sister, Juanita. Of all the Haynes children, Juanita had always seemed like the one on whom fortune had smiled the most. As the only girl in the family, she had been spared the worst aspects of adolescence in the Robert Taylor Homes, and had gotten the most love and attention from her father, even after he and her mother split up. She was pretty and smart. When she was five years old and a woman from the school board came by the family's apartment to talk to Ruby about whether she was ready to enter school, Juanita was able to answer all the woman's questions herself. She always got good grades. Ruby pampered her: the only extravagance she allowed herself during the years when she was on public aid was an occasional trip to the Loop to buy Juanita a dress or a pair of shoes at Marshall Field's or Carson Pirie Scott. Juanita didn't have a firmly worked-out plan for her life, but she wanted to get a white-collar job one day—something in a hospital or a bank—and move to the North Side, far away from the project.

The first of Juanita's girlfriends in 5135 to have a child out of wedlock was Thomas Chairs's sister. Ruby didn't see this as a signal for her to start worrying about the same thing happening to Juanita. She disapproved of the Chairs family and couldn't imagine that its doings would serve as an example for her own children; she especially disapproved of Thomas, whom she saw as a bad boy to the core, and didn't want to do anything to encourage his relationship with Juanita. Other mothers in

5135 were getting their teenage daughters on the pill, but Ruby told Juanita that she considered that to be simply an invitation to have sex. Juanita had sex with Thomas anyway, starting when she was fifteen, in his mother's apartment, without using contraceptives. In her junior year at DuSable she got pregnant and dropped out.

Robert got a girl in 5135 pregnant at about the same time. He and Thomas both reacted to the news in the same way: they felt good about it, taking their incipient fatherhood as an emblem of mature masculinity. One evening while Juanita was pregnant, Thomas and Robert were hanging around the grounds of the project, drinking wine and talking. They ran into an old playground friend of theirs known as Boswell, who introduced them to a friend of his called Vamp, who was just out of a juvenile detention center. After a while Vamp said he had to pick something up at an apartment in 5001 South Federal where he was staying. The four of them walked over to the building together. Thomas and Robert held the elevator while Boswell and Vamp went inside; when they got back and the elevator started moving, they hit the emergency stop button, pulled guns, and demanded that Thomas and Robert hand over their money. Inside the airless metal box, suspended somewhere between floors so that no one could possibly come to their rescue, looking down the barrels of guns, Thomas and Robert both experienced some surge of inexplicable bravery, and they began to fight. Vamp panicked and shot Thomas in the chest, at a point just below his heart. Thomas had had enough to drink that he didn't go into shock. The fight continued. Boswell's gun, fortunately, turned out not to be loaded. Thomas was able to wrestle Vamp's gun away. He put it to Vamp's head and pulled the trigger, but — fortunately again, for both of them — it didn't go off. Robert got the elevator going again. When it got to the ground floor, Robert carried Thomas back to 5135, laid him on a bench, and called an ambulance. It took two operations before he was better.

Robert and Thomas soon realized at least one of their shared ambitions by getting namesakes. Robert's son was named Robert Junior; Thomas and Juanita's daughter was Tomesha. On the day she was born, Thomas and Robert were off at a party on the South Side, and Ruby went to the hospital with Juanita to attend the birth. Thomas showed up the next day, and for the next few weeks he made fatherly gestures. When Tomesha was three months old, he bought her a pair of earrings. He was on his way to deliver them when he encountered a group of gang members in the entryway of 5135, shooting dice. One of them was Robert

Shaw, who ran 5201 South Federal for the Blackstone Rangers and had recently done harm to several of Thomas's friends and relatives. They exchanged insults and started to fight. A friend of Thomas's who happened to be passing by came over and pulled a gun, which gave Thomas the chance to escape. Wild with anger and adrenaline, he ran up to his mother's apartment and told her he was going to go back downstairs and get Robert Shaw. She begged him to stay inside and forget about it. He wouldn't listen; "I was so mad I couldn't think," he says. "I just wanted to get respect." He grabbed a gun, ran back downstairs, and found Robert Shaw still in the entryway, with three of his friends. Shaw grabbed a two-by-four and took a swing at Thomas. Thomas shot him dead, and ran off into the night.

Juanita, in her mother's apartment, heard the shot. The next day Thomas called and told her what had happened. By then he was hiding out in a friend's apartment in a high-rise project elsewhere on the South Side. He asked Juanita to come see him, and she agreed, but by the time she got there the police had caught up with him; it turned out that Robert Shaw's girlfriend had a sister who was dating a friend of Thomas's, and she snitched. Thomas was convicted of first-degree murder, and sentenced to thirty years in a state penitentiary in downstate Illinois. For Juanita, all the glow of new motherhood was instantly gone, and along with it the plans she had been cultivating for marrying Thomas, finishing school, and getting a job. She always felt that the murder of Robert Shaw was the big turning point in her life — a blow that took away her pride, her confidence, her hope, and her optimistic picture of Thomas, and from which she never really recovered.

JOHNNIE SPENT most of his military service stationed in West Germany. Even before he came home, Connie suspected that he was up to something suspicious, because he never sent home any of his pay, as he had promised to do. He brought a stereo back to Chicago with him, and when he got home he took it apart and pulled out a large stash of hashish. That ushered in a period when Johnnie would have friends over every day to play cards, listen to music, drink, and take drugs. They tried what was, at the time, the entire pharmacopoeia of the Robert Taylor Homes: LSD, cocaine, PCP, amphetamines, barbiturates, and, finally, heroin. Connie, whose previous experience with drugs had been limited to marijuana, used everything that Johnnie and his friends did, but when, after a few months, she became pregnant, she stopped. Johnnie didn't: soon he was a heroin addict.

The money they were getting from public aid wasn't enough to live on, especially with Johnnie's drug habit to support, so Johnnie got a job as a security guard at a hospital. His paycheck almost never got back to the family; most of it was already owed to the dope man, who was known to deliver severe, and sometimes fatal, beatings to customers who got behind on their accounts. Connie and Johnnie began to fight a lot. She would fuss at him for not bringing any money home, and he would counter by constantly criticizing her cooking and housekeeping, wanting, Connie felt, to take the offensive as a way of demonstrating that he was still the authority figure in their apartment. The birth of their son Melvin, in the spring of 1975, didn't bring about any improvement in their relationship. One day in 1976 Connie came home to the apartment from a shopping trip and found a woman there wearing Johnnie's bathrobe. Connie kicked Johnnie out and filed for divorce.

Ruby Haynes had for years been a loyal member of the lowest rung of the Chicago Democratic machine, helping to turn out the vote on election day. She never had any of the objections to Mayor Daley that were common among middle-class blacks; to her, he was the man who had built her home and her children's elementary school. By the 1970s, she was a precinct captain: Third Ward, Fourth Precinct, one of several precincts wholly contained within the Robert Taylor Homes that always produced a nearly unanimous vote for the machine. In return for her efforts, Ruby acquired a little influence within the project. She knew and had easy access to her alderman, Tyrone Kenner, and at least a casual acquaintanceship with Harold Washington, then a member of the state legislature, who had started his political career as a precinct captain in the Third Ward. She got word of jobs that were available with the city and with some of the big private employers in town, and distributed them to her friends. She had some say over who got what apartment in her building.

When some maintenance men working on the roof of Connie's building broke a water main, causing water to come pouring in through the ceiling of Connie's apartment, Ruby was able to arrange for her to move into 5135 South Federal. After Melvin was born, Ruby helped Connie take advantage of a regulation that allowed families in the Robert Taylor Homes to have separate bedrooms for their boys and girls, and move to a large corner apartment in 5135, number 610. Connie's breakup with

Johnnie didn't at all damage her friendship with Ruby, who had been displeased with Johnnie for years and took Connie's side in their marital troubles — just as some of Luther's female relatives had taken Ruby's side in their divorce, and remained close to Ruby. Connie, Ruby, and Juanita, all single now and all living in 5135, formed a warm family, sharing resources, helping each other with child care, and weathering the constant round of crises together. By now Connie's sister Charlene was also living in the Robert Taylor Homes, in another building, and so was Ruby's eldest son, George.

When Ruby's son Larry returned from Vietnam, he moved back into her apartment in the project. Larry was still the good son. He had tried heroin a couple of times in Vietnam but hadn't gotten hooked, and he had been wounded in the back by a piece of shrapnel, but, unlike his brothers, he came back from the service with a good record and a feeling that the discipline of military life and the broadening effect of exposure to the world outside the ghetto had left him a stronger, more capable person. Just in the time he had been away, the Robert Taylor Homes had changed alarmingly: more guns, heavier drugs, fewer families. "I wasn't going to come back and get into a society that was really going down," he says. "I wanted to go *up*. I couldn't see staying in the projects. I've got common sense."

Larry got a job as a custodian for Illinois Bell, left that after he didn't get promoted to installer even though he had passed the test for it, worked at a laundry for two years, and then got a job as a security guard at a hospital in Evanston, a large suburb at the northern border of the city of Chicago. Evanston was a long trip from the project, and, as the bearer of a black face, Larry was regularly harassed by the police there when he got off his train at night and walked to work. On the other hand, it was blissfully green and peaceful compared to the Robert Taylor Homes, and there was a good-sized, stable, middle-class black community of long standing in the less affluent section of the town. Convinced that his whole future depended on his getting as far away from the project as possible, Larry decided to pursue a career in Evanston. After his second year of working at the hospital, he got a custodian's job at the Evanston Post Office, and after a year at that he was promoted to mechanic — a real "position," as opposed to just a job. Shortly after that he moved to Evanston, married, and had two children. He is still with the Post Office. Quite often in a ghetto family, one of the children will emerge as the person with the best chance to "clear," that is, make a life outside the ghetto. Of Ruby Haynes's children, Kermit, Terrell, Johnnie, and Robert were all, by the mid-1970s, just moving around Chicago from job to job and from woman to woman; Juanita was a welfare mother; Kevin, undersized and barely able to speak intelligibly, was handicapped in some way Ruby never understood and unable to live on his own. Larry was the one who cleared. In the new generation of the family that was now growing up in the Robert Taylor Homes, the word "Evanston" became the emblem for what they all aspired to.

Larry was right about the Robert Taylor Homes: they kept getting worse. After he left, there were no adult men permanently in residence on Ruby's floor in 5135. The unemployment rate in their section of the project rose during the seventies from 18.6 per cent to 31.4 per cent. Several times in the late 1960s and early 1970s police were fired upon by snipers in the windows of high-rise public-housing projects; in 1975, a policeman was killed by a sniper in the Henry Horner Homes, on the West Side. Visitors to the project from the outside world — firemen, emergency medical technicians, poll takers, bill collectors, delivery men, salesmen, social workers, maintenance workers, truant officers, sociologists — were often robbed or roughed up, and as a result most of these people found excuses not to go there any more.

When gang members and other vandals incapacitated the elevators, they weren't speedily repaired; at one point, three-fourths of the elevators in the Robert Taylor Homes were not operating. Problems with the heat, water, electricity, and fire alarms were also slow to be fixed. The project was becoming a world unto itself, completely cut off from the institutions and mores of the wider society. During the time of the riots, Chicago as a whole felt directly threatened by conditions in the ghettos. Now the city had reorganized itself in such a way that the only people in real danger were the residents of the ghettos themselves, and for them the peril was unrelenting. The rest of the city had nervously edged away.

To the people living in the Robert Taylor Homes, its conditions were a miserable fact of life for which there was no good explanation. Anger, at least articulated anger at whoever was to blame, was relatively rare. The traditional ghetto animus against white exploiters was far below the level it had reached in earlier decades, largely because, with the exception of a dwindling number of white policemen, there were no longer any visible white exploiters. The little price-gouging stores in the neighborhood had been bought up by Palestinians. A white person in the project was an extremely rare sight, except on television. "People didn't talk about white people," Robert Haynes says. "You couldn't *conceive* of what they'd do except put you in jail. If a white person showed up, lots of people would just put up their hands and drop their guns. You were just taught survival, and you didn't have to be taught survival among whites. White people weren't an issue. Stuff was always happening, every day. 'So and so's trigger-happy.' 'Somebody says you're doing this.' Nobody ever said, 'The white people are coming to get you all.' " The lack of any evident reason for the horrifying state of the Robert Taylor Homes only made life there more horrifying; it encouraged people to turn on each other, and on themselves.

One day in 1977, Ruby Haynes was walking down State Street in front of the project, in broad daylight, when she noticed that an unfamiliar man was walking along next to her. He slung an arm around her neck and told her to keep on walking and get all her money out of her purse and give it to him. When she did, he disengaged himself and walked on as if nothing had happened. Ruby found a policeman and pointed the man out to him. The policeman, looking bored, said he had to write out a complaint before he could do anything, and pulled out a pad and pencil. By the time he was finished, the robber was gone. At about the same time, Robert was out walking one evening when three men accosted him and demanded his money. When he refused to give it up, one of them pulled a gun and shot him in the stomach—just a flesh wound, but frightening all the same.

George, Ruby's oldest son, who for years had been leading a modest but stable existence as a butcher in ghetto grocery stores, began to have marital problems that, for some reason, had a devastating effect on him. Ruby thought it was all the fault of George's wife, Sandy, who in her opinion was a no-good woman who drank too much and hung around with gang members. George started drinking too. In the summer of 1977, George's wife put him out of their apartment in the Robert Taylor Homes, and he moved in with Ruby. Shortly after that he turned up at the emergency room of a South Side hospital, having overdosed on barbiturates. The doctors saved his life, and ruled that he had attempted suicide. He entered a mental hospital in Los Angeles, and, after he was released, wound up living on the downtown skid row there. Robert went out to Los Angeles, got George, cleaned him up, and brought him back to Chicago for Thanksgiving.

George begged his wife for a reconciliation, but she wouldn't hear of it; she filed for divorce, and tried to keep him even from coming over to visit their children. On February 26, 1978, the day their divorce became final, George told his mother he was going to Sandy's apartment to see the kids. It was a bitterly cold winter day—the temperature was below zero. George didn't come home. Ruby became alarmed and called the police, but they told her not to worry about it, he would turn up.

He didn't turn up. When the spring thaw came in early April, George's naked body was found along the South Side shoreline of Lake Michigan.

The police listed George's death as a suicide, but Ruby always suspected that he had been murdered. Why would he have taken all his clothes off? Her suspicion was that when he had arrived at Sandy's apartment building, some of the gang members living there had jumped him, and that they had brought him out to the Forty-ninth Street beach, beaten him up, stripped him, taken him out beyond the ice, and thrown him in the lake. There was nothing she could do to prove it, though; George was simply gone, severely mourned by her but unavenged.

Shortly after George's death, Ruby's financial situation improved drastically. She had worked nights, on and off, for years, in hospitals and hotels, but at the time she was unemployed. Her children were old enough that she no longer qualified for Aid to Families with Dependent Children, and she had to subsist on the stipend of the state's General Assistance program for single poor people, which was only seventy-eight dollars a month. After Kevin turned eighteen, though, she was able to get him declared eligible for Supplemental Security Income, the Social Security program for disabled nonelderly people that Congress enacted during the Nixon administration, in the heyday of Daniel Patrick Moynihan's "income strategy." In November 1978, Ruby turned sixty-two and became eligible for Social Security herself. To switch from being a single beneficiary of the welfare system to a double beneficiary of the Social Security system was to enter an entirely different class economically. Welfare, generally thought of as a payment to the undeserving (and mostly black) poor, was extremely unpopular with the public, and its benefits had lagged all through the 1970s, ever since Ronald Reagan, as governor of California, succeeded in persuading Nixon to stop requiring the states to raise welfare payments to keep up with inflation. But Social Security had the reputation of being an insurance program from which every working American would sooner or later benefit, and was consequently very popular. The benefits, always higher than welfare's, were legally tied to the inflation rate during the Nixon administration. Now Ruby was getting two monthly checks of more than $300 each.

At the end of 1978, Ruby went down to Clarksdale to visit her relatives — her first trip home since 1954. A cousin of hers showed her around, and she was amazed to see that, in an area on the outskirts of town that she remembered as a cotton patch, brand-new housing projects were going up. They were nothing like the Robert Taylor Homes: the buildings were only two stories high, with just four apartments each, and they were in the middle of a new black neighborhood of ranch-style brick suburban tract houses, rather than in an isolated ghetto. Ruby was heartily sick of what the Robert Taylor Homes had become, and since George's death she had felt only bitterness toward Chicago as a whole. She went to see her friend Otha Haynes, a cousin of her ex-husband Luther's who was a social worker in Clarksdale, and asked if she could get an apartment in one of the new projects. Otha said she'd see what she could do. In January 1979, Otha called Ruby in Chicago and said she had a place lined up for her. The date it would be ready for her was April 5, 1979, which itself seemed to Ruby like a signal, since it was the first anniversary of George's wake. She decided to move back to Mississippi.

Ruby arranged for her apartment in 5135, her rented furniture, and also her duties as precinct captain, to be turned over to Juanita. Tyrone Kenner gave her a going-away party. With Kevin in tow, she took a bus back to Clarksdale. Her life in the North was over.

THE POLITICAL boss of the Third Ward, Ralph Metcalfe, was for most of his career as trusty an apparatchik of Mayor Daley's machine as could be found. Metcalfe had made his name on the South Side as an athletic hero. He was a teammate of Jesse Owens on the 1936 U.S. Olympic team — Metcalfe won the silver medal in the hundred-meter dash while Owens was winning the gold. He was a Catholic — always a great plus for a black politician who aspired to a place in Daley's good graces — and, even better from Daley's standpoint, he was never a member of Bill Dawson's organization. Over Dawson's objections, Daley made Metcalfe ward committeeman, and then alderman, in the Third Ward, as part of his strategy of cutting down on Dawson's power by taking control over patronage away from him. When Dawson died in

1970, Daley anointed Metcalfe as his successor as congressman from the South Side. Metcalfe was anything but a reformer. He had his office in a members-only gambling club, and he kept his distance from the civil rights movement. When Martin Luther King came to Chicago, Metcalfe told the press, "We have adequate leadership here."

In the spring of 1972, a black dentist named Herbert Odom, who was chairman of the Citizens' Committee for Metcalfe, left his office in Englewood one evening, got into his Cadillac, and set out for his home in Hyde Park, a middle-class integrated South Side neighborhood next to the University of Chicago. A police car pulled him over. The policemen, who were white, asked him for his driver's license. Odom hadn't been doing anything wrong, and he was angry at being stopped; in his words, he "gave them some lip." The policemen grabbed him roughly, pushed him over the hood of his car, put him in handcuffs, and took him to the Englewood police station. There he was never booked for any crime, but he was kept waiting around for several hours and told he could make only one phone call. He called Ralph Metcalfe.

At about the same time, another black dentist, Herbert Clairborne, was driving through the middle-class black neighborhood of Avalon Park when he suffered a stroke. He swerved and hit a parked car; white policemen stopped him and charged him with drunken driving and leaving the scene of an accident, and held him in a police station for five hours without calling a doctor or his family. He went into a coma.

If the victims in these incidents had been poor blacks from the projects, nothing would have happened. That they were substantial citizens caused their treatment by the police to hit a nerve in middle-class black Chicago. Throughout the twentieth century, the African-American middle class has suspected that, in the eyes of whites, a nigger is a nigger — that whites have a fundamental incapacity to distinguish between members of the disorganized lower class and solid, educated, hardworking people, as long as they all belong to the black race. The stories of the two dentists made a perfect example. Ralph Metcalfe, previously the soul of discretion on racial issues, changed overnight. He demanded that Daley come to his office to hear his complaints. Daley, who as a matter of principle did not go to other people's offices, refused. Daley announced that he would hold his own meeting at City Hall to discuss police misconduct; Metcalfe did not attend.

Black Chicago, at the time, was organizationally quite complex and diffuse. The machine was still strong, especially in the slums. The black independent—that is, antimachine—political movement was continuing to gain strength in the better-off areas of the South Side. Such traditional forces in the black community as the leading ministers, the *Defender*, the Urban League, and the NAACP wielded a good deal of power. Elijah Muhammad was past the peak of his influence, perhaps, but he was still in control of a small empire of mosques, shops, publications, and rental properties on the South Side. Some of King's lieutenants were still around, most notably Jesse Jackson, whose organization at the time, Operation PUSH, held Saturday morning meetings in a converted synagogue on the South Side (which Ruby Haynes sometimes attended) that were a cross between a political rally and a Baptist church service. Radical groups like the Black Panthers had small memberships but high visibility in the white press. Metcalfe's new crusade against the police galvanized all these disparate forces into a commonality of purpose that they had never had before. The lesson that King had learned in 1966 still applied: the most likely source of an effective black rebellion against the established order in Chicago was not the slums or the projects or the gangs, but the solid middle class, when it felt that its dignity was affronted and its aspirations thwarted.

The Metcalfe forces produced a list of changes they wanted in police procedures. Daley appointed a commission, which eventually suggested several much more minor measures. In the fall election season, Metcalfe got even: he endorsed a liberal Republican named Bernard Carey for state's attorney instead of the incumbent, Edward Hanrahan, the Democratic nominee and a special favorite of Daley's. Hanrahan was the official who had ordered the police raid in December 1969 on the West Side ghetto apartment of Fred Hampton, Illinois chairman of the Black Panther Party, in which Hampton and another Panther named Mark Clark had been killed. The Panther murders had a tremendous impact on black Chicago, where they were received, for the most part, not as the Sarajevo of the black revolution but as another case of the police killing black people and getting away with it, as they surely wouldn't have if the victims had been white. Hampton was well known locally (although not nationally) as the former youth chairman of the NAACP in the working-class black suburb of Maywood—in other words, he was a child of mainstream black Chicago, not a Lawndale gang-banger. In the panoply of the Chicago machine's high officialdom, Hanrahan was, because of the Panther case, the person most vulnerable to a black political rebellion.

Hanrahan lost, thanks to a heavy black vote for Carey. It was by far the most important electoral defeat suffered by the machine since Daley first took its reins in the early 1950s. Metcalfe won his reelection campaign for Congress by a wider margin than any other Democrat in the Chicago delegation.

In 1975, Metcalfe endorsed Daley's opponent for mayor, a white liberal reformer from the North Side named William Singer. Daley retaliated by stripping Metcalfe of his patronage powers in the Third Ward and turning them over to Tyrone Kenner. Then he had the Cook County Democratic Central Committee refuse to endorse Metcalfe for reelection in 1976; on its slate, the machine put up Erwin France, head of the city's antipoverty programs. In the old days, Daley had been able to remove a disobedient incumbent congressman almost effortlessly — not that the occasion arose very often. This time, Metcalfe won; even the machine's ward committeemen and other operatives on the South Side, who had officially lined up behind France (even Harold Washington, who is now the symbol of independent black political power in Chicago, endorsed France), were afraid to make an all-out effort to beat Metcalfe, because voter sentiment was running so strongly in his direction that they were afraid it might sweep them away too.

Daley died, in office, six weeks after the 1976 election. All the attempted depredations of the reformers and Washington bureaucrats and blacks over the years had left him a harder man than he used to be. He was no longer on speaking terms with such fair-haired former associates as David Stahl, his deputy mayor, who had told the press that Daley had ordered him to give some of the city's insurance business to his son John. People sometimes heard him speak angrily or dismissively about blacks as a race. The rising black rebellion against the machine never got to the point where it imperiled his own hold on the mayor's office, but it is significant that in his last reelection campaign, he failed for the first time in his career to carry the black vote in Chicago — the black vote that had made him mayor in the first place and that had been his unassailable base during his first decade in City Hall.

Harold Washington was one of the candidates for mayor in the special election to succeed Daley, but he lost to Michael Bilandic, the machine's man. Bilandic lost in 1979, though, because the black vote went overwhelmingly against him; after a crippling snowstorm, he had done a miserable job of getting the city's services going again, and the black parts of town were noticeably the last to be cleared of snow. Jane Byrne, who beat Bilandic, was a former antipoverty bureaucrat who had gotten most of the black politicians on her side in the campaign. Byrne's fall after one term, like Bilandic's, was attributable to her having alienated the black vote, which she did by trying to replace two blacks on the school board and two on the Chicago Housing Authority board with whites. A black-organized boycott of a city jazz festival in 1982 helped transform the black discontent with Byrne into a real political movement, which then contributed greatly to Washington's election as mayor in 1983.

There was so much overt racial hostility surrounding Washington's campaign, his term in office, and the race to succeed him after he died in 1987, that the achievement of the milestone of black political power at the highest levels of Chicago politics was slightly obscured. As late as the early 1980s, there were still wards on the West Side that were controlled by whites who didn't live there, and the idea that the primary role of black politicians in Chicago was as the machine's operatives in the black neighborhoods was still in full force. Today Richard M. Daley seems to be settled in for a reign as mayor of Chicago that could go on for as long as his father's, but unlike the old man, he obviously governs in the realization that a unified black opposition could topple him.

G EORGE HICKS served as an assistant manager of the Robert Taylor Homes for a year, and then he got the big promotion that he had been aiming for, to manager. The first housing project he ran was Wentworth Gardens, a small low-rise complex that was built back in the forties in the old South Side black belt. From there he moved up to manager of Stateway Gardens, the high-rise project immediately north of the Robert Taylor Homes.

While he was at Stateway, he got into trouble with the Chicago Housing Authority. One of the people on his staff had to be out of town for a couple of days on pressing personal business, and he talked George into filling out a time sheet indicating that he had been working during the period when he was away. Someone snitched, and George was made to resign. He got a job at a factory that made barbecue sauce, and then opened a grocery store called the Busy Bee, but these jobs paid much less than the housing authority. After he had been away for a year and a half, some of his friends at the housing authority talked him into applying for reinstatement there. He did, and he was rehired as an assistant manager at a project for elderly people. After a year he was promoted to manager again and put in charge of another small older project, Lawndale Gardens, on the West Side. In 1978 he got a big job: manager of the Henry Horner Homes, a notorious high rise on the Near West Side. He spent six years there, and then was put in charge of the Ida B. Wells Homes on the South Side, one of the biggest projects in Chicago.

The Wells Homes, which opened in 1941, were the first housing project for blacks in Chicago. Named for an early black crusader, prodded along by large, orderly protest rallies that helped vanquish white real estate interests' opposition to its construction, built by black construction crews, the Wells Homes were, like DuSable High School, a bedrock institution of black Chicago during the 1940s, a symbol of pride and ambition. They were sturdy and attractive low-rise brick buildings, surrounded by playgrounds and athletic fields. When they opened, 18,000 families applied for the 1,662 apartments there. In *Black Metropolis*, published in 1945, St. Clair Drake and Horace Cayton wrote about the Wells Homes, "Its 2,000 families are the envy of the whole South Side. . . . When a common laborer or a relief client tried to 'get in The Project' he was attempting to take the first step toward living middle-class. Those who got in had gone one rung up the ladder."

A relentlessly ameliorative atmosphere prevailed there, with the encouragement of the housing authority. Devereux Bowly, Jr., in *The Poorhouse: Subsidized Housing in Chicago*, describes the tone of social uplift at the project when it opened:

> At Ida B. Wells . . . 17 per cent of the early tenants received relief, as well as 23.5 per cent who got WPA payments. An early endeavor of the tenants at Wells was a "Get off and keep off the WPA and Relief" club. This group gathered job vacancy listings and made them available to project residents. In the early years CHA accepted only "complete families" with children, except for a small quota of elderly couples for its two-room apartments. An elaborate investigation was made of CHA applicants that included: 1) an office interview by a social worker, 2) employment verification, 3) check for a police record, 4) home visit by an investigator. . . .

By the time George got to the Wells Homes in 1984, those days were long gone. In 1955, at the peak of the black migration, the housing authority added ten high-rise buildings to the project and began to cut back on the screening procedures. Over the years the familiar story of deterioration was played out; the Wells Homes over which George presided was a small city of fifteen thousand people, all of them poor and almost all of them living in female-headed families, and the high rises in particular were a nest of problems: gangs, broken elevators, crime, vacant apartments. Perhaps a truly heroic manager might have been able to make a difference, but for George, running the project was a job, not a mission, and he believed he was doing the best he could under the circumstances, which were insufficient funding for repairs and maintenance, shoddy screening, difficult tenants, and a slow-moving bureaucracy downtown. He tried to keep the buildings fixed up as well as he could. He got to know a few of the tenants, mainly the ones on the housing authority's building councils, but most of the residents of the Wells Homes were strangers to him.

Occasionally George would see a familiar face in the project — someone from Clarksdale. He did not, in these cases, rush to introduce himself to the person as someone from the same hometown. Back at the Henry Horner Homes, one of the tenants — a woman from Clarksdale who had been a gifted athlete growing up but as an adult was obviously mentally unbalanced — had learned that George was from Clarksdale too, and she had become a pest, constantly coming by his office to complain about something. Anyway, the people he recognized from Mississippi at the Wells Homes were not from his own circle of friends in the Brickyard. Usually, he had known them as sharecroppers on the plantations in the country — people he had seen while driving around with his father collecting burial-insurance premiums in the 1940s. As George saw it, the cotton-picking machine had thrown them out of work, they had come to Chicago, and, lacking the education that he had been fortunate enough to have, they had landed on welfare and in the projects. Like his father, George had wound up making his living serving the black poor simply because that was the best career open to him, and he felt bad for them, but he knew that their fundamental problems were far beyond his ability to solve.

Only a few times during his career at the Chicago Housing Authority did George get his name in the papers. In 1987, a renegade tenants' group in the Wells Homes began organizing protests against the conditions there — the broken windows, balky elevators, and unreliable heating. They got a little publicity, and one of the executives from downtown came to the project to meet with them. The *Tribune* published a photograph of her touring the Wells Homes, and quoted her expressing concern. She ordered George to prepare a report responding to the group's complaints, and he did. The whole situation quickly died down. A few repairs were made. The *Tribune* and the people from headquarters didn't come around again. The tenants' group, which George considered a bunch of self-appointed troublemakers who should have simply joined their building councils if they wanted to help the project, lapsed into quiescence. In 1988 George was promoted to the highest level in the housing authority's civil service system, at a salary of $45,000 a year, and given a job supervising all the housing projects for the elderly on the West Side. He worked at an administrative office at Forty-seventh and State, on the grounds of the Robert Taylor Homes and just at the edge of the formerly glorious commercial strip that he had been shown on his first visit to Chicago.

George had a rich life outside of work. In 1969, two years after the death of his first wife, he married a woman who was a schoolteacher and a fellow migrant from Mississippi. His parents moved back to Clarksdale in 1971, when his grandmother took sick, but two of his sisters stayed in Chicago. For many years George was head of the large Chicago chapter of the Alcorn College alumni association. With a group of his friends from home, he started the Clarksdalians Club, which was one of hundreds of associations for people from a shared Southern hometown that sprang up in Chicago in the 1970s, as the people who had made the great migration became middle-aged and nostalgic. One of them, the Greenville Club, owns a building on the far South Side that serves as its clubhouse; the Clarksdalians Club, like most of the rest, has no permanent location, but it holds regular meetings, puts on large dinner dances, gives scholarships and community service awards, and rents a fleet of buses once a year to take its members back to Clarksdale for a reunion.

The members of the Clarksdalians Club are mostly middle-class government employees — teachers, policemen, bus drivers, bureaucrats. Like George, they no longer live in the ghetto, but most of them drive back there every day to go to work. They keep in close touch with each other. At a place called the Glass House Lounge at Seventy-ninth and Halsted on the South Side, just across the street from the offices of the Muslim newspaper, *The Final Call*, and a few blocks from George's house, people from Clarksdale like to congregate informally after work. George doesn't go there much any more, but his phone at home is always ringing, and often the caller is someone from Clarksdale bearing gossip, news from home, or the tale of a misfortune that has befallen a Clarksdalian and that the members of the club might help rectify.

When George gets back from work in the afternoon, he runs a chain and padlock through the steering wheel of his mini-van (it has been broken into a couple of times; the neighborhood to the north of his has gotten a little slummy), goes inside, and drinks a beer in his easy chair. There are two ten-year-old Cadillacs inside the garage in back of the house; in the living room, stuffed poodles and china dolls sit in neat rows on the shelves, and there is a stack of purple napkins on a table imprinted with the legend "Have Cocktails with Armentra & George." George's two daughters have long since graduated from school and left home — one works in the Post Office, and the other, who is married to a deputy sheriff, in a social service agency — but they stop by regularly. George has one grandchild, a four-year-old boy named Jamel, who spends a lot of time at his house. He gives every indication of being a contented man — contented with the way his own life has turned out, that is; not with the general state of affairs in Chicago.

The living room conversation in the Hicks home is consistent with what you can hear, in the evenings, all over black middle-class Chicago: in Chatham and Pullman, Pill Hill and Morgan Park, South Shore and Harvey. The overall tenor is much more overtly racial than it is in the projects; middle-class blacks are the only relatively prosperous English-speaking ethnics in America whose cultural identity is still strong enough to support a wide array of commercial institutions — magazines, radio stations, record companies — that are aimed solely at them. Black achievement is often noted, and so are the barriers to it. Although the process of neighborhood transition from white to black in Chicago has, twenty years after the migration, slowed to a crawl, there are still plenty of white neighborhoods and suburbs where a black family can't buy a house and where a lone black pedestrian is liable to be called a nigger and even to be beaten up. Black families were fire-bombed in the white neighborhood of Bellwood in 1973, in Chicago Lawn and Broadview in 1975, in Forest Park in 1976, in Gary in 1979, in Palos Heights in 1980, in South Chicago in 1983, in the Island, Ashburn, and the Southeast Side in 1984, and in Gage Park in 1985. Ford City, a shopping mall on the Southwest Side, is famously inhospitable to black customers.

Stories abound about white people in the Loop crossing the street when they see you approaching, or leaving the bus when you sit down next to them, or getting fatter paychecks than you for doing the same job. Older people who grew up in the South still privately refer to superior-acting white people by the old plantation nicknames "Mister Charlie" and "Miss Ann." The proceedings on television are minutely analyzed for evidence of discrimination. When a black figure gets in trouble, it's usually pointed out that if a white boy had done the same thing, nothing would have happened to him. There are loud complaints about cartoonish, or infantilized, black characters on the prime-time series, and cheers for blacks like Bill Cosby and Jesse Jackson who have made it big via strong, proud, dignified personae. When white people appear discussing the problems of the black family, it strikes a nerve: there always seems to be a note of condemnation of the entire race, as if the speaker doesn't realize there are millions of middle-class black parents who harangue their teenage children about the virtues of chastity, and besides, everybody has friends who are struggling with family problems that engender empathy, not censoriousness. In every black neighborhood in Chicago, the percentage of female-headed families is higher than it is in white neighborhoods at the same income level.

The parlous state of the black slums in Chicago is a constant looming presence in the consciousness of the black middle class. The reactions it provokes are complicated. On the one hand, the views about welfare and crime that can be heard inside George Hicks's immaculate bungalow, and places like it, are quite similar to what they'd be in the white lower-middle-class neighborhoods of the far Southwest Side: criminals get off too easily and ought to be in jail; public aid is a transfer of money from the hardworking to the lazy.

On the other hand, the larger social vision is entirely different. Middle-class blacks with Southern roots constantly compare the people in the projects to the sharecroppers back home: they're the worst historical victims of white racism, they've always been poor and led disorganized lives, and they never had a real chance to make it. America is run by white people, so the way it is is the way white people want it to be. If it were white folks who were living in the projects, the projects would be maintained properly. Especially since the Reagan administration's deep budget cuts in social programs, which were a direct hit on the black middle class's employment base, the concept of white genocide against the black poor is routinely discussed. The drug business, in particular, is often described as being masterminded by whites, sometimes up to and including President Bush. Although black nationalism is not the creed of the ordinary black middle class, black solidarity is, and nationalists like

Louis Farrakhan win points for their appealing, if unlikely, vision of a reunited, economically independent black America, and for daring to attack whites directly. What Drake and Cayton wrote in the 1940s about the forebears of Farrakhan still holds true:

> Frustrated in their isolation from the main streams of American life, and in their impotence to control their fate decisively, Negroes tend to admire an aggressive Race Man even when his motives are suspect. They will applaud him, because, in the face of the white world, he remains "proud of his race and always tries to uphold it whether it is good or bad, right or wrong."

George Hicks, like many people of his generation, harbors a certain nostalgia for the state of black society in the days before the end of segregation. He recognizes that the ripple effects of the civil rights movement are responsible for his being able to pursue his career in government and achieve relative prosperity, but he misses the sense of community that the South Side had when he first arrived there. "They did what I call opening up the pasture," he says. "They let us out of the pasture. We were all fenced in — all the big shots, everybody, was in the neighborhood. Our kids could see black entertainers walking down the street. Joe Louis, Sugar Ray Robinson — they used to walk Forty-seventh Street, or be at Killer Johnson's on Sixty-first Street, or the Evans Hotel on Forty-seventh. They lived there. Now, they don't live on the South Side, period. None of those guys live in a black neighborhood. I'm still in the general area where black folks are able to migrate. I'm not saying we shouldn't go for something better. But the top white folks all live in white neighborhoods. They don't live in black neighborhoods. And all the top black folks live in white neighborhoods. When that happened, it broke down a lot of things we had going."

The situation for middle-class blacks in Chicago, as George sees it, is not quite so good as it might appear to be. If a black person opened a store in a white neighborhood, whites wouldn't trade there, unless it was selling something that is seen as the province of blacks, like barbecue or sporting goods. If a black celebrity like Michael Jordan of the Chicago Bulls were to marry a white girl, he would probably see his endorsement deals begin to dry up. Once blacks began to achieve high positions in the housing authority and on the school board, whites began to blame black leaders for the age-old problems of the government institutions in the ghettos, and they still can't differentiate the average black person from the ghetto street criminal. The projects, which in George's view might still be saved, are in danger of being dismantled — especially Cabrini-Green, the first place he worked at the housing authority, which occupies valuable real estate near the Loop on the North Side that is potentially useful to white people. "They want Cabrini *bad,*" he says. "They think about it in their sleep. If black folks don't hold on, they'll lose what they have."

In the old days, the better-off blacks tended to live in an all-black world defined by black institutions like churches and businesses and well-to-do residential pockets inside the black belt, while poor blacks, with their jobs as field hands and domestics, bore the brunt of the difficulties that went along with regular daily contact with white authority figures. Today the situation has been reversed: the black poor are in isolated ghettos and often aren't working, while the black upper class experiences the difficult racial climate in white suburbs, white university campuses, and white corporations. The day-to-day tension of race relations has shifted toward the higher end of the economic scale.

There is a picture on George Hicks's mantelpiece of a niece who is a student at Howard, which makes her the member of the family with the highest-status credential and so the one most likely to enter a sphere where she will have frequent dealings with whites. George and his immediate family belong to that substantial portion of the black middle class that has very little contact with whites, at work, at school, or in the neighborhood. Black consciousness is not the wrenching issue for them that it is for blacks whose life-trajectories have been such as to introduce them to the difficulties of assimilationism. Of the members of the Clarksdalians Club, it is the one with the most prestigious job — Taylor Cotton, Jr., who runs an office of the Chicago Urban League that promotes affirmative action plans in the construction industry — whose political vision is the most nationalist; he used to work with the Black Panthers in a ghetto social program. George was unaffected by the black-power movement, thought the Panthers were punks (though he was outraged by the murders of Fred Hampton and Mark Clark), and has chosen to make his own stand by staying firmly rooted in the black community. Oprah Winfrey, a Mississippian by birth, may live on the Gold Coast of the North Side; Mr. T., who grew up in the Robert Taylor Homes and built the bluff male style of the projects into a successful acting career, may live in a white suburb; but George's heroes are black millionaires like Dempsey Jack Travis, a real estate man, and Edward Gardner, a cosmetics king, who remained on the South Side. George, by now, has enough money to move to the suburbs himself, but he is going to stay put.

I N 1962, in a little book called *Challenge to Affluence*, Gunnar Myrdal (the Swedish author of *An American Dilemma*) predicted that rising unemployment in the United States might "trap an 'under-class' of unemployed and, gradually, unemployable and underemployed persons and families at the bottom of a society." In a footnote he said, apologetically, "The word 'under-class' does not seem to be used in English."

It took nearly two decades for the word to become a standard part of the national language, and when it did, it was generally understood as a synonym for the population of the black slums. The idea of the underclass was a departure from the main currents of American thought since the New Deal. It implied that poverty, for the poorest of the black migrants to the cities, had become a permanent condition. This was a common idea at the turn of the century, when white immigrants from Southern and Eastern Europe were streaming into the cities—Jacob Riis wrote in 1890 that Jews and Italians "carry their slums with them wherever they go"—but when the white urban ghettos began to disappear, slum life came to be regarded by most Americans as mainly the temporary lot of the immigrant generation, to be escaped by its children. The underclass was not an explicitly racial term, either, and so it carried the message that direct racial discrimination was not the prime cause of the conditions in the ghettos. Something else must have caused it; meanwhile, the connotation was that the forward march of the black poor had, only a few years after the great civil rights victories, ground to a halt.

Explorations of the idea of the underclass went on in a minor way through the 1960s and 1970s, usually without Myrdal's strict linkage of it to unemployment. Herbert Gans, the sociologist, wrote in 1965 that "public housing is home to the underclass." Andrew Brimmer, the black economist insulted behind his back by the dying Lyndon Johnson, said in a commencement address in 1971, "The simple fact is that the accelerated growth of dependency upon public welfare is creating a permanent 'underclass' in America." In 1975 Eleanor Holmes Norton, a leader of the younger generation of civil rights activists, was asked to deliver the keynote address at the annual conference of the National Urban League.

She had recently seen statistics showing that the percentage of black births that occurred out of wedlock was rising rapidly—a phenomenon that she and most of her audience, as members of the middle class, hadn't personally seen taking place, and that, because of the furor that followed the Moynihan Report, was still an extremely touchy subject among black opinion-makers. "I didn't want to be declared a traitor," Norton says. "The issue has to be addressed carefully. So I wrote the speech as a love letter from a black woman to a black man." In the speech, after going through the numbers about poor blacks' families, she said, "I suspect that these doleful statistics reveal that urban ghetto life is ever so much more devastating than the less concentrated and less vicious poverty of rural black life from which we are so rapidly converting."

Mitchell Sviridoff, the former director of the New Haven Gray Areas Program, was by then an official at the Ford Foundation, and he heard about Norton's speech, circulated copies of it widely through the social welfare world, and began to use the term "underclass" in his own writing. In 1978, Senator Edward Kennedy, in an address to the annual convention of the NAACP that was written by his brother Robert's speechwriter, Adam Walinsky, called for a focusing of national attention on "the great unmentioned problem of America today—the growth, rapid and insidious, of a group in our midst, perhaps more dangerous, more bereft of hope, more difficult to confront, than any for which our history has prepared us. It is a group that threatens to become what America has never known—a permanent underclass in our society." In 1982, Ken Auletta, a leading journalist, wrote a book called *The Underclass*, which was in part a description of a job-training program funded by Sviridoff and in part a review of the debate about ghetto poverty; it had the effect of putting the term into general use.

The underclass is not a precise, scientific concept: there is no sure way of determining whether a particular person is a member of it or not. For that reason estimates of its size vary widely, from two million people up to more than ten million. Nonetheless, some points of agreement about the underclass have emerged. It is plain that the ghettos deteriorated most severely, and the black middle class began to pull away from the black poor, during the late 1960s and early 1970s. The unemployment rate of black male sixteen- and seventeen-year-olds rose from 22.5 per cent in 1966 to 39 per cent in 1974, though school enrollments in that age group barely increased at all. The welfare rolls grew from 3 million in 1960 to 6.7 million in 1969, to 10.9 million in 1972; of single mothers,

29 per cent were on welfare in 1964 and 63 per cent in 1972. The arrest rate for black males between the ages of thirteen and thirty-nine rose by 49 per cent between 1966 and 1974. The percentage of black children born out of wedlock went from 16.9 in 1966 to 27.1 in 1976 and kept rising, passing 50 per cent in 1980; female-headed families accounted for 34.8 per cent of the black poor in 1965 and 60.6 per cent in 1973. Meanwhile, the income of black married couples rose steadily toward parity with whites, while their birth rate dropped below that of whites.

The disagreement is about why the ghettos fell apart when they did. The leading liberal theorist of the underclass in the 1980s was William Julius Wilson, who as chairman of the University of Chicago's sociology department held what was by tradition the most prominent position in American sociology. Wilson was a great admirer of Bayard Rustin, and he shared Rustin's long-deferred vision of the future of the civil rights struggle: the real cause was establishing a centrally managed, full-employment social-democratic economic order under which the black poor would be brought into the work force; the elimination of racial discrimination had been largely accomplished and was no longer central; strategically, it was crucial to avoid policies aimed specifically at blacks, because the country as a whole would never accept them, whereas the labor movement and the Democratic Party could be mobilized behind color-blind economic policies.

Wilson's views necessarily made his relations with the mainstream civil rights movement tense, just as Rustin's with King had been. In 1978 Wilson published a book called *The Declining Significance of Race*, in which he argued against "race-specific" policies like affirmative action and minority set-asides, which were gospel for organizations like the NAACP. He often discussed out-of-wedlock childbearing by the black poor, and even wrote about the Moynihan Report in a favorable tone. As a result he was constantly attacked by other black scholars, as well as by fringe political figures like Steve Cokely, a Chicago activist who won brief fame by suggesting that Jewish doctors were injecting blacks with the AIDS virus (in a speech that was mostly devoted to calling Wilson a "nigger" and other names).

In his major work on the underclass, *The Truly Disadvantaged*, published in 1987, Wilson took pains to construct a position that did not romanticize the state of the ghettos or explain away the crime and single-parent family structure there. At the same time, the broader argument set off by the Moynihan Report — Whose fault was ghetto poverty, the poor people's or society's?—was very much on his mind, and on the minds of most other poverty experts. Wilson went to great lengths to avoid the sin of victim-blaming. He attributed the ghettos' social deterioration to the outmigration of the middle class, which left poor people isolated and deprived of the beneficial effects of the old ghetto institutional structure, and, even more important, to unemployment.

Drawing on the work of John Kasarda, a sociologist, and Frank Levy, an economist, Wilson showed that the bountiful inner-city unskilled industrial jobs that had been the prime attraction of the urban North for millions of rural black migrants had essentially disappeared, most dramatically after 1970. Chicago lost 47 per cent of its manufacturing jobs between 1972 and 1982. Jobs generally were moving to the suburbs and the Sunbelt, physically away from the black poor; manufacturing jobs were going overseas or disappearing altogether, as the country shifted to a service economy that was split between minimum-wage jobs and work that required a high school or college degree. The overall economic slowdown that followed the 1973 OPEC embargo hit unskilled urban blacks especially hard. Within a couple of miles of Wilson's office at the university, the evidence of the change was readily visible. The stockyards were closed, steel mills were shutting down, and many of the smaller red-brick factories that dotted the South Side stood empty.

Culture was a tricky issue for Wilson. His argument assumed that the ghettos had a particular social structure that was not conducive to success. He wrote about the ghettos' being "increasingly socially isolated from mainstream patterns of behavior," and used terms like "social isolation" and "ghetto-specific culture" to explain the patterns of behavior that did exist there. But his determination not to blame people in ghettos for their predicament led him to attack the idea of a "culture of poverty" that would "continue to influence behavior even if opportunities for social mobility improve." At every turn Wilson looked for ways to demonstrate that poor people were not the authors of their own problems. Thus the real cause of out-of-wedlock childbearing in the ghettos, to Wilson, was a lack of "marriageable" (that is, employed) males, rather than an autonomous social custom; and the solution to the problem was "changing the social and economic situations, not the cultural traits, of the ghetto underclass." Wilson had partially loosened the bonds imposed on intellectuals by the reaction to the Moynihan Report: he made concern about the state of the black family a respectable subject again. But not entirely, for "culture of poverty" was still considered an offensive term in the universities, and social programs aimed at acculturation, such as intensive education and job training, took a back seat to the mission of structural economic change.

The leading conservative to emerge with a sweeping explanation of the deterioration of the ghettos was Charles Murray. Murray was a formerly liberal social scientist who had become disillusioned during the course of a career spent evaluating antipoverty programs for foundations and government agencies, and entered the new world of conservative policy-studies institutes, privately funded and outside the universities, that had sprung up during the 1970s. In *Losing Ground*, published in 1984, Murray presented, in a tone of sorrowful recognition of hard truths, an explanation for the underclass that was entirely at odds with Wilson's. It was no coincidence, to Murray, that the underclass first became discernible during the heyday of the Great Society; he believed it was created by the Great Society. The poor black family had fallen apart, and black unemployment had risen, he argued, because welfare had become more generous, removing the incentive to marry or to look for work. Crime had gotten worse because various liberal reforms had driven down the probability of punishment. Educational achievement had dropped because schools stopped imposing tough standards on their students. In general, the liberal tendency to excuse the antisocial behavior of the black poor had served to encourage more antisocial behavior. He ended *Losing Ground* by calling for the complete abolition of welfare.

Murray's book provoked a furious and voluminous liberal counterattack. His critics pointed out that out-of-wedlock childbearing continued to rise long after real welfare benefits began to fall in the early 1970s, and that it was rising just as rapidly in low-benefit states like Mississippi, where working clearly paid better than welfare, as in high-benefit states like Illinois. The black illegitimacy *rate* (that is, the percentage of black women of childbearing age who give birth out of wedlock) had actually fallen dramatically during the late sixties and early seventies, while the black illegitimacy *ratio* (the percentage of black babies who are born out of wedlock) was rising, because on the whole black women were having fewer babies — that is, moving closer to white social norms. William Julius Wilson criticized Murray for not acknowledging the importance of the broad economic trends that were at the heart of his own theory. The controversy over *Losing Ground* obscured one important similarity between Murray's work and Wilson's: Murray carefully avoided blaming the victim, too, by scrupulously laying all responsibility for the underclass at the feet of white liberals, so that the entente about avoiding the term "culture of poverty" ran all the way across the political spectrum. (A few years after *Losing Ground*, in what seemed a reversal of field, Murray embarked on a study that sought to explain blacks' lower economic and social status by examining the differences between the races in performance on intelligence tests. In a way this represented the migration to the North, a generation after the black migration itself, of white Southern opinion of the Cohn-Percy variety, but it seemed at odds with the scrupulously nonracial, economic-determinist position of *Losing Ground*.)

A third explanation for the underclass came from Christopher Jencks, a prominent sociologist who wrote long critical reviews of both *Losing Ground* and *The Truly Disadvantaged*. Jencks said the underclass had been created by economic and cultural trends that had swept through all of American society, not just the ghettos, in the late 1960s and early 1970s. Because of feminism, the sexual revolution, and the growing respectability of divorce, the white family had been breaking down too; in fact the illegitimacy ratio was rising even more rapidly among whites than blacks. White crime increased. White respect for authority lessened. The white teenage male unemployment rate rose and fell in tandem with the black rate, because both were being driven by the state of the labor market nationally, not in the inner cities. Because poor blacks had less education, higher unemployment, and higher indices of social disorganization to begin with, all these trends affected them more dramatically than they did whites — as the old saying goes, when white America gets a cold, black America has pneumonia. However, by Jencks's logic, as the national culture swung back toward more conservative mores, the underclass would begin to shrink; he pointed out that in the 1980s, black high school dropout rates, murder rates, and (as the labor market tightened) unemployment rates were falling, so it might already be happening.

A final important change that was taking place in the late 1960s, when the underclass began to become noticeable, was the end of the great black migration to the North. On the whole, of course, the migration was a success: most migrants found a much better life than they would have if they had stayed home in the South. But the similarities between the social ills of the vanished black sharecropper world of the rural South — out-of-wedlock childbearing, unstable marriages, high rates of violent crime, poor education, rampant substance abuse — and those of the new Northern ghetto underclass are so striking that it's impossible not to wonder whether they were directly related.

The connection between the end of the migration and the emergence of the underclass may have simply been that, as E. Franklin Frazier said, a period of social disorganization following arrival in the North was to be expected for at least some of the black migrants, as they left a rural church-centered environment for a modern urban one. It is really a separate question, though, whether black migrants with a background in the sharecropper system (who made up a minority of the great migration) had special disadvantages that caused them to do less well in the North than migrants who had, back in the South, more experience with town life, more education, and more stable families. Was George Hicks, in other words, able to find a more comfortable place in Chicago than Ruby Haynes partly because of the differences in their experiences before they ever got to Chicago?

Most of the hard data on the great migration consists of comparisons between black migrants to the North and blacks born in the North. These consistently show migrants doing slightly better economically than non-migrants. With white migrants to cities, the pattern is exactly the reverse: the urban-born do better, and it's easy to see why—they've attended better schools, they're operating on familiar turf, and they have better access to informal job-placement networks. Why shouldn't this be the case for black migrants too? It's especially odd that having had more years of schooling, which generally is a strong predictor of success in American society, seemed to provide no economic advantage to blacks at the time the great migration was ending.

There are two possible explanations for the greater success of black migrants as a group than non-migrants. First, the cities could have been so unwholesome as environments for blacks that having grown up in them would have conferred a special disadvantage; as Larry Long of the U.S. Census Bureau, author of several papers comparing migrants to non-migrants, once put it, "in Northern ghetto areas daily exposure to drugs, crime, violence, and overcrowded living conditions makes growing up and leading stable adult lives especially difficult." But in a city like Chicago, the whole notion of a difficult ghetto life that was completely unrelated to the great migration seems contrived. Many of the "non-migrants" in the statistical studies were surely people like Kermit and Robert Haynes, who were children of migrants and who grew up in what was essentially an immigrant community—one whose geography and economy had been profoundly shaped by the panicked white reaction to the great migration. Without the migration there would have been no Robert Taylor Homes.

The second explanation for black migrants' doing better than non-migrants is that opportunity for blacks in the North might have been so severely limited at the time of the migration that an eagerness to devote oneself to any job, no matter how bad, was the greatest inherent advantage a person could have, greater even than a high school or college degree. Migrants, who had Southern-bred low expectations combined with enough motivation to move across the country in search of opportunity, would have been more likely to have this quality than non-migrants. Even so, by the end of the 1960s middle-class jobs for blacks were opening up so rapidly that education was well on its way to becoming the kind of economic advantage for blacks that it has long been for whites. This development would have put at least the very last wave of displaced and uneducated sharecroppers to depart the South at a severe disadvantage.

By the 1960s the sharecropper system as such was mostly dead in the South, but a lot of black former sharecroppers were still working on plantations as day laborers, chopping cotton. They lost their jobs quite suddenly: in 1967, the federal government extended the minimum wage to farm workers, and as a result most Southern planters, faced with the prospect of paying $1.15 an hour to people who had been making $3 a day, immediately began using the chemical defoliants that were then becoming available, rather than black field hands with hoes, to get the weeds out from between their cotton plants. The switch from choppers to chemicals was the final, most dramatic step in the long process of black disengagement from Southern agriculture, and it caused a burst of migration to the cities, which by then were far less hospitable than they had been when former sharecroppers like Ruby Haynes and Uless Carter got there.

Everybody who took part in the intense intellectual debate about the underclass in the 1980s at least agreed that they were addressing an issue of great urgency that required some dramatic national response; but there was almost no response at all.

The work on the underclass being produced in universities and think tanks did not create much of a spark in the general public. It was overwhelmingly statistical—none of the best-known academic underclass experts did field work — and the intellectual pirouetting involved in discussing a phenomenon defined by cultural indices like family structure while avoiding the issue of culture per se gave the arguments an elaborate, recondite quality. During the second half of the 1980s, when the underclass debate was at its peak, the two causes of the underclass most often cited by the experts, welfare payments and unemployment, were both diminishing.

Among black politicians and the leaders of civil rights organizations, the idea of the underclass was still not widely accepted; even William Julius Wilson, who traveled in those circles, announced in 1990 that he would henceforth try to use the term "ghetto poor" instead of "underclass." When Jesse Jackson, an illegitimate child himself, was asked about the underclass, he would usually draw himself up and say, "*I* am the underclass." There was a feeling that raising the underclass issue would bring out all the old white prejudices about innate black laziness, criminality, stupidity, and immorality, and that it would distract attention from the race-based political agenda of the black middle class. Bayard Rustin, speaking shortly before he died about the relative silence of Benjamin Hooks of the NAACP and John Jacob of the Urban League on the issue, said, "Do you think Hooks and Jacob don't know this? They're not idiots. But they are set up to deal with problems of color and have to act as if they still exist." Most black leaders were by now sufficiently separated from the black poor in their daily lives that the full realization of what life in the ghettos had become was slow in dawning. Eleanor Norton was surprised by the figures on the black family that she discovered in the 1970s — "I had never seen the female-headed black family," she says. Marian Wright Edelman, who had conceived the Poor People's Campaign and now is head of the Children's Defense Fund, says, "In the early 1980s, I asked for the figures on the black family, and I got back that fifty-five per cent of black kids were born out of wedlock. I couldn't believe it. I sent it back."

By now, there is a great deal of concern about the black family among the black leadership, but it is regarded as a touchy issue, to be handled with great delicacy. The Urban League has begun addressing the issue in its annual reports; Alpha Phi Alpha, the most prominent black fraternity, has a teenage pregnancy prevention program. Everyone is convinced, though, that an open call for action to help the ghettos would surely run afoul of white racism. "If they thought it was a poor black problem, they'd give you $2.98," Edelman says. "If they thought it was people like them, they'd have all kinds of ideas about how to help. People move from self-interest." So the focus is kept on deracialized proxy issues: children, welfare reform, economics, drugs, homelessness.

For the past decade or so, minor stirrings of what might be called the Booker T. Washington tendency in black America have begun to reappear. Washington, the founder of the Tuskegee Institute and a former slave on a plantation, proposed in a famous speech in Atlanta in 1895 that blacks set aside the goal of legal rights and concentrate instead on self-help, so that the great mass of poor rural blacks could become economically self-sufficient workers, farmers, artisans, and small businessmen without arousing white hostility. Washington's archenemy was W. E. B. DuBois, whose family had been free for generations and who, as the leading figure in the NAACP, fought to put legal equality, rather than solving the problems of the black lower class, at the top of the black agenda. For many years the feud between DuBois and Washington was the defining struggle in black intellectual and political life, and, in terms of setting the course for black organizations, the DuBois side clearly won.

When the issue of the underclass arose, it created an opening for a revival of Washingtonism: legal equality had been achieved, and the problem of the black poor still remained. Civil rights and the war on poverty hadn't healed their wounds, so wasn't it now time for a revival of self-help? There were some strains of Washington sympathy among left-wing black nationalists, such as Harold Cruse of the University of Michigan and Louis Farrakhan, but the revival mainly involved black conservatives who were allied with the larger conservative movement and with the Republican Party, where their program of an end to affirmative action, forced integration, and liberal social welfare programs found its natural audience. Robert Woodson, a former community action worker, started an organization called the National Center for Neighborhood Enterprise that promoted tenant ownership of housing projects; Woodson had warm relations with Republican officialdom, and Jack Kemp, secretary of HUD in the Bush administration and the coordinator of all the administration's antipoverty programs, embraced his ideas. On the day his appointment to the Cabinet was announced, and frequently thereafter, Kemp called for a new war on poverty, based on the principle of the regeneration of the ghettos through self-help and "empowerment" — which, though Kemp didn't seem to realize it, was exactly the principle that hadn't worked in the first war on poverty. Glenn Loury, a young professor at Harvard (and a product of the South Side of Chicago) who, along with Shelby Steele of San Jose State University, was the most eloquent writer on behalf of the Washington revival, was appointed to the number-two job in the Department of Education during Reagan's second term, but a personal scandal forced him to withdraw just before he was supposed to take office.

The black leadership did not warmly embrace the idea of self-help as the key to black progress. After Loury published a sweeping statement of his views in *The New Republic*, he got a call from Benjamin Hooks. Loury says, "He said, 'Look, I'm a civil rights leader. Sure, I know these problems exist, but my job is to hold white people's feet to the fire. In these years of Ronald Reagan and turning the clock back, how can I go around criticizing little black kids?' Then I had a private meeting with a group of black leaders: Carl Holman, of the National Urban Coalition; John Jacob; Walter Fauntroy [then the District of Columbia's represen- tative in Congress]; Joseph Lowery of the SCLC; Coretta King. I made a one-hour presentation. I said the real problem is the problem of the black poor, and civil rights activism is largely irrelevant — though not if you want to own a TV station. I said, 'You people have exhausted a lot of moral capital with your whining.' The reaction was quite amazing. I got no real rebuttal. They said, 'We appreciate your contribution. We're proud of you. A young black scholar like you being on the faculty at Harvard is what we were fighting for in the '60s. But you have to be careful of when and how you say these things.'"

The black self-help movement is far more vibrant in intellectual and political circles, and in the hearts of middle-class blacks, than it is in the ghettos it is supposed to repair. In a place like Chicago, self-help for most people inside the ghettos still means moving out, and in the middle- class neighborhoods, people practice the creed of self-improvement in their own lives but are not eager to see further cuts in the government programs that provide most of them with their livelihood. The social isolation and erosion of institutions that Wilson wrote about has pro- gressed to the point where there is no real mechanism in place for the revival of the worst neighborhoods through the reunification of the black classes. There are quite a few successful community development orga- nizations in black neighborhoods, but they are subsidized by philanthro- pists, and located in areas that people with jobs haven't left yet. The high-rise projects are operating at such a heavy loss that simply turning them over to their tenants is impracticable.

In American public life, the underclass is stuck in the antechamber where policy issues rest until they become political crusades. The times are conservative. The magnitude of the federal deficit has taken major government undertakings out of the realm of political debate. Most people believe that all the federal government's past efforts to help the black poor failed miserably. The underclass itself is, as always, relatively quiescent politically, and the payoff to the country as a whole for addressing its problems — better race relations, a restoration of the fabric of city life, a more optimistic national spirit, a rise in economic productivity — is an abstract one that does not easily motivate voters to support an expensive solution. The black poor have become the victims of the dissolution of the national mood of optimism and consensus, which has been proceeding steadily ever since they arrived in the Northern cities. The country is fragmented into constituencies that look out for their own interests. To the public as a whole, the underclass lacks a human face — its most publicized members are criminals, and otherwise it is a mass of frightening statistics. What the underclass most needs is to move closer to the mainstream of American life, socially and economically, but assimilation is no longer the national creed.

There have certainly been times in the past when the country's main racial problem was widely recognized, but when the possibility of a solution appeared remote. What worked best then was the formulation of the issue in a way that touched the deep disquiet about race in the national conscience. Harriet Beecher Stowe did that for slavery. Martin Luther King did it for segregation. Political support for a concerted effort to help the underclass is not likely to materialize until it is understood as a moral cause.

A FEW MONTHS before Ruby Haynes left the Robert Taylor Homes for Clarksdale, her daughter Juanita, tired of the life of a prison widow, began seeing a man named Harold Yates, who lived in the next building in the project. She got pregnant, and had a son she named Johnnie, after her brother. The relationship with Harold didn't last; Juanita settled into single motherhood in Ruby's old apartment in 5135 South Federal.

In 1980, Thomas Chairs was released from the state prison where he had been doing time for the murder of Robert Shaw, having been the unintended beneficiary of a new Illinois law that attached fixed sentences to major crimes in order to prevent liberal judges from letting criminals out on parole. He moved in with Juanita for a while, but they didn't get along; he was upset that she had had a child by another man, and he nagged her about it constantly. Soon he moved down the hallway to his mother's apartment.

Thanks to her political connections, Juanita got a part-time job with a federal program as a "community organizer" in the project, meaning that she would perform minor tasks such as chaperoning children's trips to parks and museums. Thanks to the continuing vitality of the community development idea and to the ability of organized labor to keep federal jobs programs from dispensing real work, jobs like Juanita's typically were situated inside ghettos and didn't impart any skills that would be useful in the outside world. The work was pleasant, though, and Juanita was allowed to keep her public-aid grant. After eighteen months the job ended—the CETA program, her employer, was designed as a temporary work experience, and anyway its funding was heavily cut in the first year of the Reagan administration—and she was just at home with her children again.

Juanita had a friend named Linda Walton who had grown up in 5135 South Federal but had gotten enough education to get a good job, as a secretary, and escape the project. Linda got paid every two weeks, and on payday she got into the habit of buying cocaine and snorting it with Juanita. Up to that point Juanita hadn't had much experience with drugs. She smoked marijuana as a teenager, but once she was given a "Thai stick"—a joint laced with PCP—that caused her to pass out. She wound up being taken to a hospital emergency room by her brothers, and after that she stayed away from drugs for years.

Linda Walton got married in 1984. Shortly afterward, Juanita went over to her apartment one weekend and found a group of people smoking cocaine in a pipe. They asked Juanita if she wanted to try it. She said sure. It was a much more intense experience than snorting—there was an immediate strong rush to the head that lasted for only a minute or so, and then you'd take a rest and smoke some more. Soon Linda and Juanita were smoking cocaine every weekend, and after a few months of that Juanita started smoking on her own, almost every day, with her friends in 5135.

The project had remained on its downward course. One day in 1984, Juanita saw a murder committed in broad daylight in the entranceway to 5135: two men were arguing, and one of them pulled a gun and shot the other. Cocaine was becoming an important part of the life of the building.

Most of Juanita's girlfriends in 5135 were on it. Because Juanita was the only member of her social circle with her own apartment (the others still lived with their mothers, who weren't on drugs), her place became the group's cocaine-smoking center, which meant that Juanita often got her cocaine free. Somebody would buy half a gram, which cost fifty dollars, from the dope man, whose parents lived in the building. Then, in Juanita's apartment, they would mix the cocaine with baking soda and put a little bit in a test tube with a few drops of water. They would soak a cotton ball (which looked not too different from the ones Juanita's mother used to pick on Delta plantations) in grain alcohol, hold it under the test tube, and light it, which made the ingredients form into a ball. Then they'd put the test tube in cold water, and the cocaine would crystallize, so that it looked like a piece of hard candy, colored light pink or mint green. They'd dig it out of the test tube, put it in a pipe, and smoke. Five or six people would go through a half gram in fifteen minutes; then somebody would have to try to get the money to buy some more.

When she was smoking, Juanita would send her daughter Tomesha out on the porch to play, but it wasn't hard for Tomesha to figure out what was going on. Her playmates would tell her, "Your mama and my mama are getting high together." It became obvious to Juanita that her drug use was taking its toll on Tomesha, because she began acting moody and sullen. Juanita brought her down to Clarksdale and left her with Ruby.

By 1985, Juanita realized that she had become a drug addict. She had gotten back together with Thomas and become pregnant again, and she smoked cocaine all through her pregnancy. Her brother Johnnie moved into her apartment and got on cocaine too. Thomas wasn't on drugs, but he was drinking too much, and fighting with Juanita and with Johnnie. Once Thomas pulled a gun on Johnnie, Juanita called the police, and Thomas wound up in jail for a few days. Just before Juanita was due to give birth, the usual crowd came over to smoke cocaine, and Thomas tried to kick them out. He got in a tussle with one of Juanita's girlfriends, and she called the police; he was back in jail on the day that his and Juanita's second daughter, Thomasine, was born. Miraculously, Thomasine was healthy—two of Juanita's friends gave birth to addicted "drug babies" at around the same time; one died in infancy, and the other had to be in intensive care for several months—but she seemed to cry constantly. Juanita brought her and Johnnie, her son, down to Clarksdale and stayed with Ruby for a couple of months, but Thomas persuaded her to come back to Chicago again.

By this time Juanita was buying her own cocaine. She got to the point where she turned her public-aid identification card over to the dope man. When her check came, she would meet him at a local "currency exchange" — a storefront operation that received welfare checks directly from the public-aid department, so that they wouldn't be stolen from the project's mailboxes, and then cashed them, for a small commission — and turn all the money over to him in payment for her drug debts. She would sell her food stamps at the little "Arab stores" in the area, which paid seventy cents on the dollar for them, and then beg food from other people in 5135. A friend taught her how to go to Field's and Carson's in the Loop, pop the plastic tags off the merchandise, and spirit it away in a shopping bag; she would bring the clothing she stole back to the project and sell it for a quarter of the retail price. All the money went to cocaine. She stopped paying her rent and her electric bill, but the housing authority, desperate to keep tenants in the Taylor Homes so that its federal subsidies would continue flowing, didn't kick her out. The only thing Juanita wouldn't do to get money for drugs was sell her body, but several of her friends in the building did.

Juanita broke up with Thomas again and became pregnant by a man named Walter Stewart, who lived in 5100 South Federal and worked in a fast-food fried chicken place on Forty-seventh Street. She kept smoking cocaine. One evening a friend came over with a batch that was laced with amphetamines. They smoked together from ten in the evening until two in the morning, and then Juanita went into cardiac arrest. Her friend got a neighbor to call an ambulance, and Juanita was rushed to the hospital. She recovered, but she was badly shaken; even through the haze of her addiction — the urge for one more perfect high that was so strong it led the mind to rationalize away nearly any sensible thought — she could see that she was endangering the life of her unborn child, and probably her own life as well. On April 14, 1986, Juanita was lying in her bed at night, thinking that in the morning the welfare checks would arrive at the currency exchange, which meant that a big group would probably be coming over to smoke. Suddenly she heard a voice in her head, saying, Stop! Go down South!

The next day Juanita met the dope man at the currency exchange, as usual. She owed him only $150, which meant that she had $192 in cash left over. She went down to the Loop, bought new jogging suits for her children, and then went to the Greyhound bus station and got a ticket for Clarksdale. The bus left late that night. The next day she arrived at her mother's apartment unannounced, confessed the whole story of her drug addiction, and moved in. She was clean and healthy when her new son, Jacorey, was born.

Juanita's brother Johnnie stayed on in the apartment in 5135. It wasn't in his name, and couldn't have been—it was a violation of the rules for a single man to have such a big place—but the housing authority rarely checked the building any more, so he got away with it. A friend of his moved in, and they began dealing cocaine out of the apartment together. The business didn't last long. Johnnie and his friend were both skimming cocaine out of the pouches they sold, cheating their customers and each other. They got into a wrangle about it one afternoon that ended with Johnnie's friend setting the apartment on fire. Somebody called the fire department, and they came and broke the door down and got Johnnie out before he got hurt, but he couldn't stay there any more. The housing authority never got around to fixing the place up again. Apartment 902, home to the Haynes family in Chicago for a quarter century, was now just a burnt-out, unoccupied shell.

Three floors down, in Apartment 610, Connie was still living with her five children, the last member of the clan left in the Robert Taylor Homes. It was quite possibly the worst place in the country in which to raise a family. Federal census tract 4002, which includes 5135 South Federal, is the third poorest in the country; the poorest is census tract 3817, which is immediately to the north and also wholly within the Robert Taylor Homes. In the context of the rest of the world, the social disorder in the project is even worse than the poverty: plenty of places outside the United States have lower per capita incomes, but very few can match it in such measures as infant mortality, birth weight, life expectancy, crime, and family structure.

The entrance to 5135 is bleak and forbidding. Most of the time it is littered with empty bottles and piles of uncollected garbage. Gang symbols are spray-painted all over the lobby. The open plaza on the State Street side is barren of greenery. The elevators, stripped of their emergency-stop buttons, are jerky and unreliable, sometimes stopping on the designated floor and sometimes not. All the access points to the building—the elevator cabs, the stairwells, and the hallways—reek of urine and cheap wine. Gang members regularly shoot out the lights in the breezeways and stairwells, so coming home to 5135 after dark is a terrifying experience.

Of the 160 apartments in the building, fifty are vacant; there are three vacant apartments on Connie's floor, which is one of the better ones because it is relatively close to the ground. The vacant apartments are centers of gang activity, drug dealing, weapons storage, and illegal residency by homeless men and freshly released criminals. The Disciples now control 5135; a "falcon," or building captain, and a lieutenant live there, and hold weekly meetings in one of the vacant apartments. The Cobra Stones control the building next door, which ensures a constant round of gang warfare in the area. At the age of eight or nine, boys in the building will begin to receive the attentions of gang recruiters. They are asked to prove their fitness for gang membership by stealing, selling drugs, and publicly "showing out," or denouncing the authority of, their mothers (unless their mothers have agreed to become "den mothers" and let the gangs use their apartments), all of which are signs of their having attained manhood; if they don't join, they are taunted, provoked, and sometimes beaten. In the buildings to the south of 5135, there are gangs for girls as well as for boys.

Crack cocaine made its first appearance in 5135 in 1986, when a woman brought some back from a trip to California, and it became generally available in 1988. It didn't fundamentally alter the life of the building, because so many other drugs were already around. Smoking cocaine, in the way that Juanita did, is still considered preferable to smoking crack, although it is more expensive. Carachi, a black substance that is a powerful form of heroin, is another popular new drug in the building, and of course the substance most widely abused there is still alcohol. Minor crime never stops, and major crime is not especially rare. In the course of one year, 1988, a girl who lived on the ninth floor at 5135 was taken to a vacant apartment and shot by a group of young men; in 5201, a boy was killed on one of the breezeways on Halloween night by a shot to the head from a .357 magnum; in 5001, a boy was shot in the head and left to die on a breezeway, a pair of twin girls were shot but survived, and a boy was shot and killed in one of the elevators. Quite often the perpetrators of murders in the project are never brought to justice, in large part because the witnesses are afraid that if they cooperate with the police, the gangs will kill them later.

The Chicago Police Department's Second District headquarters is just a stone's throw from 5135 South Federal, and there is a police substation inside the Robert Taylor Homes, but the police walk through each building only twice a week, during daylight hours; at night, all the police in the district are in cars. Social workers from the public-aid department have long since stopped coming into the Robert Taylor Homes, because so many of them were mugged there in the 1970s; people go downtown every six months to have their welfare status recertified. A few years ago, the public-aid department stopped sending out all its welfare checks on the same day, because there were so many robberies outside the currency exchanges. Illegal loan-sharking operations, which charge 100 per cent interest and hold people's welfare cards as security, are scattered through the neighborhood.

After Juanita's departure, a woman on the first floor took over as the precinct captain of 5135, but after a couple of years she moved out of the project, and now there is no precinct captain. The Third Ward alderman who gave Ruby her going-away party, Tyrone Kenner, was convicted of extortion in 1983 – it turned out that he had been collecting hundred-dollar commissions from the people for whom he got city jobs. His replacement, Dorothy Tillman, is well known in Chicago as an outspoken member of the black independent-politics movement, but she isn't much of a presence inside 5135. When people call her office with complaints about their heat or water, they are usually told to call the project's management office, which typically pleads insufficient money and manpower. Harold Washington, when he was mayor, was a genuine hero in 5135, a former Third Ward politician much loved and admired for keeping in touch with his roots. He visited the building regularly; when he died, all through the Chicago projects people could be seen standing outside crying. No one has replaced him as a symbol of official concern for the residents of the Robert Taylor Homes.

DuSable High School became briefly famous in 1985 as the first high school in America to dispense birth control; at the time, nearly a third of its female students were pregnant. It has steadily lost students as people have left the neighborhood – there were more than 5,000 in the early 1970s, and today there are fewer than 2,000. More than half of each freshman class fails to graduate. Only 60 per cent of the parents come in to sign their children's report cards, which are issued three times a year. Of the male students, one in eight is a former inmate of a home for juvenile criminals. Six police officers are on duty inside the school every day. Inside the classrooms, the students do mostly routine copying, and are given A's for such work as this description of Ernest Hemingway's story "A Clean, Well-Lighted Place": "He old man is a deaf man who is tiring to make a living." Even the elementary schools that serve the Robert Taylor Homes have problems with gang activity and student pregnancies.

Connie, through immense force of will, has been able to create a home life in this environment that got her children on the way to something better. Maxine, her oldest daughter, graduated from DuSable and from a community college on the South Side, and is now studying computer science. Marlo, the next daughter, is a student at a secretarial college in the Loop. In 1987 she had a son out of wedlock, making Connie a grandmother at the age of thirty-six, but Connie was not displeased about it — Marlo had waited until she was nineteen to get pregnant, and she has a good steady relationship with her boyfriend, a former resident of the project who is now living on the North Side, has a job on a loading dock, and helps a lot with the baby.

Melanie, the next daughter, is the star of the family. She was valedictorian of the DuSable class of 1987, and is majoring in psychology at the University of Illinois' Chicago campus. Like Maxine, she has never been pregnant. When Melanie graduated from DuSable, she got a brand-new Plymouth Horizon from a program run by the Reverend T. L. Barrett, pastor of the Life Center Church of Universal Awareness on Michigan Avenue and himself a child of the Robert Taylor Homes. In accordance with his philosophy of "black wealth, black health," Barrett had persuaded businesses to make substantial material gifts to outstanding students at DuSable. When the news of Melanie's new car appeared in the newspapers and in *Jet* magazine, she got a call from her long-absent father, Charles Mays, who wanted to borrow it. She refused, sold the car to help pay for her education, and never heard from him again.

The child Connie has the most trouble with is Melissa, her youngest daughter. When Melissa was fifteen, she got pregnant. Connie talked her into getting an abortion and scraped together $100 to pay for it, but a year later Melissa was pregnant again. Connie felt that Melissa's girlfriends had put the idea in her head that she could get her own welfare check if she had a baby, and that her primary motive in getting pregnant was money, not love. Connie disapproves of the baby's father, another former resident of the project, because he doesn't have a job, doesn't come around very often, and doesn't offer Melissa any financial help — in fact, Connie herself attended the birth of Melissa's daughter because he wasn't around, and afterward she and Melissa took him to court to make him pay child support. Since Melissa was under eighteen and living at home when the baby was born, she could get on welfare only if Connie signed for her, which Connie refused to do. She put Melissa and her daughter on her own grant, and told Melissa she had to stay in school.

Melvin, Connie's only son and youngest child, is the one she worries about the most. Growing up in the project is harder for a boy than a girl, because a boy is under constant pressure to demonstrate his masculinity in destructive ways (chief among them, joining a gang) and doesn't have a parent of the same sex around, as girls do. Connie's sister, who got a transfer from the Robert Taylor Homes to Altgeld Gardens in 1988 after one of her neighbors beat her up in the elevator, has two sons who are in the Disciples. By the time he was in the eighth grade at Farren elementary school, Melvin was already being harassed by the gangs. "They pick on me a lot," he says. "They come into my face, say I'm a coward, taunting me, pushing me, any time I come around. They say they're going to kick my ass if they catch me bothering one of their boys again. I know they've got guns and knives. If it's a whole group of them, I might get a little fear in my heart, but most of the time I'm not afraid of them." By the time he was thirteen years old, Melvin was already more than six feet tall; he decided to avoid DuSable altogether and go to high school instead at Simeon, a school in George Hicks's neighborhood with a famous basketball team. In 1985 Simeon's star basketball player, Benjy Wilson, was shot and killed on the street in broad daylight by two gang members, one of whom was the grandson of the great blues impresario Willie Dixon. Still, Simeon is regarded as much safer than DuSable.

Connie's strategy for dealing with the life of the Robert Taylor Homes is to try to tune it out as much as possible. She doesn't socialize with her neighbors much; when she passes them in the lobby or the breezeway, she nods and keeps on walking. She has instructed her daughters, who are regularly hooted at and called "bitches" by the other girls in the project because of their good study habits, to do the same. Her apartment looks different from the others in the building even from the outside, because there is a glued-on number, instead of graffiti, on the door. Inside, the atmosphere is calm and orderly. On the walls are hung pictures of Isaac Hayes, Prince, the Last Supper, and Garfield the cat. In the early 1980s Connie got a job, at $4.50 an hour, as a maid at the Westin Hotel in the Loop, but she quit and went back on welfare in 1985 because she had begun to hear reports from neighbors that her children were acting up during the hours when she was gone, and she decided to keep a closer eye on them as they entered their teens. She is getting a check of $386 a month, which keeps her decently supplied for about three weeks, at which point she has to put the family on a diet of spaghetti, hot dogs, and chicken necks until the next check arrives. On weekend nights she goes to lounges around the South Side, where she stays out until one or two in the morning listening to music and trying to meet men. She has had a few relationships, but nothing serious; she has found that once you tell a man you live in the Robert Taylor Homes, he usually loses interest, because visiting the projects in the evenings is not a prospect that most South Siders relish.

For the most part, Connie has no faith that any agency of government is interested in helping her. There are a couple of much-appreciated exceptions. The Women's, Infants', and Children's nutrition program provided her with formula, baby cereal, milk, beans, cheese, and juice for Melvin, when he was a baby, and for her two grandchildren. From the age of two and a half until he entered kindergarten, Melvin was in Head Start at the Farren school; as a condition of his enrollment, Connie had to work there as a volunteer two days a month. She felt he was much better prepared for school than kids who hadn't been in Head Start. On the other hand, Connie's least favorite government program is WIN, a federal work-incentive scheme created during the seventies to encourage welfare mothers to get jobs. When Melvin turned six, Connie got a letter saying she had to come to the WIN office downtown and register. She was hoping to get job training there, but instead they just talked to her about job-hunting techniques and told her to come back in two weeks. On that visit she got a list of ten employers she had to go see, but she was looking for night work, and none of them had any. She found her job at the Westin on her own. Once her two grandchildren were put on her welfare check, she was, thankfully, out of the WIN program again. When Melissa graduates from DuSable and turns eighteen, she will get a check of her own, and Connie's grant will be reduced to $150 a month. At that point she plans to go for another hotel job and get off welfare for good.

Connie's divorce from Johnnie became final in 1980. By that time he was living outside the project with a woman named Valerie. In 1981 they had a son, Johnnie Junior; they split up, Johnnie married someone else, got divorced, and got back together with Valerie. They had an apartment together on the South Side, but were frequently separated. Johnnie was still on drugs, and he worked, sporadically, as a laborer at McCormick Place, the big convention center in Chicago. He and Connie found that they were able to maintain cordial relations after the divorce, and he comes around 5135 South Federal every now and then to see his children.

In 1987, Juanita moved back to Chicago from Clarksdale with her children, telling herself that if she stayed away from the Robert Taylor Homes she would be all right. She took a room in a friend's apartment, but she found it impossible to keep up with the rent payments, so she moved in with Johnnie and Valerie. There she quickly got back on cocaine. In early 1988, another friend of hers, a deeply religious woman named Darlene Peterson, offered her a free room if she would promise to stop using drugs, get a job, and attend church every Sunday. Juanita gratefully accepted; she felt that if Darlene hadn't come along, she would have ended up in a center for drug addicts. Darlene found her a job as an order-filler for the Spiegel catalogue.

Then Thomas Chairs crossed Juanita's path again. By this time he had become a cocaine addict. His mother had kicked him out of her apartment in 5135, and he was living by his wits out on the streets. Darlene wouldn't let Thomas in her house, so when Juanita wanted to see him they had to meet in Washington Park. She still felt, after all these many years, that Thomas was the love of her life, and even though he was hardly the world's greatest prospective mate, she wanted to be with him. Knowing that he was never going to amount to anything as long as he was in Chicago, she asked him to move back South with her. He agreed. In September 1988, Juanita's brother Larry loaded Juanita, Thomas, and the kids into his van and drove them down to Clarksdale, where Ruby was waiting to take them into her care.

THE HISTORICAL tide that had brought Ruby to the Chicago ghetto forty years earlier is now visibly receding. Statistically, the movement of blacks back to the South is insignificant, but so is movement in the other direction. The black population of Chicago rose by 300,000 during the sixties, the last decade of the great migration, reaching a total of more than a million; since then it has grown much more slowly and only by virtue of the excess of births over deaths. The Illinois Central station at Twelfth Street and Michigan Avenue was torn down in 1970. The palpable presence of the South in black Chicago is growing fainter, although many people still go home once or twice a year, and the ghetto

grocery stores still sell such Southern merchandise as confections im-
ported from Memphis and the small packets of Argo Starch that pregnant
women, in accordance with a longstanding folk custom, like to chew, and
black politicians still use a Delta metaphor—"plantation politics"—as
their standard term of opprobrium for white rule.

The traditional ghettos are home to hundreds of thousands of people,
but they are taking on a vestigial feeling. On the West Side, Little Village, the commercial strip along Twenty-fourth Street that is the major
center of Chicago's biggest contemporary immigrant group, Mexican-
Americans, has the crowded, bustling atmosphere Forty-seventh Street
had in the forties; eight blocks to the north, Sixteenth Street, which runs
through the heart of Lawndale and is probably the worst area in Chicago
outside the projects, is horribly run-down and half abandoned. The most
active live-blues scene in the city is now in an affluent white neighborhood on the Near North Side. The Muslims, who in their day may have
been the largest organization made up primarily of the ghetto poor, and
who were much admired in black Chicago for their ability to turn around
even prison inmates and prostitutes, are down to an active membership
of several hundred people at best, and most of the old Muslim businesses—the bakeries and the restaurants—are gone. Wallace Muhammad, the son of Elijah, who took over the leadership of the Nation of
Islam after his father's death in 1975, moved closer to the conventional
Islamic faith, lost power to Farrakhan, who continues to preach a religion
specific to the African-American experience, and finally moved to California; and Farrakhan is more a popular orator than the leader of an
organization. Elijah's most famous disciple, Muhammad Ali, has long
since removed himself from Chicago to rural Michigan.

It is no longer possible to think of the worst-off ghetto neighborhoods
as being the heart of black Chicago, which has become essentially a very
large ethnic community whose organizational focus is on political power
rather than the social welfare of the poor. The larger society is making
no great effort to improve living conditions in the ghettos; instead the
main goal is keeping the disorder there down to a manageable level and,
most of all, contained. Inside the ghettos, the overwhelming preoccupation of most ambitious people, especially if they are young, is with
leaving.

Probably the most common escape route is military service, and in
second place are the parochial schools, which, with much lower salaries
and smaller administrative staffs than the public schools, produce far

better educational results; in both cases, the common thread is a strict system of rules, requirements, and high expectations of a kind that the projects, the public schools, and the social agencies have long since abandoned, which serve to introduce into young people's lives an alternative to the ghetto culture. Back in 1963, in *Dark Ghetto*, Kenneth Clark somewhat apologetically proposed establishing a paramilitary "cadet corps" in Harlem, because of "the relative ease with which uniforms, disciplined organizations, and regulations can be used to bolster the self-esteem of young people." The Muslims, an organization completely out of sympathy with Clark's gospel of integration, were the closest thing to an embodiment of that idea of Clark's, with their dress codes, strictures on behavior, and heavy work requirements. Many of the successful social institutions in the Chicago ghetto today have a similar spirit. For example, the elementary school of the Holy Angels Catholic Church, which is right across the street from the Ida B. Wells Homes, uses a regimen that its principal, a black priest named George Clements, describes this way:

> We bear down hard on basics. Hard work, sacrifice, dedication. A twelve-month school year. An eight-hour day. You can't leave the campus. Total silence in the lunchroom and throughout the building. Expulsion for graffiti. Very heavy emphasis on moral pride. The parents must come every month and pick up the report card and talk to the teacher, or we kick out the kid. They must come to the PTA every month. They must sign every night's homework in every subject. The kids wear uniforms, which are required to be clean, pressed, no holes. We have a waiting list of over a thousand, and the more we bear down, the longer the list gets. We have achieved honors as an academic institution above the national norms in all disciplines.

Clements is a great believer in black pride and self-help, and has no faith in the ability of government programs to treat poor blacks as anything but deficient, dependent people. Still, there are plenty of programs, in Chicago and elsewhere, that under government auspices and with government funding succeed in preparing kids from the ghetto for school, helping them along while they are there, and training them for the job market, always by stressing the importance of pride and standards. The domestic agencies of the federal government could apply the same principle in a truly comprehensive way, through jobs programs tied to the welfare system and special educational efforts beyond the Head Start years, but they haven't, yet.

At the very end of the eighties, there was a small sign of change for the better at 5135 South Federal Street. For years the Chicago Housing Authority had been embroiled in a series of scandals. When Harold Washington became mayor, he appointed Renault Robinson, a former police officer and the founder (with George Clements) of the Afro-American Patrolmen's League, as the first black chairman of the Chicago Housing Authority. Various black executives—including, for a while, Erwin France—came in to run the housing authority under Robinson, but problems of crime, sloppy accounting, questionable subcontracting, and poor maintenance persisted; the housing authority lost some federal monies because of its poor performance. The scandals played differently with different constituencies: project residents like Connie saw them as just more of the same, whites felt that self-aggrandizing black politicians were screwing up the projects and hurting their own people, and middle-class blacks took them as proof of the proposition that powerful blacks in government were held to a higher standard than their white predecessors had been. Finally, in 1987, Robinson resigned, and a black developer of subsidized housing named Vincent Lane replaced him and immediately began to clean house.

Lane moved toward reviving screening and tenant eviction, and toward reformulating rent policies so that tenants with jobs would no longer have a financial incentive to leave. He cleaned out dusty corners of the housing authority bureaucracy by abolishing jobs en masse and then requiring managers to reapply for their old positions—an exercise that led to George Hicks's being demoted, in 1990, from manager to assistant manager; George, bitter and hurt, took early retirement. In the Robert Taylor Homes, Lane started setting up security systems in the buildings, in which a doorman stationed in the lobby would have to approve the entrance of all tenants (who had to show an identification card) and visitors (who had to be vouched for by a tenant). As one of the better buildings in the project, 5135 South Federal was one of the first to be converted to the new system. Connie, having heard many promises of reform over the years that hadn't come true, was cynical about it. She appreciated the presence of the doorman, but at night, when the building's security sergeant went home, the guards on duty would often slip away to dalliances they were having with women who lived in 5135, leaving the front desk unattended. There was still crime and drug dealing, in part because some of the perpetrators were residents of the building, not interlopers from the outside; Connie had once caught her own next-door neighbors trying to break into her apartment.

Connie's long-term plans didn't change. For years she has had an application on file for Section 8, a federal program that gives poor people grants to find private housing on their own. The state of Section 8's funding is such that preference must go to people who don't live in public housing, which the government presumes to be decent; people inside the project like to say that if you apply when your children are young, your grant won't come through until they are grown up. Connie hopes that time is coming for her. As an alternative to Section 8, she would like to move into a small project outside the ghetto, but there are hardly any of them in Chicago; the housing authority's office in charge of building scatter-site housing was inactive for many years, and when Renault Robinson took the authority, he actually abolished it. Eventually, Connie hopes, something will come through. Perhaps when she gets a job she will be able to afford to rent an apartment in one of the good areas of the South Side; perhaps when her daughters enter the white-collar work force, one of them will find something for her. After nearly two decades in the Robert Taylor Homes, she is weary and depressed, and what she wants more than anything is to get out.

CLARKSDALE

THE MECHANIZATION of cotton picking and the phasing out of the sharecropper system had been substantially completed in Clarksdale by 1960, and race relations in the town had settled, for the moment at least, into an uneasy and unsatisfying equilibrium. Chicago was still drawing people away, although the magnitude of the exodus was diminishing. For black people who stayed in the Delta, the options were the same as they had always been: if you had an education, you usually served the needs of the black poor, by teaching in the black school system, or preaching, or operating a small business on the black side of town; if you didn't, you worked for white people as a household servant in town or as a day laborer, chopping cotton on the plantations.

The situation was roughly the same all over the South. In the years since 1954, when the Supreme Court handed down its decision in the case of *Brown* v. *Board of Education* declaring legally segregated school systems to be unconstitutional, not only had the Southern schools not desegregated, segregation as an all-encompassing way of life appeared to be even stronger than it had been before the decision, because a well-organized white resistance had sprung up. Public facilities were still segregated. All the social customs that went along with segregation were unchanged. Thanks to the poll tax and other means, the overwhelming majority of Southern blacks still couldn't vote. In Mississippi, in the same year as the *Brown* decision, the state legislature passed a law requiring anyone who wanted to become a registered voter to interpret a passage from the state constitution chosen at random by the county registrar — a requirement that in practice applied only to blacks, whose constitutional interpretations were almost invariably found wanting. Five per cent of the black adult population of Mississippi was registered to vote in 1960. As late as 1963, Coahoma County, whose seat was Clarksdale, had only 1,371 black registered voters out of an eligible black population of 14,604, and most of them were registered only through the intercession of planters to whom they had promised control over their votes.

In 1956, the Mississippi legislature created the State Sovereignty Commission, a quasi-public body with the power to engage in surveillance and other covert activities to stop the forces of integration. The Citizens Council, a middle-class white organization devoted to disabling integrationist efforts in the South, was especially strong in Mississippi, where it received funding from the Sovereignty Commission; the Clarksdale chapter of the Citizens Council was run by the president of the biggest bank in town and had virtually the entire white businessman class as members. After the *Brown* decision, when Aaron Henry circulated a petition among blacks in Clarksdale asking the school board to desegregate, the Citizens Council arranged for all the banks in town to deny credit to anyone who had signed. In 1955, while Charles Diggs, the black congressman from Detroit, was staying in Henry's house to help him plan an effort to register black voters, the house was fire-bombed. The Mississippi Regional Council of Negro Leadership, an organization Henry and a few of his friends had founded in 1950 to fight segregation in the Delta, was moribund by the late 1950s, and even within the black community there was not a wholly unified front against segregation: black preachers would circulate in the countryside soliciting contributions from white planters to help fund efforts of anti-integrationist organizations they claimed to run.

The Southern civil rights movement didn't become truly galvanized at the small-town level until 1961, when a series of sit-ins and, especially, the journey of the Freedom Riders, who traveled through the South sitting in at segregated bus stations, generated national newspaper and television coverage that dramatically demonstrated the courage of the people in the movement and the gruesome violence of the white resistance. Aaron Henry's efforts to wake Clarksdale up finally began to bear fruit. In August 1961, three black teenagers staged a brief sit-in at the Illinois Central station in Clarksdale to protest the segregation of the waiting rooms there. In December of that year another small group sat in at the white waiting room of the Greyhound bus station. Then the Chamber of Commerce created a grievance that led to Clarksdale's first important protest of the civil rights era. It abruptly withdrew its invitations to two black high school bands to participate in the town's Christmas parade — an insult that struck at the heart of Clarksdale's black middle class, which had been looking forward to seeing its children march. In response the NAACP, under the slogan "No Parade, No Trade," organized a boycott of all the white-owned stores in Clarksdale, during which nearly all the blacks in town bought their groceries and clothing elsewhere for several weeks. After the boycott, Aaron Henry's wife was fired from her teaching job in the county school system, and Henry himself was arrested twice, first for leading the boycott and then on a charge that he had sexually molested a white boy he had picked up hitchhiking on a country road. In 1962, the town Christmas parade was canceled.

In 1963, two white kids broke Henry's living room window in the middle of the night and threw in a Molotov cocktail. Neither was convicted. The window of his drugstore, in which copies of the Declaration of Independence and the Emancipation Proclamation were on display, was smashed in several times, and then the store was bombed; the sheriff's office ruled that the cause was a bolt of lightning. It is difficult, from the vantage point of a generation later, to grasp how perilous Henry's position was at the time, when civil rights figures in the South were regularly beaten, jailed, and killed. In June 1963, Medgar Evers of the NAACP was assassinated at the front door of his house as he was coming home from work. James W. Silver's *Mississippi: The Closed Society*, published in 1964, described Henry as "the most likely candidate in Mississippi for the next Medgar Evers treatment." Henry never wavered. In the summer of 1963, the NAACP picketed the white churches in Clarksdale (which didn't admit blacks), the daily newspaper (which referred to whites as "Mr." and "Mrs." and to blacks by their unadorned last names), the city hall, the telephone company, and the Post Office (where blacks couldn't hold clerical jobs), the swimming pool, the public library (where blacks couldn't check out books), and the segregated lunch counters, restaurants, theaters, and other public places. The city responded, in most cases, simply by taking integration out of the realm of possibility: the pool was drained, and then sold to the American Legion; the lunch counters were closed; the library removed all its chairs. Through all this turmoil, Clarksdale retained a reputation for being, after Greenville, the most notable island of racial calm in the Delta, because it was controlled by high-class white folks who kept the Ku Klux Klan, which since the *Brown* decision had been in one of its periods of resurgence all through the South, at bay — there were no civil rights fatalities in Clarksdale.

Aaron Henry became head of the state chapter of the NAACP and also of the Council of Federated Organizations, the umbrella group set up to coordinate all civil rights activities in Mississippi in 1963 and 1964. In the fall of 1963 he was the COFO candidate for governor and waged a campaign whose purpose was, necessarily, only symbolic, since COFO's constituency couldn't vote — but COFO mock-registered eighty thousand black voters. In 1964 he was officially in charge of managing the hordes of Northern college students and civil rights movement ground troops who descended on Mississippi for Freedom Summer, a duty that kept him in a whirlwind of traveling, marching, bailing people out of jail, shepherding visiting dignitaries like Martin Luther King and Allard Lowenstein (the indefatigable liberal-activist head of the National Student Association, who was arrested in Clarksdale for violating the curfew), and keeping the tensions between the NAACP and SNCC down to a manageable level. He was one of the founders of the Mississippi Freedom Democratic Party, which was an offshoot of COFO and was the organization that sent a delegation to the 1964 Democratic National Convention in Atlantic City demanding to be seated instead of the regular Mississippi delegation. When Henry agreed to participate in the compromise under which he and one other member of the Freedom Democratic Party would agree to join the regular delegation, he became an invaluable resource to the Johnson administration: he was one of the few respected civil rights leaders in the South who were still firmly in place on the field of battle, and still willing to deal in good faith with the federal government.

As a KID growing up in Clarksdale, Bennie Gooden used to sit around with a friend of his named Jesse Epps having long talks about what Gooden calls their "dreams of glory." In high school Gooden was president of the student council and Epps vice president; along with campus politics, they would discuss the changes they'd bring to Clarksdale one day, the businesses they'd start, the money they'd make. Because they came of age before the civil rights movement, they had to put these dreams on hold. Gooden came home after college and got a teaching job; Epps wound up in Syracuse, New York, as an official of the electrical workers' union. Still, Epps would write Gooden long letters that were full of talk about, as Gooden puts it, "changing the Delta from a Hell to a Living Oasis."

Shortly before the passage of the Economic Opportunity Act of 1964, Jesse Epps reappeared in Clarksdale with a plan to start an adult literacy program in the Delta that he said would be funded by the Ford Foundation and the AFL-CIO. Gooden set up a meeting for him with the local black leadership, which went well, and soon Epps had moved to Clarksdale. He chartered an organization called the Southern Educational and Recreational Association, hired Gooden as his deputy, and, changing course slightly, applied to the brand-new Office of Economic Opportunity for a grant to operate a Head Start program in Clarksdale in the summer of 1965.

White Clarksdale was not keen on Jesse Epps. His organization was, first of all, entirely black, and Epps had hopes of getting it declared the sole community action agency in Coahoma County, so that there would be no white involvement whatsoever in the local war on poverty. There was a feeling that Epps, who after all was a professional labor organizer, would eventually use SERA as a political organization to help topple the entirely white officialdom of Clarksdale. In the view of whites Epps was, by virtue of his long residence in the North, an outsider, and he was pretentious. He spoke in an affected quasi-British accent and often boasted about the top-flight education he had received at the University of Chicago and Syracuse University, and about his connections to the upper level of the Eastern establishment. Also, in a rural area like the Delta, grants from the war on poverty were big money; in Chicago, the OEO had a financial impact on local government but was beneath the notice of the barons of the private economy, whereas in Clarksdale the community action agency would be instantly one of the biggest economic entities in town, and, as an employer, it would directly compete with every business that used a black labor force. The prospect of Epps running the show was extremely disconcerting to whites.

The Coahoma County board of supervisors decided to put together its own community action board and compete with SERA for federal funds. The board included several blacks but, significantly, not Aaron Henry. The black board members demanded that Henry be appointed, and when the whites wouldn't agree, all but one of the blacks quit the board. Henry began to get in touch with his East Coast contacts on behalf of SERA's grant application, and soon it was approved. Still, the situation was a mess. The school board wouldn't let SERA use its classrooms or buses, so it was difficult for the Head Start program to operate. On the larger question of who was going to be declared the Clarksdale community action agency, the OEO was unhappy with both of the current competitors, because neither one was integrated enough. There were never any illusions in Washington about the war on poverty in Mississippi serving the white poor, but it was crucial to the fate of the OEO's budgets in Congress that the Southern community action boards be neither all-white nor all-black—especially the latter.

Fortunately for the OEO, a few whites in Clarksdale were willing to work with the likes of Aaron Henry on a community action board. Most notable among them were the Carr brothers, Oscar and Andrew, who together ran a cotton plantation out on New Africa Road. The Carrs were impeccably respectable Delta planters—long-established, prominent in cotton-industry and social organizations, athletic, and popular—but both of them had spent time in the East and had returned home as civil rights sympathizers. In the early 1960s, Oscar Carr helped to found the First National Bank of Clarksdale, which was known as "the nigger bank" because it broke the prevailing custom of refusing loans to black farmers and businessmen. Carr went before the board of supervisors and pleaded with its members to join forces with SERA in creating the community action board, but the supervisors refused.

On June 1, 1965, Oscar Carr, Aaron Henry, and Jesse Epps met in Washington with Sargent Shriver himself—a sign of how much this one little town's antipoverty program meant to the OEO—and agreed to try to put together a new, integrated community action board in Clarksdale. When they came home, Carr made another presentation to the board of supervisors in which he insisted that Henry be involved, and announced that he would not serve on the board himself, so that nobody would suspect him of pursuing the hidden agenda of getting the OEO's money deposited in the First National Bank. Within a month, a new organization called Coahoma Opportunities Incorporated had been formed, with a fully integrated board whose members included Aaron Henry and Andrew Carr. Its chairman was Semmes Luckett, an old-school conservative white lawyer who also served on the board of the State Sovereignty Commission; Andrew Carr had run against Luckett for the chairmanship and lost by one vote.

It didn't bother Shriver that Luckett was running the board—in fact it was a plus, because, to his natural press agent's turn of mind, having an archsegregationist at the head of an integrated community action board in Mississippi made for a better story. In August 1965, just after the bloody Watts riot had badly shaken the Johnson administration's faith that the country's racial problems were rapidly being solved, Shriver wrote a memo to Bill Moyers in the White House crowing about the new board in Clarksdale as "an extraordinary example of progress in the anti-poverty program" — a much better example, he said, than the board in Los Angeles. He went on: "And it seems to me that Clarksdale could well serve as a symbol and an inspiration to all American communities. As I said to the press, '. . . if Clarksdale, Mississippi can solve its problems in a cooperative way, Los Angeles can do it just as well.' It occurs to me, therefore, that an effective way to publicize Clarksdale's achievements would be to invite its anti-poverty Board to the White House in the near future." The invitation was extended; Andrew Carr remembers wondering whether the Johnson administration really knew what it was getting into when Lady Bird Johnson told him how happy she was that the racial problems of the South were over now, so that they could move on to new challenges.

Jesse Epps had expected to be given the biggest piece of the pie available to Coahoma Opportunities Incorporated, the Head Start contract, but he ran into trouble. He didn't complete the government-required audit of his summer Head Start program on time. The OEO in Washington became concerned. Andrew Carr, who had cosigned the mortgage on Epps's house in Clarksdale and so had his trust, went to his office to have a talk with him. While he was there, Aaron Henry called and said he wanted to talk about the audit too. Epps told him that Carr was there on the same mission; "Well, now you've got it in black and white," Henry said.

Then it turned out that Epps had lied about his record — he hadn't finished college at all, let alone gotten degrees from Chicago and Syracuse. Bennie Gooden and Epps had worked out an informal understanding by which Gooden would go to work for Coahoma Opportunities as deputy director and use the position to ensure that Epps got the Head Start money. Now Gooden found it impossible to swing that deal, and instead Epps was given a minor position with Coahoma Opportunities. Soon afterward he left Clarksdale, moved to Memphis, and got a job with the municipal employees' union (when Martin Luther King came to Memphis during the sanitation workers' strike in 1968, Epps ferried him around town). Gooden began to hear stories around town to the effect that he had stepped on his old friend to get ahead, which he thought Epps was spreading or at least wasn't bothering to correct. Before long their friendship was over, and each man felt wounded by the other; as Gooden saw it, Epps should have realized there was nothing he could have done to help him once all the damaging information came out, and it was unfair for Epps to expect him to pass up, out of blind loyalty, his one big chance to do something besides spend his whole life teaching.

Gooden's new boss, the director of Coahoma Opportunities, couldn't have been more different from Epps: he was Gus Roessler, a white stockbroker who had grown up in Pennsylvania, moved to Clarksdale following his marriage to the daughter of a farmer there, and served a term in the 1950s as president of the Clarksdale chapter of the Citizens Council. Roessler had converted to integrationism since then, and anyway, Gooden badly wanted to make his new situation work. They got along.

It quickly became clear that Sargent Shriver's ebullient announcement of the success of Coahoma Opportunities had been premature. In November 1965, the fourteen white conservative members of the board (including Semmes Luckett, the chairman) abruptly resigned in a group. Their complaint was that the OEO, in its eagerness to make Coahoma Opportunities its showplace of integrated community action in Mississippi, was trying to make the program much bigger than it ought to have been, by indiscriminately pouring in money that was sure to be wasted and to screw up the existing economic arrangements in Clarksdale. The final straw for the conservatives came when the OEO asked Coahoma Opportunities to start a large program to train poor people for a wide array of jobs, many of which didn't exist in the Delta. "It was *fruitless*," says Joseph Ellis, publisher of the Clarksdale newspaper and one of the fourteen who resigned. "Textile-mill worker. Aerospace engineer. I wouldn't sign the request for the funds. Shriver's office called me and asked if they could sign my name so they could get the money. I said no."

With the white conservatives gone, Coahoma Opportunities didn't look like an integrated community action program any more — it looked like a black program with three token whites on the board, which was not the appearance the OEO wanted it to have. All the generous grants that were being made ready in Washington were contingent on the board's being restocked with whites. "So Andy Carr and I had to go out and replace those whites who'd left with other whites," Gus Roessler says. "We were driving the country roads, meeting people one on one.

That spell was the major crisis of our organization. If we hadn't found the whites, we would have gone down the drain." They found the whites. In the first half of 1966, Coahoma Opportunities got $1.2 million in grants from the OEO.

The money went primarily for education programs: early childhood development for preschool children, Head Start for kindergarteners, and adult education for illiterate people who were past school age. There was also a credit union to help poor people get loans when the banks turned them down, a legal aid program, and a program to enroll elderly people in Medicare. Several neighborhood centers were set up. On their own terms the programs gave rise to very little grumbling, even among white conservatives, but as was the case with the war on poverty everywhere, probably their greatest effect was significantly expanding the black middle class. The early childhood development program alone, in its first year, had 253 people on its staff — more than 1 per cent of the population of Clarksdale. Most of them didn't have the credentials to get jobs with the traditional provider of white-collar jobs to blacks, the school system, so otherwise they would have been working with their hands.

Joining the middle class is a psychological passage as well as an economic one, and Coahoma Opportunities was a seminal institution in that sense too. For the first time in Clarksdale's history, blacks and whites worked side by side officially as equals (even the black school superintendent, in the old days, ultimately always had to go to the white superintendent hat in hand). Merely to be addressed by whites by courtesy titles (other than "Reverend") was a new experience for blacks in Clarksdale. To the whites in Coahoma Opportunities, the amount of mister and missussing that went on was almost a joke — it was impossible to get anyone to call you by your first name. The regular interaction among blacks and whites that Coahoma Opportunities created simply hadn't existed before, and the achievement of several civil rights milestones, such as the newspaper's giving blacks courtesy titles in print, was a direct result. The legal aid program helped many elderly blacks who had been sharecroppers to create neat progressions of legal divorces out of their tangled and informal marital histories, so that they could become eligible for Social Security survivors' pensions and so join the decent middle-class division of the American welfare state. "It was completely important," says Aaron Henry. "Blacks for the first time became masters of their own fate in terms of how a program was run. It gave a way for whites to sell to their peers the idea of whites participating with blacks.

They felt that if we don't get over that, the niggers are gonna spend all the money. It was a brand new vision and light."

SINCE THE MID-1950S, representatives of chemical companies had been traveling through the Delta, trying to sell planters and county agricultural agents on the virtues of a new generation of defoliants that were being developed in their laboratories. The planters were initially wary. The chemicals were, in the early days, extremely powerful and unpredictable; one year in the 1950s, several planters used a brand-new and untested defoliant that caused their entire cotton crop to die in the seedling stage when an unseasonable spring cold front came through. They were so expensive that the old Delta rule of thumb, according to which anyone who could produce a yield of one bale of cotton per acre made a nice profit, no longer applied to the planters who used them. Anyway, black labor was still abundantly available to do the same thing as the chemicals—weed the cotton fields—at a much lower price. For the uneducated children of the sharecropper system, there wasn't much choice but to chop cotton. Good-paying unskilled jobs in Chicago were drying up. Welfare payments in Mississippi were the lowest in the country and impossible to live on.

Gradually, the planters started to look more favorably on the chemicals. The first one to be widely accepted was Treflan, manufactured by DuPont, a "pre-emerge" that was worked into the soil just before planting and that retarded the growth of weeds for about six weeks. After that some chopping was required, although chemical sprays that would kill the weeds but not the cotton plants were coming on the market by the mid-1960s. Other chemicals were developed that would get rid of the Johnson grass that grew up in the fields late in the summer, that would make the cotton plants grow bigger, and that would loosen the bolls from the stems just before picking time. By 1965, a planter who wanted to participate fully in the chemical revolution might wind up giving his cotton crop as many as a dozen separate treatments between cultivation and harvest, at an expense so great that he had to get his yield up to two bales an acre in order to make money. At the same time, more advanced (and more expensive) farm machines, such as eight-row tractors and four-row pickers, were constantly coming on the market.

What made the chemical revolution complete, with a suddenness that the mechanical revolution never had, was the institution of the federal minimum wage for farm laborers in February 1967, a reform that had been championed by Northern liberals like Robert Kennedy and his fellow senator from New York, Jacob Javits. In an instant, the pay for cotton choppers more than tripled and the economic rationality of switching over to chemical farming became irrefutable. In Coahoma County, by Andrew Carr's estimate, a thousand black farm laborers — 5 per cent of the black population of the county — were put out of work. In the Delta as a whole, according to a confidential memo that an HEW official wrote to the White House in 1967, "Following the inauguration of the new farm minimum wage provisions, it is conservatively estimated that an additional 11,000 farm workers, representing families of in excess of 50,000 members, have lost or will lose their jobs." The minimum wage finally forced the planters of the Delta to drop their long-cherished self-conception as landed gentry presiding over a mild paternalistic system that lacked the relentless economic logic of capitalism. "After that, it was like running a factory up North," says Eugene Doyle, who ran the office operations of the enormous King & Anderson plantation. "It was never the same. It was *fun* before that. Life was easy. They enjoyed it. We enjoyed it."

Most of the displaced black farm workers wouldn't have agreed with Doyle's assessment of how much fun they were having under the old system, but it was inarguable that they were now in a crisis. In Greenville, even before the imposition of the minimum wage, a group of displaced black farm workers took over an abandoned Air Force base and had to be forcibly removed by military police. The incident became a minor national issue; Martin Luther King got involved in the effort to help the farm workers. In a long telegram to President Johnson, King urged him to turn the air base into a housing project and job-training center for poor blacks:

> Some fled to Northern ghettos. Some burdened already over-crowded Mississippi kinfolk. Others are trying desperately to survive. . . . Callous disregard of the federal government for their plight and the plight of tens of thousands of other poor Mississippi Negroes makes a mockery of all the humanitarian ideals this nation espouses throughout the world. . . . These people, United States citizens, want only an opportunity to participate in and become a productive part of the society from which they have thus far been excluded.

In the view of the White House, it was politically impossible to meet King's demand, because Mississippi's powerful senators, John Stennis and James Eastland, opposed it. Harry McPherson wrote to Johnson, "Enter Senator Stennis. He told Wilbur Cohen that unless the property is returned to Greenville 'my only recourse will be through the HEW appropriations bill,'" whose fate he, a member of the Senate Appropriations Committee, could substantially affect. The community action agency in Greenville, embroiled in a seemingly hopeless racial wrangle, was unable to enter the fray effectively. Desperately in need of some way to respond, the White House got in touch with the OEO, the Labor Department, the Commerce Department, HEW, the Agriculture Department, and even the Ford Foundation, asking for their help. Shriver mounted an emergency food-distribution effort, and eventually a new job-training program got under way, but such jury-rigged and Washington-originated activities were not the way the war on poverty was supposed to work.

Clarksdale, whose newly resuscitated community action board was just getting to work when the agricultural minimum wage came in, was one of the few bright spots that Washington could point to in the Delta, and that further enhanced Coahoma Opportunities' favored position with the OEO. The adult education program, which started in March 1966 and by August had gotten $400,000 from the OEO and had an enrollment of 932 people, served as a safe harbor for most of the displaced farm workers in the county, to which they proceeded directly from their old jobs chopping cotton. Among the attractions of adult education was that it paid its enrollees $30 a week, about double what they had been making on the plantations before the minimum wage came in. Many of their children went into early childhood development or Head Start at the same time. The adult education program taught reading and writing in particular, and in general the mores of town life — "personal habits, cleanliness, dress, and attitude," as one report on the program put it. Certainly not everyone who passed through it wound up with a good job — for many people it served as a transition to life on welfare, which became sustainable when the benefits were raised slightly and the food stamp program began — but it saved Clarksdale from the kind of major disruption that in other places attended the final severing of the centuries-old link between black Southerners and the cotton fields.

The Civil Rights Act of 1964 brought a conclusive end to the segregation of public facilities in Clarksdale, although in the particularly sensitive case of the municipal swimming pool, where the half-clad bodies of black men and white women might be in close physical proximity, the town fathers decided they were better off without one. After years of boycotts, the downtown businesses hired some black sales clerks and cashiers. The Voting Rights Act, by abolishing the poll tax and the constitutional-interpretation requirement, made it possible for most blacks in Clarksdale to become registered voters at last; Washington officials, like John Doar of the Justice Department, regularly passed through town to make sure the transition went smoothly. On one occasion when Doar was speaking in Clarksdale, Semmes Luckett sat in the audience and hissed him, but Luckett was an unusually resistant member of the town's business establishment. For the most part, economic forces were pushing Clarksdale, and Mississippi, in the direction of disengagement from the forces of white resistance, because segregation had changed from an economic necessity (as it had been in the days when it was essential that most blacks have no option besides farm labor) to a hindrance, scaring Northern capital and factories away. In February 1965, the Mississippi Economic Council issued a declaration that "Mississippi is not an island unto itself, but an integral and responsible part of the United States," which was the first serious sign of trouble for the Citizens Council.

The one area in which white Clarksdale took the course of absolute resistance to integration was in the schools, in large measure because the person in charge of the issue was Semmes Luckett. Most towns in Mississippi, when the federal government began requiring them to enforce the 1954 Supreme Court decision, came up with "freedom of choice" plans that were instantly struck down in court. In Clarksdale, Luckett drew up a system of geographical zones, a tactic that effectively maintained segregation, since there were no integrated neighborhoods in town, but that caught the forces of integration off guard, because they had been promoting zoned systems elsewhere. During the 1964–65 school year Aaron Henry sent his daughter Rebecca to register at one of the white schools in Clarksdale. She was turned away, officially on the grounds that she lived in the wrong zone, and the NAACP Legal Defense Fund filed suit. The case of *Rebecca E. Henry* v. *The Clarksdale Municipal Separate School District* was in court from 1965 until 1971. Luckett won in Federal District Court in 1965, lost in the Fifth Circuit Court of Appeals in 1969, appealed to the Supreme Court (which wouldn't hear the case), submitted a series of modified, slightly integrated zoned plans to the Fifth Circuit, and finally gave up when the Fifth Circuit ordered

Clarksdale to provide only one locus of public education at each grade level, so that full integration would be inescapable.

The lawyer in charge of the Legal Defense Fund's efforts in the latter stages of the case was Melvyn Leventhal, who must have been a figure out of Luckett's nightmares — a left-wing Jew from Brooklyn, and a miscegenationist to boot, since he was married at the time to the black novelist Alice Walker. Nonetheless, Luckett was unfailingly cordial to Leventhal, in the old Southern manner. "What a character!" Leventhal says. "He was a segregationist zealot, but very sophisticated, and always a gentleman. He would offer me rides places. Once he had me over to dinner. Semmes always said that segregation was a natural way of life, and, very nicely, why didn't I go back to New York and solve the problems in my own backyard. After the final court order, I'll never forget, Semmes called me up and congratulated me. He said, 'I guess you beat me.' That only happened one other time in all the desegregation cases I tried. And I never had an answer to Semmes about the problems in my own backyard. It was a valid criticism."

The prosperous white citizenry of Clarksdale, unwilling to put complete faith in Luckett's ability to win his case, began working on a contingency plan during the long wait for the Fifth Circuit's decision. The decision came down in March 1969; in September, a brand-new private school called Lee Academy (many of the new "seg academies" in the South were named after Confederate heroes) opened for business. It has never had a black student. Meanwhile a local committee worked out the details of integrating the public schools. Andrew Carr was the chairman, but the real power was Aaron Henry, who wasn't even on the committee, because the Justice Department and the Legal Defense Fund relied on his judgment as to the acceptability of the integration plan. Eventually the eight elementary schools in town were paired off, with each matched set teaching only two grades under a strict racial quota system. After sixth grade, all the public school students in Clarksdale went to the one middle school in town (housed in the former quarters of the black high school), and then to the one high school.

In 1983 Henry gave his assent to the reconversion of the elementary schools to a zoned system, so that children could stay in one school in their neighborhood for all seven years. As a result, the elementary schools became substantially resegregated, though some black students are assigned to the schools in white neighborhoods. In 1986 the school board built a second middle school, again only after having won Henry's blessing, which meant that the old middle school was entirely black and the new one two-thirds white. Clarksdale High School, which is located in the main affluent white neighborhood in town, is about 60 per cent black and 40 per cent white. That makes it one of the most integrated public schools in the Delta.

AARON HENRY did what was probably the most important of all his favors for the Johnson administration and the OEO in 1966, during the worst crisis of the war on poverty in Mississippi.

During Freedom Summer, a psychologist in New York named Tom Levin had helped organize a team of doctors to go down to Mississippi and provide medical support to the civil rights movement. Levin, a merry, elfish man, was the son of an ardently unionist hat-blocker and had himself, in his younger days, been a member of the Young Communist League (until the Hitler-Stalin pact of 1939) and the Socialist Workers Party. "I'm a New York Jewish radical, that's who I am," he says now, guilelessly. After Levin came home from Mississippi that summer, he got a call from the famous radical lawyer William Kunstler's daughter, who was in Greenville organizing a strike; she asked him to come back down and set up a day care center for the children of the people on the picket line. He did, and while he was there, working closely with SNCC, inspiration struck: "I got the idea of a Lenin School to set up black revolutionaries, in which the ego, the superego, and id of the child would all be SNCC, to be clinical about it." As he put it to an interviewer from an oral-history project years later, "These people would be the kamikaze revolutionaries that would change the self.... I thought it worth putting in ten or fifteen years to turn out hardened social revolutionaries." Levin set about starting four of these training schools, with twenty-five students each.

In the fall of 1964 Polly Greenberg, who was the OEO official in charge of Head Start in the South, got in touch with Levin. "Polly said to me that the notion of four training schools was not significant," he says. "The OEO had a great deal of funds. I should consider doing it as a larger project." At first Levin was resistant, but Greenberg pursued him ardently and promised that the OEO would not interfere with his work. By that time SNCC, the sponsor Levin originally had in mind for his schools, was becoming hostile to white involvement, so he was in need of organized support anyway. In March 1965, Levin set up a headquarters in an abandoned Seventh-day Adventist camp in the town of Edwards, just past the southern edge of the Delta. The Citizens Crusade Against Poverty, Dick Boone's group, gave him a $5,000 grant to write his proposal. "It was like a radical's dream put on paper," Levin says. "We asked for centers in sixty-five communities, and a million and a half dollars, for the summer of sixty-five. They thought I was a Quaker, and I kept my Machiavellian Leninist side under my belt. The only thing they cut was the training-film budget, from a hundred thousand to twenty-five thousand. So we had more than a million dollars in May! We organized all over the place. We ended up starting eighty-seven centers, serving six thousand children. It was astonishing!"

Levin called his organization the Child Development Group of Mississippi. It was the largest Head Start program in the country.

In one sense, CDGM was an immediate success. From a standing start, it quickly became an enormous going concern that performed a noble function and that was, at the community level, almost entirely run by thousands of black people who had never been in charge of anything in their lives (professional schoolteachers were actually banned from working for CDGM at first). But in almost every other way, the organization was in trouble from the beginning. During the first week of training, a white nut came to the headquarters in Edwards and fired off a few rounds of warning shots with his revolver. Shortly thereafter, while Levin was driving home alone from a meeting at the CDGM center in Rolling Fork, the Delta town where Muddy Waters was born, a man in a pickup truck tailgated him for a few miles, and then forced him off the road. Somebody fired a gun at the Rolling Fork center a few days later.

The CDGM centers kept sloppy records, and by the end of the summer there were already problems with the OEO over unaccounted-for funds. Relatives of board members were on the payroll. Rumors began to circulate about wild sexual goings-on in the dormitories in Edwards. ("People fucked, it was nothing!" Levin says.) A few CDGM employees were arrested at an antiwar demonstration in Jackson. There were stories about the centers' training people to take part in civil rights protests (Levin doesn't deny them: "I saw this as a base for black people to organize communities for social change. Oh, I was quite a madman!") and refusing to admit white children. Senators Stennis and Eastland were up in arms, officially for all these reasons and, more fundamentally, because they had no say in what had quickly become one of the main federal programs in their state. The White House could ill afford to offend them; Eastland, as chairman of the Senate Judiciary Committee, could single-handedly hold up all appointments of federal judges.

At the end of the summer of 1965, the OEO called a meeting of CDGM's board at a junior college in a small town halfway across the state from the headquarters in Edwards. There one member of the board, Marian Wright, who was then an NAACP lawyer in Jackson and wasn't yet married to Peter Edelman, told Levin he would have to move the headquarters to Jackson and establish separate chaperoned dormitories for the men and women on the staff. The OEO in Washington was so concerned about the outcome of the meeting that it maintained an open phone line to the junior college; at one point, one official got Levin on the phone and told him that if he agreed to the terms, he could have any job with the OEO he wanted, except for Shriver's. He refused. The board decided to take a vote, and Marian Wright won. A few days later, the board met again and relieved Levin of his duties.

Wright was convinced that with a new director, CDGM could be made to run smoothly, and she is still bitter that Washington refused to give her a chance to prove it. Stennis scheduled Senate hearings to investigate CDGM, and Shriver concluded that the organization was a lost cause politically. CDGM's application for the renewal of its grant, held up for months, was finally approved, for a small fraction of the amount requested, in February 1966, but Stennis and Eastland kept hammering away. After a few more months, Shriver put in a call to Aaron Henry, whom Levin had befriended back in the early days and who had lobbied his contacts in Washington on behalf of the initial grant to CDGM. "Sarge said, you got me into this," Henry says. "He said Stennis and Eastland had infiltration into CDGM and knew everything that was going on. Sarge was of the position that he really couldn't defend it if they went public. He said either we'll shut it down, or you start a new organization that will follow the rules."

On September 13, 1966, in the town of Yazoo City, a group called Mississippi Action for Progress was incorporated as an applicant for Head Start funding from the OEO. Its board members included Aaron Henry and several of the leading patrician white moderates of the Delta: Oscar Carr; Hodding Carter III, the son, namesake, and heir of the legendary publisher of the *Delta Democrat-Times* in Greenville, which was the main integrationist newspaper in Mississippi; LeRoy Percy, cousin of William

Alexander Percy and inheritor of his cotton plantation (but not his political views); and Owen Cooper, the head of a big fertilizer-manufacturing company in Yazoo City.

Concern about CDGM was running so high in Washington that the White House was closely monitoring the situation over Shriver's shoulder. In those days Lyndon Johnson was constantly hearing from Southern members of Congress that what was going on now in their districts was like Reconstruction all over again. The comparison was in his mind anyway, because he had come of age hearing all the standard Southern stories about the humiliations of the post–Civil War years, and he used to tell his aides that if he overplayed the power of the federal government even a little, the result could be a permanent occupation of the South, or, in the event of a counterrevolution, the restoration of segregation. In that context, CDGM looked like the modern version of the Freedmen's Bureau and the Loyal League, organizations of the 1870s that were enshrined in white Southern lore as examples of schemes run by radical whites from the North that, under the guise of social improvement, whipped up the freed slaves into a frenzy of revolutionary political activity. Because Bobby Kennedy was its leading supporter in official Washington, CDGM activated another of Johnson's obsessive fears as well, the fear of being politically and morally upstaged by Kennedy. A politically active young lawyer in Greenville, Douglas Wynn, was the son-in-law of one of Lyndon Johnson's closest political confidants in Texas, Edward Clark, and Wynn more than once traveled to Washington and met personally with Harry McPherson in the White House to apprise him of MAP's progress as it was getting organized.

In late September, the OEO announced that it was revoking CDGM's grant, on grounds of fiscal irresponsibility, and making MAP the major recipient of Head Start funds in Mississippi. The whites on the MAP board were so prominent that the problem of the senators from Mississippi was neatly circumvented. As Patricia Derian, who was MAP's director, says, "They knew how to handle Eastland and Stennis. They were *above* Eastland and Stennis. Those guys would have to *go* if they impeded it." Aaron Henry's participation, though, was the real key to MAP's credibility as a replacement for CDGM: he was the one black leader in Mississippi whose civil rights credentials were so unassailable that no organization he lent his name to could be convincingly portrayed as a mere tool of the white power structure. Henry had decided once again to side with the liberal elements in the federal government instead of the forces of independent black radicalism, and in so doing, he had saved Sargent Shriver's neck.

Aided and abetted by the Citizens Crusade Against Poverty, CDGM fought back. On October 19, 1966, a full-page ad appeared in *The New York Times* with a headline that said, in two-inch-high type, "Say it isn't so, Sargent Shriver." Dick Boone knew his mark: there was nothing Shriver disliked more than bad publicity, especially in that forum, and a few days later he gave CDGM a scaled-down grant. Over the next few years, relations between CDGM and MAP were extremely bitter. In 1967, two MAP centers were burned down, an MAP recruiter was shot at, another MAP employee's car was burned, and another was threatened at knife point—all the work of CDGM people, in the view of the OEO officials in Washington who were monitoring the situation. Several times, CDGM people broke up MAP meetings and warned people not to send their children to MAP centers. In 1968, during another battle over CDGM's funding, one of Johnson's aides received a message from his secretary that read: "A Mr. Richard Boone of the Citizens Crusade Against Poverty called at 5:07 p.m. and asked that you *be sure* to call him back *today*. If he does not get in touch with you today, there will be 'new problems.'" All these tactics backfired: over the years, CDGM shrank and finally disappeared altogether, but MAP is still the largest recipient of Head Start funds in Mississippi; its small yellow buses are a common sight on country highways in the mornings through much of the state.

AFTER A few years at Coahoma Opportunities, Bennie Gooden began looking around for something else to do. As soon as Richard Nixon became president, the newspapers were full of stories predicting that the OEO was going to be severely cut back or eliminated entirely; to Gooden, the long-term viability of Coahoma Opportunities was questionable. His family was growing—eventually he had six children—and he needed more money and more security.

Gooden was a controversial figure at Coahoma Opportunities. Everybody acknowledged that he was smart, hardworking, honest, and a gifted administrator, but he made white people uneasy. He lacked the spirit of selflessness that whites thought of as part of the psychological equipment of an administrator of a social program; he was restless, driven, a mass of wants. There seemed to be an irritating grain of sand lodged deep in his soul that kept him from being able to embrace the ethic of interracial affection that, in the minds of white liberals, should have infused the war on poverty. On one occasion he came close to being fired. Three women working for Coahoma Opportunities, two white and one black, called Andrew Carr, who is a strict Catholic, and complained that Gooden had tried to seduce them. Carr convened an all-day meeting of the Coahoma Opportunities board and confronted Gooden with the charges. By that time most of black Clarksdale had heard what was going on and had closed ranks around Gooden; as Vera Mae Pigee, a local beautician and NAACP stalwart, wrote in her self-published memoir of the civil rights days in Clarksdale, the prevailing attitude among blacks was that "if he is fired all of us will be fired and can go back to the low paying jobs we had before where ever in the cottonfields."

The board took a vote on whether to dismiss Gooden, which came out strongly in his favor; Carr was one of only two dissenting votes. Gooden stayed on, but kept his eyes open for other opportunities. In the summer of 1969, a friend of his introduced him to a man named William Martin, a housing consultant who happened to be passing through Clarksdale. Martin told Gooden about a federal program under which nonprofit groups could get loans from HUD to build subsidized housing for the poor, and suggested that they work together to start such a project in Clarksdale. Gooden agreed. He got his church, Chapel Hill Baptist, to act as sponsor, and, in his spare time, worked with Martin on an application to send to HUD. HUD rejected the application; it turned out that the problem was Martin, who had previously gotten into trouble with HUD over a subsidized project he was running in California. As he had previously parted company with Jesse Epps, Gooden now disengaged himself from William Martin and refiled the application. This time HUD approved it.

Purely by chance, Gooden had found his metier. He taught himself the ins and outs of federal grantsmanship, building construction, and property management, and soon Chapel Hill Heights, a compound of two-story apartment buildings, was going up on a tract of farm land at the edge of town. At the same time, an organization founded by Owen Cooper in association with the Catholic Church was building a similar subsidized project nearby, called Eastgate Gardens. Gooden got himself appointed manager of both projects when they were finished, and, reasoning that since both had forty-year guaranteed mortgages he now had a position that was far more secure than anything the war on poverty could offer, he quit his job with Coahoma Opportunities and went into the subsidized-housing business full time.

He prospered. Gooden is a great joiner, booster, and keeper up of contacts, and he maintained close ties to the nonprofit organizations that could sponsor new housing projects: Owen Cooper's Catholic operation, the Baptist churches, the Knights and Daughters of Tabor (of which he was a loyal member), and the Mississippi State Federation of Colored Women's Clubs, a venerable social improvement agency whose national organization was founded by Margaret Murray Washington, the wife of Booker T. Washington. He built half a dozen projects in Clarksdale alone, including the immodestly named Bennie S. Gooden Estates, and by the late 1980s he was managing an empire that included sixty projects spread across Mississippi, Arkansas, and Tennessee (one of Gooden's partners was Vincent Lane, before he became head of the Chicago Housing Authority).

Gooden's projects in Clarksdale are completely different from the public housing in Chicago. They are well maintained and surrounded by green space. He knows many of the tenants personally, and the managers who work for him are well acquainted with everyone who is living in their projects. Crime is negligible. Gooden is sufficiently well connected in the black community that he has the confidence to screen new residents simply on the basis of keeping people out "once the word gets out on them," as he puts it, rather than according to their credit or employment histories (or even whether they had a criminal record), and it seems to work. Rather than being isolated like the public housing in Chicago, most of Gooden's projects are adjacent to the new middle-class subdivision in town where most of the black teachers and government employees live. Gooden's own home, a brick French Provincial mansion that he built in the 1980s and that is, if not the biggest house in Clarksdale, certainly the biggest built since World War II, is just a stone's throw from Chapel Hill Heights and Eastgate Gardens.

In late middle age, Gooden is widely known as the richest black man in Clarksdale, a big, broad-faced, unruly paterfamilias who spends his days working the phone in his office, whose walls are covered with plaques and citations honoring him, or cruising around town in his late-model Cadillac checking on his properties. Black people admire him for his success, his role as a provider of good cheap housing, his civic work, and his attractive family; white people resent him for having used the war on poverty as a road to personal wealth and because they sense that he doesn't like them.

The whole white notion of the state of Clarksdale is rather bleak. The cotton business is not in good shape; the acreage planted to cotton in the county is at half of its historic peak, as planters turn their land over to other crops, like soybeans. Children of prominent white families only rarely seem interested in making their careers in Clarksdale. Several venerable plantations have passed out of the hands of the families that owned them for a century. King & Anderson, lacking a willing heir, was sold to the Prudential Insurance Company in 1980; Mrs. W. K. Anderson, the widow of one of the former owners, who lives alone in her elegant plantation house out on the place, says, "My feeling now, seeing everything in shambles, the commissary torn down, is — *Gone With the Wind* didn't happen only in antebellum times. It's happening again." The Hopson plantation, where the mechanical cotton picker was field-tested, was broken up because of a family dispute; the last of the Hopsons left in Clarksdale runs a place called the Hopson Antique Mall, which is housed in what used to be the state-of-the-art headquarters of the plantation. In town, such monuments of the great days of Clarksdale as the Illinois Central station and the Alcazar Hotel, the tallest building in town, are empty and boarded up.

As white Clarksdale sees it, black Clarksdale is a welfare colony floating on a tide of federal transfer payments, sapped of the will to work. Most of the blacks who were displaced from the cotton fields by machines and chemicals have moved to town, where, in the whites' view, they are either doing nothing or holding down make-work jobs with Coahoma Opportunities, performing no useful function except for providing Bennie Gooden with the tenant base on which his empire is built. The federal government is by far the leading source of income in the Delta. Most of the whites have become Republicans; a white planter from Clarksdale named Leon Bramlett, who was one of the group that quit the Coahoma Opportunities board back in 1965, was the Republican candidate for governor of Mississippi in 1983.

There is a feeling among the more conservative white Clarksdalians that the federal government intentionally decided to create a welfare-and-social-program reservation for blacks in the Delta in order to stanch the migration to the North; Clarksdale was sacrificed for the sake of keeping the peace in Chicago. Back in the 1960s, a graduate student who interviewed Semmes Luckett summarized his version of this theory:

Luckett believes that the solution to the race problem in the South is the outmigration of Negroes. This belief seems to be the basis for his primary objection to the anti-poverty program. He thinks that the real purpose of the OEO in Coahoma County is to interfere with the normal laws of supply and demand and to negate the outmigration of Negroes from the Delta. He concedes that this interference may be self-defeating because after receiving adult education, Negroes may not be satisfied with cooking in the kitchen or working on the plantation.

Today, Joseph Ellis, the publisher of the paper, says, "What really checked the outmigration was the institution of the government welfare entitlement programs. I think it was planned. Had they not created a welfare economy here, people would have had to go somewhere else or starve. Politically, we had no power. It was decided that it was easier to deal with them down here than up there. And cheaper."

In black Clarksdale, the condition of the town seems far better than it was in the old days, even though most black people are still much worse off than most of the white people in town. The past quarter century has been a period of uninterrupted black progress such as has never been seen before in Mississippi. Now, when families come home from Chicago for their July Fourth reunions, they book blocks of rooms at the best hotel in town, the new Best Western on Highway 61. George Hicks's Clarksdalians Club rented the Clarksdale Civic Auditorium for one of its functions. The transition from a plantation economy to a welfare economy doesn't look like such a bad trade from the black perspective, especially since along with it came the end of segregation, many new white-collar jobs, and, finally, political power. The white suspicions about blacks' using the poverty program as an opening wedge into electoral politics have been, to some extent, borne out. Coahoma Opportunities' community centers have registered thousands of black voters. For specially important elections — the 1972 presidential campaign, when Sargent Shriver was on the Democratic ticket; the 1976 campaign, during which Aaron Henry was personally courted by Jimmy Carter; and, especially, the 1979 campaign when Henry was elected to the Mississippi legislature — the Head Start buses rolled through the black neighborhoods, picking people up and taking them to the polls.

As the owner of a drugstore in the age of Medicare and Medicaid, Henry presumably could have done well financially by the Great Society, as Bennie Gooden has, but he is a political leader, not a businessman. The Fourth Street Drugstore is a dusty emporium that looks as if it hasn't changed much since its opening in 1950. Rather than signs advertising sales, the main item of decoration inside the store is poster-sized photographs of James Chaney, Mickey Schwerner, and Andrew Goodman, the three civil rights workers murdered in Mississippi during Freedom Summer. Henry is often out of town, in Jackson, where the legislature meets and the state NAACP is headquartered, or in Washington, or delivering a speech somewhere. Still imperturbable, solid, and energetic in his late sixties, he is Clarksdale's most honored citizen. A street (in one of Gooden's housing projects) and a community health center are named after him, and he was the inaugural member of the Clarksdale Hall of Fame. At the same time, he is an active political power in town, and helped to achieve the black electoral milestones that followed his own election to the legislature. In 1986 Mike Espy, of the Century funeral homes family, was elected Mississippi's first black congressman since Reconstruction, from a Delta district. In 1988, Andrew Thompson beat a white candidate to become Clarksdale's first black sheriff since John Brown disappeared during the race riot of 1875. In 1989, Mike Espy's older brother Henry was elected Clarksdale's first black mayor.

It looks to blacks in Clarksdale as if, even now, there are more civil rights victories to be won. There are no black real estate agents in town. There are no black casualty insurance agents. There is only one black bank vice president, and one black car salesman. It is next to impossible for a black family to buy a house in the white neighborhoods. Some of the white teachers in the high school have a reputation for treating black students insultingly. Blacks are still underrepresented in government jobs. Stories circulate about incidents of blacks' being turned away from white institutions — for example, a woman who works for Bennie Gooden bought two burial plots in the white cemetery, and the owner tried to give her money to the man who runs the black cemetery, who refused to take it. Unlike the whites' grievances, though, blacks' are correctable, and therefore they do not give rise to feelings of despair.

An agricultural area disguises its true condition better than a city can. The Delta, a large area not served by interstate highways, commercial jets, or passenger railroads, home to only one town of more than 25,000 people, is sleepy and remote. Its chief feature, still, is its miles and miles of rich dark fields bracketed by ruler-straight roads, rows of trees in single file, and banks of clouds sitting low in the sky, all conveying a sense of horizontality. There isn't any bustle in any of the towns — certainly not in Clarksdale, where, as in every place in the Delta, the downtown is quiescent and the old black commercial district is nearly ghostly, a casualty of integration and the removal of commerce to drive-in strips along the highways. Only one Delta town, Indianola, the place that Hortense Powdermaker and John Dollard studied, has a major new homegrown industry, a catfish farm and processing plant; in Clarksdale, the coming of businesses with big payrolls remains a distant dream. It is easy to see the Delta as a place that, after changing from wilderness to cotton kingdom to sacred battleground of the civil rights revolution over the course of less than a century, is now essentially finished, quietly winding down, its emblem the abandoned sharecropper cabin rotting in the sun. Or it can look like an arena of nearly miraculous racial progress, and, especially if the economy were ever to improve, even hope — a place whose recent history is more truly symbolized by the new black neighborhood of ranch-style tract houses that sits at the edge of every town. It all depends on your vantage point.

I N 1985, after having lived in Flint, Michigan, for six years, Uless Carter moved back to Clarksdale. He got an apartment in Bennie Gooden's newest and biggest housing project, Federation Towers, a three-story building for the elderly sponsored by the Federation of Colored Women's Clubs. Federation Towers is a pleasant place, with commodious apartments that have small private balconies, and it seemed to Uless to be an especially fitting final home for him, since as a boy he had briefly lived in a sharecropper cabin and worked in the cotton fields on the very spot where Federation Towers now stood. Uless keeps a branch from a cotton plant on a shelf in his living room to remind himself of the way things used to be. Otherwise his apartment is mostly decorated with religious paraphernalia; half a dozen well-thumbed Bibles rest on various table tops.

Nearly everybody living in Federation Towers is a former sharecropper, and the overall mood there is one of happiness bordering on disbelief over the comfort of the accommodations. The place is serenely peaceful, except during the tub-thumping church services that are held twice a week in the downstairs common room; for the most part, people spend their days visiting, watching television, housekeeping, and doing volunteer work for the Federation or the Taborians. Sometimes Uless is called upon to lead the services in the building, or at a little church in town, but he is starting to slow down. In 1989 an episode of internal bleeding put him in the hospital for a while, and after that he could feel his energy ebbing and his memory beginning to deteriorate. Generally he stays in his apartment, dressed in a necktie and a smoking jacket, listening to classical music on the radio and reading Scripture.

Ruby Haynes is still living in Eastgate Gardens, the project she moved into from Chicago in 1979; her building is on a cul-de-sac called Martin Luther King Boulevard. Juanita and her children, after staying with Ruby for a while when they relocated to Clarksdale in 1988, got their own apartment in Eastgate, in the building next door to Ruby's. Ruby's youngest child, Kevin, had never left home, and now he is the main source of trouble in her life. They don't get along well. He drinks, and when he has had too many beers he rages at his mother, telling her that he hates Clarksdale and that the departure of his father from their household back in 1965 was all her fault. Ruby's friends have told her she ought to have Kevin committed to Whitfield, the state mental hospital. Once she tried to, but when the people from the hospital came over to examine him he was all sweetness and light and talked about nothing but how much he loved his mother, so they turned him down as a patient. Now he is enrolled in a program in Clarksdale that is supposed to rehabilitate alcoholics and train them for jobs; every day a bus picks him up, carries him there, and deposits him back home in the afternoon. A more recent addition to the household is Ruby's fifteen-year-old grandson, Robert Haynes, Jr., whom her son Larry brought down to Clarksdale for Ruby to raise after finding out that the boy's mother, who was living in the Robert Taylor Homes, had become a heroin addict.

Ruby has longstanding ties to the Stringer family, which owns one of the black funeral homes in Clarksdale. Back in the 1940s, she lived briefly in the Stringer funeral home when she was married to Kermit Butler, who drove the ambulance there, and even now the first bill she pays every month is the premium of $21.72 on her burial insurance with the Stringers. The wife of the head of the funeral home operates a flower shop in Clarksdale. Shortly after returning to Clarksdale, Ruby got a part-time job there assembling bouquets for weddings, funerals, church services, and holidays. In her mid-seventies, trim and in good health, she is still working there, though her and Kevin's Social Security checks are her real means of support.

Juanita's boyfriend, Thomas Chairs, got two jobs when he arrived in Clarksdale, one as a janitor in a doctor's office and the other unloading boxes at the big new Kroger's grocery store on Highway 61. Just before Christmas, 1988, he took a VCR out of the storeroom at Kroger's and hid it, intending to take it with him when he left work and sell it to buy presents for his children. A coworker saw him and told the night manager, and Thomas wound up serving a one-year sentence in the county jail. There he found Jesus, as prisoners often do. On September 9, 1989, he was baptized in jail. He asked Juanita to marry him, and she said she would after he got out. They set Valentine's Day, 1989, as their wedding date, but just before Thomas was to be released another inmate stole a piece of cake off his tray in the lunchroom and called him a "dick-sucking mother-fucker." Thomas lost his temper and attacked the man, and they gave him another six months; the wedding was put off.

Juanita and her four children were living on a welfare check of $168 a month, along with $368 in food stamps. Juanita has stayed off drugs. Tomesha, her oldest child, is a junior high school student, and so is entering the zone of maximum danger for poor black kids, but she seems to be on a steady course. She is a cheerleader at school, and, with Ruby as her chaperone, an enthusiastic churchgoer. Juanita feels reasonably confident that she will finish school and avoid getting pregnant; in fact Tomesha frequently urges Juanita to study for her high school equivalency certificate. Johnnie, Juanita's next child, is an A student in elementary school, and the two smallest kids are flourishing in Head Start. During the Christmas season of 1989, Juanita got a minimum-wage job in an Exxon station, which put her in a little better shape financially (even though her food stamp grant was cut) and made her feel that she was doing something with her life. She is pleased, on the whole, with the way her move to Clarksdale is working out.

Early in 1990, Robert Haynes turned up in Clarksdale. Out of work, the father of three out-of-wedlock children by three different women, an alcoholic who had done a stretch in a drying-out clinic, he now announced to his skeptical mother that he was going to turn over a new leaf. He found a girlfriend and moved into her apartment in another one of Bennie Gooden's projects, and founded a theatrical troupe called The Love, Truth & Reality Company. He spends most of his time at the civic auditorium putting small groups of friends and relatives through rehearsals of plays he has written. In the spring he put on a production called "I, Too, Have a Dream," in which he played himself—an alcoholic ghetto street-corner man who finds salvation through God, the inspiration of black history, and the speeches of Martin Luther King.

In the crucial scene in the play, Robert, abandoned by his girlfriend and children, stands alone on stage, swigging from a bottle, and delivers a despairing stream-of-consciousness monologue infused with a traumatized and self-loathing slum's-eye view of what it means to be black:

> Being black is getting down loud and wrong it's getting holy and sanctified and grabbing a whole hand fulla the sister next to you when she start speaking in tongues it's hitting the number or having you palm read and getting the short end of the stick and no glory it's grabbing a fat mama having her smell like ham fat hot biscuits and black eye peas it's buying what you don't want begging for what you don't need and stealing what's yours by right being black has a way of making you mad most of the time hurt all the time having so many hang ups till the problem of suicide don't even enter your mind. . . .

Then he falls to his knees and cries out for God; an offstage voice reads the passage from the Book of John in which Jesus, on the night before his crucifixion, assures his apostles that "In my father's house there are many mansions"; his family returns; his children sing an inspirational song about the Head Start program; and, at the end, Robert delivers King's most famous speech in an eerily perfect imitation of the great man's voice and cadence, finishing with that ringing celebration of America's coming racial redemption: "Free at last, free at last, thank God Almighty we're free at last."

K ING'S DREAM has not yet quite come true for poor black people in Clarksdale. The social ills of the Chicago ghettos are beginning to appear in the Delta. In Greenville and Clarksdale, in the poorer black neighborhoods, the spray-painted symbols of the Disciples and the Vice Lords can be seen here and there on the sides of buildings; in Jackson, the Chicago gangs have substantial branches, sustained by the constant movement of teenagers back and forth between the two cities, and have gotten into the drug business. In 1985, in the town of Canton, just north of Jackson, a phalanx of Cadillacs decorated with Vice Lords symbols came down for the funeral of a gang member who had been killed when a fight in a bar escalated to gunplay. In Clarksdale the gangs aren't so flagrant, but everybody has heard stories about their activities. Their heads are two men in their twenties, one from Chicago, the other from Clarksdale. In 1990, one gang member shot another in the neck in the local McDonald's. The gangs broke up a black school prom. They slashed all the tires on the cars parked along one street. A group of boys wearing gang jackets threw rocks at Uless Carter's car while he was driving down the street in broad daylight.

Teenage pregnancy, always high in Clarksdale, doesn't seem to be getting any lower; in the apartment next door to Ruby's there is a fifteen-year-old girl with two children. Cocaine is available even in the junior high schools. Black-on-black crime, which traditionally was confined to drunken brawls and lovers' quarrels, is moving out into the streets. There are muggings at mailboxes in poor neighborhoods on the first and third of every month, when the welfare and Social Security checks arrive. It is not supposed to be completely safe any longer to walk around the housing projects, or along Issaqueena Street, at night. There are occasional incidents of interracial violence — two white kids shot by blacks, two blacks beaten by whites at the Greyhound station, a white farm couple and their two children brutally murdered in their home by two blacks — and after each one people say they can feel a rise in the level of racial hostility in the everyday life of the town. In the old days, such crimes would never have been brought to trial: the black perpetrators would have been lynched and the white ones let off. Now they are processed in a gingerly manner, because, it is said, the authorities fear that police misconduct or a well-publicized unpopular court verdict might lead to a riot.

Within the black community, people are starting to worry whether the comity of the civil rights years will fray as class divisions become more pronounced. In an incident much gossiped about, and resented in the poor parts of town, the mayor's wife refused to act as hostess of the annual black debutante ball; some of the girls she would have had to introduce were daughters of single mothers, not married couples. Even Bennie Gooden confesses to sensing a little resentment directed at him by some of the residents of his projects. But on the whole, the center still holds in black Clarksdale. Ruby Haynes sees people like Gooden and Aaron Henry in church. Nearly everybody has the feeling of being on a communal upward trajectory. Black disunity really belongs, with crime, economic problems, and the vestiges of segregation, on the list of things hovering in the middle distance of the tableau of life in black Clarksdale — not overwhelmingly problematic right now, but threateningly positioned between the place on the road where most people find themselves and the longed-for territory of true fulfillment that shimmers off on the horizon.

Ruby is settling into old age with a sense of contentment about the circumstances she has found, but her feelings about her life as a whole are more mixed. She is as well off materially as she ever has been. The two great wounds of her life, her divorce from Luther and the death of her son George, have healed, somewhat, with the years. She has seen the part of the world that she inhabits change almost unimaginably for the better. Something is missing, though: she has made it through difficulties that would have defeated most people, but she hasn't been rewarded with inner peace. There has always been that nagging sensation of incompleteness, which had made itself felt most directly in her relationships with men.

Now that men play no romantic or financial role in her life, Ruby finds that she is much happier than she used to be. It is odd, because she believes that as a matter of principle, God made man to have dominion over everything, to rule his home and family — but in her own life she has never been able to stand it when a no-good man tried to tell her what to do. She is enduringly exasperated with her sons, except for Larry, and with most of their fathers too. Luther is still married to Dorothy Johnson, the woman he left Ruby for, owns a home on the far South Side of Chicago, and has worked for years as a parking-lot attendant; only recently have he and Ruby found that they can speak civilly to each other on the phone. Ruby's boys, when they call, generally speak to her in one of two modes, both annoying: in her imitation of their voices, they are either blusteringly gruff ("You quit fussing at me!") or, when they want money, cloying ("Hey, mama. Just called to see how you're doing. Any bills you can miss this month?"). Over and above all the specific frustrations that men have visited on Ruby, they represent something larger: a sense that for some reason she has been denied access to a pleasant social order, a way that ordinary life is supposed to fit together.

At night Ruby likes to stay up late stretched out on her sofa, working on the Bible quizzes that her pastor, the Reverend Willie Morganfield of Bell Grove Baptist Church, a cousin of Muddy Waters, passes out to his parishioners every week. Answering each question on a quiz requires poring through hundreds of pages of Scripture to find a specific chapter and verse; filling them out week after week has made Ruby more specifically familiar with the Bible than she has ever been in her life. She is especially drawn to the several books of the Old Testament during which the prophets are leading their people toward the land of Canaan that God has promised them, but haven't arrived yet. It is a resonant image for a poor black American who has lived through nearly all of the twentieth century and seen the end of sharecropping and segregation and the rise and fall of Chicago as a glorious symbol of hope: the other side of the Jordan River is now clearly visible, but unattained.

Martin Luther King, on the last night of his life, preached a sermon in Memphis based on the last section of the Book of Deuteronomy, in which Moses climbs to the top of Mount Pisgah to die and God says, "This is the land of which I swore to Abraham, to Isaac, and to Jacob, 'I will give it to your descendants.' I have let you see it with your eyes, but you shall not go over there." A more obvious Biblical parallel comes to mind for King, a young minister on the eve of martyrdom, but he chose to compare himself explicitly to Moses: "He's allowed me to go up to the mountain, and I've looked over, and I've seen the promised land," he said. "I may not get there with you. But I want you to know tonight that we, as a people, will get to the promised land."

Ruby's favorite passage on the subject is a different one, the section of the Book of Genesis where God speaks to Abraham, and first makes the great promise: "As an everlasting possession I will give you and your descendants the land in which you are now aliens, all the land of Canaan. . . ." The land in which Ruby and her descendants are now aliens is the United States, at least in the sense of what the whole world understands its promise to be. It isn't their land yet.

AFTERWORD

Thinking about the history of American race relations can easily give rise to bitterness and fatalism, but it is encouraging to remember how often in the past a hopeless situation, which appeared to be completely impervious to change, finally did change for the better. The framers of the Constitution, idealists though they were, couldn't imagine an American nation without slavery—but in the long run slavery was ended. In this century legal segregation looked like an unfortunate given, impossible to eliminate, until well after the end of World War II. That black America could become predominately middle class, non-Southern, and nonagrarian would have seemed inconceivable until a bare two generations ago.

Today the racial problem that is regarded as insuperable is the condition of the black slums in big cities. At the level of conversation, if not of political oratory, there seems to be a conviction that we don't know what can possibly help the ghettos, that even if we did know it couldn't be done for lack of political support, and that some unbridgeable gap between blacks and whites makes the amelioration of any problem related to race unlikely. These sentiments are not, in fact, either clear-eyed or realistic; they really belong on the long list of dolorous racial attitudes that turn out to be merely resistance to change wearing the garb of pessimism.

One reason for the prevailing gloom is that we've focused on the ghettos as places, and mistakenly used their condition as a symbol of the state of black America as a whole. Because we have a short historical memory, we think of the ghettos and the American dilemma generally as having been on a hopeful course in the early 1960s, and as having then plunged into despair. It is true that the ghettos have deteriorated badly in the past three decades, but an important part of the explanation is that millions of people left them and found better lives elsewhere. Also, even in the days before the ghettos' problems became so obvious, everyone who bothered to look at the lives of the poorest of the black poor, rural *and* urban, came away alarmed by the deprivation, ignorance, ill health, and social disorganization they found.

All through the nineteenth century, white Southerners claimed that poor blacks were fundamentally unassimilable as full-fledged Americans, and they used this idea to justify slavery, and then the ending of Reconstruction, and then the institution of the Jim Crow laws. In order to prove that the claim was wrong, Booker T. Washington, more than a century ago, embarked on his life's work as an educator. In the black slums of the big cities, firsthand observers from W. E. B. DuBois to E. Franklin Frazier to Richard Wright to Kenneth Clark voiced concern about the condition of the social fabric there. In other words, this is really an old problem that has become more isolated and concentrated and, as a result, become worse and more obvious. For most of this century, racial reformers put off its solution so that the goal of black freedom from discrimination could receive full attention. Now it is the most significant remaining piece of unfinished business in our country's long struggle to overcome its original sin of slavery.

The one concerted national attempt to address the woes of the black slums came during the period between 1964 and 1972. The events in Washington described in this book did not at all end in abject failure, as many people now believe. Clearing away some of the dense mythic fog surrounding the war on poverty and its successor programs is essential before we can try to complete the work those programs started. The war on poverty was a political failure mainly because it made enemies of local elected officials. Its main program, community action, was a conceptual failure in the sense that it raised expectations about the revival of the ghettos that couldn't be met, and presumed a link between political empowerment and individual economic advancement that doesn't exist. Rhetorically, the war on poverty was made to sound more sweeping than it really was, and so set itself up to seem as if it had ended in defeat when it didn't vanquish all poverty. But to say that the experiences of the late 1960s and early 1970s prove for all time that federal social welfare programs can't work, or that they cause ghetto poverty to worsen, is to cross over into the realm of political fantasy.

The lives of the millions of participants in the great black migration to the cities have been limned by sweeping historical trends: the mechanization of the cotton fields, the end of legal segregation, World War II and the booming labor market it created in the urban North, the death of consensus liberalism as America's reigning creed, and the collapse of our manufacturing economy. The federal government's response to the migration, which didn't come until the migration was approaching its end, affected the migrants but was hardly the main determinant of their fate. Of the people whose life stories are told in this book, one, Uless Carter, had no interaction with the government at all until he reached the age of eligibility for Social Security and subsidized senior citizens' housing. At the other extreme, George Hicks, who had the benefit of a stable upbringing and a college education, was in a position to take advantage of the expansion of government services that began with the war on poverty. His social welfare bureaucrat's career gave him a comfortable middle-class life in Chicago; the government programs enabled him to achieve his initially impossible-seeming ambition.

Ruby Haynes and her circle of friends and relatives all grew up in very harsh circumstances and lived mostly in areas, whether in Mississippi or in Chicago, that were set aside for the black poor and avoided by everyone else. From Ruby's perspective, opportunity presented itself dramatically three times during the course of her life: first, in the form of the booming job market in Chicago in the 1940s; second, with the opening of the Robert Taylor Homes; and third, when she was able to move back to Clarksdale and live in a safe housing project there. The great attempt to tear down the barriers to black progress — the civil rights and Great Society laws of the 1960s — had no effect at all on Ruby and her family; being poor, uneducated, and caught up in the ongoing chaos of ghetto life, they weren't positioned to take advantage of the changes in the way that George Hicks was.

The war on poverty passed through the Haynes family's life like a faint breeze: various family members were briefly clients of its programs, but for all of them it was an interlude, not a turning point in either direction. A few antipoverty programs, like Head Start and infants' nutrition, have been a much appreciated help in the raising of the family's children. Ruby, her daughter Juanita, and her daughter-in-law Connie have been on and off of welfare for most of their lives, so welfare is a more significant government program for them than is any part of the war on poverty, but it doesn't seem to have given them any decisive push toward success or failure. Welfare has a reputation for causing poor black couples to break up, but in the case of Ruby, Connie, and Juanita, the female-headed family pattern long predated their going on welfare and doesn't seem to have much to do with it.

The one government program that can fairly be accused of having gone wrong in a way that deeply harmed the Haynes family is public housing, especially the deadly effect of having no tenant screening in massive high rises that are segregated and filled with large families. Living in public housing doesn't absolutely doom people — Ruby's son Larry got out thanks to his jobs in the Army and the Post Office, and Connie's children are plainly on their way out thanks to Connie's iron will. But the atmosphere of these federally funded projects — the rampant crime, the drugs, the sense of absolute apartness from the rest of American society, the emphasis on an exaggerated and misguided version of masculinity that glorifies gang membership and sexual conquest — clearly helped to cause the troubles of most of Ruby's children.

The baseline against which Ruby Haynes measures her progress is the rural peonage in which she grew up, in which people didn't have enough food, clothing, or shelter, barely went to school, couldn't vote, moved constantly from plantation shack to plantation shack, and experienced nuclear family life only occasionally. The idea that the black poor have made no progress simply makes no sense to her, because things are so much better now; and the idea that government programs have been the main force shaping the course of her life also seems absurd, because for her — as for Uless Carter, and George Hicks — the true main force has been the simple fact of being black. George now lives the life of a member of an American ethnic group with an extremely strong identity; Ruby and her family, for all practical purposes, are still part of a caste system.

THE GHETTOS partake in the fluidity of American society, even as they are kept at arm's length from it. As the country changes, the ghettos will keep changing too. They have continued to lose population. Their condition improves in tight labor markets and worsens in more competitive ones. They react to changing mores and to the ongoing process of racial assimilation. Like the idea that the problems of the ghettos are new, the idea that they can be solved in a single dramatic stroke — by welfare reform, or by the emergence of new black leaders (or white leaders), or by the construction of more jails, or by eliminating drugs, or by changing the schools — seems to be irresistibly appealing. But racial breakthroughs in this country have always entailed major, sustained efforts, and the next one will too. Left alone, the ghettos are likely to become smaller and more isolated. A better outcome is possible, but it won't come from pushing some magic button.

Of all the simple ideas for helping the ghettos, probably the most common and persistent for the past quarter century has been the idea that they can be turned around, "developed" into thriving ethnic enclaves. The idea of ghetto development originated on the left, but it is remarkably appealing across the ideological spectrum. For years it has been the official vision of Republican administrations in Washington. Along with it goes a conviction that federal government efforts to help the ghettos must be locally based: tax incentives will cause businesses to start up there, tenant management will save the housing projects, community-development corporations will shore up the housing stock, parents will fix the schools, and the Washington bureaucracy should be kept out. All this has a powerful emotional attractiveness. It envelops the ghettos in the romanticized aura Americans attach to small-town life. By treating the issue of racial integration as irrelevant, it neatly removes from the agenda the most divisive racial remedies of the past generation, such as busing, scatter-site public housing, and affirmative action. For blacks drawn to nationalism, it contains the promise of a reunified, self-determining, economically independent community removed from the agonies of assimilationism.

The clear lesson of experience, though, is that ghetto development hasn't worked. Community-development efforts in the ghettos have the advantage of doing no harm, and it is vitally important to bring to the ghettos the ordinary qualities of most American neighborhoods, especially safe streets and good schools. But poor ethnic ghettos are usually temporary communities, rising in population during times of migration and falling when the residents begin to move up the ladder. Black ghettos have emptied out especially dramatically over the last generation. Most of them have essentially no employment base and, because they have such high crime rates and poor schools, they aren't likely to attract new residents. The impressive record of black success in America's cities since the 1960s has been almost entirely bound up with leaving the ghettos rather than improving them; with finding work in big organizations, not in inner-city start-ups; with participating in the wider system of electoral politics, not community organizing. To assume that a federal government retreat and a renaissance in the ghettos will together prove to be the answer is to stand on its head the obvious moral of all our urban racial progress of the past generation, which is that educated people in the ghettos will seize upon government jobs as a way to exit.

The danger in the notion of ghetto development is not in the ghettos themselves but in the realm of ideas. The advocacy of community-development projects has a crowding-out effect, causing discussion of other, better remedies to cease. Without ending any efforts to improve the ghettos that are now under way, we should change our reigning idea about what will help most: we should be trying to bring the ghetto poor closer to the social and economic mainstream of American society, not encouraging them to develop a self-contained community apart from the mainstream.

American society in the wider sense is not now a real presence in the ghettos, except via television, which only creates a continuous cognitive dissonance between everyday slum life and overall American life. Police officers don't walk the beat, most schools don't teach, fathers don't live at home, crime goes unpunished, the ward and precinct bosses who once offered a link to the political system are disappearing, and the old-fashioned settlement-house and social-agency training functions have withered away. Outside the ghettos, especially in the black middle class, sentiment has begun to run strongly in favor of reestablishing the social linkages between poor blacks and the rest of black society, but right now there is no mechanism in place to bring that about. The number of middle-class people who voluntarily return to the ghettos to live and help — or who move there for the first time — is always going to be tiny. Given the poverty and dispiritedness in the slums, it is unlikely that their residents will suddenly mobilize around some new figure who preaches moderation and bourgeois values. Any planned undertaking that would have a chance of affecting the ghettos substantially would have to be of enormous scope. For both practical and moral reasons, the institution by far best suited to the task is the federal government.

THE PROSPECT of federal involvement in local community affairs usually elicits two fears. The first, the traditional white Southern one, is of Washington's imposing its (usually liberal, and usually racial) will on the finely wrought social organization of faraway communities; the second, the newer black one, is of whites' trying to colonize and subjugate quasi-independent black communities.

Neither of these need be severely worrisome when we think about new ghetto social programs. Most of the government offices in ghetto neighborhoods are already operated under local auspices and would continue to be so. The revival of the maximum feasible participation clause, so as to bypass local government in search of "authentic leaders" to receive federal funds, is the remotest of all political possibilities, especially since so many local officials now are black. The federal function would be to provide more money and to direct what should be done with it. Past experience tells us that while this wouldn't be wildly popular, it would not amount to Washington's forcibly taking over local institutions. As for the racial issue, it would not be nearly so serious now as it was in the time of the war on poverty, because today most of the government employees who work in the ghettos are black; as a practical matter, the social welfare bureaucrats staffing any new social programs in the ghettos would be mostly black, so the programs would also help to achieve some of the longed-for bringing together of a bifurcated black America, and would incidentally strengthen the economic base of the black middle class.

Another doubt about new federal programs is the now pervasive skepticism about the ability of the federal government to take on any task without botching it. It is in large measure the shortcomings of the government's response to the black migration in the first place that accounts for the overall loss of faith in government domestic policy. Right now poor black people are paying a heavier price for this defeatism than anyone else, but sooner or later all the citizens of a great nation that simply gives up on its government will suffer adverse consequences.

In the specific case of the ghettos, the idea that the government can't accomplish anything is a smokescreen obscuring the useful and encouraging results of a quarter century's worth of research on antipoverty programs—research of a kind that didn't exist when the war on poverty began. We now know that the easiest problem to solve is simple material need: the food stamps program plainly reduces hunger, for example. In the ghettos, where material need is only part of the problem, the mission is more complicated, and the kind of programs that would help are less dramatically successful. Still, programs that come under the banner of "intervention," in which the government becomes a guiding presence in the lives of the ghetto poor, do demonstrably work.

Programs offering education, counseling, and birth control devices in high school clinics can reduce teenage pregnancy rates. Programs that send nurses and social workers to the homes of expectant mothers to provide prenatal care or food reduce infant-mortality rates and the incidence of low-birth-weight babies. Head Start consistently produces better early school performance, though after a few years the benefits it confers seem to wear off and its graduates drop to the level of other students; but this problem makes clear the need for even more sustained intervention in the educational lives of young children. One such program, conceived by James Comer of the Yale University Child Study Center, has impressively raised the achievement scores of ghetto elementary school students through a system of unusually intense school involvement in the lives of students and their parents. Various job training programs, including the Job Corps (which is now in much better shape than it was during its early years), increase the long-term likelihood of their graduates' being employed.

All these programs are relatively expensive per participant, and their payoff is not immediate and tangible, but in the long run they can save the government money that would have gone to welfare and incarceration. The work of planning them and carrying them out could provide a locus where many thousands of blacks and whites can work together to bring something new and worthy into being; this would be a far better public dialogue about race than one consisting mainly of squabbling over the distribution of resources and arguing about whose fault it is that things are so bad. Short of the kind of major cataclysm that wholly reorders a society, such as a war, an ambitious wave of new programs of this kind is the best chance we have to make a real difference in the ghettos.

It is not at all difficult to sketch out the framework of such a wholesale government effort—an effort so comprehensive that it would stand a good chance of substantially affecting the life of everyone who lives in the ghettos. The rather casual official attitude toward street crime, for example, which has existed ever since there have been ghettos, could finally end, and police officers could be put back on the streets and criminals quickly punished. Welfare could become a temporary program leading to a job. Housing projects could begin screening tenants again, and kicking out bad ones. We could try to improve the chances that every ghetto child is born healthy, learns to read and write in elementary school, graduates from high school, gets trained for the job market as it now exists, puts off parenthood until he or she can manage a family, and has a job waiting at the end of the process. The government could provide the job itself, in the form of New Deal–style projects that produce tangible results and impart real work experience. Obviously the precise conception and the management of all the programs require painstaking, detailed work, but the overall concept is simple and direct: the government should be trying to break the hold on individuals of those aspects of the ghetto culture that work against upward mobility, by providing a constant, powerful force that encourages the people of the ghettos to consider themselves part of the social structure of the country as a whole.

In the current political climate, this may all sound almost fantastic, but it is fully in accord with the thinking of most of the leading experts in the field. (Only the idea of the government's guaranteeing everyone a job, and requiring long-term welfare recipients to work, is not a matter of consensus at this point.) Besides its not being a daring leap into the unknown conceptually, as it was in the mid-1960s, a major expansion of the government's social programs (again, excepting the guaranteed-job idea) would not be so expensive. Most estimates put the cost in the range of $10 billion to $25 billion a year, which even at the high end is less than one-thirtieth of the federal budget. Whether that is exorbitant depends on what it accomplishes and how it is understood. If it could make a significant improvement in what we all know is the principal problem in American domestic life — a problem that poisons not just race relations but also our attitudes toward education, law enforcement, and city life itself — it would be a bargain.

Obviously the public is not now clamoring for a major increase in government spending on the ghettos. That should not be a cause for despair. Racial progress has almost never been a populist or popular cause, except, of course, among blacks. The alliance that in the past has produced racial reform is one between blacks and white liberals, and they have been able, in the best cases at least, to bring a recalcitrant public around to agreement with their views. That the next important step in American race relations now appears politically perilous is entirely typical, and it need not prevent progress from taking place. The real impediment in the short run is not a lack of political support — which in racial matters always comes after the fact, if it comes at all — but a weakness of spirit.

For most of our history, the issue of race has been linked to the issue of nationhood. During periods of fragmentation — periods when a multiplicity of local, ethnic, and economic interests held sway — racial problems have been put on the shelf. It is during the times when there has been a strong sense of *national* community that the problems have been addressed. The Civil War was one such time, at least in the Union states, and the long stretch between the New Deal and the Vietnam War was another; these periods brought us emancipation and civil rights. It has always been the federal government, not local governments or private business, that has led the way on race relations (though often the government had to be prodded into action by a political movement); the personal involvement of the president himself has usually been necessary. Like national defense and foreign policy, the management of racial issues seems to require a capability for national action. That the idea of the federal government's ameliorating race relations seems strange today is only a symptom of a much broader problem, which is that we are insufficiently unified as a society to be able successfully to undertake ambitious, organized national projects of any kind. If we can heal the ghettos, which are the part of the country most hurt by our current fragmentation, it will be a sign that we are on the way to a restoration of our spirit of community.

It is essential that any attempt to address racial issues quickly win public support, even if it doesn't have public support to begin with. Otherwise, it will suffer the fate of Reconstruction and the war on poverty — a short life followed by a period of reaction. The most straightforward way for new federal programs to win acceptance is to show that they work, not in the sense of dramatically eliminating the underclass overnight, but in the sense of being demonstrably honest, well run, committed to mainstream values, and devoid of the punitive, ram-it-down-their-throats quality that the shortest-lived reforms have had. The forces of practicality can be made to move from opposition to support of government programs if it becomes clear that a better work force and calmer cities would be the result. State and local governments would feel a pull to create social programs of their own once they saw that ghetto conditions are susceptible to improvement. Yet another argument for the federal government's centrality in the first wave of new programs is that it is best equipped to maintain their quality and ensure consistency of purpose. A radically decentralized approach, like the community action program, is bound to produce at least some disasters among its thousands of independent agencies, and these cause the whole idea of social welfare programs to lose legitimacy.

The way new programs are received depends not only on how they are run, but also on the way the case is stated for them. Our lack of faith in Americans' ability to put aside selfish concerns and address the big problems has produced a conviction, even among people who want to mount a new assault on ghetto poverty, that it would have to be camouflaged in some way. So the call to action is always couched as something else: as a new family policy, or children's policy, or drug policy, or civil rights policy. New antipoverty initiatives are thought to be doomed to failure unless they are buried in the tax code or loaded up with middle-class beneficiaries to give political cover. Those aspects of ghetto life that are characterized by self-destructive behavior rather than by victimization of the innocent — drug use, out-of-wedlock childbearing, dropping out of school — are, quite often, played down for fear that Americans will leap to the conclusion that the black ghetto poor are undeserving and should be written off. The old threat has not quite died out that riots will occur unless there are new programs, because there is a feeling that only the self-preservative urge can motivate the public to support anything aimed specifically at the ghettos.

The result of all this well-intentioned fuzzing up of the true nature of the tragedy in the ghettos is a loss of moral urgency, and all causes need moral urgency if they are to be fulfilled. The ghettos, and race relations in general, are the one area in American domestic life where the whole country agrees that there is something terribly wrong, where the vocabulary of crisis and national responsibility is not in the least trumped-up. The United States has an undeniable strain of racial prejudice in its character, but it also has a racial conscience, which periodically comes to the fore. What brings it out is the demonstration of conditions in black America that are intolerable and that are clearly linked to the country's history of departing from its democratic ideals in the case of blacks.

The ghettos bear the accumulated weight of all the bad in our country's racial history, and they are now among the worst places to live in the world. Programs for middle-class blacks — affirmative action and minority set-asides — are never going to set the country aflame with a sense of righteous purpose. Neither will family allowances or an increase in the Earned Income Tax Credit. The conditions that now prevail in the ghettos, honestly presented and openly discussed, could. To be born into a ghetto is to be consigned to a fate that no American should have to suffer. The more clearly we can be made to see that and to understand the causes of the situation, the less likely it is that we will let it stand.

Acknowledgments

THIS BOOK has been in the works for some years, so I have incurred a substantial load of debts. The first and greatest is to William Whitworth, the editor of *The Atlantic*. He and I began discussing this project even before I went to work for him in 1983. For all that time, he has been unfailingly encouraging and patient, even when it wasn't at all clear whether there would be any useful result to him from the research I was doing. By publishing several long articles of mine along the way, he allowed me to field-test my thinking over a long period. The questions and suggestions he has offered, always gently, have been extremely helpful — especially the suggestion that I use Chicago as my main setting. Also at *The Atlantic*, Corby Kummer edited the articles out of which this book grew, Sue Parilla checked them for accuracy, and Barbara Wallraff ridded them of grammatical errors; all did their work so well that watching them in action taught me lessons that have been essential to the writing of this book.

The main help I got while doing my research was from all the people who spoke with me, often repeatedly, as interview subjects — especially the people whose life stories are told here, who gave me a great deal of their time. I'd like to thank, also, Grace Jones Cleveland of Chicago and several other members of her family (Charmella Cleveland, Chaun Cleveland, Tommie Cleveland, Arjell Jennings, and Churie Shelby), who went through the whole lengthy process of telling me their family history but don't appear in the book.

In the earliest stages of my research, I was planning to write about migrants to Chicago from the town of Canton, Mississippi, rather than Clarksdale. Among the Cantonians in Chicago who helped me, Mildred

Nichols Burton, Alice Dunlap, and the Reverend J. B. Sims were particularly generous.

After my first article about migration to the North appeared in *The Atlantic*, two remarkable people in Chicago got in touch with me and offered to help in any way they could. I took both of them up on it. Jack Connelly, who runs a successful antipoverty program called Jobs for Youth/Chicago, arranged for me to meet dozens of graduates of his program whose family roots were in Mississippi. John Spikner, a saintly man who lives alone in the Lawndale ghetto and has devoted his life to volunteer work, took me around his neighborhood, introducing me to people and, again, helping me to locate migrants from Mississippi. In Clarksdale, the managers of Federation Towers, Willie Gregory and the Reverend Michael Myles, and of Eastgate Gardens, Elsa Pittman, put a good deal of effort into getting me in touch with former sharecroppers and with returned migrants from Chicago among the tenants of their housing developments. Bennie Gooden, whose career I describe in this book, and Vivian Johnson, who works for him at Southland Management in Clarksdale, also helped with this part of the research. Also in Clarksdale, Jean Cauthen did me the great favor of loading me into her car one day and driving me around town introducing me to interview subjects.

Several people provided me with unpublished manuscripts or collections of papers. Mrs. W. K. Anderson of Clarksdale gave me a short typed history of the King & Anderson cotton plantation. Martin Anderson turned over to me a stack of memoranda and personal notes about welfare policy from the 1968 Nixon presidential campaign and the first years of the Nixon administration. Patrick Anderson, who worked at the President's Committee on Juvenile Delinquency in the early 1960s, gave me an unpublished essay he wrote about that experience. James Butler showed me papers about the Hopson family's cotton plantation and the development there of the mechanical cotton picker, and Howell Hopson sent me some additional material, including photographs, on the same subject. Constance Henry Daniels (whose life story is told in this book) and Patricia Derian let me go through old scrapbooks that contained valuable material. Adam Yarmolinsky gave me an unpublished essay he wrote about the early planning sessions for the war on poverty. Sharon Hicks-Bartlett let me read a sheaf of comments she had written, as part of her work as a graduate student in sociology at the University of Chicago, on the academic literature on black ghettos. Pierre DeVise, of Roosevelt University in Chicago, gave me part of an unpublished work-in-progress on segregation in Chicago. Finally, two of my subjects, Harry McPherson and Sargent Shriver, took the time to write me letters clearing up detailed questions I raised about their time in government.

Some of the oral history interviews at the John F. Kennedy and Lyndon Johnson presidential libraries are available to researchers only with the permission of the subject. For granting me such permission, I thank Peter Edelman, James Farmer, Myer Feldman, David Hackett, Frank Mankiewicz, and Adam Yarmolinsky. While I'm on the subject of libraries, there are a few librarians to whom I'm especially grateful: Joan Howard and Scott Parham at the Nixon Presidential Materials Project, Aloha South at the National Archives, Linda Hanson and Nancy Smith at the Johnson Library, Henry Gwaizda and Ron Whealan at the Kennedy Library, Linda Smith at the Carnegie Public Library in Clarksdale, Larry Jones and Pete Daniel at the Smithsonian Institution, and Polly Gadsden at my hometown library in Pelham, New York, who processed interlibrary loan requests for me.

Because they read all or part of this book before publication and offered comments, suggestions, and corrections, I am deeply grateful to Alan Brinkley (whose efforts were especially copious), Hodding Carter, Peter Edelman, John Ehrlichman, James Fallows, Henry Hampton, Frederick Hayes, Corby Kummer, Frank Levy, Larry Long, Joseph Nocera, John Palmer, Charles Peters, and William Julius Wilson.

Several people worked for me over the years as research assistants, tirelessly running down information in libraries and on the telephone in return for too-low wages; without their help, this book would have taken years longer to finish. They are Meg Jacobs, Elizabeth Leonard (whose tour of duty was the longest), Andrew Reinhardt, and Caroline Young.

As book projects often do, this one went through two generations of editors. Robert Gottlieb signed me up and Lee Goerner watched over the early stages of my research; then both left Knopf for greener pastures and Elisabeth Sifton became my editor. With great firmness, understanding, and enthusiasm, she supervised the completion of the research, the writing, and the alchemic process by which a typescript is made into a book. Her assistant, George Andreou, and Katherine Hourigan, Knopf's managing editor, were also tremendously helpful and supportive. Carol Carson and Archie Ferguson spent hour upon hour of extra time to get jacket design exactly right. My agent, Amanda Urban, was, as usual, absolutely on the case throughout.

It would have been impossible for me to bring this project to fruition if I hadn't had the constant love and encouragement of my wife, Dominique Browning. Her suggestions have been indispensable, but what I have valued even more is her unwavering conviction that what I was doing was worthwhile, and was a treasured aspect of our life together.

A Note on Sources

THERE IS an enormous wealth of material that at least touches on the broad subjects of this book, American race relations and social welfare policy—fiction, poetry, history, sociology, biography, music, photography, and memoirs. Rather than attempt to list all of it, I have tried in the notes that follow to mention all the specific sources for my information (except for information that is a matter of general public record, such as quotations from presidential speeches and descriptions of events that were widely reported in the press), and to name along the way a few books that were especially useful to me. Most of the books about the black migration to the North, though, do not deal with the period during and after World War II, when the bulk of the migration took place. I have been able to find only one book of nonfiction solely about the post-1940 phase of the migration, and I should mention it here: *The Black Migration: The Journey to Urban America*, by George Groh (Weybright and Talley, 1972). Claude Brown's *Manchild in the Promised Land* (Macmillan, 1965), besides having been part of the inspiration for the title of this book, is a superb memoir of the ghetto life lived by the children of the migrants.

In researching the sections of this book about the federal government, I spent time at four document collections: the John F. Kennedy Library in Boston, the Lyndon Johnson Library in Austin, Texas, the Nixon Presidential Materials Project in Alexandria, Virginia, and the National Archives in Washington, D.C. There is a wealth of primary source material about the making of national social policy in all these places. The Kennedy and Johnson libraries both maintain large and useful collections of oral history interviews with members of the two administrations, and they also contain most of the paperwork generated by the White House planners of the war on poverty and the succeeding Great Society programs. The material in the Kennedy Library is less extensive, and easier to get at — it is concentrated in the papers of Walter Heller, Theodore Sorensen, Daniel Knapp, and Richardson White, Jr. The Johnson Library's material on domestic policy-making is vast and spread through many different collections, and so it requires a greater time commitment from researchers. The papers of the Office of Economic Opportunity are at the National Archives, but they are voluminous and still substantially unsorted, so it is impossible to go through them comprehensively. I did find that the records on a few specific subjects, such as field inspectors' reports on particular programs in Mississippi and Chicago, contained valuable information.

The Nixon Project — a warehouse rather than a presidential library, run by people with no evident commitment to maintaining their subject's reputation — has material that is especially useful. There is very little in the Kennedy and Johnson libraries that indicates what the president himself was thinking, but Richard Nixon as president was an inveterate scribbler in the margins of the material in his in-box; by reading the "President's Handwriting" files, it is usually possible to see what his personal reaction was to what he was reading. Also, both of Nixon's top aides, H. R. Haldeman and John Ehrlichman, took detailed notes by hand during meetings, and most of these notes are available at the Nixon Project. It is a great historical luxury to have two blow-by-blow accounts, and sometimes more if other aides were present and taking notes, of every important discussion of domestic policy in which Nixon took part. Finally, the hundreds of pages of memoranda at the Nixon Project from Daniel Patrick Moynihan to Nixon comprise a much more copious record of the thinking of a key adviser on social policy than is available for either the Kennedy or Johnson administration.

Most of the material in this book comes from my own interviews. Perhaps I'm displaying a reporter's bias here, but it seemed to me that as rich in information about the black migration and its consequences as the archives and published sources were, the memories of the people involved were even richer.

Notes

3 DEMONSTRATION OF THE MECHANICAL COTTON PICKER: James Butler, a Hopson in-law in Clarksdale, maintains a collection of papers relating to the development of the picker that are the best source on the subject, and from which all my description of the demonstration comes. Particularly useful are Hopson Planting Company, "Mechanization of a Delta Cotton Plantation," privately published, October 1944; Howell H. Hopson, Jr., "Memorandum of a Plantation Episode," typescript, dated January 1, 1963; "Mechanical Cultivation and Picking of Cotton, Dream of Industry, Comes True," Acco Press, November 1944; "Revolution in Cotton," *Collier's*, July 21, 1945; "King Cotton's Scepter Falls to Machinery," *Chicago Tribune*, October 10, 1944; and "Robot Field Hands Successfully Invade Southland," *Memphis Commercial Appeal*, October 15, 1944.

RUST BROTHERS: See John Rust, "The Origin and Development of the Cotton Picker," West Tennessee Historical Society Papers, Volume VII (1953), pp. 38–56; James H. Street, *The New Revolution in the Cotton Economy: Mechanization and Its Consequences* (University of North Carolina Press, 1957), pp. 116–134; Frank E. Smith, *The Yazoo River* (Rinehart & Co., 1954), p. 332. The Rust brothers were also involved in the "Delta Cooperative Farm," an interracial, socialized 2,300-acre cotton plantation outside the town of Hill House (which was Ruby Daniels's first home in the Delta) that was founded in 1936 under the auspices of a national board of blue-chip liberals (such as Reinhold Niebuhr), and folded five years later. See Wirt A. Williams, editor, *History of Bolivar County, Mississippi* (The Reprint Company, 1976), pp. 261–264. For more information on the movement to reform the cotton plantation system, see Howard Kester, *Revolt Among the Sharecroppers* (Arno Press, 1969); and Donald H. Grubbs, *Cry from the Cotton* (University of North Carolina Press, 1971).

4 QUOTATIONS FROM HOWELL HOPSON: Hopson, "Memorandum of a Plantation Episode."

DESCRIPTION OF HOWELL HOPSON: Interview with Hopson's son, Howell H. Hopson III, of Gainesville, Florida; the younger Hopson provided me with a copy of the photographs referred to.

5 NOBODY BOTHERS TO SAVE OLD FARM EQUIPMENT: One buyer of a first-gen-

eration International Harvester cotton picker, a California company called Producers Oil, did save it, and donated it to the Smithsonian Institution's Museum of History and Technology in 1970.

QUOTATION FROM HOWELL HOPSON: Hopson, "Memorandum of a Plantation Episode."

6 SHARECROPPING AND SEGREGATION: John W. Cell, *The Highest Stage of White Supremacy: The Origins of Segregation in South Africa and the American South* (Cambridge University Press, 1982) contains the best recent summary of the history of the South during the years following the end of the Civil War. The classic on the subject of the segregating South is C. Vann Woodward, *Origins of the New South, 1877–1913* (Louisiana State University Press, 1951). Also see Woodward's *The Strange Career of Jim Crow* (Oxford University Press, 1966).

STATISTICS ON BLACK MIGRATION: U.S. Department of Commerce, Bureau of the Census, *Historical Statistics of the United States, Colonial Times to 1970, Part One,* pp. 22 (percentage distribution of black population), 95 (number of migrants to the North), 105–106 (number of immigrants from other countries).

7 RUBY LEE DANIELS: Except where noted, this and all subsequent details about her life come from interviews with her.

PICKING COTTON: On this and other matters pertaining to Mississippi agriculture and the sharecropper system, I have relied primarily on material from interviews with planters and former sharecroppers who are, for the most part, not named or quoted in the text. The former sharecroppers who were most useful were Reather Blisset, Uless Carter, Viola Coley, Viola Davis, Jessie Dobbins, Frank Henry, Arjell Jennings, Zeala Johnson, Dovie King, Mary Malone, Mamie Marshall, Reba McAllister, Lucille Roark, Marie Robinson, Churie Shelby, Mattie Siggers, J. B. Sims, Edna Stapleton, and Grace Terrell. The planters were Leon Bramlett, Andrew Carr, R. V. Casilli, Eugene Doyle, James Furr, Edwin Mullens, LeRoy Percy, and Carter Stovall.

10 JOHN CLARK: "Clarksdale–Coahoma County 1836–1936: One Hundred Years of Progress in the Mississippi Delta," unpublished manuscript in the Mississippi Collection of the Carnegie Public Library, Clarksdale, Mississippi, p. 15.

STREETS, RAIL LINE, INCORPORATION, PAVING: "Clarksdale–Coahoma County 1836–1936," pp. 2–4.

11 PEAK OF COTTON ACREAGE: *Statistical Abstract of the United States 1942* (Government Printing Office, 1942), p. 775.

NUMBER OF TENANT FARMERS: Charles S. Johnson, Edwin R. Embree, and W. W. Alexander, *The Collapse of Cotton Tenancy: Summary of Field Studies and Statistical Surveys 1933–35* (University of North Carolina Press, 1935), p. 4.

THOMAS DIXON: See especially *The Leopard's Spots: A Romance of the White Man's Burden* (Doubleday & Page, 1902).

DAVID COHN: David L. Cohn, *Where I Was Born and Raised* (University of Notre Dame Press, 1967), p. 120.

WILLIAM ALEXANDER PERCY: William Alexander Percy, *Lanterns on the Levee: Recollections of a Planter's Son* (Alfred A. Knopf, 1941), p. 275.

12 THE "RACE RIOT": Material collected by the Works Progress Administration in the 1930s and now on file in the Mississippi Collection of the Carnegie Public Library in Clarksdale is my chief source of information on the riot. In particular: Wilber T. Gibson, "The Riot in Coahoma County," undated typescript; George F. Maynard, untitled typescript dated May 12, 1925; "Historical Research Project of Coahoma County," interviews with Mrs. Mary Fisher Robin-

son, "an old citizen," Mr. T. S. Aderholt, Mr. G. F. Maynard, Sr., and Mr. J. D. Smith. In 1880, a U.S. Senate Committee conducted a lengthy interview about the riot with John Brown, the former county sheriff, who was then active in helping black migrants settle in Kansas and who, of course, had a version of the "race riot" that is completely at variance with the white version. See U.S. Senate, 44th Congress, 1st Session *Senate Report No. 527,* Vol I, pp. 351–393.

13 "THE TIDE OF IGNORANCE": Mabel B. Fant and John C. Fant, *History of Mississippi* (The Mississippi Publishing Company, 1920), quoted in "Historical Research Project of Coahoma County," Assignment #22.

"THIS TURNED OUT LIKE THINGS GENERALLY DO": Gibson, "The Riot in Coahoma County."

14 "DO NOT SHOOT THESE NEGROES": Maynard, typescript.

THE END OF RECONSTRUCTION: James Wilford Garner, *Reconstruction in Mississippi* (Macmillan, 1901) has an unabashed bias against Reconstruction, but it is a good source of details about the period.

15 ILLINOIS CENTRAL RAILROAD: Robert L. Brandfon, *Cotton Kingdom of the New South: A History of the Yazoo Mississippi Delta from Reconstruction to the Twentieth Century* (Harvard University Press, 1967), is a valuable work in general, and it contains a wealth of interesting material on the Illinois Central's activities in the Delta. An interesting tidbit is that the Illinois Central owned a 10,000-acre cotton plantation outside Clarksdale and gave an interest in it to the Speaker of the U.S. House of Representatives, Joseph Cannon of Illinois, in hopes of inducing him to look favorably on the railroad's legislative agenda.

16 ROBERT S. ABBOTT: Roi Ottley, *The Lonely Warrior* (H. Regnery, 1955), a biography, is the best source on Abbott. The information on Abbott's role in promoting black migration comes from Chapter 10, "The Uneasy Exodus." Other useful books about the World War I–era black migration include Allen B. Ballard, *One More Day's Journey: The Story of a Family and a People* (McGraw-Hill, 1984); Arna Bontemps, . . . *They Seek a City* (Doubleday, Doran & Co., 1945); Neil Fligstein, *Going North: Migration of Blacks and Whites from the South, 1900–1950* (Academic Press, 1981); James R. Grossman, *Land of Hope: Chicago, Black Southerners, and the Great Migration* (University of Chicago Press, 1989); and Florette Henri, *Black Migration: Movement North, 1900–1920* (Anchor, 1975).

QUOTATION FROM E. FRANKLIN FRAZIER: E. Franklin Frazier, *The Negro Family in Chicago* (University of Chicago Press, 1932), p. 80.

BLACK POPULATION GROWTH OF CHICAGO: The commission I refer to here issued an excellent report, *The Negro in Chicago* (University of Chicago Press, 1922); Charles S. Johnson, the author of *Shadow of the Plantation* (see below), was the chief investigator. These figures appear on page 79.

POLICE ROLE IN PREVENTING MIGRATION: Cohn, *Where I Was Born and Raised,* p. 336.

17 SOUTH IS BETTER FOR NEGRO: *The Negro in Chicago,* p. 104.

BLACK POPULATION GROWTH OF CHICAGO IN 1930S: Arnold R. Hirsch, *Making the Second Ghetto: Race and Housing in Chicago, 1940–1960* (Cambridge University Press, 1983), p. 17.

MARTIN LUTHER KING'S VISIT TO A PLANTATION: Stephen Oates, *Let the Trumpet Sound: The Life of Martin Luther King, Jr.* (Harper, 1982), p. 345.

18 TEACHERS' SALARIES: Cohn, *Where I Was Born and Raised,* p. 347.

19 20 PER CENT INTEREST: Cohn, p. 124.

"WHEN SELF THE WAVERING BALANCE HOLDS": Interview with Carter Stovall.

HORTENSE POWDERMAKER: Hortense Powdermaker, *After Freedom: A Cultural Study of the Deep South* (Russell & Russell, 1968), p. 86.

20 QUOTATION FROM JOHN DOLLARD: John Dollard, *Caste and Class in a Southern Town* (Yale University Press, 1937), p. 119.

24 "SIMPLE AND AFFECTIONATE": Percy, *Lanterns on the Levee*, p. 300.

QUOTATIONS FROM DAVID COHN ABOUT BLACK INFERIORITY: Cohn, *Where I Was Born and Raised*, pp. 115 ("emotionally unstable"), 116 ("childlike"), 81 ("long moral holiday").

25 "GNAWING PAINS AND TERRORS OF REMORSE": Cohn, p. 111.

"WORK WITH HIS HANDS": Cohn, p. 157.

ROY FLOWERS: Interview with James Furr.

"NONE OF US WAS INFLUENCED BY WHAT THE NEGROES THEMSELVES WANTED": Percy, *Lanterns on the Levee*, p. 258.

"CAMPAIGN OF VILIFICATION": Percy, p. 263.

"EMBITTERING INFLUENCE": Percy, p. 265.

26 "A STATE OF WILD EXCITEMENT": Percy, p. 266.

PERCY'S SPEECH IN THE BLACK CHURCH: Percy, pp. 267–268.

"ONLY UNDER COMPULSION": Cohn, *Where I Was Born and Raised*, p. 55.

"SEXUALLY COMPLETELY FREE": Cohn, p. 79.

27 GUNNAR MYRDAL: Gunnar Myrdal, *An American Dilemma: The Negro Problem and Modern Democracy* (Harper & Brothers, 1944), pp. 587–588.

"WE DO NOT GIVE THE NEGRO CIVIC EQUALITY": Cohn, *Where I Was Born and Raised*, p. 161.

"IT IS THE SEXUAL FACTOR": Cohn, p. 294.

28 "IF YOU COULD BE A NIGGER ONE SATURDAY NIGHT": Interviews with James Furr and Hodding Carter III.

CHARLES S. JOHNSON: Charles S. Johnson, *Shadow of the Plantation* (University of Chicago Press, 1934), pp. 68 (181 illegitimate children), 31 (152 female-headed families, 231 first marriages), 53 ("Sex, as such"), 188 (35 per cent). One contemporary journalistic account of out-of-wedlock childbearing in Washington, D.C., Leon Dash, *When Children Want Children* (Morrow, 1989), has a chapter exploring its subjects' roots in the sharecropper system in North Carolina and cites Johnson's work in support of the argument that the prevailing family structure in black city slums today is an outgrowth of the family structure that was common among sharecroppers.

ARTHUR RAPER: Arthur F. Raper, *Preface to Peasantry: A Tale of Two Black Belt Counties* (University of North Carolina Press, 1936), p. 71.

29 HORTENSE POWDERMAKER: Powdermaker, *After Freedom*, pp. 143 ("the typical Negro family"), 146 ("personnel of these matriarchal families"), 68 (common-law marriages).

JOHN DOLLARD: Dollard, *Caste and Class in a Southern Town*, p. 397.

GUNNAR MYRDAL: Myrdal, *An American Dilemma*, pp. 177 ("extremely high illegitimacy"), 933 ("The census information").

MARRIAGE AND TRADITIONAL CULTURES: Letter from Douglas R. White, professor of social science, University of California, Irvine, and editor of *World Cultures*, January 30, 1989.

30 JOHN DOLLARD: Dollard, *Caste and Class in a Southern Town*, pp. 402 ("They are satisfied"), 404 ("The furnish system").

HORTENSE POWDERMAKER: Powdermaker, *After Freedom*, pp. 173 (jealousy), 369 ("Perhaps the most severe result").

31 "OUTSIDE THE LAW": Powdermaker, *After Freedom*, p. 173.

CHARLES JOHNSON: Johnson, *Shadow of the Plantation*, pp. 49 ("extreme isolation"), 50 ("unique moral codes"), 90 (disorganization), 209 ("This group").

STATES WITH HIGH MURDER RATES: Powdermaker, *After Freedom*, p. 170.

COCAINE: Cohn, *Where I Was Born and Raised*, p. 279.

"AMONG THE LOWEST CLASS": W. E. B. DuBois, *The Philadelphia Negro: A Social Study* (Schocken Books, 1971), p. 192.

32 QUOTATION FROM *The Souls of Black Folk*: W. E. B. DuBois, *Writings* (The Library of America, 1986), p. 461.

COOK COUNTY HOSPITAL: Frazier, *The Negro Family in Chicago*, pp. 180–181.

34 BLACK PEOPLE IN CLARKSDALE: In describing race relations in Mississippi during segregation, I have relied primarily on material from interviews with, in addition to the people named in this chapter, Johnnie Bennett, Thea Bowman, Jack Brinson, Eddie Brown, Oresa Brown, Robert Chinn, LeEtta Clark, Oliver Clark, Patricia Derian, Annie Devine, Robert Divine, Alice Dunlap, Mike Espy, Beatrice Evans, Reba Harris, Leonard Henderson, Frank Henry, Robert Jackson, Leroy Jones, Louisa Jones, Leandrew Love, Mamie Marshall, Samuel McCray, Mildred McGee, William Meeks, Bill Mosby, Ray Mosby, Blanche Nichols, Mildred Nichols, Lucille Roark, J. B. Sims, Marion Stringer, Deborah Terrell, James Thompson, Ezra Towner, and ViEthel Wells.

35 DR. HILL'S WIFE: Interviews with Jessie Dobbins, Earl Gooden, and Dr. P. W. Hill, Jr.

37 QUOTATION FROM JOHN DOLLARD: Dollard, *Caste and Class in a Southern Town*, p. 397.

QUOTATION FROM *Invisible Man*: Ralph Ellison, *Invisible Man* (Random House, 1952), p. 45.

38 "IN THE DILAPIDATED SHACKS": Powdermaker, *After Freedom*, p. 133.

CENTURY FUNERAL HOMES: Interview with Mike Espy; Vera Pigee, *The Struggle of Struggles, Part Two* (Art-Type Company, 1979), p. 13.

39 TWO BLACK FUNERAL-HOME SCIONS: The other one is Marion Stringer, son of Charles Stringer.

40 "JOHN'S DOING VERY WELL WITH GENERAL MOTORS": Interview with John Lewis, the former civil rights leader who is now a U.S. Representative from Georgia. While in general I haven't provided citations for general impressions about black life in the South before the civil rights movement, because they're assembled from many interviews, in this case I do because I'm quoting Lewis word for word.

41 WILLIAM ALEXANDER PERCY: Probably Percy's most important legacy as a writer is the influence he had on his cousin and ward, Walker Percy. In Walker Percy's early novels, there is an interplay between the young, alienated hero and an older relative who has the comfort of absolute belief in a system of morality that the hero is unable to subscribe to. It's tempting to conclude that William Alexander Percy's racial paternalism was, in particular, the code that Walker Percy couldn't accept, so that he was forced to explore the territory of loss of faith in society. If so, it would be another example of the tendency of the issue of race relations in America to induce in people who contemplate it at length a generalized feeling of disillusionment.

CARTER STOVALL AND MUDDY WATERS: Interview with Carter Stovall.

MUDDY WATERS'S MOVING TO CHICAGO: Mike Rowe, *Chicago Breakdown* (Da Capo Press, 1979), p. 66.

GEORGE HICKS: Except where noted, this and all subsequent details about his life come from interviews with him.

44 BENNIE GOODEN: Except where noted, this and all subsequent details about his life come from interviews with him.

45 AARON HENRY: Except where noted, the biographical information on Henry in this section comes from interviews with him.

46 HENRY'S SERVING IN AN INTEGRATED UNIT AND READING *Native Son*: Donald C. Mosley and D. C. Williams, Jr., "An Analysis and Evaluation of a Community Action Anti-Poverty Program in the Mississippi Delta" (unpublished Ph.D. thesis at Mississippi State University, 1967), p. 21.

47 "NEGROES ARE NECESSARY": Powdermaker, *After Freedom*, p. 23.

QUOTATION FROM JAMES K. VARDAMAN: James W. Silver, *Mississippi: The Closed Society* (Harcourt, Brace & World, 1966), p. 19.

KING & ANDERSON PLANTATION: Private history of King & Anderson plantation, typescript, September 1959.

MANAGERS' TRIP TO CHICAGO: Cohn, *Where I Was Born and Raised*, pp. 340–345.

J. H. JACKSON'S CHANGING THE ADDRESS OF HIS CHURCH: Interview with Louis Martin.

48 GREENVILLE VETERANS: Interviews with Melvin Taylor, Odell Wells, and ViEthel Wells, officers of the Greenville Club of Chicago.

49 MORE BLACK PEOPLE IN COAHOMA COUNTY: Cohn, *Where I Was Born and Raised*, p. 24.

QUOTATION FROM AARON HENRY: Interview with Henry.

QUOTATION FROM RICHARD HOPSON: Letter from R. N. Hopson to Mrs. Dorothy Lee Black, office manager of the Delta Council, April 21, 1944, Hopson papers.

50 PATERNALISTIC PLANTERS: Interviews with Eugene Doyle (former office manager of King & Anderson), Carter Stovall, and LeRoy Percy.

51 QUOTATION FROM DAVID COHN: Cohn, *Where I Was Born and Raised*, pp. 329–330.

52 QUOTATION FROM RICHARD WRIGHT: Richard Wright, *12 Million Black Voices: A Folk History of the Negro in the United States* (Viking, 1941), p. 93.

53 "INTO THESE KITCHENETTES": St. Clair Drake and Horace Cayton, *Black Metropolis: A Study of Negro Life in a Northern City* (Harcourt, Brace and Company, 1945), pp. 576–577.

ULESS CARTER: Except where noted, this and all subsequent details about his life come from interviews with him.

56 HISTORY OF KING & ANDERSON: Private history of King & Anderson; interviews with Eugene Doyle and Mrs. W. K. Anderson.

57 THE ANDERSON FAMILY DID NOT WANT THE MATTER PRESSED: Interview with Mrs. W. K. Anderson.

CHICAGO

61 "THE POOREST AND MOST UNSTABLE ELEMENTS": Drake and Cayton, *Black Metropolis*, p. 576. In general, *Black Metropolis* is not only a superb source on black Chicago in the 1940s, but perhaps also the best comprehensive description of black life in an American city ever written.

64 ELIJAH MUHAMMAD: Malcolm X with Alex Haley, *The Autobiography of Malcolm X* (Grove Press, 1966), and C. Eric Lincoln, *The Black Muslims in America* (Beacon Press, 1961), are the best books on the Muslims. In Lincoln's book, Chapter 1 gives the Muslims' early history; for a description of the Muslim theology, see *The Autobiography of Malcolm X*, pp. 164–168.

65 RICKETY THREE-STORY TENEMENTS: Wright, *12 Million Black Voices*, provides an especially vivid portrait of the worst of the South Side slums at that time, accompanied by photographs from the famous Farm Security Administration file.

POLICY: Drake and Cayton, *Black Metropolis*, Chapter 17, describes the South Side policy wheels in great detail. Drake and Cayton estimated that the policy business employed five thousand people in the 1940s.

JOBS CLOSED TO BLACKS: Interviews with Samuel Bernstein, James Bevel, Arthur Brazier, Philip Hauser, Louis Martin, and Richard Newhouse; also, Allan H. Spear, *Black Chicago: The Making of a Negro Ghetto, 1890–1920* (University of Chicago Press, 1967), p. 155.

QUOTATION FROM E. FRANKLIN FRAZIER: E. Franklin Frazier, *The Negro Family in the United States* (University of Chicago Press, 1966), p. 229.

67 "AND AS MOSES LIFTED UP THE SERPENT": John 3:14–16, Revised Standard Version.

LUTHER HAYNES: Except where noted, this and all subsequent details about his life come from interviews with him.

70 BLACK POPULATION OF CHICAGO: Hirsch, *Making the Second Ghetto*, p. 17.

2,200 PEOPLE A WEEK: Interview with Erwin France.

CARDINAL STRITCH AT THE ILLINOIS CENTRAL STATION: Interview with Nicholas Von Hoffman, who accompanied Stritch.

40 PER CENT ROMAN CATHOLIC: Felician O. Foy, editor, *The 1949 National Catholic Almanac* (Doubleday, 1949), p. 187. The almanac's figures change over the years, rising as high as 48 per cent for 1959, but 40 per cent seems to be the average for the postwar period.

71 1919 RIOT: Spear, *Black Chicago*, pp. 214–222; *The Negro in Chicago* also describes the riot in detail.

AIRPORT HOMES RIOT: Devereux Bowly, Jr., *The Poorhouse: Subsidized Housing in Chicago, 1895–1976* (Southern Illinois University Press, 1978), p. 50; Hirsch, *Making the Second Ghetto*, pp. 56–60, 76, 88–91.

QUOTATION FROM KALE WILLIAMS: Interview with Williams.

RACE AND THE DUMPING OF MAYOR KELLY: Interviews with Don Rose (a veteran liberal political consultant in Chicago) and Nicholas Von Hoffman; Mike Royko, *Boss: Richard J. Daley of Chicago* (New American Library, 1971), pp. 55–56; Martin Myerson and Edward Banfield, *Politics, Planning, and the Public Interest* (The Free Press, 1955), p. 129.

72 KELLY AND ROBERT WEAVER: Interview with Robert Weaver.

KELLY AND THE ICKES RULE: Myerson and Banfield, *Politics, Planning, and the Public Interest*, p. 124; Bowly, *The Poorhouse*, p. 27; interview with Devereux Bowly, Jr.

REAL ESTATE TRADE ASSOCIATION'S CODE OF ETHICS: Myerson and Banfield, *Politics, Planning, and the Public Interest*, p. 20.

FERNWOOD PARK RIOT: Bowly, *The Poorhouse*, p. 50; Myerson and Banfield, *Politics, Planning, and the Public Interest*, p. 127; Hirsch, *Making the Second Ghetto*, pp. 54–55.

Shelley v. *Kraemer*: Hirsch, p. 30; Bowly, *The Poorhouse*, p. 56; Myerson and Banfield, *Politics, Planning, and the Public Interest*, p. 22.

73 PARK MANOR RIOT: Hirsch, pp. 58–59.

ENGLEWOOD RIOT: Hirsch, p. 55. In addition to all the violent resistance to neighborhood integration in Chicago during the 1950s, there was a famous case in the Chicago suburbs as well. Morris Milgram, a liberal real estate developer, made plans to build an integrated subdivision in Deerfield, north of Chicago; the town fought him, not with rocks and bottles but with legal documents, and eventually succeeded in turning the land into a park and remaining segregated. Milgram's lawyer, by the way, was Willard Wirtz, soon to become secretary of labor. See Harry and David Rosen, "But Not Next Door" (Obolensky, 1962).

CONTROVERSY OVER HOUSING SITES: This is essentially the subject of Myerson and Banfield, *Politics, Planning, and the Public Interest*, which is the authoritative source on it. See also Bowly, *The Poorhouse*, pp. 77–80, and Hirsch, *Making the Second Ghetto*, pp. 223–228.

"IMPROVEMENT ASSOCIATION": Myerson and Banfield, *Politics, Planning, and the Public Interest*, p. 107.

BUZZERS ON TAVERN DOORS: Interview with Nicholas Von Hoffman.

CICERO RIOT: Hirsch, *Making the Second Ghetto*, pp. 53–55.

74 TRUMBULL PARK RIOT: Bowly, *The Poorhouse*, pp. 80–83; Hirsch, *Making the Second Ghetto*, p. 41.

WILLIAM DAWSON: Interviews with Devereux Bowly, Jr., Erwin France, Louis Martin, Don Rose, Kenneth Smith, and Nicholas Von Hoffman. There is some discussion of Dawson in James Q. Wilson, *Negro Politics: The Search for Leadership* (The Free Press, 1960); in Edward C. Banfield, *Political Influence* (The Free Press, 1961); in Drake and Cayton, *Black Metropolis*; in Royko, *Boss*; and in Myerson and Banfield, *Politics, Planning, and the Public Interest*.

75 DAWSON'S ADVISING KENNEDY'S STAFF NOT TO USE "CIVIL RIGHTS": Harris Wofford, oral history interview, Kennedy Library, p. 51.

"DAWSON USED TO SAY YOU LIVE AND DIE IN POLITICS": Interview with Erwin France.

76 DAWSON AND THE POLICY KINGS: Myerson and Banfield, *Politics, Planning, and the Public Interest*, p. 77.

QUOTATION FROM DAWSON: Myerson and Banfield, *Politics, Planning, and the Public Interest*, p. 79.

"SO THEY BUILT A LITTLE WOODEN CLOSED OFFICE": Wofford, oral history, p. 44.

QUOTATION FROM MIKE ROYKO: Royko, *Boss*, pp. 62–63.

77 DALEY'S LICENSE PLATE NUMBER: Eugene C. Kennedy, *Himself! The Life and Times of Mayor Richard J. Daley* (Viking, 1972), p. 2.

"JACK-LEG" PREACHERS: In Drake and Cayton, *Black Metropolis*, pp. 629–632, there is an unsympathetic account of the modus operandi of jack-leg preachers.

78 QUOTATION FROM RICHARD WRIGHT: Wright, *12 Million Black Voices*, p. 135.

79 AID TO DEPENDENT CHILDREN: James T. Patterson, *America's Struggle Against Poverty, 1900–1985* (Harvard University Press, 1986), is an authoritative source on this and most of the rest of the history of American social welfare policy.

MAN-IN-THE-HOUSE RULE: The rule was abolished by the Supreme Court in 1968, in its decision in the case of *King* v. *Smith*.

80 HEADQUARTERS OF THE CHICAGO BLUES: Rowe, *Chicago Breakdown*, p. 216, has

a map showing the location of the leading blues clubs in the 1950s. There are other books about the blues that are more felicitously written—for example, Robert Palmer, *Deep Blues* (Viking, 1981), but nobody can top Rowe for specific details about the blues in Chicago during their heyday.

CHESS BROTHERS: Rowe, *Chicago Breakdown*, p. 63.

81 RACIAL TRANSITION IN LAWNDALE: The Chicago Fact Book Consortium, *Local Community Fact Book Chicago Metropolitan Area* (Chicago Review Press, 1984), p. 80. In accordance with Chicago vernacular, I use "Lawndale" as the name for the neighborhood the *Local Community Fact Book* calls "North Lawndale."

PANIC-PEDDLERS: Interviews with Anthony Downs, John Egan, Edward Marciniak, and Kale Williams; Hirsch, *Making the Second Ghetto*, pp. 31–34.

82 LAWNDALE'S POPULATION'S GROWING: *Local Community Fact Book*, p. 80.

TWENTY-FOURTH WARD: David K. Fremon, *Chicago Politics Ward by Ward* (Indiana University Press, 1988), pp. 157–161; interviews with Samuel Bernstein, John McDermott, Don Rose, and Nicholas Von Hoffman.

83 GEORGE COLLINS AND CARDISS COLLINS: Interview with Don Rose.

HOWLIN' WOLF: Interview with Jim O'Neal (editor of *Living Blues* magazine); Rowe, *Chicago Breakdown*, pp. 134–139.

84 CONSTANCE HENRY: Except where noted, this and all subsequent details about her life come from interviews with her. (Ms. Henry now goes by her married name, Constance Daniels.)

85 "LISTEN, BABY": Letter from Lillian Henry to Charles Henry, undated, in family papers in the possession of Constance Daniels.

86 LILLIAN HENRY'S NOTEBOOK ENTRIES: In family papers.

87 "THIS BED IS SO LONESOME": Letter from Lillian Henry to Ferris Luckett, May 3, 1957, in family papers.

89 RICHARD DALEY: Interviews with Anthony Downs, Jack Egan, Erwin France, Edward Marciniak, Louis Martin, Don Rose, and David Stahl; Royko, *Boss*; Kennedy, *Himself!*; Milton Rakove, *Don't Make No Waves—Don't Back No Losers: An Insider's Analysis of the Daley Machine* (Indiana University Press, 1975); and Len O'Connor, *Clout—Mayor Daley and His City* (H. Regnery, 1975).

JAKE ARVEY NOT ALLOWED TO BE A CONVENTION DELEGATE: Interview with Don Rose.

90 DALEY'S LIMITING DAWSON'S POWER: Fremon, *Chicago Politics Ward by Ward*, p. 30; interview with Don Rose.

DALEY'S GREETING CITY WORKERS BY NAME AND CONSIDERING MINOR REQUESTS: Interview with David Stahl.

DALEY'S SUITS: Interview with David Stahl; Royko, *Boss*, p. 17.

ISAAC ROSENFELD: Isaac Rosenfeld, "Life in Chicago," *Commentary*, June 1957, pp. 523–534.

KENNEDY BROTHERS: During his 1968 presidential campaign, for example, Robert Kennedy expected to have Daley's support, although we now remember the two men as having exemplified the two warring camps in the Democratic Party. Interviews with Peter Edelman and Frank Mankiewicz; Arthur Schlesinger, Jr., *Robert Kennedy and His Times* (Ballantine Books, 1979), pp. 928–929.

DALEY'S BLACK SUBALTERNS: Royko, *Boss*, p. 147.

91 JESSE JACKSON: Royko, p. 26.

TEXTBOOK-WRITING SCANDAL: Interview with Francis Keppel.

"WILLIS WAGONS": Interviews with Edward Marciniak, John McDermott, Al Raby, and Kenneth Smith.

92   CHICAGO HOUSING AUTHORITY'S MASSIVE BUILDING PROGRAM: Bowly, *The Poorhouse*, p. 112.

LE CORBUSIER: Bowly, p. 64; Le Corbusier, *The Radiant City: Elements of a Doctrine of Urbanism to Be Used as the Basis of Our Machine-Age Civilization* (Orion Press, 1933).

HENRY HORNER HOMES: Bowly, pp. 112–114.

STATEWAY GARDENS: Bowly, p. 115.

CABRINI-GREEN: Bowly, pp. 116–118.

ROBERT TAYLOR HOMES: Bowly, pp. 124–129.

93   THE INTRICATE SYSTEM OF DEALS BY WHICH CHICAGO OPERATED: Interviews with Samuel Bernstein and Richard Newhouse.

94   THE BLACK ANTIMACHINE POLITICAL MOVEMENT: Interview with Don Rose.

1963 NAACP CONVENTION: Royko, *Boss*, p. 134.

DALEY'S LOSING THE WHITE VOTE IN 1963: Royko, p. 132.

DALEY'S SHORING UP HIS SUPPORT AMONG WHITES: Interviews with Edward Marciniak, Louis Martin, Don Rose, and David Stahl.

95   GATHERING PLACES FOR CLARKSDALIANS: Interviews with Jack Brinson, Oliver Clark, Leonard Henderson, and Edward James. The Bedford Hotel, 1310 West Jackson Boulevard, and the Crest Hotel, 1510 West Adams Street, both cheap places on the Near West Side catering to transients, were the first Chicago homes of many single men from Clarksdale.

CITIZENS COUNCIL OFFER OF FREE TRANSPORT TO CHICAGO: Interview with Ken Lawrence, a researcher who has devoted years to uncovering the activities of the organized white resistance in Mississippi; see also Neil R. McMillen, *The Citizens Council: Organized Resistance to the Second Reconstruction, 1954–64* (University of Illinois Press, 1971), pp. 229–234.

T. R. M. HOWARD AND THE EAGLE EYE: Interview with Taylor Cotton, Jr.; Seth Cagin and Phillip Dray, *We Are Not Afraid: The Story of Goodman, Schwerner, and Chaney and the Civil Rights Campaign for Mississippi* (Macmillan, 1988), p. 135.

BILBO'S BLACK CHILDREN: Interview with Uless Carter.

97   ALINSKY AND THE WOODLAWN ORGANIZATION: Interviews with Arthur Brazier, John Egan, Tracy O'Sullivan, Robert Squires, and Nicholas Von Hoffman; Sanford D. Horwitt, *Let Them Call Me Rebel: Saul Alinsky, His Life and Legacy* (Alfred A. Knopf, 1989), Chapter 23.

98   QUOTATION FROM NICHOLAS VON HOFFMAN: Interview with Von Hoffman.

99   ROBERT MOSES AND FRANKIE LYMON: Interview with Moses.

QUOTATION FROM ROBERT MOSES: Interview with Moses.

100   "FATHER, I THINK YOU SHOULD BE CAREFUL": Interview with John Egan.

"LOOK, GO SEE MY GUYS": Interview with Nicholas Von Hoffman.

101   SCHOOL BOYCOTT: Horwitt, *Let Them Call Me Rebel*, p. 406.

102   FOUNDING OF BLACKSTONE RANGERS: Interviews with Robert Squires and Nicholas Von Hoffman.

"WELL, TELL THEM": Interview with Nicholas Von Hoffman.

CHARLES SILBERMAN: Charles Silberman, *Crisis in Black and White* (Random House, 1967), pp. 318–350.

"IN MANY WAYS THE MOST IMPRESSIVE EXPERIMENT": *Fortune*, March 1962, p. 140.

103   SPIRITUALIST CHURCHES: Drake and Cayton, *Black Metropolis*, pp. 641–646, provide a skeptical description of the Spiritualist churches on the South Side.

106 "THE EARTH IS THE LORD'S": Psalms 24:1, Revised Standard Version.

"DREAM BOOKS": Drake and Cayton, *Black Metropolis*, p. 475.

4,400 APARTMENTS IN ROBERT TAYLOR HOMES, AND EARLY COMPLETION: Bowly, *The Poorhouse*, pp. 124–125.

107 THE HOLE: Interview with Constance Daniels.

QUOTATION FROM LARRY DANIELS: Interview with Larry Daniels.

WASHINGTON

111 JOHN F. KENNEDY AND THE JURY-TRIAL AMENDMENT: Hubert Humphrey, oral history interview, Johnson Library, Part I, p. 29; Wofford, oral history, p. 7.

112 QUOTATION FROM *Business Week*: "The Vicious Cycle of Poverty," *Business Week*, February 1, 1964, p. 38.

KENNEDY'S DEBT TO BLACK PUBLISHERS: Interview with Louis Martin; also, the Theodore Sorensen papers at the Kennedy Library contain some correspondence from the late 1950s between Sorensen, then the top staff member in Kennedy's Senate office, and black publishers.

SIMEON BOOKER'S COLUMN: Simeon Booker, oral history interview, Kennedy Library, p. 15.

113 "GOD, I HATE THAT": Peter Edelman, oral history interview, Kennedy Library, Part I, p. 21.

ROBERT KENNEDY'S ASKING LYNDON JOHNSON TO TURN DOWN THE VICE-PRESIDENTIAL NOMINATION IN 1960: Edwin O. Guthman and Jeffrey Shulman, editors, *Robert Kennedy in His Own Words: The Unpublished Recollections of the Kennedy Years* (Bantam Books, 1988), p. 22. This book consists of the oral history interviews Kennedy gave to the Kennedy Library and is a valuable direct look at his thinking.

"I THINK THOSE RUNNING FOR OFFICE": Guthman and Shulman, *Robert Kennedy in His Own Words*, p. 67.

QUOTATION FROM LOUIS MARTIN: Interview with Martin.

POWELL "ALWAYS EXACTS A PRICE": *Robert Kennedy in His Own Words*, p. 72.

POWELL'S ENDORSING EISENHOWER: Michael Harrington, *The Other America: Poverty in the United States* (Macmillan, 1962), p. 70.

114 POWELL'S OFFER TO SPEAK FOR KENNEDY IN THE SOUTH: Interview with John Siegenthaler.

MARTIN LUTHER KING AND NIXON: Martin Luther King, Jr., oral history interview, Kennedy Library, p. 12.

"SHRIVER WAS THE HOUSE COMMUNIST": Wofford, oral history, p. 98.

"THE DEFINITION OF GOOD AND BAD": Wofford, oral history, p. 7.

"HE GOT INTO THE ROOM": Wofford, oral history, p. 25. Wofford's memoir, *Of Kennedys and Kings: Making Sense of the Sixties* (Farrar, Straus & Giroux, 1980), also contains a detailed account of the Kennedy phone call.

115 "NOW YOU BOMB-THROWERS HAVE DONE TOO MUCH": Wofford, oral history, p. 26.

SHRIVER'S DRESSING-DOWN: Taylor Branch, *Parting the Waters: America in the King Years 1954–1963* (Simon & Schuster, 1988), p. 364.

VANDIVER AND ROBERT KENNEDY: Guthman and Shulman, *Robert Kennedy in His Own Words*, p. 70. The official version of the call to the judge can be found in Schlesinger, *Robert Kennedy and His Times*, pp. 234–235.

"HE DIDN'T QUITE HAVE THE EMOTIONAL COMMITMENT": King, oral history, p. 3.

"THE MORAL PASSION IS MISSING": Wofford, oral history, p. 63. Further evidence of Kennedy's caution on civil rights comes from interviews with Peter Edelman, Richard Goodwin, Nicholas Katzenbach, Francis Keppel, Robert Lampman, Hugh Sidey, Robert Weaver, and Harris Wofford; and from the Kennedy Library's oral history interviews with Berl Bernhard, Clarence Mitchell, and Joseph Rauh.

"HE WAS DRIVING VERY FAST": Wofford, oral history, p. 10.

116 "WOFFORD WAS VERY EMOTIONALLY INVOLVED": Guthman and Shulman, *Robert Kennedy in His Own Words*, p. 78.

ROBERT KENNEDY'S ISSUING THE HOUSING ORDER: Interview with Robert Weaver.

ROBERT KENNEDY'S ASKING KING TO POSTPONE THE FREEDOM RIDES: King, oral history, p. 24.

ROBERT KENNEDY'S OFFERING TAX BREAKS TO JAMES FARMER: James Farmer, oral history interview, Johnson Library, Part II, p. 19.

QUOTATION FROM FRANCIS KEPPEL: Francis Keppel, oral history interview, Kennedy Library, p. 15.

BEATING OF SIEGENTHALER: Interviews with Richard Goodwin and John Siegenthaler; Clarence Mitchell, oral history interview, Kennedy Library, p. 15.

ROSS BARNETT: Interview with Robert Weaver.

"I'M TOUGH": Adam Yarmolinsky, oral history interview, Johnson Library, p. 20.

"WEAK": Guthman and Shulman, *Robert Kennedy in His Own Words*, p. 159.

117 *The Affluent Society* AND RACE: John Kenneth Galbraith, *The Affluent Society* (Houghton Mifflin, 1958), p. 327.

DOUGLAS'S STUDY OF POVERTY: Interviews with Walter Heller and Robert Lampman; the study itself is Robert J. Lampman, "The Low Income Population and Economic Growth," for consideration by the Joint Economic Committee (Government Printing Office, 1959).

118 U.S. COMMISSION ON CIVIL RIGHTS: Interview with Harris Wofford; the report is *Report of the United States Commission on Civil Rights 1959* (Government Printing Office, 1959).

GLAZER AND MOYNIHAN: Interviews with Nathan Glazer and Daniel Patrick Moynihan; Nathan Glazer and Daniel Patrick Moynihan, *Beyond the Melting Pot: The Negroes, Puerto Ricans, Jews, Italians, and Irish of New York City* (MIT Press, 1970).

LEONARD DUHL AND THE SPACE CADETS: Interviews with Leonard Duhl and Lee Rainwater.

119 *The Urban Villagers:* Herbert J. Gans, *The Urban Villagers: Group and Class in the Life of Italian-Americans* (The Free Press, 1982).

QUOTATION FROM GANS: "The Failure of Urban Renewal," by Herbert J. Gans, *Commentary*, April 1965, p. 30.

Tally's Corner: Elliot Liebow, *Tally's Corner: A Study of Negro Street-Corner Men* (Little, Brown, 1967).

Behind Ghetto Walls: Lee Rainwater, *Behind Ghetto Walls: Black Families in a Federal Slum* (Penguin, 1973).

BIOGRAPHICAL INFORMATION AND QUOTATION FROM PAUL YLVISAKER: Interview with Ylvisaker.

THE FUND FOR THE REPUBLIC: Frank K. Kelly, *Court of Reason: Robert Hutchins and the Fund for the Republic* (The Free Press, 1981), pp. 63–76.

GRAY AREAS PROJECT IN NEW HAVEN: Interviews with Mitchell Sviridoff and Paul Ylvisaker; Peter Marris and Martin Rein, *Dilemmas of Social Reform: Poverty and Community Action in the United States* (Routledge and Kegan Paul, 1972), pp. 170–175.

120 MOBILIZATION FOR YOUTH: Interviews with Richard Cloward and Lloyd Ohlin. Daniel Patrick Moynihan, *Maximum Feasible Misunderstanding: Community Action in the War on Poverty* (The Free Press, 1970), pp. 38–60, contains an extremely skeptical account of the origins of Mobilization. On the war on poverty in general, see also Allen J. Matusow, *The Unraveling of America: A History of Liberalism in the 1960s* (Harper Torchbooks, 1986), which is only partly about the war on poverty but is nonetheless the most complete work by a historian on that under-covered subject; Frances Fox Piven and Richard Cloward, *Regulating the Poor: The Functions of Public Welfare* (Pantheon, 1971); Daniel Knapp and Kenneth Polk, *Scouting the War on Poverty: Social Reform Politics in the Kennedy Administration* (Heath Lexington Books, 1971); and James L. Sundquist, editor, *On Fighting Poverty* (Basic Books, 1969), especially Sundquist's own essay, "Origins of the War on Poverty."

ROBERT PARK AND ERNEST BURGESS: Interviews with Philip Hauser and Nicholas Von Hoffman.

CHICAGO NEIGHBORHOODS AND DELINQUENCY: This theory is laid out in Clifford R. Shaw, *Delinquency Areas: A Study of the Geographical Distribution of School Truants, Juvenile Delinquents, and Adult Offenders in Chicago* (University of Chicago Press, 1929).

121 JOSEPH LOHMAN: Interviews with Richard Boone, Richard Cloward, and Lloyd Ohlin.

QUOTATION FROM RICHARD BOONE: Interview with Boone.

Delinquency and Opportunity: Richard Cloward and Lloyd Ohlin, *Delinquency and Opportunity: A Theory of Delinquent Gangs* (The Free Press, 1960).

122 QUOTATION FROM RICHARD CLOWARD: Interview with Cloward.

QUOTATION FROM LEONARD COTTRELL: Marris and Rein, *Dilemmas of Social Reform*, p. 170. There is useful background information on Cottrell in Matusow, *The Unraveling of America*, pp. 112–119.

123 DAVID HACKETT: Interview with David Hackett; Schlesinger, *Robert Kennedy and His Times*, pp. 48–49, 440–448.

124 "WE WERE BOTH, IN A WAY, MISFITS": David Hackett, oral history interview, Kennedy Library, p. 4.

"NORMAL BEHAVIOR": Interview with David Hackett.

HACKETT'S MARGINALITY AT THE JUSTICE DEPARTMENT: Interviews with Nicholas Katzenbach, Anthony Lewis (who covered the Justice Department for *The New York Times*), Burke Marshall, and John Siegenthaler.

EUNICE SHRIVER'S INTEREST IN JUVENILE DELINQUENCY: Interview with Sargent Shriver.

125 QUOTATIONS FROM DAVID HACKETT: Interview with Hackett.

RICHARD BOONE: Interviews with Patrick Anderson, Hyman Bookbinder, Richard Boone, William Capron, Richard Cloward, Peter Edelman, Peter Goldmark, David Hackett, and Lloyd Ohlin; also, oral history interview with Christopher Weeks, Johnson Library.

ACTIVITIES OF PRESIDENT'S COMMITTEE ON JUVENILE DELINQUENCY: Interviews with Leonard Duhl and David Hackett; Hackett, oral history, Kennedy Library. There is some material on this also in the papers of Daniel Knapp and Richardson White, Jr., at the Kennedy Library.

126 "I'D BE A PARATROOPER": Interview with Hugh Sidey.

QUOTATION FROM DAVID HACKETT: Interview with Hackett.

ROBERT KENNEDY AND JAMES BALDWIN: Interviews with Kenneth Clark, Burke Marshall, and John Siegenthaler; Schlesinger, *Robert Kennedy and His Times*, pp. 355–359; Guthman and Shulman, *Robert Kennedy in His Own Words*, pp. 223–226.

127 JEROME SMITH: Interview with Donald Wendell, a fellow CORE member.

KENNEDY'S FIRST MEETING WITH SIEGENTHALER: Interview with John Siegenthaler.

KENNEDY AND RICHARD HARWOOD: Interviews with David Hackett and Harwood.

128 "MOST OF THE PROGRAMS IN ACTION": Memorandum from David Hackett to Robert Kennedy, August 5, 1963, Knapp papers, Kennedy Library.

"THE FEDERAL GOVERNMENT IS TERRIBLE": Interview with David Hackett.

"THE GUERRILLAS": Matusow, *The Unraveling of America*, p. 114.

"OPPORTUNITIES FOR CONFORMITY": Moynihan, *Maximum Feasible Misunderstanding*, p. 111.

HARYOU: Interviews with Kenneth Clark and David Hackett; Moynihan, *Maximum Feasible Misunderstanding*; Marris and Rein, *Dilemmas of Social Reform*; Matusow, *The Unraveling of America*; and the Office of Economic Opportunity's self-produced Administrative History, in the Johnson Library, all cover HARYOU.

129 "I WOULD GET RID OF SHULER": Robert Kennedy, handwritten note on a memorandum from David Hackett dated September 27, 1963, White papers, Kennedy Library.

"IN DREAMS BEGIN RESPONSIBILITIES": Delmore Schwartz, "In Dreams Begin Responsibilities" (New Directions, 1938).

LLOYD OHLIN'S BRIEFING THE KENNEDY BROTHERS: Interview with Ohlin.

WALTER HELLER'S BACKGROUND: Interview with Heller.

130 SOMETHING FOR POOR PEOPLE: Heller's papers at the Kennedy Library are the best primary source on the war on poverty during 1963, before it was given the name.

DWIGHT MACDONALD'S REVIEW: Dwight Macdonald, "Our Invisible Poor," *The New Yorker*, January 19, 1963, pp. 82–132.

131 KENNEDY'S READING MACDONALD'S ESSAY: Interviews with William Capron and Walter Heller.

MEMORANDA FROM HELLER TO KENNEDY AND LAMPMAN: Heller papers, Kennedy Library.

LAMPMAN'S DOUBTS: Interview with Robert Lampman.

LAMPMAN'S MEMORANDUM TO HELLER: Heller papers, Kennedy Library.

HELLER'S LUNCH AT THE WHITE HOUSE MESS: Interview with Walter Heller.

132 HELLER'S MEMORANDUM TO KENNEDY: Heller papers, Kennedy Library.

HELLER AND THE REPUBLICAN CHURCH WOMEN THEORY: Interviews with Myer Feldman, Walter Heller, and Theodore Sorensen.

CAPRON'S INTERAGENCY TASK FORCE: Interviews with William Cannon, William Capron, Walter Heller, Charles Schultze, and Theodore Sorensen; some material on the task force is in the Heller papers at the Kennedy Library.

133 QUOTATION FROM WALTER HELLER: Interview with Heller.

QUOTATION FROM WILLIAM CAPRON: Interview with Capron.

134 "I HEAR YOU'RE WORKING ON THE PROBLEM OF THE POOR": Interview with Walter Heller.

HELLER'S NOTES: Heller papers, Kennedy Library.

HELLER'S FINAL MEETING WITH KENNEDY: Interview with Walter Heller; Heller papers, Kennedy Library.

135 QUOTATION FROM THEODORE SORENSEN: Theodore Sorensen, oral history interview, Kennedy Library, p. 168.

"AN AMBER LIGHT TINTED GREEN": Interview with William Capron.

QUOTATION FROM WALTER HELLER: Interview with Heller.

LYNDON JOHNSON: On general issues of Johnson's character, interviews with Horace Busby, Joseph Califano, David Ginsburg, Arthur Goldschmidt, Richard Goodwin, Nicholas Katzenbach, Francis Keppel, Lawrence Levinson, Louis Martin, Harry McPherson, Bill Moyers, Hugh Sidey, and Elizabeth Wickenden; especially useful among the oral history interviews at the Johnson Library are the ones with Wilbur Cohen, Francis Keppel, and Christopher Weeks; and also interesting is a typescript by Katharine Graham describing a weekend visit to Johnson at his ranch in 1964.

136 "AN EFFORT TO SET UP A POLICE STATE": Merle Miller, *Lyndon: An Oral Biography* (G. P. Putnam's Sons, 1980), p. 118.

QUOTATION FROM HORACE BUSBY: Interview with Busby.

MARY MCLEOD BETHUNE: Interview with Harry McPherson.

MONEY TO BLACK COLLEGES: Interview with Horace Busby. The college was Prairie View A&M, and the governor was James Allred.

QUOTATION FROM HORACE BUSBY: Interview with Busby.

QUOTATION FROM DAVID GINSBURG: Interview with Ginsburg.

CAMPAIGN STOP IN CLEVELAND, TEXAS: Interview with Horace Busby.

QUOTATIONS FROM BILL MOYERS: Bill Moyers, "Second Thoughts," a speech delivered at Hofstra University, April 11, 1986, p. 9.

WOODROW WILSON: Interview with Bill Moyers.

138 QUOTATION FROM ROBERT WEAVER: Interview with Weaver.

QUOTATION FROM WILLARD WIRTZ: Interview with Wirtz.

"IT WAS A PRETTY BRUTAL BUSINESS": Jack Conway, oral history interview, Johnson Library, Part II, p. 69.

QUOTATION FROM LOUIS MARTIN: Louis Martin, oral history interview, Johnson Library, pp. 17–18.

139 QUOTATION FROM JOHNSON-SORENSEN CONVERSATION: "Edison Dictaphone Recording, LBJ – Sorensen, June 3, 1963," Theodore Sorensen papers, Kennedy Library, pp. 4–5.

140 QUOTATION FROM ROBERT KENNEDY: Guthman and Shulman, *Robert Kennedy in His Own Words*, p. 178.

HELLER'S NOTES: Heller papers, Kennedy Library.

141 "THAT'S MY KIND OF PROGRAM": Interview with Walter Heller.

HELLER'S NOTES: Heller papers, Kennedy Library.

QUOTATION FROM ARTHUR SCHLESINGER: Arthur Schlesinger, Jr., "A Eulogy: JFK," *Saturday Evening Post*, December 14, 1963, p. 32.

142 FRAMED PIECE OF NOTE PAPER: Arthur Schlesinger, Jr., *A Thousand Days: John F. Kennedy in the White House* (Fawcett, 1971), p. 923; interview with Peter Edelman.

QUOTATION FROM ELIZABETH WICKENDEN: Interview with Wickenden.

JOHNSON'S LETTER TO THE AMERICAN PUBLIC WELFARE ASSOCIATION: *New York Times*, December 5, 1963, in Heller papers, Kennedy Library.

143 QUOTATION FROM WALTER HELLER: Interview with Heller.

HACKETT'S PROPOSAL: Memorandum from David Hackett to Theodore Sorensen, December 3, 1963, Sorensen papers, Kennedy Library.

HELLER'S MEMORANDUM TO SORENSEN: Heller papers, Kennedy Library.

QUOTATION FROM WILLIAM CANNON: Interview with Cannon. Heller, in his interview with me, confirmed that Johnson was skeptical about community action.

144 QUOTATION FROM HORACE BUSBY: Interview with Busby.

BUSBY'S MEMO TO JOHNSON: Memorandum from Horace Busby to Johnson, December 30, 1963, Welfare files, Johnson Library.

WICKENDEN'S LETTER TO MYER FELDMAN: Letter from Elizabeth Wickenden to Feldman, January 4, 1964, Welfare files, Johnson Library. Sorensen's deputy's deputy was Lee White; his reply is dated January 14, 1964.

QUOTATION FROM HORACE BUSBY: Interview with Busby.

SORENSEN AS AUTHOR OF 1964 STATE OF THE UNION ADDRESS: Interview with Horace Busby; the early drafts of the address in the Johnson Library are signed with Sorensen's initials, TCS.

145 JOHNSON'S RESEARCH STUDY: Carl M. Brauer, "Kennedy, Johnson, and the War on Poverty," *Journal of American History*, June 1982, p. 118.

ECONOMIC REPORT OF THE PRESIDENT: 1964 Economic Report of the President (Government Printing Office, 1964), p. 17.

SARGENT SHRIVER: Interviews with Patrick Anderson, Richard Boone, William Cannon, William Capron, David Hackett, Frederick Hayes, Frank Mankiewicz, Louis Martin, Harry McPherson, Bill Moyers, Charles Peters, Sargent Shriver, Harris Wofford, Adam Yarmolinsky, and Paul Ylvisaker; oral history interviews with Jack Conway, William Phillips, Norbert Schlei, and Christopher Weeks, Johnson Library.

146 "WHAT BOBBY THINKS": Interview with Horace Busby.

MOYERS'S HOPING TO BE MADE PEACE CORPS DIRECTOR: Interview with Bill Moyers.

ROBERT KENNEDY'S WANTING THE ANTIPOVERTY JOB AND THE VICE-PRESIDENCY: Schlesinger, *Robert Kennedy and His Times*, pp. 689, 697–718.

SHRIVER'S VICE-PRESIDENTIAL AMBITIONS: Interview with Frank Mankiewicz; Moynihan, *Maximum Feasible Misunderstanding*, p. 82.

147 QUOTATION FROM SARGENT SHRIVER: Interview with Shriver.

CHEVROLET DIVISION OF GENERAL MOTORS: Jack Conway, oral history, Part I, pp. 9–10.

"NOT BIG ENOUGH!": Interview with Richard Boone.

"THE KENNEDYS KNOW WHEN TO QUIT": Interview with Adam Yarmolinsky.

"THE WHITE HOUSE HAS A PLAN": Interview with Sargent Shriver.

"IT'LL NEVER FLY": Interview with Adam Yarmolinsky.

148 GANDHI AND THE CHICAGO SCHOOL SYSTEM: Wofford, oral history, p. 4.

"WHO'S THAT? GET HIM IN": Interview with Frank Mankiewicz.

"A *big* BET WAS BEING MADE": Moynihan, *Maximum Feasible Misunderstanding*, p. 170.

149 QUOTATION FROM ADAM YARMOLINSKY: Interview with Yarmolinsky.

QUOTATION FROM FRANK MANKIEWICZ: Interview with Mankiewicz.

QUOTATION FROM LLOYD OHLIN: Interview with Ohlin.

ADDING ANOTHER ZERO: Interview with Paul Ylvisaker.

"YOU TELL SHRIVER, NO DOLES": Moyers, "Second Thoughts," p. 17.

LESTER THUROW: Interviews with Bill Moyers and Thurow.

150 QUOTATION FROM JOHN KENNETH GALBRAITH: Galbraith, *The Affluent Society,* pp. 325–326.

QUOTATION FROM OSCAR LEWIS: Oscar Lewis, *La Vida: A Puerto Rican Family in the Culture of Poverty—San Juan and New York* (Random House, 1966), pp. xliii, xlv. The initial statement of the culture of poverty thesis is in Lewis, *Five Families: Mexican Case Studies in the Culture of Poverty* (Basic Books, 1959).

LEWIS: *La Vida,* p. xlv.

151 OSCAR LEWIS'S PRESENCE AT SHRIVER'S MEETINGS: Interview with Robert Lampman.

MICHAEL HARRINGTON'S PRESENCE: Interview with Frank Mankiewicz.

QUOTATION FROM RICHARD BOONE: Interview with Boone.

"DICK BOONE WAS CAREFUL NOT TO RAISE WITH SHRIVER": Weeks, oral history, Part I, p. 18.

152 SVIRIDOFF'S PRESENCE AT MEETINGS: Interview with Mitchell Sviridoff.

"LADIES BOUNTIFUL": Interview with Adam Yarmolinsky.

MANKIEWICZ AND COMMUNITY ORGANIZING: Interview with Frank Mankiewicz.

NOT ENTIRELY SUCCESSFULLY: Interview with Charles Peters.

BOONE'S CLOSENESS TO ALINSKY: Interview with Richard Boone.

QUOTATION FROM WILLIAM CAPRON: Interview with Capron.

QUOTATIONS FROM RICHARD BOONE: Interviews with Boone.

THEORY ABOUT ROBERT KENNEDY, AND SHRIVER'S DENIAL: The chief proponents of this theory are William Cannon and David Hackett; Schlesinger accepts it in *Robert Kennedy and His Times.* Shriver denied it at length, and I think convincingly, in a letter to me dated September 2, 1988.

153 QUOTATION FROM SARGENT SHRIVER: Interview with Shriver.

QUOTATION FROM ADAM YARMOLINSKY: Yarmolinsky, oral history interview, Johnson Library, Part I, p. 11.

QUOTATION FROM ADAM YARMOLINSKY: Interview with Yarmolinsky.

154 MARRIAGE OF WIRTZ'S SON: Interview with William Cannon.

COST OF WIRTZ'S PROPOSALS: Interview with William Cannon.

WIRTZ AND THE CIGARETTE TAX: Interviews with Daniel Patrick Moynihan, Willard Wirtz, and Adam Yarmolinsky.

155 ORIGINS OF MOYNIHAN'S "ONE-THIRD OF A NATION" REPORT: Interviews with Daniel Patrick Moynihan. A biography of Moynihan, Douglas E. Schoen, *Pat: A Biography of Daniel Patrick Moynihan* (Harper & Row, 1979), is a useful general source on his career.

MOYNIHAN'S MISSING THE PRESS CONFERENCE: Interview with Paul Barton.

SHRIVER'S AIDES' OPINION OF MOYNIHAN: Interviews with William Cannon and Adam Yarmolinsky; Weeks, oral history, p. 41.

WIRTZ'S OPINION OF MOYNIHAN: Interviews with Paul Barton and Willard Wirtz; Schoen, *Pat,* pp. 88–90.

156 TALK IN WASHINGTON ABOUT RACIAL PROBLEMS OUTSIDE THE SOUTH: Burke Marshall, the assistant attorney general for civil rights under Robert Kennedy, was an especially strong proponent of this view.

QUOTATION FROM ADAM YARMOLINSKY: Interview with Yarmolinsky.

JAMES SUNQUIST AND W. R. POAGE: Interview with Sunquist.

WILBUR MILLS: Weeks, oral history, Part II, p. 16.

157 LAND REFORM: Interviews with William Cannon, Joseph Doherty, and James Sunquist.

QUOTATION FROM ADAM YARMOLINSKY: Adam Yarmolinsky, "Johnson's Anti-Poverty Program," unpublished manuscript, p. 23.

ECONOMIC OPPORTUNITY ACT DRAFTED IN JUSTICE DEPARTMENT: Interviews with Hyman Bookbinder, Richard Boone, and William Cannon. The office where it was drafted was that of Norbert Schlei, head of the department's Office of Legal Counsel.

158 QUOTATION FROM ELIZABETH WICKENDEN: Letter from Wickenden to Walter Jenkins, May 4, 1964, Bill Moyers papers, Johnson Library.

"THE PRESIDENT THINKS": Yarmolinsky, "Johnson's Anti-Poverty Program," p. 25.

"I SHOULD HAVE LISTENED TO WICKY": Interview with Elizabeth Wickenden.

BAYARD RUSTIN AND THE MARCH ON WASHINGTON: Interview with Rustin.

159 "WHAT ARE WE GOING TO DO WITH MARTIN NEXT?": Interview with Harris Wofford.

"THE KIDS": Interview with Bayard Rustin.

SHERMAN'S MARCH THROUGH GEORGIA: Conway, oral history, p. 81.

INTERNAL POLITICS OF SNCC: Interviews with John Lewis, Robert Moses, Kwame Ture, and Bob Zellner; see also Clayborne Carson, *In Struggle: SNCC and the Black Awakening of the 1960s* (Harvard University Press, 1981).

160 QUOTATION FROM JOHN LEWIS: Interview with Lewis.

HARRIS WOFFORD AT HOWARD LAW SCHOOL: Interview with Wofford.

161 QUOTATION FROM ROGER WILKINS: Roger Wilkins, *A Man's Life: An Autobiography* (Simon & Schuster, 1982), p. 184.

ILL WILL BETWEEN NAACP AND SNCC DURING FREEDOM SUMMER: Interviews with Aaron Henry; there are some allusions to this in Pigee, *The Struggle of Struggles, Part One*, pp. 69–78.

QUOTATION FROM BOB ZELLNER: Interview with Zellner.

162 MEDGAR EVERS OWNED A GUN: Interview with Robert Moses.

GUN IN KING'S ARMCHAIR: Bayard Rustin, oral history interview, Johnson Library, Part I, p. 17.

KENNETH CLARK, KING, AND MALCOLM X: Interview with Clark.

BALDWIN'S TELLING CLARK HIS MEETING WAS TAPED: Interview with Clark.

ADMINISTRATION OFFICIALS' ANNOYANCE AT CIVIL RIGHTS LEADERS: Interview with Nicholas Katzenbach.

QUOTATION FROM LOUIS MARTIN: Interview with Martin.

163 BALDWIN'S TELLING CLARK HIS MEETING WAS TAPED: Interview with Clark.

ADMINISTRATION OFFICIALS' ANNOYANCE AT CIVIL RIGHTS LEADERS: Interview with Nicholas Katzenbach.

QUOTATION FROM LOUIS MARTIN: Interview with Martin.

164 CONTROVERSY OVER MOBILIZATION FOR YOUTH: Interview with Richard Cloward; Moynihan, *Maximum Feasible Misunderstanding*, pp. 102–127.

165 QUOTATION FROM THEODORE MCKELDIN: Confidential letter from McKeldin to Lyndon Johnson, January 20, 1965, Marvin Watson papers, Johnson Library.

QUOTATION FROM CHARLES SCHULTZE: Memorandum from Schultze to Johnson, September 18, 1965, Welfare files, Johnson Library.

QUOTATION FROM HUBERT HUMPHREY: Memorandum from Humphrey to Johnson, December 2, 1965, Welfare files, Johnson Library.

QUOTATION FROM JOSEPH CALIFANO: Memorandum from Califano to Johnson, December 18, 1965, Welfare files, Johnson Library.

166 REPUTATION OF DALEY: Interviews with William Cannon and Adam Yarmolinsky.

QUOTATION FROM MYER FELDMAN: Myer Feldman, oral history interview, Kennedy Library, p. 298.

QUOTATION FROM ROBERT KENNEDY: Guthman and Shulman, *Robert Kennedy in His Own Words*, p. 208.

QUOTATION FROM WILLIAM CANNON: Interview with Cannon.

167 QUOTATION FROM FREDERICK HAYES: Interview with Hayes.

"WHAT IN THE HELL ARE YOU PEOPLE DOING?": Moyers, "Second Thoughts," pp. 19–20.

QUOTATION FROM BILL MOYERS: Interview with Moyers.

KENNETH O'DONNELL AND DALEY: Interview with Louis Martin.

SHRIVER'S POSSIBLE SENATE RACE: In the Marvin Watson papers at the Johnson Library there is a dossier on this subject.

JOHN CONNALLY'S COMPLAINTS ABOUT THE OEO: Interviews with Bill Moyers.

EDITH GREEN'S CRITICISM OF THE OEO: Edith Green, oral history interview, Johnson Library; Matusow, *The Unraveling of America*, pp. 265, 269.

QUOTATION FROM JOSEPH DOHERTY: Interview with Doherty.

WILBUR COHEN AND THE OEO: See, for example, his memoranda of December 26, 1963, to Theodore Sorensen (Sorensen papers, Kennedy Library); January 10, 1964, to Walter Heller and Kermit Gordon (Cohen papers, Johnson Library); March 9, 1968, to Johnson (Welfare files, Johnson Library); a memorandum from James Gaither to Joseph Califano regarding "HEW proposal for OEO reorganization," August 8, 1967 (James Gaither papers, Johnson Library); and a memorandum from Bill Moyers to Joseph Califano, August 5, 1966 (Welfare files, Johnson Library).

QUOTATION FROM DANIEL PATRICK MOYNIHAN: Interview with Moynihan.

168 NOTE FROM LLOYD CUTLER: Undated handwritten note from Cutler to Sargent Shriver (filed June 23, 1966), Moyers papers, Johnson Library.

POWELL'S BANNING OEO EMPLOYEES FROM HIS COMMITTEE'S OFFICES: William Phillips, oral history interview, Johnson Library, p. 68.

THE RESEARCH DIVISION AND THE EVALUATION DIVISION: Interviews with Peter Goldmark, William Haddad, and Frederick Hayes. Haddad ran the evaluation division, whose official name was the Office of Inspection; Sanford Kravitz ran the research division.

SHRIVER BOOED: *New York Times*, April 15, 1966, p. 1.

169 "TO SCORE A HUNDRED": Interview with Frederick Hayes.

JOB CORPS ENROLLEES' SLEEPING IN GYMNASIUMS: Weeks, oral history, Part I, p. 60.

QUOTATION FROM FREDERICK HAYES: Interview with Hayes.

HARYOU'S TROUBLES: OEO Administrative History, pp. 45–57, Johnson Library.

ALINSKY: Matusow, *The Unraveling of America*, p. 248.

OEO REPORT ON CHICAGO: Memorandum from Joseph Genovese to Director of Audits, OEO, May 13, 1965, Moyers papers, Johnson Library.

INCIDENTS OF VIOLENCE AT JOB CORPS CAMPS: OEO Administrative History, Johnson Library.

170 JOKE AMONG THE OEO'S LOBBYISTS: Phillips, oral history, Part I, p. 81.

ATHLETES AGAINST POVERTY: Interview with Patrick Anderson.

"LI'L ABNER": A series of sketches of Li'l Abner fighting poverty can be found in Box 26 of the Welfare files, Johnson Library.

QUOTATION FROM SARGENT SHRIVER: Memorandum from Shriver to Johnson, November 13, 1967, Welfare files, Johnson Library.

SHRIVER'S SUPPORT FOR A GUARANTEED INCOME, AND QUOTATION FROM SHRIVER: Interview with Shriver; also, interview with Robert Lampman, and Ben Heineman, oral history, Johnson Library, p. 29.

171 TALK ABOUT MOVING NORTH DURING THE SELMA CAMPAIGN: Interviews with James Bevel and John Lewis; David J. Garrow, *Bearing the Cross: Martin Luther King, Jr., and the Southern Christian Leadership Conference* (Morrow, 1986), p. 427.

172 STANLEY ELKINS: Interview with Elkins; the book is Stanley Elkins, *Slavery: A Problem in American Institutional and Intellectual Life* (University of Chicago Press, 1959). See also Ann J. Lane, editor, *The Debate Over Slavery: Stanley Elkins and His Critics* (University of Illinois Press, 1971).

GLAZER'S GIVING MOYNIHAN A COPY OF *Slavery*: Interview with Stanley Elkins.

173 QUOTATION FROM STANLEY ELKINS: Interview with Elkins.

WIRTZ'S TELLING JOHNSON THAT MOYNIHAN CAMPAIGNED FOR KENNEDY: Interview with Harry McPherson.

MOYNIHAN'S NOT TELLING WIRTZ ABOUT HIS POLITICAL AMBITIONS: Interview with Wirtz.

QUOTATION FROM PAUL BARTON: Interview with Barton.

E. FRANKLIN FRAZIER: See Frazier, *The Negro Family in the United States*.

KENNETH CLARK: See Kenneth B. Clark, *Dark Ghetto: Dilemmas of Social Power* (Harper & Row, 1965), Chapter 5.

174 "THE TANGLE OF PATHOLOGY": The entire Moynihan Report is reprinted in Lee Rainwater and William Yancey, *The Moynihan Report and the Politics of Controversy* (MIT Press, 1967), which in general is an authoritative source on the report.

"THE NUMBERS WENT BLOOEY ON ME": Interview with Daniel Patrick Moynihan. Paul Barton is my source for saying that work on the report was well under way before its authors were aware of the disaggregation of the unemployment rate and the opening of new welfare cases.

QUOTATION FROM WILLARD WIRTZ: Interview with Wirtz.

TWICE-A-DAY MAIL DELIVERY: Kermit Gordon made a similar proposal in his memorandum to Johnson of January 13, 1965, discussed on page 195 of the text.

RICHARD GOODWIN'S READING OF THE MOYNIHAN REPORT: Interview with Goodwin. Moynihan wrote the initial draft of the Howard speech, which Goodwin rewrote into the form in which Johnson delivered it. MOYNIHAN AND THE REPORT'S RELEASE: Interviews with Paul Barton, Richard Goodwin, and Willard Wirtz.

175 JOHN DOLLARD: Interview with Moynihan; see also Daniel Patrick Moynihan, "Remembering John Dollard," *The New York Times Book Review*, November 9, 1980, p. 1.

DESCRIPTION OF THE MOYNIHAN REPORT IN *The New York Times*: John D. Pomfret, "Drive for Negro Family Stability Spurred by White House Panel," *New York Times*, July 19, 1965, p. 1. An internal White House memorandum from Lee White to Bill Moyers, dated August 12, 1965 (Harry McPherson papers, Johnson Library), about the question of whether to make the report public makes it clear that the *Times* story (which had been joined, by then, by another story about the report in *Newsweek*) essentially made it impossible for the White House not to release the report.

QUOTATION FROM WILLARD WIRTZ: Interview with Wirtz.

EVANS AND NOVAK: Rainwater and Yancey, *The Moynihan Report and the Politics of Controversy*, pp. 375–377.

QUOTATION FROM RICHARD GOODWIN: Interview with Goodwin.

WILLIAM RYAN: Rainwater and Yancey, *The Moynihan Report and the Politics of Controversy*, pp. 197–199; the book is William Ryan, *Blaming the Victim* (Pantheon, 1971).

176 REACTION AGAINST THE MOYNIHAN REPORT BY BAYARD RUSTIN AND JAMES FARMER: Interviews with Farmer, Harry McPherson, and Rustin.

177 QUOTATION FROM JOYCE LADNER: Joyce Ladner, *tomorrow's tomorrow: The Black Woman* (Doubleday, 1971), p. 238.

"THE FAMILY IS A CREATURE OF SOCIETY": Andrew Billingsley, "Black Families and White Social Science," in *Journal of Social Issues*, Summer 1970, p. 130.

"ALL THE MAJOR INSTITUTIONS": Andrew Billingsley, *Black Families in White America* (Prentice-Hall, 1968), p. 157.

QUOTATION FROM BERL BERNHARD: Rainwater and Yancey, *The Moynihan Report and the Politics of Controversy*, p. 248.

QUOTATION FROM BOB ZELLNER: Interview with Zellner.

178 THE ANTI-SEMITIC STRAIN IN THE BLACK-POWER MOVEMENT: Jonathan Kaufman, *Broken Alliance: The Turbulent Times Between Blacks and Jews in America* (Scribner, 1988), has a great deal of information on this. Probably the crucial incident here was the New York teachers strike of 1968, which pitted the nationalist leadership of the black Ocean Hill–Brownsville ghetto against the mainly Jewish teachers and principals in their school district, and in which anti-Semitic flyers were circulated at one point. Another famous incident in New York was the publication in 1967 of the catalogue for the Metropolitan Museum of Art's exhibition "Harlem on My Mind: Cultural Capital of Black America 1900–1968," which contained an essay by a Harlem high school senior named Candice Van Ellison that said, "Our contempt for the Jew makes us feel more completely American in sharing a national prejudice." Also, SNCC embraced the Palestinian cause in the late 1960s — and many of the whites kicked out of SNCC were Jewish (as, for that matter, were many of the whites involved in the civil rights movement generally).

THE EXPERIENCE OF EDWARD BANFIELD: Interview with Banfield; the book is Edward C. Banfield, *The Unheavenly City: The Nature and the Future of Our Urban Crisis* (Little, Brown, 1970).

179 "WOULD THEY HAVE PREFERRED A WATTS?": OEO Administrative History, Johnson Library, p. 48.

QUOTATION FROM KWAME TURE: Interview with Ture.

QUOTATION FROM BOB MOSES: Interview with Moses.

180 IF THERE HAD BEEN NO BLACK-POWER MOVEMENT: Interviews and correspondence with Frederick Hayes.

ORIGINS OF THE BLACK PANTHER PARTY: Bobby Seale, *Seize the Time: The Story of the Black Panther Party and Huey P. Newton* (Random House, 1970), pp. 13–69.

LEROI JONES: Matusow, *The Unraveling of America*, p. 259.

POWELL'S RENOUNCING THE USE OF "NEGRO": Memorandum from Louis Martin to Harry McPherson, September 7, 1966, McPherson papers, Johnson Library.

KWAME TURE'S JOB OFFER: Interview with Ture.

181 INTERNAL MEMO TRAFFIC: This is available at the National Archives, in the files of the OEO's Office of Inspection.

"IF MY HEAD WERE STICKING ON A PIKE": Letter from Daniel Patrick Moynihan to Harry McPherson, September 22, 1966, McPherson papers, Johnson Library, p. 5.

MOYNIHAN AND FAMILY ALLOWANCES: "The Case for a Family Allowance," reprinted transcript of Moynihan's testimony before the Senate Government Operations Committee, *New York Times Magazine*, February 5, 1967, p. 13.

"OBVIOUSLY ONE CAN NO LONGER ADDRESS": Letter from Moynihan to McPherson, September 22, 1966, McPherson papers, Johnson Library, p. 3.

MOYNIHAN'S BOOK ON THE BLACK FAMILY: "Random House will publish his forthcoming book on the Negro family some time in 1967," says *Commentary* in its author's identification of Moynihan in the February 1967 issue, p. 31.

MOYNIHAN'S ARTICLE FOR *Commentary*: Daniel P. Moynihan, "The President & the Negro: The Moment Lost," *Commentary*, February 1967, pp. 31–45.

182 "I DON'T KNOW WHAT WAS IN THERE": Interview with Bill Moyers.

"LOOK AT THE *strength* IN THAT FACE!": Interview with Hugh Sidey.

JOHNSON ON SUNDAY AT CAMP DAVID: Interview with Nicholas Katzenbach.

"GET THOSE COONSKINS UP ON THE WALL": Keppel, oral history, p. 7; Weeks, oral history, Part I, p. 71.

183 FOUR THOUSAND SOUTHERN SCHOOL DISTRICTS: Keppel, oral history, p. 19; interview with Keppel.

"WELL, CAN'T YOU GET ANOTHER ONE OR TWO": Cohen, oral history, Part III, p. 17.

"EVERY DAY WHILE I'M IN OFFICE": Cohen, oral history, Part III, p. 16.

"I WILL PROBABLY LOSE A MILLION VOTES A MONTH": Interview with Francis Keppel.

"I THINK WE JUST GAVE THE SOUTH TO THE REPUBLICANS": Interview with Bill Moyers.

184 QUOTATION FROM HARRY MCPHERSON: Memorandum from McPherson to Johnson, June 24, 1965, McPherson papers, Johnson Library.

"THAT BOY RODE AROUND THIS TOWN IN A MAROON CONVERTIBLE!": Interview with Bill Moyers. Patrick Anderson, a staff member of the President's Council on Juvenile Delinquency in the early 1960s and another Texan of modest origins, vividly remembers Kennedy riding around town in a powder-blue convertible. Whatever color the convertible was, it certainly made an impression.

"THE PRESIDENT" AND "JOHNSON": These references appear throughout Guthman and Shulman, *Robert Kennedy in His Own Words*.

185 "PEN USED TO SIGN": The picture with this inscription hangs in John Doar's law office in New York City.

JOHNSON'S SERVANTS: Interviews with James Farmer, Harry McPherson, and Bill Moyers.

"I WAS SITTING IN THE TOILET": Martin, oral history, p. 26.

"ALL THEY EVER HEAR AT ELECTION TIME": The official text, which can be found in Public Papers of the Presidents, Lyndon Johnson, 1963–64 (Office of the Federal Register, 1965), pp. 1281–1288, says "Negro, Negro, Negro," but Horace Busby, who was there, says he really said, "nigger, nigger, nigger."

JOHNSON'S USING THE WORD "NIGGER" IN PRIVATE: Interviews with Arthur Goldschmidt and Hugh Sidey; Nicholas Katzenbach, in his interview with me, remembered hearing Johnson call black employees at his ranch "boy." See also

Richard Goodwin, *Remembering America: A Voice from the Sixties* (Little, Brown, 1988), p. 395.

"THE CROWN PRINCE OF THE VIETNIKS": Memorandum from Harry McPherson to Johnson, April 4, 1967, McPherson papers, Johnson Library.

"INFORMALLY AND QUIETLY": Memorandum from Nicholas Katzenbach to Harry McPherson, September 17, 1966, McPherson papers, Johnson Library.

"THERE IS NO LONGER ANY NEED": Memorandum from Harry McPherson to Johnson, September 12, 1966, McPherson papers, Johnson Library.

186 "VOTE POWER": Interview with Bill Moyers.

QUOTATION FROM LOUIS MARTIN: Interview with Martin.

"IF THEY GIVE BLACKS THE VOTE": Interview with Elizabeth Wickenden.

"IT'S TOO BAD": Interview with Arthur Goldschmidt.

QUOTATION FROM ROBERT KENNEDY: Schlesinger, *Robert Kennedy and His Times*, p. 681.

APPOINTMENT OF HENRY FOWLER: Interview with Burke Marshall.

ROBERT WOOD'S TELEGRAM FROM JOHNSON: Interview with Wood.

TASK FORCE ON URBAN AFFAIRS: Interview with Wood. As Wood tells the story, when the list of the task force's members was published, Johnson, who was nearly fanatical about the secrecy of appointments, even minor ones, called Wood from his Texas ranch to chew him out; Wood pointed out that the dateline on the news stories containing the list was Austin, and Johnson quickly got off the phone.

187 QUOTATION FROM WILLIAM LEUCHTENBERG: Letter from Leuchtenberg to Joseph Califano, July 6, 1966, Welfare files, Johnson Library.

QUOTATION FROM ROBERT EISNER: Letter from Eisner to Joseph Califano, July 25, 1966, Welfare files, Johnson Library.

QUOTATION FROM ROBERT WOOD: Interview with Wood.

QUOTATION FROM VICTOR PALMIERI: Interview with Palmieri.

188 JOHNSON'S BELIEVING KENNEDY WOULD ATTACK HIM FROM THE RIGHT ON VIETNAM: Interview with Horace Busby.

QUOTATION FROM ROBERT WOOD: Interview with Wood.

"BOBBY IS AN EMOTIONAL FELLOW": Memorandum from James Rowe to Johnson, January 16, 1968, Marvin Watson papers, Johnson Library.

"HE IS AN ARROGANT LITTLE *schmuck*": Memorandum from John P. Roche to Johnson, January 26, 1968, Watson papers, Johnson Library.

JOHNSON AND KENNEDY'S MEMORIAL: Memorandum from Daniel Patrick Moynihan to Richard Nixon, February 1, 1969, President's Handwriting file, Nixon Presidential Materials Project.

"SHRIVER'S GROUP": Interview with Bill Moyers.

QUOTATION FROM HARRY MCPHERSON: Memorandum from McPherson to Joseph Califano, July 19, 1967, McPherson papers, Johnson Library. There is one more intriguing sentence that follows the passage quoted: "Just remember A.H.N.I.A.L.N. and it always will be with them so watch it and try to talk about something else when you have to." What do the initials stand for? McPherson says he can't remember.

189 QUOTATION FROM JOSEPH CALIFANO: Memorandum from Califano to Johnson, June 27, 1967, James Gaither papers, Johnson Library. Johnson's interest in things being named after him was very familiar to his aides; in fact Johnson was well known to hope that people working for him who had male babies would consider the name Lyndon.

PERMISSION FOR A FIVE-MINUTE SPEECH: Memorandum from Joseph Califano to Johnson, February 13, 1967. Califano's caution on the subject can be conveyed by a brief quotation from the memo: "I have told Sarge that I was not sure I could make it. I have no strong feeling either way. Do you want me to speak?"

"THEY'RE NOT AGAINST POVERTY": Interview with Bill Moyers.

"START KEEPING A FILE": Handwritten note from Johnson to Marvin Watson, Watson papers, Johnson Library. In the file that Watson started keeping is a 1961 memo from the commissioner of the Internal Revenue Service about Robert Kennedy's plans to tap the phones of suspected racketeers — information Watson (and Johnson) must have considered leaking in order to make Kennedy look like a trampler of civil liberties.

JOHNSON'S REMARKS TO WILBUR COHEN: Cohen, oral history, Part III, p. 10.

THE CANDIDACY FOR THE NUMBER-TWO JOB AT HEW: Cohen, oral history, Part III, p. 11; the candidate was Bertrand Harding, and the Texas crony was James McCrocklin.

WORK ON BEAUTIFYING PARK OPPOSITE JOHNSON'S RANCH: Letter from Bertrand Harding to Johnson, June 26, 1968, Watson papers, Johnson Library. Johnson wrote on top of the letter, "Put on my desk," and in the margin put down queries about such matters as how many bluebonnet seeds would be planted along the LBJ Trail.

QUOTATION FROM JOSEPH CALIFANO: Memorandum from Califano to Johnson, December 4, 1967, Welfare files, Johnson Library.

THE IDEA OF THE GREAT SOCIETY: Memorandum from "GER" (George Reedy) to "Juanita," September 13, 1968.

190 JOHNSON'S WATCHING *Seven Days in May*: Interview with Horace Busby.

"CURRENT RACIAL DEVELOPMENTS": Many of these reports can be found in the Watson papers, Johnson Library.

"THE FBI ALWAYS KNEW": "Papers of Katharine Graham," Johnson Library, p. 20A.

SHRIVER'S REASSURING JOHNSON: Memorandum from Sargent Shriver to Johnson, September 12, 1967, Welfare files, Johnson Library.

QUOTATION FROM DAVID GINSBURG: Interview with Ginsburg.

SCHULTZE'S SLIPPING MONEY TO THE KERNER COMMISSION: Interview with Schultze; see also Schultze's memorandum to Johnson of January 25, 1968, Califano papers, Johnson Library.

191 THE KERNER REPORT: Interviews with Anthony Downs, David Ginsburg, Peter Goldmark, and Victor Palmieri.

"I JUST CAN'T SIGN": Memorandum from Harry McPherson to Johnson with attached notation of Johnson's response, March 13, 1968, Confidential File, Johnson Library.

CALIFANO'S MEMO TO JOHNSON: Memorandum from Joseph Califano to Johnson, April 10, 1968, Confidential File, Johnson Library.

192 SHRIVER'S APPOINTMENT AS AMBASSADOR TO FRANCE: Interview with Horace Busby.

QUOTATION FROM FRED HAYES: Interview with Hayes.

QUOTATION FROM SARGENT SHRIVER: Interview with Shriver.

193 QUOTATION FROM ROBERT KENNEDY: Guthman and Shulman, *Robert Kennedy in His Own Words*, p. 204.

QUOTATION FROM PETER EDELMAN: Edelman, oral history, Part I, p. 98.

"BECAUSE PEOPLE LIKE YOU ARE ASKING ME TO": Interview with John Siegenthaler.

194 KENNEDY AND HOMOSEXUALS: Edelman, oral history, Part VIII, p. 54.

"WHAT'S A REPERTORY COMPANY?": Mankiewicz, oral history, p. 39.

KENNEDY'S LEGISLATIVE AGENDA: Interviews with Peter Edelman and Adam Walinsky.

195 QUOTATION FROM PETER EDELMAN: Interview with Edelman.

KERMIT GORDON'S MEMO TO JOHNSON: Memorandum from Gordon to Johnson, January 13, 1965, Moyers papers, Johnson Library. The theory about the memo's signals for Johnson to turn the proposal down comes from William Capron, to whom I sent the memo for bureaucratic deciphering.

196 QUOTATION FROM PAT BROWN: *New York Times*, December 29, 1966, p. 14, quoted in Matusow, *The Unraveling of America*, p. 214.

"YOU SEE, THESE PEOPLE": Interview with Bill Moyers.

QUOTATION FROM BEN WATTENBERG: Memorandum from Wattenberg to Johnson, November 21, 1967, Watson papers, Johnson Library.

QUOTATION FROM FRANCIS KEPPEL: Interview with Keppel.

QUOTATIONS FROM WILBUR COHEN: Cohen, oral history, Part IV, pp. 9–11.

197 QUOTATION FROM FRANCIS KEPPEL: Interview with Keppel.

HAROLD HOWE STRIPPED OF HIS RESPONSIBILITIES: Interview with Howe.

QUOTATION FROM ROBERT WEAVER: Memorandum from Weaver to Johnson, May 22, 1966, Legislative Background Model Cities papers, Johnson Library.

"I THINK YOU WILL HAVE TO OVERCOME": Memorandum from Henry H. Wilson, Jr., to Johnson, May 30, 1966, Legislative Background Model Cities files, Johnson Library.

DEBATE WITH EUGENE MCCARTHY: Interview with McCarthy; Schlesinger, *Robert Kennedy and His Times*, p. 979.

KENNEDY'S COUNTING ON MAYOR DALEY'S SUPPORT: Interview with Frank Mankiewicz.

198 BEDFORD-STUYVESANT PROJECT'S FAILING TO CREATE JOBS: Interview with John Doar.

"I FEEL THAT THE COMMUNITY ACTION PROGRAM": Memorandum from Fred Bohen to Joseph Califano, May 6, 1968, Gaither papers, Johnson Library.

QUOTATION FROM ROBERT WEAVER: Memorandum from Weaver to Johnson, May 22, 1966, Legislative Background Model Cities files, Johnson Library.

QUOTATION FROM A YOUNG INTELLECTUAL: Charles M. Haar, "Thinking the Unthinkable About Our Cities: A Scenario in Four Parts," Califano papers, Johnson Library, p. 11.

199 QUOTATION FROM VERNON JORDAN: Interview with Jordan.

200 REBELLION OF WOMEN IN SNCC: The leading rebels were Mary King and Casey Hayden; see King, *Freedom Song: A Personal Story of the 1960s Civil Rights Movement* (Morrow, 1987), Chapter 12.

201 THE GREAT SOCIETY AS A GENERATOR OF JOBS FOR BLACKS: Michael K. Brown and Steven P. Erie, "Blacks and the Legacy of the Great Society: The Economic and Political Impact of Federal Social Policy," *Public Policy*, Volume 29, Number 3 (Summer 1981), pp. 299–330. On the reduction of poverty during the Great Society in general, see John E. Schwarz, *America's Hidden Success: A Reassessment of Public Policy from Kennedy to Reagan* (Norton, 1988).

PERCENTAGE OF BLACKS EMPLOYED BY GOVERNMENT: Bernard E. Anderson, "Economic Patterns in Black America," in National Urban League, "State of Black America 1982," p. 7.

DROP IN BIG-CITY MANUFACTURING EMPLOYMENT: Daniel Patrick Moynihan, "Employment, Income, and the Ordeal of the Negro Family," *Daedalus*, Fall 1965, p. 753.

202 SCHULTZE'S URGING JOHNSON TO THINK OF THE OEO AS A JOBS PROGRAM: See, for example, Schultze's memoranda to Johnson of September 18 and November 6, 1965, Welfare files, Johnson Library.

"WELFARE COLONIALISM": Stokely Carmichael and Charles V. Hamilton, *Black Power: The Politics of Liberation in America* (Random House, 1967), p. 183.

"I HAVE BEEN AN ACTIVE DEMOCRAT": Memorandum from Daniel Patrick Moynihan to H. R. Haldeman, October 1, 1969, Haldeman papers, Nixon Project.

203 QUOTATION FROM VERNON JORDAN: Interview with Jordan.

QUOTATION FROM JAMES FARMER: Interview with Farmer.

A PROTÉGÉ OF STROM THURMOND: His name is Harry Dent. For a complete description of these machinations, see Lewis Chester, Godfrey Hodgson, and Bruce Page, *An American Melodrama: The Presidential Campaign of 1968* (Viking, 1969).

NIXON'S PERCENTAGE OF BLACK VOTES: Memorandum from Moynihan to Nixon, March 19, 1969, Oversize Federal Government files, Nixon Project, p. 1.

"30% WHO ARE POTENTIALLY ON OUR SIDE": Handwritten comment by Nixon on a memorandum from Moynihan, January 16, 1970, President's Handwriting file, Nixon Project.

QUOTATION FROM JOHN EHRLICHMAN: Interview with Ehrlichman.

204 QUOTATION FROM JOHN EHRLICHMAN: Interview with Ehrlichman. Ehrlichman also discusses Nixon's views about black intelligence in his book *Witness to Power: The Nixon Years* (Simon & Schuster, 1982), p. 223.

QUOTATION FROM DANIEL PATRICK MOYNIHAN: Letter from Moynihan to Harry McPherson, April 15, 1966, McPherson papers, Johnson Library.

"THE COMPLETE DECADENCE": Handwritten comment by Nixon on a memorandum from Moynihan, January 16, 1970, President's Handwriting file, Nixon Project. Nixon's comment provides the answer to the rhetorical question Tom Wolfe raised in *Radical Chic and Mau-Mauing the Flak Catchers* (Farrar, Straus & Giroux, 1970), p. 92: "Couldn't you just see Nixon sitting in the Oval Room and clucking and fuming and muttering things like 'rich snob bums' as he read [about Leonard Bernstein's party]?"

"EVEN SO, I'M STICKING HERE": Memorandum from Moynihan to Nixon, May 9, 1970, President's Handwriting file, Nixon Project.

MOYNIHAN'S TEN-YEAR-OLD SON: Memorandum from Moynihan to Nixon, December 2, 1970, President's Handwriting file, Nixon Project.

205 "YOUR TASK, THEN, IS CLEAR": Memorandum from Moynihan to Nixon, January 3, 1969, quoted by Moynihan in a memo to John Ehrlichman and H. R. Haldeman, July 24, 1970, Ehrlichman papers, Nixon Project, p. 8.

"*To be blunt*": Memorandum from Moynihan to Nixon, August 4, 1970, President's Handwriting file, Nixon Project, p. 4.

"HE'S SO STIMULATING": John Ehrlichman, notes of a meeting with Nixon, August 11, 1972, Ehrlichman papers, Nixon Project.

A CONSTITUTIONAL CONVENTION: Memorandum from Moynihan to Nixon, July 17, 1969, President's Handwriting file, Nixon Project. ("The risks are great. So are the possibilities," Moynihan wrote, displaying a keen understanding of Nixon's self-concept as a political leader.)

A NIXON ARCHITECTURAL POLICY: Memorandum from Moynihan to Nixon, June 21, 1969, President's Handwriting file, Nixon Project.

DEPARTMENT OF HIGHER EDUCATION AND RESEARCH: Memorandum from Moynihan to Nixon, December 17, 1969, President's Handwriting file, Nixon Project, p. 4.

FEMINISM AS A MAJOR SOCIAL FORCE: Memorandum from Moynihan to Nixon, August 11, 1970, President's Handwriting file, Nixon Project.

A SERIES OF URBAN FISCAL CRISES: Memorandum from Moynihan to Nixon, November 30, 1970, President's Handwriting file, Nixon Project, p. 2..

OTHER DISTINGUISHED FIGURES: Memorandum from Moynihan to Nixon, January 3, 1969, quoted in Moynihan's memo to Ehrlichman and Haldeman, July 24, 1970, p. 6 (Lincoln, Roosevelt, and Wilson); letter from Moynihan to Nixon, November 23, 1971, President's Handwriting file, Nixon Project, pp. 3–4 (Churchill).

"IT IS REASSURING TO HAVE A TRUE INTELLECTUAL": Handwritten note by Nixon on a memorandum from Moynihan, June 20, 1969, President's Handwriting file, Nixon Project.

"YOU BELONG IN THE EXCITING THINGS": John Ehrlichman's notes of a meeting with Nixon, Moynihan, and Haldeman, October 8, 1969, Ehrlichman papers, Nixon Project.

"YOUR GREAT INAUGURAL ADDRESS": Memorandum from Moynihan to Nixon, June 19, 1970, p. 3, President's Handwriting file, Nixon Project.

"YOUR BRILLIANT FIRST YEAR IN OFFICE": Letter from Moynihan to Nixon, March 8, 1971, President's Handwriting file, Nixon Project, p. 2.

"WHAT YOU HAVE DONE FOR RACIAL EQUALITY": Memorandum from Moynihan to Nixon, June 30, 1970, President's Handwriting file, Nixon Project, p. 2.

"NEW FEDERALISM": Memorandum from Moynihan to Nixon, September 18, 1969, President's Handwriting file, Nixon Project.

206 PATRICK BUCHANAN'S MEMO: A. Waldron, "Critique of the Welfare Program," July 1, 1968, with handwritten notes by Nixon and a covering memorandum by Buchanan, personal papers of Martin Anderson.

"NO INCREASE IN ANY POVERTY PROGRAM": Handwritten comment by Nixon on a memorandum from John Ehrlichman, March 19, 1969, President's Handwriting file, Nixon Project.

"I WANT IMMEDIATE ACTION": Handwritten comment by Nixon on a list of the presidential appointees at the Office of Economic Opportunity, March 23, 1969, President's Handwriting file, Nixon Project.

"WAIT TILL THE OEO TYPES GET TO ME!": Memorandum from Moynihan to Nixon, January 31, 1969, President's Handwriting file, Nixon Project.

"AVOID, AT WHATEVER IMMEDIATE COSTS": Memorandum from Moynihan to Nixon, February 20, 1969, President's Handwriting file, Nixon Project.

NEW INTRODUCTION TO *Maximum Feasible Misunderstanding*: Moynihan, *Maximum Feasible Misunderstanding*, p. ix.

207 QUOTATION FROM EDWARD BANFIELD: Interview with Banfield.

RESTORING FUNDS FOR ROBERT KENNEDY'S MEMORIAL: Memorandum from Moynihan to Nixon, February 1, 1969, President's Handwriting file, Nixon Project.

DUBOIS'S WIDOW: Memorandum from Moynihan to Nixon, May 12, 1970, President's Handwriting file, Nixon Project.

QUOTATION FROM RICHARD NATHAN: Interview with Nathan.

QUOTATIONS FROM TASK FORCE REPORT ON WELFARE POLICY: Report of the

Task Force on Public Welfare, Transitional Task Force Reports file, Nixon Project, pp. 15, 24, 29. Edward Banfield headed a task force on urban affairs whose report is much more conservative.

208 "VERY BAD ADVICE '60 TO IKE": John Ehrlichman, notes of a meeting with Nixon, Moynihan, and Haldeman, October 8, 1969, Ehrlichman papers, Nixon Project.

QUOTATION FROM LEONARD GARMENT: Interview with Garment.

EXECUTIVE ORDERS DECLARING MARTIAL LAW: Interview with John Ehrlichman.

"DISGRACEFUL IN PAST 100 YEARS": John Ehrlichman, notes of a meeting with Nixon and a group of other officials, April 21, 1971, Ehrlichman papers, Nixon Project.

"THEY EXPLOITED THEM": John Ehrlichman, notes of a meeting with Nixon (interrupted so that Nixon could take a phone call from Reagan), February 12, 1972, Ehrlichman papers, Nixon Project.

"DON'T LET THE FEDERAL GOVERNMENT BE HEROIC": Ehrlichman, notes of meeting, April 21, 1971, Ehrlichman papers, Nixon Project.

QUOTATIONS FROM HALDEMAN ON DESEGREGATION: Memorandum from Haldeman to Nixon, August 4, 1970, President's Handwriting file, Nixon Project.

209 "THE TIME MAY HAVE COME": Memorandum from Moynihan to Nixon, January 16, 1970, President's Handwriting file, Nixon Project, p. 7.

LEON PANETTA AND JAMES ALLEN: Interviews with John Ehrlichman and Stanley Pottinger; Panetta tells the story of his time in the Nixon administration in Leon E. Panetta and Peter Gall, *Bring Us Together: The Nixon Team and the Civil Rights Retreat* (Lippincott, 1971).

"SUBURBAN INTEGRATION": Memorandum from Ehrlichman to Nixon, President's Handwriting file, Nixon Project.

REPUBLICAN NATIONAL COMMITTEE'S FAKED LETTERS: These are in the files of the RNC at the Nixon Project, and there is no indication of whether or not they were ever sent.

"BLACK PROBLEM": Ehrlichman, notes of a meeting with Nixon and James T. Lynn, November 28, 1972, Ehrlichman papers, Nixon Project.

210 "IS DE FACTO SEGREGATION OK": Handwritten note by Nixon on memorandum from Patrick J. Buchanan, January 30, 1970, President's Handwriting file, Nixon Project.

"NO GOOD POLITICS": John Ehrlichman's notes of a meeting with Nixon, March 19, 1970, Ehrlichman papers, Nixon Project.

QUOTATION FROM JOHN EHRLICHMAN: Interview with Ehrlichman.

QUOTATION FROM RICHARD NATHAN: Interview with Nathan.

211 JOHNSON'S TASK FORCE: The task force's report is at the Johnson Library, in the collection of reports from the many secret task forces Johnson set up.

MOYNIHAN'S TASK FORCE: It was run by John R. Price, an assistant to Moynihan, and its records are in the papers of Egil Krogh at the Nixon Project.

MOYNIHAN'S DENIAL: Interview with Moynihan. "I never went anywhere *near* that discussion. They never went to the cities for welfare," he told me.

"NO MORE WILL POOR PERSONS": Moynihan, *The Politics of a Guaranteed Income: The Nixon Administration and the Family Assistance Plan* (Random House, 1973), p. 162.

NIXON'S FIRST SPEECH ABOUT THE PLAN: It was delivered on August 11, 1969.

QUOTATION FROM *The Economist*: Moynihan, *The Politics of a Guaranteed Income*, p. 174.

212 "INCOME STRATEGY": Memorandum from Moynihan to Nixon, May 17, 1969, President's Handwriting file, Nixon Project, p. 3.

NIXON'S EYES LIT UP: Interview with Martin Anderson.

QUOTATION FROM JOHN PRICE: Interview with Price.

BURNS'S TRYING TO CHANGE NIXON'S SPEECH: Interview with Martin Anderson; typescript titled "Approved by Ray Price — 8/7/69 — 6:45 p.m.," Anderson's personal papers. Anderson was Burns's deputy, and his papers are full of material produced in the course of his and Burns's unsuccessful attempts to derail the Family Assistance Plan.

QUOTATION FROM MARTIN ANDERSON: Interview with Anderson.

"IN CONFIDENCE I HAVE DECIDED": Handwritten comment by Nixon on a memorandum from Moynihan, April 11, 1969, President's Handwriting file, Nixon Project.

213 "*A guaranteed income will never be enacted*": Memorandum from Moynihan to Melvin Laird, September 4, 1973, President's Handwriting file, Nixon Project, p. 1.

"*Addressed to the cultural strata*": Memorandum from Moynihan to Laird, September 4, 1973, p. 3.

"WILL COME TO BE ACCEPTED": Memorandum from Moynihan to Laird, September 4, 1973, p. 7.

QUOTATION FROM MOYNIHAN, AND NIXON'S COMMENTS: Memorandum from Moynihan to Nixon, July 24, 1970, President's Handwriting file, Nixon Project.

"JUST GET SOMETHING DONE": John Ehrlichman, notes of a meeting with Nixon, August 27, 1970, Ehrlichman papers, Nixon Project.

214 "I QUIT — GO ON WELFARE": John Ehrlichman, notes of a meeting with Nixon, August 30, 1972, Ehrlichman papers, Nixon Project.

"THE INTEGRATION INTO THE LARGER SOCIETY": Memorandum from Moynihan to Nixon, March 19, 1969, Oversize Federal Government files, Nixon Project, pp. 7, 13.

215 "THE NEGRO POOR HAVING BECOME MORE OPENLY VIOLENT": Memorandum from Moynihan to Nixon, March 19, 1969, pp. 24–26.

"*The militant middle class*": Memorandum from Moynihan to Nixon, March 19, 1969, p. 28. It's worth noting that elsewhere (p. 19) in this same memo, Moynihan told Nixon, "You should know [about] . . . a rather pronounced revival — in impeccably respectable circles — of the proposition that there is a difference in genetic potential between the two populations. . . . I personally simply do not believe this is so, but the truth is that it is an open question." He included a table comparing white and black IQ scores.

216 QUOTATION FROM PETER EDELMAN: Edelman, oral history, Part III, p. 331.

KING'S BURSTING INTO TEARS IN MARKS: Interviews with Robert Jackson, Samuel McCray, and Ezra Towner.

217 POOR PEOPLE'S CAMPAIGN AT THE WHITE HOUSE: This description comes from "Notes for the President's File, Urban Affairs Council, 13 May 1969," by Raymond K. Price, Jr., President's Office files, Nixon Project; from notes made at the meeting by Martin Anderson, in Anderson's personal papers; and from interviews with Anderson and Ehrlichman.

"A CRUEL HOAX": Interview with Peter Edelman.

"A POMPOUS, TIRED CHARLATAN": Price, "Notes for the President's File," p. 21.

QUOTATION FROM RALPH ABERNATHY: Price, "Notes for the President's File," p. 21.

QUOTATION FROM JOHN EHRLICHMAN: Interview with Ehrlichman.

218 "MODEL CITIES — FLUSH IT": John Ehrlichman, notes of a meeting with Nixon, November 14, 1972, Ehrlichman papers, Nixon Project.

"OEO — LEGAL SERVICES": John Ehrlichman, notes of a meeting with Nixon, December 1, 1972, Ehrlichman papers, Nixon Project.

"TAKE THE HEAT": John Ehrlichman, notes of a meeting with Nixon, December 7, 1972, Ehrlichman papers, Nixon Project.

"FLUSH MODEL CITIES": John Ehrlichman, notes of a meeting with Nixon, November 28, 1972, Ehrlichman papers, Nixon Project.

NIXON'S INSTRUCTIONS TO HOWARD PHILLIPS: Interview with Phillips.

219 QUOTATION FROM DAVID STOCKMAN: William Greider, *The Education of David Stockman and Other Americans* (Dutton, 1982), p. 12.

DESCRIPTION OF JOHNSON AT CIVIL RIGHTS SYMPOSIUM: Interviews with Horace Busby and Harry McPherson.

220 WALTER HELLER'S VISIT TO JOHNSON: Interview with Heller.

QUOTATIONS FROM JOHNSON: Interview with Walter Heller.

CHICAGO

226 KERMIT AS A GANG LEADER: Interviews with Thomas Chairs, Juanita Haynes, and Robert Haynes.

CHICAGO GANGS: A good overall source on present-day Chicago gangs is Chicago Police Department, "Guide for the Identification of Chicago Street Gangs," unpublished typescript, undated. On early-twentieth-century gangs, Shaw, *Delinquency Areas*, is useful. Royko, *Boss*, pp. 36–37, discusses the rumors about Daley's youthful gang membership. A long letter to the author from David Dawley, chairman of The National Center for Gang Policy, was also very helpful.

227 JEFF FORT: Tom Brune and James Ylisela, Jr., "The Making of Jeff Fort," *Chicago Magazine*, November 1988. Stories about Fort appear regularly in the Chicago newspapers, too.

LESSER-KNOWN GANG LEADERS: Interviews with Robert Haynes, Norman Smith, and Antoine Williams.

GANG CRIME IN THE ROBERT TAYLOR HOMES: Aside from interviews with the people whose life stories appear in this book, it was also especially useful to talk with Mamie Marshall, a former resident; Ron Tate, a writer who grew up in the Taylor Homes; and with Chicago police officers Gerald Creed, Leroy Grant, Mardren Johnson, Robert Robinson, Nick Williams, and Bill Wright.

228 SCREENING PROCEDURES AT THE ROBERT TAYLOR HOMES: Interviews with Devereux Bowly, Jr., James S. Fuerst, and Joseph Gardner.

231 CABRINI-GREEN: Interviews with Leonard Henderson, Sharon Hicks-Bartlett, Edward Marciniak, and Al Sims; Bowly, *The Poorhouse*, pp. 116–119.

232 POWER OF HEADQUARTERS AT CHICAGO HOUSING AUTHORITY: Interviews with Robert Keeley and Vincent Lane.

233 THE GAUTREAUX CASE: Bowly, *The Poorhouse*, pp. 189–194; interviews with Mary Davis and Kale Williams.

234 COORDINATING COUNCIL OF COMMUNITY ORGANIZATIONS: Interviews with James Bevel, Edward Marciniak, John McDermott, and Al Raby; Garrow, *Bearing the Cross*, pp. 431–525, comprehensively covers the activities of the civil rights

movement in Chicago. Also useful was Pierre de Vise, *Descent from the Summit: Race and Housing in Chicago Since the Summit Agreement of 1966*, unpublished manuscript.

POWELL'S NOT WANTING KING IN NEW YORK: Garrow, *Bearing the Cross*, p. 435.

235 QUOTATION FROM JAMES BEVEL: Interview with Bevel.

RUSTIN'S DOUBTS ABOUT THE "END SLUMS" CAMPAIGN: Garrow, *Bearing the Cross*, p. 455.

236 DEATH OF DESSIE MAE WILLIAMS: Arna Bontemps and Jack Conroy, *Anyplace But Here* (Hill and Wang, 1966), pp. 340–342.

DAN ROSTENKOWSKI: Memorandum from Lawrence O'Brien to Lyndon Johnson, August 11, 1965, Local Government papers, Johnson Library.

237 POLICE GUARD FOR PHILIP HAUSER: Interview with Hauser.

238 QUOTATION FROM JOHN McDERMOTT: Interview with McDermott.

JOHN DOAR AND ROGER WILKINS IN CHICAGO: Interviews with Doar and Wilkins; memorandum from Wilkins to Harry McPherson, July 27, 1966, McPherson papers, Johnson Library.

"THE SITUATION IN CHICAGO IS EXTREMELY BAD": Memorandum from Harry McPherson to Johnson, August 5, 1966, McPherson papers, Johnson Library.

239 CONTRACT BUYERS' LEAGUE: Interview with John Egan; Dempsey J. Travis, *An Autobiography of Black Chicago* (Urban Research Institute, 1981), pp. 165–172.

240 MOB SCENE AT THE LEADERSHIP COUNCIL: See, for example, Michael Arndt, "Housing Subsidy Office Overwhelmed by Crowd," *Chicago Tribune*, January 24, 1984, section 2, page 1.

242 WILLIS WAGONS AT FARRAGUT HIGH SCHOOL: Interview with Arlene Daggs.

243 QUOTATION FROM MIKE ROYKO: Royko, *Boss*, pp. 168–169. The quotation from Daley appears there too.

WELFARE FOR SINGLE MEN AND WOMEN: It's called General Assistance in most places, including Illinois.

245 "THEY DO NOT PERMIT ANY TYPE OF COMMUNITY ORGANIZATION": Memorandum from John Daum to Edgar May, March 29, 1966, OEO Office of Inspection papers, National Archives.

"OUR BELOVED DETON BROOKS": Memorandum from Ted Jones to Edgar May, June 13, 1966, OEO Office of Inspection papers, National Archives.

"THE POVERTY PROGRAM DOES NOT REACH THE PEOPLE": Memorandum from Sherwin Markham to Lyndon Johnson, February 1, 1967, Welfare files, Johnson Library.

"THERE IS NO REAL ATTEMPT": Memorandum from Art Follman to Wally Quetsch, May 29, 1967, OEO's Office of Inspection papers, National Archives.

DALEY'S KILLING HEW'S GRANT TO KING: Memorandum from Wilbur Cohen to Johnson, August 24, 1967, Local Government files, Johnson Library; memorandum from Steve Clapp to Edgar May, July 28, 1967, OEO Office of Inspection papers, National Archives; interviews with Edward Marciniak and Harold Howe.

BROOKS'S KEEPING URBAN PROGRESS CENTERS OPEN: Memorandum from Clapp to May, July 28, 1967.

JOHN FRY: Fry has written two books that cover his association with the Blackstone Rangers: *Fire and Blackstone* (Lippincott, 1969), and *Locked-Out Americans* (Harper & Row, 1973).

246 QUOTATION FROM LOUIS MARTIN: Interview with Martin.

JEREMIAH BERNSTEIN AND ARTHUR BRAZIER: Interview with Brazier.

"WHILE MEMBERS OF THE GROUP ENGAGE IN CONSTANT SOCIAL DEVIANCE": Memorandum from W. C. Lawrence to Lloyd Ohlin, June 11, 1962, Knapp papers, Kennedy Library.

247 QUOTATION FROM WILLIAM HADDAD: Interview with Haddad.

"TWO WILL PUT THE BLACKSTONE RANGERS": Letter from Sargent Shriver to Joseph Califano, June 7, 1967, Gaither papers, Johnson Library.

QUOTATION FROM DAVID STAHL: Interview with Stahl.

DALEY'S SUSPICIONS OF A SECRET DEAL BETWEEN THE WOODLAWN ORGANIZATION AND THE UNIVERSITY OF CHICAGO: Interview with Edward Marciniak.

SEVENTY-SIX OF EIGHT HUNDRED PARTICIPANTS PLACED IN JOBS: Irving A. Spergel, "Youth Manpower: What Happened in Woodlawn," unpublished report by the School of Social Service Administration, University of Chicago, April 1969, p. 212.

"MUCH TIME SEEMED TO BE SPENT": Spergel, "Youth Manpower," p. 116.

"FOR THE MOST PART": Spergel, p. 98.

248 ARRESTS OF PARTICIPANTS IN PROGRAM: Memorandum from Bill Farrell (no recipient listed), January 6, 1968, Welfare files, Johnson Library.

Chicago Tribune HEADLINES: *Chicago Tribune*, December 22, 1967 (OEO AIDS; the *Tribune* then was still using its own eccentric spellings of several words, including "aides"); December 23, 1967 (NAPS, DICE; the figure $972,000 is the *Tribune*'s mistake, and should be $927,000); and December 26, 1967 (QUIT SCHOOL).

MCCLELLAN'S HEARINGS: See "Hearings Before the Permanent Subcommittee on Investigations of the Committee on Government Operations, United States Senate, July 3, 9, and 10, 1968" (Government Printing Office, 1968).

QUOTATION FROM BERTRAND HARDING: Memorandum from Harding to Johnson, June 25, 1968, Welfare files, Johnson Library.

249 FORT'S PREVENTING A RIOT: See, for example, Spergel, "Youth Manpower," p. 143.

SENATOR PERCY: Interview with Erwin France; Brune and Ylisela, "The Making of Jeff Fort."

THE FORD FOUNDATION: Interview with Eamon Kelly, then a Ford Foundation official.

QUOTATION FROM SARGENT SHRIVER: Interview with Shriver.

DESCRIPTION OF EL RUKN HEADQUARTERS: At a time when Fort was incarcerated in a federal prison in Bastrop, Texas, I called the warden's office there to request an interview with him. Five minutes later, my call was returned by someone from the Chicago headquarters, who told me that while I would not be allowed to see Fort, I could visit there; my description is based on that visit.

FORT IN MILWAUKEE: F. Richard Ciccone, "Jeff Fort's 'Nation': Allah Gets a Chief Priest," *Chicago Tribune*, April 11, 1976.

250 BACKGROUND OF ERWIN FRANCE: Interviews with France.

QUOTATION FROM LOUIS MARTIN: Interview with Martin.

QUOTATION FROM ERWIN FRANCE: Interview with France.

ACTIVITIES OF MODEL CITIES IN CHICAGO: Interviews with Erwin France, Edward Marciniak, and David Stahl; also, the *Chicago Tribune* covered Model Cities extensively over the years, most notably in a series of articles that appeared during the week of February 20, 1972.

LEON FINNEY'S RELATIONSHIP TO HUDDLESTON: Interview with Mike Espy, who is Finney's first cousin.

251 ERWIN FRANCE'S BUDGET AND PAYROLL: Interviews with France.

POPULATION LOSS IN MODEL CITIES NEIGHBORHOODS: *Local Community Fact Book*, pp. 7 (Uptown), 80 (Lawndale), 104 (Grand Boulevard), 115 (Woodlawn).

FIRES IN WOODLAWN: Interview with Father Tracy O'Sullivan, a Catholic priest whose parish is in Woodlawn.

WOODLAWN'S POPULATION LOSS: *Local Community Fact Book*, p. 115.

BLACK POPULATION GROWTH IN CHICAGO SUBURBS: Larry Long and Diana DeAre, "The Suburbanization of Blacks," *American Demographics*, September 1981, p. 20.

STATISTICS ON GRAND BOULEVARD: *Local Community Fact Book*, pp. 104–105.

QUOTATION FROM LOUIS MARTIN: Interview with Martin.

252 DALEY'S DEAL WITH BLACK LEADERS IN 1968: Interview with Louis Martin.

HEW AND BUSING IN CHICAGO: Interviews with Harold Howe, Francis Keppel, and Stanley Pottinger.

QUOTATION FROM STANLEY POTTINGER: Interview with Pottinger.

255 VITO MARZULLO: Fremon, *Chicago Politics Ward by Ward*, pp. 157–161.

256 EDMOND BLAIR: See Manuel Galvan, "Minister, 58, Found Shot to Death in Car," *Chicago Tribune*, May 25, 1980.

257 DUSABLE HIGH SCHOOL: Interviews with Walter Anglin, Anthony Eirich, Meldin Goodman, Luke Helm, and Gwendolyn Jones, all on the staff at DuSable.

258 DUSABLE'S PTA: Interview with Brenda Homes, head of Parents United to Save DuSable.

REPUTATION OF CAMP ATTERBURY: Christopher Weeks, oral history, part I, p. 67.

259 LIFE HISTORIES OF THOMAS CHAIRS AND ROBERT HAYNES: Except where noted, these and all subsequent details about their lives come from interviews with them.

265 QUOTATION FROM LARRY DANIELS: Interview with Daniels.

266 UNEMPLOYMENT RATE IN THE ROBERT TAYLOR HOMES: *Local Community Fact Book*, p. 110.

BROKEN ELEVATORS IN THE ROBERT TAYLOR HOMES: Douglas Frantz, "Design Problems, Vandals Also Haunt CHA's Elevators," *Chicago Tribune*, January 30, 1984, p. 1.

269 THIRD WARD POLITICS: Fremon, *Chicago Politics Ward by Ward*, pp. 34–39.

270 QUOTATION FROM RALPH METCALFE: Garrow, *Bearing the Cross*, p. 444.

QUOTATION FROM HERBERT ODOM: Interview with Odom.

271 HAMPTON AS NAACP YOUTH CHAIRMAN: Interview with Conrad Worrill, a boyhood acquaintance of Hampton's.

272 DALEY'S NO LONGER SPEAKING TO DAVID STAHL: Interview with Stahl. Another old friend to whom Daley stopped speaking was Anthony Downs, a land-use policy expert whose father, Jim Downs, was head of a real estate research organization and very close to Daley; the Downses wrote a report on the Chicago assessor's office that displeased Daley.

DALEY'S SPEAKING DISMISSIVELY ABOUT BLACKS: Interviews with Sam Bernstein and John Connelly.

274 QUOTATION FROM DRAKE AND CAYTON: Drake and Cayton, *Black Metropolis*, pp. 660–661.

QUOTATION FROM DEVEREUX BOWLY: Bowly, *The Poorhouse*, pp. 31–33.

275 GEORGE HICKS'S GETTING HIS NAME IN THE PAPERS: See *Chicago Tribune*, January 30, 1987, section 2, page 8; April 20, 1987, section 1, page 7; and June 26, 1988, section 1, page 14.

277 CHARACTERIZATION OF THE TENOR OF BLACK MIDDLE-CLASS CONVERSATION IN

CHICAGO: Besides interviews with George Hicks, especially helpful were interviews with Mildred Nichols Burton, LeEtta Clark, Taylor Cotton, Jr., Alice Dunlap, Weedell McIntosh, Al Sims, J. B. Sims, Deborah Terrell and her family, and ViEthel Wells and other members of the Greenville Club of Chicago.

FIRE-BOMBINGS OF BLACK FAMILIES: *Chicago Tribune*, April 13, 1975 (Broadview); January 16, 1976 (Forest Park); June 20, 1979 (Gary); August 7, 1980 (Palos Heights); January 26, 1983 (South Chicago); November 9, 1984 (The Island); November 21, 1984 (Ashburn); April 24, 1984 (Southeast Side); and June 2, 1985 (Gage Park).

279 QUOTATION FROM DRAKE AND CAYTON: Drake and Cayton, *Black Metropolis*, pp. 394–395.

281 QUOTATION FROM GUNNAR MYRDAL: Gunnar Myrdal, *Challenge to Affluence* (Pantheon, 1962), p. 34.

QUOTATION FROM JACOB RIIS: Jacob Riis, *How the Other Half Lives: Studies Among the Tenements of New York* (Hill and Wang, 1957), p. 20.

QUOTATION FROM HERBERT GANS: Gans, "The Failure of Urban Renewal," p. 33.

QUOTATION FROM ANDREW BRIMMER: Moynihan, *The Politics of a Guaranteed Income*, p. 343.

282 QUOTATION FROM ELEANOR HOLMES NORTON: Interview with Norton.

"I SUSPECT THAT THESE DOLEFUL STATISTICS": "Remarks of Eleanor Holmes Norton, Commissioner of Human Rights of New York City, at the 65th Annual Conference of the National Urban League, Atlanta, Georgia, Wednesday Evening, July 30, 1975," typescript, p. 9.

MITCHELL SVIRIDOFF AND NORTON'S SPEECH: Interview with Sviridoff.

QUOTATION FROM EDWARD KENNEDY: Ken Auletta, *The Underclass* (Random House, 1982), p. 26.

SIZE OF THE UNDERCLASS: The pioneer researchers here are Erol Ricketts, of the Rockefeller Foundation, and Isabel Sawhill, of the Urban Institute. To arrive at their measurement, they add the total populations of all census tracts that are one standard deviation above the national average in all of four indices: proportion of high school dropouts, proportion of working-age men who are not in the labor force, proportion of welfare recipients, and proportion of female-headed households. See Erol R. Ricketts and Isabel V. Sawhill, "Defining and Measuring the Underclass," Urban Institute research paper, December 1986.

BLACK MALE UNEMPLOYMENT RATE: Charles Murray, *Losing Ground: American Social Policy, 1950–1980* (Basic Books, 1984), p. 272.

SCHOOL ENROLLMENTS: Murray, p. 278.

WELFARE ROLLS: *Social Security Bulletin: Annual Statistical Supplement 1989* (Government Printing Office, 1990), p. 341.

PERCENTAGE OF SINGLE MOTHERS ON WELFARE: Christopher Jencks and Kathryn Edin, "The Real Welfare Problem," *The American Prospect*, Spring 1990, p. 45.

283 ARREST RATES: Murray, p. 285.

ILLEGITIMACY RATIO: Murray, p. 289.

PERCENTAGE OF POOR LIVING IN FEMALE-HEADED FAMILIES: Murray, p. 290.

WILLIAM JULIUS WILSON'S ADMIRATION FOR BAYARD RUSTIN: Interviews with Wilson.

WILSON'S BOOKS: *The Declining Significance of Race* (University of Chicago Press, 1980); *The Truly Disadvantaged: The Inner City, the Underclass, and Public Policy* (University of Chicago Press, 1987).

284 JOHN KASARDA AND FRANK LEVY: See, for example, Kasarda, "The Regional and Urban Redistribution of People and Jobs in the U.S.," prepared for the National Council Committee on National Urban Policy, June 1986, and Levy, *Dollars and Dreams: The Changing American Income Distribution* (Norton, 1987).

CHICAGO'S LOSS OF MANUFACTURING JOBS: Kasarda, "The Regional and Urban Redistribution," p. 29.

QUOTATIONS FROM WILLIAM JULIUS WILSON: Wilson, *The Truly Disadvantaged*, pp. 60 ("social isolation"), 91 ("marriageable"), 137 ("ghetto-specific culture," "continue to influence"), 138 ("changing the social and economic situations"), 58 ("increasingly socially isolated").

285 LIBERAL COUNTERATTACK TO MURRAY: See, for example, "Losing Ground: A Critique," Institute for Research on Poverty, University of Wisconsin–Madison, Special Report Series, August 1985.

286 CHRISTOPHER JENCKS'S THEORY: Christopher Jencks, "Which Underclass Is Growing? Recent Changes in Joblessness, Educational Attainment, Crime, Family Structure, and Welfare Dependency," unpublished paper, October 1989.

DATA ON THE GREAT MIGRATION: See Daniel O. Price, "Rural-Urban Migration and Poverty: a Synthesis of Research Findings, With a Look at the Literature," a report done for the Office of Economic Opportunity (Tracor, 1971), which is an excellent overview. Among the particular studies that are most useful are: Stanley Lieberson, "A Reconsideration of the Income Differences Found Between Migrants and Northern-Born Blacks," *American Journal of Sociology*, January 1978; Stanley Lieberson and Christy A. Wilkinson, "A Comparison Between Northern and Southern Blacks Residing in the North," *Demography*, May 1976; Larry H. Long, "Poverty Status and Receipt of Welfare Among Migrants and Nonmigrants in Large Cities," *American Sociological Review*, February 1974; Larry H. Long and Lynne R. Heltman, "Migration and Income Differences Between Black and White Men in the North," *American Journal of Sociology*, May 1975; and Stanley H. Masters, "Are Black Migrants From the South to the Northern Cities Worse Off Than Blacks Already There?", *The Journal of Human Resources*, Fall 1972.

For material that addresses, to some extent, the question of which black migrants did best in the North (rather than whether migrants as a group did better than non-migrants), see: David Featherman and Robert Hauser, *Opportunity and Change* (Academic Press, 1978), especially Chapter Six, "Race and Opportunity," and Chapter Seven, "Regional Development, Migration, and Socioeconomic Assimilation"; Gladys K. Bowles, A. Lloyd Bacon, and P. Neal Ritchey, "Poverty Dimensions of Rural-to-Urban Migration: A Statistical Report," a paper prepared for the U.S. Department of Agriculture; Karl E. Taeuber and Alma F. Taeuber, "The Changing Character of Negro Migration," *American Journal of Sociology*, January 1965; and Ronald Freedman, "Cityward Migration, Urban Ecology, and Social Theory," in Ernest W. Burgess and Donald J. Bogue, editors, *Contributions to Urban Sociology* (University of Chicago Press, 1964).

For a critique of this book's overall treatment of the black migration, followed by a debate between the author and a critic, see David Whitman, "The Great Sharecropper Success Story," *The Public Interest*, Summer 1991; Nicholas Lemann, "The Underclass and the Great Migration," and David Whitman, "The Migrants' Tale and Ghetto Culture," *The Public Interest*, Fall 1991.

289 QUOTATION FROM BAYARD RUSTIN: Interview with Rustin.

QUOTATION FROM ELEANOR HOLMES NORTON: Interview with Norton.

QUOTATIONS FROM MARIAN WRIGHT EDELMAN: Interview with Edelman.

290   HAROLD CRUSE: See Cruse's books *The Crisis of the Negro Intellectual* (Morrow, 1967) and *Plural But Equal: A Critical Study of Blacks and Minorities and America's Plural Society* (Morrow, 1987).

BUSH ADMINISTRATION'S ANTIPOVERTY EFFORTS: Interviews with Charles Kolb, James Pinkerton, and Richard Porter, the members of the White House staff who coordinate these efforts.

QUOTATION FROM GLENN LOURY: Interview with Loury.

299   "HE OLD MAN IS A DEAF MAN": I saw this paper, and many others in the same vein, while sitting in on classes at DuSable.

T. L. BARRETT: See Peter Kendall, "Minister Unveils New Enterprise," *Chicago Tribune*, July 7, 1988, section 2, p. 4, and Casey Banas and Hanke Gratteau, "'Trying to Break the Welfare Cycle,'" *Chicago Tribune*, November 19, 1985, section 2, p. 2. In 1988, Barrett was accused by the Illinois attorney general's office of operating a pyramid scheme that sold memberships in his church for $1,500 apiece.

300   QUOTATION FROM MELVIN DANIELS: Interview with Daniels.

303   ACTIVE MEMBERSHIP OF THE MUSLIMS: Interviews with Farid Muhammad and Salim Muwakkil.

304   KENNETH CLARK'S CADET CORPS: Clark, *Dark Ghetto*, pp. 102–104.

QUOTATION FROM GEORGE CLEMENTS: Interview with Clements.

305   VINCENT LANE'S REFORMS: Interview with Lane.

CLARKSDALE

309   STATE CONSTITUTION INTERPRETATION REQUIREMENT: Silver, *Mississippi: The Closed Society*, p. 87. Bear in mind, though, that the same requirement was in the Mississippi state constitution of 1890, so the legislature in 1954 was merely underscoring a longstanding rule.

FIVE PER CENT OF BLACKS REGISTERED TO VOTE: Silver, *The Closed Society*, p. 86.

310   BLACK REGISTRATION IN COAHOMA COUNTY: Silver, p. 87.

CREATION OF SOVEREIGNTY COMMISSION AND CONTRIBUTIONS TO THE CITIZENS COUNCIL: Silver, p. 8.

CITIZENS COUNCIL IN CLARKSDALE: Interview with Gustave Roessler.

AARON HENRY'S PETITION: Interview with Henry.

FIRE-BOMBING OF AARON HENRY'S HOUSE: Interview with Henry.

MISSISSIPPI REGIONAL COUNCIL OF NEGRO LEADERSHIP: Cagin and Dray, *We Are Not Afraid*, p. 135.

SIT-INS IN CLARKSDALE: Vera Pigee, *The Struggle of Struggles, Part One* (Harlo Press, 1975), pp. 28–60.

311   HARASSMENT OF AARON HENRY: Interviews with Henry; Silver, *The Closed Society*, pp. 99–101; Cagin and Dray, *We Are Not Afraid*, p. 173.

CHRISTMAS PARADE CANCELED: Mosley and Williams, "An Analysis and Evaluation of a Community Action Anti-Poverty Program in the Mississippi Delta," p. 2.

QUOTATION FROM JAMES SILVER: Silver, *The Closed Society*, p. 99.

NAACP PICKETING: Pigee, *The Struggle of Struggles*, pp. 50–60.

CLOSING OF PUBLIC FACILITIES: Mosley and Williams, "An Analysis," p. 2.

312 COFO: Interviews with Aaron Henry; Silver, *The Closed Society*, p. 251; Cagin and Dray, *We Are Not Afraid*, pp. 180, 214–215, 217–218.

313 SOUTHERN EDUCATIONAL AND RECREATIONAL ASSOCIATION AND THE ORIGINS OF COMMUNITY ACTION IN CLARKSDALE: Mosley and Williams, "An Analysis," is the most useful source on this. There is some interesting material in the Mississippi files of the OEO's Office of Inspection, at the National Archives in Washington. Also, interviews with Leon Bramlett, David Califf (a founder of the First National Bank), Andrew Carr, Joseph Ellis, Bennie Gooden, Aaron Henry, Gustave Roessler, and Robert Wood (a lawyer who was involved in the legal aid program).

315 SHRIVER'S MEMO: Shriver to Bill Moyers, August 18, 1965, Moyers papers, Johnson Library.

ANDREW CARR AT THE WHITE HOUSE: Interview with Carr.

"WELL, NOW YOU'VE GOT IT IN BLACK AND WHITE": Interview with Andrew Carr.

EPPS AND MARTIN LUTHER KING: Garrow, *Bearing the Cross*, p. 605.

316 QUOTATION FROM JOSEPH ELLIS: Interview with Ellis.

QUOTATION FROM GUS ROESSLER: Interview with Roessler.

317 $1.2 MILLION IN GRANTS: Mosley and Williams, "An Analysis," p. 71.

253 PEOPLE ON STAFF: Mosley and Williams, p. 58.

QUOTATION FROM AARON HENRY: Interview with Henry.

318 CHEMICAL DEFOLIANTS: Interviews with Leon Bramlett, Andrew Carr, Edwin Mullens, and LeRoy Percy.

319 AGRICULTURAL MINIMUM WAGE: There is a brief comment on Robert Kennedy's role in Edelman, oral history, Part 7, p. 31.

A THOUSAND BLACK FARM LABORERS OUT OF WORK: Interviews with Andrew Carr.

QUOTATION FROM HEW OFFICIAL: Memorandum from Lisle C. Carter, Jr., to Lawrence Levinson, April 17, 1967, McPherson papers, Johnson Library.

QUOTATION FROM EUGENE DOYLE: Interview with Doyle.

QUOTATION FROM MARTIN LUTHER KING, JR.: Telegram from Martin Luther King to Lyndon Johnson, August 16, 1966, McPherson papers, Johnson Library.

320 QUOTATION FROM HARRY MCPHERSON: Memorandum from McPherson to Johnson, August 16, 1966, McPherson papers, Johnson Library.

WHITE HOUSE ASKING FOR HELP: Memorandum from Christopher F. Edley (a Ford Foundation executive) to Harry McPherson, May 13, 1966; memorandum from McPherson to Johnson, August 16, 1966; memorandum from Lisle Carter to Lawrence Levinson, April 17, 1967. All in McPherson papers, Johnson Library.

BUDGET AND PAYROLL OF CLARKSDALE ADULT EDUCATION PROGRAM: Mosley and Williams, "An Analysis," pp. 68, 71.

$30-A-WEEK PAY TO ADULT EDUCATION ENROLLEES: Mosley and Williams, p. 69.

INSTRUCTION IN "PERSONAL HABITS": Mosley and Williams, p. 69.

321 JOHN DOAR'S VISITS TO CLARKSDALE: Interviews with John Doar and Edwin Mullens.

DECLARATION BY MISSISSIPPI ECONOMIC COUNCIL: Silver, *The Closed Society*, p. 281.

SCHOOL INTEGRATION IN CLARKSDALE: Interviews with Andrew Carr, Aaron Henry, and Melvyn Leventhal; *Rebecca E. Henry et al., Appellants, v. The Clarksdale*

Municipal Separate School District et al., Appellees, decision of the United States Court of Appeals, Fifth Circuit, March 6, 1969.

322 QUOTATION FROM MELVYN LEVENTHAL: Interview with Leventhal.

CHANGES IN DESEGREGATION PLAN DURING THE 1980s: Interviews with Aaron Henry and Robert Ellard (the current school superintendent in Clarksdale).

323 BIOGRAPHICAL INFORMATION AND QUOTATIONS FROM TOM LEVIN: Interview with Levin.

"THESE PEOPLE WOULD BE THE KAMIKAZE REVOLUTIONARIES": Tom Levin, oral history interview, Johnson Library, p. 6.

QUOTATIONS FROM TOM LEVIN: Interview with Levin.

324 VIOLENT INCIDENTS: Interview with Tom Levin; OEO Office of Inspection files, National Archives.

SLOPPY RECORDS, RELATIVES OF BOARD MEMBERS: Interviews with Patricia Derian, Marian Wright Edelman, Peter Edelman, Aaron Henry, Harry McPherson, and LeRoy Percy. There is also material on CDGM's rocky relations with the federal government in Polly Greenberg, *The Devil Has Slippery Shoes: A Biased Biography of the Child Development Group of Mississippi* (Macmillan, 1969); Harry McPherson, *A Political Education* (Little, Brown, 1972); and Dawson Horn III, "The Politics of Social Change: What Happens When the Poor of Mississippi Go in Search of Freedom: A History of the Child Development Group of Mississippi," unpublished master's thesis, Department of Political Science, Duke University, May 1978.

QUOTATION FROM TOM LEVIN: Interview with Levin.

325 CDGM BOARD MEETING AND LEVIN'S JOB OFFER: Interview with Tom Levin.

QUOTATION FROM AARON HENRY: Interview with Henry.

326 JOHNSON'S FEARS ABOUT RECONSTRUCTION: Interviews with Horace Busby.

DOUGLAS WYNN: Letter from Harry McPherson, June 6, 1989.

QUOTATION FROM PATRICIA DERIAN: Interview with Derian.

327 INTIMIDATION AND HARASSMENT OF MAP: OEO Office of Inspection files, National Archives.

MESSAGE FOR JOHNSON'S AIDE: "Doris" to Matthew Nimetz, April 4, 1968, James Gaither papers, Johnson Library.

COMPLAINTS ABOUT BENNIE GOODEN: Interview with Andrew Carr; Pigee, *The Struggle of Struggles, Part Two,* p. 28.

329 BACKGROUND OF MISSISSIPPI STATE FEDERATION OF COLORED WOMEN'S CLUBS: Interview with Dorothy M. Latham Taylor.

QUOTATION FROM BENNIE GOODEN: Interview with Gooden.

FIFTY-TWO-ACRE PLOT: Interview with Andrew Carr.

330 SALE OF KING & ANDERSON: Interview with Eugene Doyle.

QUOTATION FROM MRS. W. K. ANDERSON: Interview with Anderson.

BREAKUP OF HOPSON PLANTATION: Interview with James Butler.

331 QUOTATION FROM SEMMES LUCKETT: Mosley and Williams, "An Analysis," pp. 31–32.

QUOTATION FROM JOSEPH ELLIS: Interview with Ellis.

CLARKSDALE CIVIC AUDITORIUM: Interviews with George Hicks.

HEAD START BUSES' TRANSPORTING VOTERS: Interview with Gustave Roessler.

332 BLACK UNDERREPRESENTATION IN WHITE-COLLAR JOBS: Interviews with Edward James and Oliver Clark.

336 QUOTATION FROM ROBERT HAYNES: Robert Haynes, "I, Too, Have a Dream," unpublished typescript.

"MANY MANSIONS": John 14:2, King James Version.

VICE LORDS IN CANTON: Interviews with Suzie Mae Green, Gabriel Henderson, Bill Mosby, Larry Ross, and Bessie Walker.

337 GANG ACTIVITIES IN CLARKSDALE: Interviews with Uless Carter, Bennie Gooden, and Juanita Haynes.

INCIDENTS OF INTERRACIAL VIOLENCE, AND FEAR OF A RIOT: Interviews with Uless Carter, James Furr, and Edward James.

339 "THIS IS THE LAND OF WHICH I SWORE TO ABRAHAM": Deuteronomy 34:4, Revised Standard Version.

"HE'S ALLOWED ME TO GO UP TO THE MOUNTAIN": Garrow, *Bearing the Cross*, p. 621.

"AS AN EVERLASTING POSSESSION": Genesis 17:8, King James Version.

AFTERWORD

347 THE OFFICIAL VISION OF REPUBLICAN ADMINISTRATIONS: A good place to get the conservative gospel on ghettos is Stuart Butler and Anna Kondratas, *Out of the Poverty Trap: A Conservative Strategy for Welfare Reform* (The Free Press, 1987).

349 RESEARCH ON ANTIPOVERTY PROGRAMS: Lisbeth B. Schorr with Daniel Schorr, *Within Our Reach: Breaking the Cycle of Disadvantage* (Anchor Books, 1989), is a compendium of evidence about intervention programs. Another useful overview is Phoebe H. Cottingham and David T. Ellwood, editors, *Welfare Policy for the 1990s* (Harvard University Press, 1989).

350 HEAD START: For a book-length study of early childhood educational intervention, see J. R. Berrueta-Clement, *Changed Lives: The Effect of the Perry Preschool Programs on Youths Through Age 19* (High/Scope Press, 1984). The Perry program is a kind of super–Head Start, which claims to have beneficial effects so long-lasting that its graduates have higher high-school graduation and employment rates and lower rates of arrest and teenage pregnancy.

351 GUARANTEED JOBS AND WORK REQUIREMENTS: Mickey Kaus, "The Work Ethic State," *The New Republic*, July 7, 1986, pp. 22–33, lays out a detailed proposal for such a program. Another endorsement of the idea of a time limit on welfare can be found in David T. Ellwood, *Poor Support: Poverty in the American Family* (Basic Books, 1988).

COST OF NEW SOCIAL PROGRAMS: A few recent social-program budget exercises are *The Common Good: Social Welfare and the American Future* (Ford Foundation, 1989); *S.O.S. America: A Children's Defense Budget* (Children's Defense Fund, 1990); and Roberta O. Barnes, Jason N. Juffras, and Joseph J. Minarik, "Policies to Help Disadvantaged Children: Financing Options for the 1990s" (The Urban Institute, 1988).

353 THE URGE TO CAMOUFLAGE ANTIPOVERTY PROGRAMS: For a statement of this position, see Theda Skocpol, "Sustainable Social Policy: Fighting Poverty Without Poverty Programs," *The American Prospect*, Summer 1990, pp. 58–70.

Index